D1267088

LUDWIG WITTGENSTEIN

PHILOSOPHICAL
GRAMMAR

LUDWIG WITTGENSTEIN

PHILOSOPHICAL GRAMMAR

PART I
The Proposition and its Sense

PART II
On Logic and Mathematics

Edited by
RUSH RHEES

Translated by
ANTHONY KENNY

BASIL BLACKWELL · OXFORD

ISBN 0 631 15220 2

Printed in Great Britain by
William Clowes & Sons Limited
London, Colchester and Beccles
and Bound at the Kemp Hall Bindery, Oxford

CONTENTS

Part I
The Proposition and its Sense

I

A sentence from the middle of a story I have not read.

The concept of understanding is a fluid one. 42

6 A sentence in a code: at what moment of translating does understanding begin?

The words of a sentence are arbitrary; so I replace them with letters. But now I cannot immediately think the sense of the sentence in the new expression.

The notion that we can only imperfectly *exhibit* our understanding: the expression of understanding has something missing that is *essentially* inexpressible. But in that case it makes no sense to speak of a more complete expression. 43

7 What is the criterion for an expression's being meant *thus*? A question about the relationship between two linguistic expressions. Sometimes a translation into another mode of representation. 45

8 Must I understand a sentence to be able to act on it? If "to understand a sentence" means somehow or other to act on it, then understanding cannot be a precondition for our acting on it. – What goes on when I suddenly understand someone else? There are *many* possibilities here. 45

9 Isn't there a gap between an order and its execution? "I understand it, but only because I add something to it, namely the interpretation." – But if one were to say "any sentence still stands in need of an interpretation", that would mean: no sentence can be understood without a rider. 46

10 "Understanding a word" – *being able* to apply it. – "When I said 'I can play chess' I really could." How did I know that I could? My answer will show in what way I use the word "can".

Being able is called a *state*. "To describe a state" can mean various things. "After all I can't have the whole mode of application of a word in my head all at once." 47

11 It is not a question of an instantaneous grasping. –

When a man who knows the game watches a game of chess, the experience he has when a move is made usually differs from that of someone else watching without understanding the game. But this experience is not the knowledge of the rules. – The understanding of language seems like a background; like the *ability* to multiply.

12 *When* do we understand a sentence? – When we've uttered the whole of it? Or while uttering it?   50

13 When someone interprets, or understands, a sign in one sense or another, what he is doing is taking a step in a calculus. – "Thought" sometimes means a process which may accompany the utterance of a sentence and sometimes the sentence itself in the system of language.   50

II

14 Grammar as (e.g.) the geometry of negation. We would like to say: "Negation has the property that when it is doubled it yields an affirmation". But the rule doesn't give a further description of negation, it constitutes negation.   52

15 Geometry no more speaks about cubes than logic does about negation.

It looks as if one could *infer* from the meaning of negation that "$\sim \sim p$" means p.   52

16 What does it mean to say that the "is" in "The rose is red" has a different meaning from the "is" in "twice two is four"? Here we have *one* word but as it were different *meaning-bodies* with a single end surface: different possibilities of constructing sentences. The comparison of the glass cubes. The rule for the arrangement of the red sides contains the possibilities, i.e. the geometry of the cube. The cube can also serve as a notation for the rule if it belongs to a system of propositions.   53

17 "The grammatical possibilities of the negation-sign". The T-F notation can illustrate the meaning of "not". The written symbol becomes a sign for negation only by the way it *works* – the way it is used in the game.   55

18 If we derive geometrical propositions from a drawing or a model, then the model has the role of a sign in a game. We use the drawing of a cube again and again in different contexts. It is this *sign* that we take to be the cube in which the geometrical laws are already laid up.   55

19 My earlier concept of meaning originates in a primitive philosophy of language. – Augustine on the learning of language. He describes a calculus of our language, only not everything that we call language is this calculus.   56

20 As if words didn't also have functions quite different from the naming of tables, chairs, etc. – Here is the origin of the bad expression: a fact is a complex of objects.   57

21 In a familiar language we experience different parts of speech as different. It is only in a foreign language that we see clearly the uniformity of words.   58

22 If I decide to use a new word instead of "red", how would it come out that it took the place of the word "red"?   59

23 The meaning of a word: what the explanation of its meaning explains. (If, on the other hand by "meaning" we mean a characteristic sensation, then the explanation of meaning would be a cause.)   59

24 Explanation can clear up misunderstandings. In that case understanding is a correlate of explanation. – Definitions.

It seems as if the other grammatical rules for a word had to follow from its ostensive definition. But is this definition really unambiguous? One must understand a great deal of a language in order to understand the definition. 60

25 The words "shape", "colour" in the definitions determine the *kind of use* of the word. The ostensive definition has a different role in the grammar of each part of speech. 61

26 So how does it come about that on the strength of this definition we understand the word?

What's the sign of someone's understanding a game? Can't he learn a game simply by watching it being played? Learning and speaking without explicit rules. We are always *comparing* language with a game according to rules. 61

27 The names I give to bodies, shapes, colours, lengths have different grammars in each case. The meaning of a name is not the thing we point to when we give an ostensive definition of the name. 63

28 What constitutes the meaning of a word like "perhaps"?

I know how it is used. The case is similar when someone is explaining to me a calculation "that I don't quite understand". "Now I know how to go on." How do I know that I know how to go on? 64

29 Is the meaning really only the use of the word? Isn't it the way this use meshes with our life? 65

30 The words "fine" ,"oh", "perhaps" . . . can each be the expression of a feeling. But I don't call that feeling the meaning of the word.

I can replace the sensations by intonation and gestures.

I could also treat the word (e.g. "oh") itself as a gesture.   66

31 A language spoken in a uniform metre.

Relationships between tools in a toolbox.

"The meaning of a word: its role in the calculus of language."
Imagine how we calculate with "red". And then: the word
"oh" – what corresponds now to the calculus?   67

32 Describing ball-games. Perhaps one will be unwilling to call
some of them ball-games; but it is clear where the boundary is to
be drawn here?

We consider language from one point of view only.

The explanation of the purpose or the effect of a word is not
what we call the explanation of its meaning. It may be that if it is
to achieve its effect a particular word cannot be replaced by any
other, just as it may be that a gesture cannot be replaced by any
other. – We only bother about what's called the explanation of
meaning and not about meaning in any other sense.   68

33 Aren't our sentences parts of a mechanism? As in a pianola?
But suppose it is in bad condition? So it is not the effect but the
purpose that is the sense of the signs (the holes in the pianola roll).
Their purpose *within* the mechanism.

We need an explanation that is *part of the calculus*.

"A symbol is something that produces this effect." – How do I
know that it is *the one I meant*?"

We could use a colour-chart: and then our calculus would have
to get along with the visible colour-sample.   69

34 "We could understand a penholder too, if we had given it a
meaning." Does the understanding contain the whole system of its
application?

When I read a sentence with understanding something happens: perhaps a picture comes into my mind. But before we call "understanding" is related to countless things that happen before and after the reading of *this* sentence.

When I don't understand a sentence – that can be different things in different cases.

"Understanding a word" – that is infinitely various.   71

35 "Understanding" is not the name of a single process but of more or less interrelated processes against a background of the actual use of a learnt language. – We think that if I use the word "understanding" in all these cases there must be some one thing that happens in all of them. Well, the concept-word certainly does show a kinship but this need not be the sharing of a common property or constituent. – The concept-word "game". "By 'knowledge' we mean these processes, and these, and *similar ones*."   74

III

36 If for our purposes we wish to regulate the use of a word by definite rules, then alongside its fluctuating use we set a different use. But this isn't like the way physics gives a simplified description of a natural phenomenon. It is not as if we were saying something that would hold only of an ideal language.   77

37 We understand a genre-picture if we recognize what the people in it are doing. If this recognition does not come easily, there is a period of doubt followed by a familiar process of recognition. If on the other hand we take it in at first glance it is difficult to say what the understanding – the recognition say – consists of. There is no one thing that happens that could be called recognition.

If I want to say "I understand it *like that*" then the "*like that*" stands for a translation into a different expression. Or is it a sort of intransitive understanding?   77

38 Forgetting the meaning of a word. Different cases. The man feels, as he looks at blue objects, that the connection between the word "blue" and the colour has been broken off. We might restore the connection in various ways. The connection is not made by a single phenomenon, but can manifest itself in very various processes. Do I mean then that there is no such thing as understanding but only manifestations of understanding? – a senseless question.

79

39 How does an ostensive definition work? Is it put to work again every time the word is used? Definition as a part of the calculus acts only by being applied.

80

40 In what cases shall we say that the man understands the word "blue"? In what circumstances will *he* be able to say it? or to say that he understood it in the past?

If he says "I picked the ball out by guesswork, I didn't understand the word", ought we to believe him? "He can't be wrong if he says that he didn't understand the word": a remark on the grammar of the statement "I didn't understand the word".

81

41 We call understanding a mental state, and characterize it as a *hypothetical* process. Comparison between the grammar of mental processes and the grammar of brain processes.

In certain circumstances both our picking out a red object from others on demand and our being able to give the ostensive definition of the word "red" are regarded as signs of understanding.

We aren't interested here in the difference between thinking out loud (or in writing) and thinking in the imagination.

What we call "understanding" is not the behaviour that shows us the understanding, but a state of which this behaviour is a sign.

82

42 We might call the recital of the rules on its own a criterion of understanding, or alternatively tests of use on their own. Or we may regard the recital of the rules as a symptom of the man's being able to do something other than recite the rules.

To understand = to let a proposition work on one.

When one remembers the meaning of a word, the remembering is not the mental process that one imagines at first sight.

The psychological process of understanding is in the same case as the arithmetical object Three. 84

43 An explanation, a chart, is first used by being looked up, then by being looked up in the head, and finally as if it had never existed.

A rule as the cause or history behind our present behaviour is of no interest to us. But a rule can be a hypothesis, or can itself enter into the conduct of the game. If a disposition is hypothesized in the player to give the list of rules on request, it is a disposition analogous to a physiological one. In our study of symbolism there is no foreground and background. 85

44 What interests *us* in the sign is what is embodied in the grammar of the sign. 87

IV

45 The ostensive definition of signs is not an *application* of language, but part of the grammar: something like a rule for translation from a gesture language into a word-language. – What belongs to grammar are all the conditions necessary for comparing the proposition with reality – all the conditions necessary for its sense. 88

46 Does our language consist of primary signs (gestures) and secondary signs (words)?

Obviously we would not be able to replace an ordinary sentence by gestures.

"Is it an accident that in order to define the signs I have to go outside the written and spoken signs?" In that case isn't it strange that I can do anything at all with the written signs? 88

47 We say that a red label is the primary sign for the colour red, and the word a secondary sign. – But must a Frenchman have a red image present to his mind when he understands my explanation "red = rouge"? 89

48 Are the primary signs incapable of being misinterpreted? Can one say they don't any longer need to be *understood*? 90

49 A colour chart might be arranged differently or used differently, and yet the words mean the same colours as with us.

Can a green label be a *sample* of red?

Can it be said that when someone is painting a certain shade of green he is *copying* the red of a label?

A sample is not used like a name. 90

50 "Copy" can mean various things. Various methods of comparison.

We do not understand what is meant by "this shade of colour is a copy of this note on the violin." It makes no sense to speak of a projection-method for association. 91

51 We can say that we communicate by signs whether we use words or samples, but the game of acting in accordance with words is different from the game of acting in accordance with samples. 92

52 "There must be some sort of law for reading the chart. – Otherwise *how would one know* how the table was to be used?" It is part of human nature to understand pointing with the finger in the way we do.

The chart does not compel me to use it always in the same way. 93

53 Is the word "red" enough to enable one to look for something red? Does one need a memory image to do so?

An order. Is the real order "Do now what you remember doing then?"

If the colour sample appears darker than I remember it being yesterday, I need not agree with my memory.   94

54 "Paint from memory the colour of the door of your room" is no more unambiguous than "paint the green you see on this chart."

I see the colour of the flower and recognize *it*.

Even if I say "no, this colour is brighter than the one I saw there," there is no process of comparing two simultaneously given shades of colour.

Think of reading aloud from a written test (or writing to dictation).   95

55 "Why do you choose *this* colour when given this order?" – "Because *this* colour is opposite to the word 'red' in my chart." In that case there is no sense in *this* question: "Why do you call 'red' the colour in the chart opposite the word 'red'?"

The connection between "language and reality" is made by definitions of words – which belong to grammar.   96

56 A gesture language used to communicate with people who have no word-language in common with us. Do we feel there too the need to go outside language to explain its signs?

The correlation between objects and names is a part of the symbolism. It gives the wrong idea if you say that the connection is a psychological one.   97

57 Someone copies a figure on the scale of 1 to 10. Is the understanding of the general rule of such mapping contained in the process of copying?

Or was the process merely *in agreement with* that rule, but also in agreement with other rules? 97

58 Even if my pencil doesn't always do justice to the model, my intention always does. 98

59 For our studies it can never be essential that a symbolic phenomenon occurs in the mind and not on paper.

An explanation of a sign can replace the sign itself – this contrasts with causal explanation. 99

60 Reading. – Deriving a translation from the original may also be a visible process.

Always what represents is the *system* in which a sign is used.

If 'mental' processes can be true and false, their descriptions must be able to as well. 99

61 Every case of deriving an action from a command is the same kind of thing as the written derivation of a result.

"I write the number '16' here *because* it says 'x^2' there."

It might appear that some causality was operating here, but that would be a confusion between 'reason' and 'cause'. 101

V

62 "That's *him*" – that contains the whole problem of representation.

I make a plan: I see myself acting thus and so. "How do I know that it's myself?" Or "How do I know that the word 'I' stands for me?"

The delusion that in thought the objects do what the proposition states about them.

"I meant the victor of Austerlitz" – the past tense, which looks as if it was giving a description, is deceptive. 102

63 *"How* does one think a proposition? How does thought use its expression?"

Let's compare belief with the utterance of a sentence: the processes in the larynx etc. *accompany* the spoken sentence which alone interests us – not as part of a mechanism, but as part of a calculus.

We think we can't describe thought after the event because the delicate processes have been lost sight of.

What is the function of thought? Its *effect* does not interest us.

103

64 But if thinking consists only in writing or speaking, why shouldn't a machine do it?

Could a machine be in pain?

It is a travesty of the truth to say: thinking is an activity of our mind, as writing is an activity of the hand. 105

65 'Thinking' 'Language' are fluid concepts.

The expression "mental process" is meant to distinguish 'experience' from 'physical processes'; or else we talk of 'unconscious thoughts' – of processes in a mind-model; or else the word "thought" is taken as synonymous with "sense of a sentence". 106

66 The idea that one language in contrast to others can have an order of words which corresponds to the order of thinking.

Is it, as it were, a contamination of the sense that we express it in a particular language? Does it impair the rigour and purity of the proposition $25 \times 25 = 625$ that it is written down in a particular number system?

Thought can only be something common-or-garden. But we are affected by this concept as we are by that of the number one. 107

67 What does man think for? There is no such thing as a "thought-

experiment". I believe that more boilers would explode if people did not calculate when making boilers. Does it follow that there will in fact be fewer? The belief that fire will burn me is of the same nature as the fear that it will burn me. 109

68 My assumption that this house won't collapse may be the utterance of a sentence which is part of a calculation. I do have reasons for it. *What* counts as a reason for an assumption determines a calculus. – So is the calculus something we adopt arbitrarily? No more so than the fear of fire.

As long as we remain in the province of true-false games a change of grammar can only lead us from one game to another, and never from something true to something false. 110

VI

69 What is a proposition? – Do we have a single general concept of proposition? 112

70 "What happens when a *new* proposition is taken into the language: what is the criterion for its being a *proposition*?"

In this respect the concept of number is like the concept of proposition. On the other hand the concept of cardinal number can be called a rigorously circumscribed concept, that's to say it's a concept in a different sense of the word. 113

71 I possess the concept 'language' from the languages I have learnt. "But language can expand": if "expand" makes sense here, I must *now* be able to specify how I imagine such an expansion.

No sign leads us beyond itself.

Does every newly constructed language broaden the concept of language? – Comparison with the concept of number. 114

72 The indeterminacy of generality is not a logical indeterminacy.

The task of philosophy is not to create an ideal language, but to clarify the use of existing language.

I'm allowed to use the word "rule" without first tabulating the rules for the word. – If philosophy was concerned with the concept of the calculus of all calculi, there would be such a thing as metaphilosophy. But there is not.   115

73 It isn't on the strength of a particular property, the property of being a rule, that we speak of the rules of a game. – We use the word "rule" in contrast to "word", "projection" and some other words.   116

74 We learnt the meaning of the word "plant" by examples. And if we disregard hypothetical dispositions, these examples stand only for themselves. –

The grammatical pace of the word "game" "rule" etc is given by examples in rather the way in which the place of a meeting is specified by saying that it will take place *beside* such and such a tree.   117

75 Meaning as something which *comes before* our minds when we hear a word.

"Show the children a game".

The sentence "The Assyrians knew various games" would strike us as curious since we wouldn't be certain that we could give an example.   118

76 Examples of the use of the word "wish". Our aim is not to give a theory of wishing, which would have to explain every case of wishing.

The use of the words "proposition", "language", etc. has the haziness of the normal use of concept-words in our language.   119

77 The philosophy of logic speaks of sentences and words in the sense in which we speak of them in ordinary life.

(We are not justified in having any more scruples about our language than the chess player has about chess, namely none.) 121

78 Sounding like a sentence. We don't call everything 'that sounds like a sentence' a sentence. – If we disregard sounding like a sentence do we still have a general concept of proposition?

The example of a language in which the order of the words in a sentence is the reverse of the present one. 122

79 The definition "A proposition is whatever can be true or false". – The words "true" and "false" are items in a particular notation for the truth-functions.

Does " 'p' is true" state anything about the sign 'p'? 123

80 In the schema "This is how things stand" the "how things stand" is a handle for the truth-functions.

A general propositional form determines a proposition as part of a calculus. 124

81 The rules that say that such and such a combination of words yields no sense.

"How do I know that red can't be cut into bits?" is not a question. I must *begin* with the distinction between sense and nonsense. I can't give it a foundation. 125

82 " How must we make the grammatical rules for words if they are to give a sentence sense?" –

A proposition shows the possibility of the state of affairs it describes. "Possible" here means the same as "conceivable"; representable in a particular system of propositions.

The proposition "I can imagine such and such a colour transition connects the linguistic representation with another form of representation; it is a proposition of grammar. 127

83 It looks as if we could say: Word-language allows of senseless combinations of words, but the language of imagining does not allow us to imagine anything senseless.

"Can you imagine it's being otherwise?" – How strange that one should be able to say that such and such a state of affairs is inconceivable! 128

84 The role of a proposition in the calculus is its sense.
It is only in language that something is a proposition. To understand a proposition is to understand a language. 130

VII

85 Symbols appear to be of their nature unsatisfied.
A proposition seems to demand that reality be compared with it.
"A proposition like a ruler laid against reality." 132

86 If you see the expression of an expectation you see what is being expected.
It looks as if the ultimate thing sought by an order had to remain unexpressed. – As if the sign was trying to communicate with us.
A sign does its job only in a grammatical system. 132

87 It seems as if the expectation and the fact satisfying the expectation fitted together somehow. Solids and hollows. – Expectation is not related to its satisfaction in the same way as hunger is related to its satisfaction. 133

88 The strange thing that the event I expected isn't distinct from the one I expected. – "The report was not so loud as I had expected."
"How can you say that the red which you see in front of you is the same as the red you imagined?" – One takes the meaning of the word "red" as being the sense of a proposition saying that something is red. 134

89 A red patch looks different from one that is not red. But it would be odd to say "a red patch looks different when it is there from when it isn't there". Or: "How do you know that you are expecting a *red* patch?" 135

90 How can I expect the event, when it isn't yet there at all? – I can imagine a stag that is not there, in this meadow, but not kill one that is not there. – It is not the expected thing that is the fulfilment, but rather its coming about. It is difficult for us to shake off this comparison: a man makes his appearance – an event makes its appearance.   136

91 A search for a particular thing (e.g. my stick) is a particular kind of search, and differs from a search for something else because of what one does (says, thinks) while searching, not because of what one finds. – Contrast looking for the trisection of the angle.

138

92 The symptoms of expectation are not the expression of expectation.

In the sentence "I expect that he is coming" is one using the words "he is coming" in a different sense from the one they have in the assertion "he is coming"?

What makes it the expectation precisely of *him*?

Various definitions of "expecting a person X".

It isn't a later experience that decides *what* we are expecting. "Let us put the expression of expectation in place of the expectation."   138

93 Expectation as preparatory behaviour.

"Expectation is a thought"

If *hunger* is called a wish it is a hypothesis that just that will satisfy the wish.

In "I have been expecting him all day" "expect" does not mean a persistent condition.   140

94 When I expect someone, – what happens?

What does the process of wanting to eat an apple consist in?   141

95 Intention and intentionality. –

"The thought that p is the case doesn't presuppose that it is the case; yet I can't think that something is red if the colour red does not exist." Here we mean the existence of a red sample *as part of our language*.   142

96 It's beginning to look somehow as if intention could never be recognized as *intention* from the outside. But the point is that one has to read off from a thought that it is the thought that such and such is the case.   143

97 This is connected with the question whether a machine could think. This is like when we say: "The will can't be a phenomenon, for whatever phenomenon you take is something that *simply happens,* not something we *do*." But there's no doubt that you *also* have experiences when you move your arm voluntarily, although the phenomena of doing are indeed different from the phenomena of observing. But there are very different cases here.   144

98 The intention seems to interpret, to give the final interpretation.

Imagine an 'abstract' sign-language translated into an unambiguous picture-language. Here there seem to be no further possibilities of interpretation. – We might say we didn't enter into the sign-language but did enter into the painted picture. Examples: picture, cinema, dream.   145

99 What happens is not that this symbol cannot be further interpreted, but: I do no interpreting.

I imagine N. No interpretation accompanies this image; what gives the image its interpretation is the *path* on which it lies.   147

100 We want to say: "Meaning is essentially a mental process, not a process in dead matter." – What we are dissatisfied with here is the grammar of *process*, not the specific kind of process.   148

101 Doesn't the system of language provide me with a medium in which the proposition is no longer dead? – "Even if the *expression* of the wish is the wish, still the whole language isn't present during this expression." But that is not necessary.   149

102 In the gesture we don't see the real shadow of the fulfilment, the unambiguous shadow that admits of no further interpretation.

149

103 It's only considering the linguistic manifestation of a wish that makes it appear that my wish prefigures the fulfilment. – Because it's the wish that just that were the case. – It is in language that wish and fulfilment meet.   150

104 "A proposition isn't a mere series of sounds, it is something more." Don't I see a sentence as part of a system of consequences?

152

105 "This queer thing, thought." – It strikes us as queer when we say that it connects objects in the mind. – We're all ready to pass from it to the reality. – "How was it possible for thought to deal with the very person *himself*?" Here I am being astonished by my own linguistic expression and momentarily misunderstanding it.   154

106 "When I think of what will happen tomorrow I am mentally already in the future." – Similarly people think that the *endless series of cardinal numbers* is somehow before our mind's eye, whenever we can use that expression significantly.

A thought experiment is like a drawing of an experiment that is not carried out.   155

107 We said "one cannot recognize intention as intention from the outside" – i.e. that it is not something that happens, or happens to us, but something we do. It is almost as if we said: we cannot see ourselves going to a place, because it is we who are doing the going. One does have a particular experience if one is doing the going oneself.   156

24

108 Fulfilment of expectation doesn't consist in some third thing's happening, such as a feeling of satisfaction. 157

VIII

109 A description of language must achieve the same result as language itself.

Suppose someone says that one can infer from a propsotion the fact that verifies it. What can one infer from a proposition apart from *itself*?

The shadowy anticipation of a fact consists in our being able already to think that *that very thing* will happen which *hasn't yet* happened. 159

110 However many steps I insert between the thought and its application, each intermediate step always follows the previous one without any intermediate link, and so too the application follows the last intermediate step. – We can't cross the bridge to the execution (of an order) until we are there. 160

111 It is the *calculus* of thought that connects with extra-mental reality. From expectation to fulfilment is a step in a calculation. 160

112 We are – as it were – surprised, not at anyone's knowing the future, but at his being able to prophesy at all (right or wrong). 161

IX

113 Is the pictorial character of thought an agreement with reality? In what sense can I say that a proposition is a picture? 163

114 The sense of a proposition and the sense of a picture. The different grammar of the expressions:

"This picture shows people at a village inn."
"This picture shows the coronation of Napoleon."   164

115 A picture's telling me something will consist in my recognizing in it objects in some sort of characteristic arrangement. – What does "this object is familiar to me" mean?   165

116 "I see what I see." I say that because I don't want to give a name to what I see. – I want to exclude from my consideration of familiarity everything that is 'historical'. – The multiplicity of familiarity is that of feeling at home in what I see.   165

117 Understanding a genre picture: don't we recognize the painted people as people and the painted trees as trees, etc.?
A picture of a human face is a no less familiar object than the human face itself. But there is no question of recognition here.   166

118 The false concept that recognizing always consists in comparing two impressions with one another. –
"We couldn't use words at all if we didn't recognize them and the objects they denote." Have we any sort of check on this recognition?   167

119 This shape I see is not simply *a* shape, but is one of the shapes I know. – But it is not as if I were comparing the object with a picture set beside it, but as if the object *coincided* with the picture. I see only one thing, not two.   168

120 "This face has a quite *particular* expression." We perhaps look for words and feel that everyday language is here too crude.   169

121 That a picture tells me something consists in its own form and colours. Or it narrates something to me: it uses *words* so to speak, and I am comparing the picture with a combination of linguistic forms. – That a series of signs tells me something isn't constituted by its now making this impression on me. "It's only in a language that something is a proposition."   169

122 'Language' is languages. – Languages *are* systems.
   It is units of languages that I call "propositions".   170

123 Certainly, I read a story and don't give a hang about any system of language, any more than if it was a story in pictures. Suppose we were to say at this point "something is a picture only in a picture-language."?   171

124 We might imagine a language in whose use the impression made on us by the signs played no part.
   What I call a "proposition" is a position in the game of language.
   Thinking is an activity, like calculating.   171

125 A puzzle picture. What does it amount to to say that after the solution the picture means something to us, whereas it meant nothing before?   172

126 The impression is one thing, and the impression's being determinate is another thing. The impression of familiarity is perhaps the characteristics of the determinacy that every strong impression has.   174

127 Can I think away the impression of individual familiarity where it exists; and think it into a situation where it does not? The difficulty is not a psychological one. *We* have not *determined* what that is to mean.
   Can I look at a printed English word and see it as if I hadn't learnt to read?
   I can ascribe meaning to a meaningless shape.   175

128 We can read courage into a face and say "now once more courage *fits* this face". This is related to "an attributive adjective agrees with the subject".

What do I do if I take a smile now as a kind one, now as malicious? This is connected with the contrast between *saying* and *meaning*. 176

129 A friendly mouth, friendly eyes, the wagging of a dog's tail are primary symbols of friendliness: they are parts of the phenomena that are called friendliness. If we want to imagine further appearances as expressions of friendliness, we read these symbols into them. It is not that I can imagine that this man's face might change so that it looked courageous, but that there is a quite definite way in which it can change into a courageous face.

Think of the multifariousness of what we call "language": word-language, picture-language, gesture-language, sound-language. 178

130 " 'This object is familiar to me' is like saying 'this object is portrayed in my catalogue'." We are making the assumption that the picture in our catalogue is itself familiar.

The sheath in my mind as a "form of imagining". – The pattern is no longer presented as an object, which means that it didn't make sense to talk of a pattern at all.

"Familiarity: an object's fitting into a sheath" – that's not quite the same as our *comparing* what is seen with a copy.

The question is "*What* do I recognize *as what*?" For "to recognize a thing as itself" is meaningless. 179

131 The comparison between memory and a notebook.

How did I read off from the memory image that I stood thus at the window *yesterday*? What made you so certain when you spoke those words? Nothing; I *was* certain.

How do I *react* to a memory? 181

132 Operating with written signs and operating with "imagination pictures".

An attitude to a picture (to a thought) is what connects it with reality.   182

X

133 Grammatical rules determine a meaning and are not answerable to any meaning that they could contradict.

Why don't I call cookery rules arbitrary, and why am I tempted to call the rules of grammar arbitrary?

I don't call an argument good just because it has the consequences I want.

The rules of grammar are arbitrary in the same sense as the choice of a unit of measurement.   184

134 Doesn't grammar put the primary colours together because there is a kind of similarity between them? Or colours, anyway, in contrast to shapes or notes?

The rules of grammar cannot be justified by shewing that their application makes a representation agree with reality.

The analogy between grammar and games.   185

135 Langauge considered as a part of a psychological mechanism.

I do not use "this is the sign for sugar" in the same way as the sentence "if I press this button, I get a piece of sugar".   187

136 Suppose we compare grammar to a keyboard which I can use to direct a man by pressing different combinations of keys. What corresponds in this case to the grammar of language?

If the utterance of a 'nonsensical' combination of words has the effect that the other person stares at me, I don't on that account call it the order to stare.   188

137 Language is not defined for us as an arrangement fulfilling a definite purpose. 189

138 Grammar consists of conventions – say in a chart. This might be a part of a mechanism. But it is the connection and not the effect which determines the meaning.

Can one speak of a grammar in the case where a language is taught to a person by a mere drill? 190

139 I do not scruple to *invent* causal connections in the mechanism of language.

To invent a keyboard might mean to invent something that had the desired effect; or else to devise new forms which were similar to the old ones in various ways.

"It is always for living beings that signs exist." 191

140 Inventing a language – inventing an instrument – inventing a game.

If we imagine a goal for chess – say entertainment – then the rules are not arbitrary. So too for the choice of a unit of measurement.

We can't say "without language we couldn't communicate with one another". The concept of language is *contained in* the concept of communication. 192

141 Philosophy is philosophical problems. Their common element extends as far as the common element in different regions of our language.

Something that at first sight looks like a proposition and is not one. Something that looks like a design for a steamroller and is not one. 193

142 Are we willing to call a series of independent signals "a language"?

Imagine a diary kept with signals. Are explanations given so that the signals are connected to another language?

A language consisting of commands. We wouldn't say that a series of such signals alone would enable me to *derive* a picture of the movement of a man obeying them unless in addition to the signal there is something that might be called a general rule for translating into drawing.

The grammar explains the meaning of the signs and thus makes the language pictorial. 194

Appendix

Part II
On Logic and Mathematics

I Logical Inference

32

IV On Cardinal Numbers

V Mathematical Proof

34

VII Infinity in Mathematics

Part 1
The Proposition and its Sense

1 How can one talk about 'understanding' and 'not understanding' a proposition? Surely it is not a proposition until it's understood?

Does it make sense to point to a clump of trees and ask "Do you understand what this clump of trees says?" In normal circumstances, no; but couldn't one express a sense by an arrangement of trees? Couldn't it be a code?

One would call 'propositions' clumps of trees one understood; others, too, that one didn't understand, provided one supposed the man who planted them had understood them.

"Doesn't understanding only start with a proposition, with a whole proposition? Can you *understand* half a proposition?" – Half a proposition is not a whole proposition. – But what the question means can perhaps be understood as follows. Suppose a knight's move in chess was always carried out by two movements of the piece, one straight and one oblique; then it could be said "In chess there are no half knight's moves" meaning: the relationship of half a knight's move to a whole knight's move is not the same as that of half a bread roll to a whole bread roll. We want to say that it is not a difference of degree.

It is strange that science and mathematics make use of propositions, but have nothing to say about understanding those propositions.

2 We regard understanding as the essential thing, and signs as something inessential. – But in that case, why have the signs at all? If you think that it is only so as to make ourselves understood by others, then you are very likely looking on the signs as a drug which is to produce in other people the same condition as my own.

Suppose that the question is "what do you mean by that gesture?" and the answer is "I mean you must leave". The answer would not have been more correctly phrased: "I mean what I mean by the sentence 'you must leave'."

In attacking the formalist conception of arithmetic, Frege says more or less this: these petty explanations of the signs are idle once we *understand* the signs. Understanding would be something like seeing a picture from which all the rules followed, or a picture that makes them all clear. But Frege does not seem to see that such a picture would itself be another sign, or a calculus to explain the written one to us.

What we call "understanding a language" is often like the understanding we get of a calculus when we learn its history or its practical application. And there too we meet an easily surveyable symbolism instead of one that is strange to us. – Imagine that someone had originally learnt chess as a writing game, and was later shown the 'interpretation' of chess as a board game.

In this case "to understand" means something like "to take in as a whole".

If I give anyone an order I feel it to be quite enough to give him signs. And if I am given an order, I should never say: "this is only words, and I have got to get behind the words". And when I have asked someone something and he gives me an answer I am content – that was just what I expected – and I don't raise the objection: "but that's a mere answer."

But if you say: "How am I to know what he means, when I see nothing but the signs he gives?" then I say: "How is *he* to know what he means, when he has nothing but the signs either?"

What is spoken can only be explained in language, and so in this sense language itself cannot be explained.

Language must speak for itself.

3 One can say that meaning drops out of language; because what a proposition means is told by yet another proposition.

"What did you mean by those words?" "Did you *mean* those words." The first question is not a more precise specification of the second. The first is answered by a proposition replacing the proposition which wasn't understood. The second question is like: "Did you mean that seriously or as a joke?"

Compare: "Did you mean anything by that gesture – if so what?"

In certain of their applications the words "understand", "mean" refer to a psychological reaction while hearing, reading, uttering etc. a sentence. In that case understanding is the phenomenon that occurs when I hear a sentence in a familiar language and not when I hear a sentence in a strange language.

Learning a language *brings about* the understanding of it. But that belongs to the past history of the reaction. – The understanding of a sentence is as much something that happens to me as is the hearing of a sentence; it accompanies the hearing.

I can speak of 'experiencing' a sentence. "I am not merely saying this, I mean something by it." When we consider what is going on in us when we *mean* (and don't just say) words, it seems to us as if there were something coupled to the words, which otherwise would run idle. As if they *connected* with something in us.

4 Understanding a sentence is more akin to understanding a piece of music than one might think. Why must these bars be played just so? Why do I want to produce just this pattern of variation in loudness and tempo? I would like to say "Because I know what it's all about." But what is it all about? I should not be able to say. For explanation I can only translate the musical picture into a picture in another medium and let the one picture throw light on the other.

The understanding of a sentence can also be compared with what we call understanding a picture. Think of a still-life picture, and imagine that we were unable to see it as a spatial representation and saw only patches and lines on the canvas. We could say in that case "we do not understand the picture". But we say the same thing in a different sense when although we see the picture spatially we do not recognize the spatial objects as familiar things like books, animals and bottles.

Suppose the picture is a genre-picture and the people in it are about an inch long. If I had ever seen real people of that size, I would be able to recognize them in the picture and regard it as a life-size representation of them. In that case my visual experience of the picture would *not* be *the same* as the one I have when I see the picture in the normal way as a representation in miniature, although the illusion of spatial vision is the same in each case. – However, acquaintance with real inch-high people is put forward here only as one possible cause of the visual experience; except for that the experience is independent. Similarly, it may be that only someone who has already seen many real cubes can see a drawn cube spatially; but the description of the spatial visual presentation contains nothing to differentiate a real cube from a painted one.

The different experiences I have when I see a picture first one way and then another are comparable to the experience I have when I read a sentence with understanding and without understanding.

(Recall what it is like when someone reads a sentence with a mistaken intonation which prevents him from understanding it – and then realizes how it is to be read.)

(To see a watch as a watch, i.e. as a dial with hands, is like seeing Orion as a man striding across the sky.)

5 How curious: we should like to explain the understanding of a gesture as a translation into words, and the understanding of words as a translation into gestures.

And indeed we really do explain words by a gesture, and a gesture by words.

On the other hand we say "I understand that gesture" in the same sense as "I understand this theme", "it says something" and what that means is that I have a particular experience as I follow it.

Consider the difference it makes to the understanding of a sentence when a word in it is felt as belonging first with one word and then with another. I might have said: the word is conceived, understood, seen, pronounced as belonging first with one word and then with another.

We can call a 'proposition' that which is conceived first in one way and then in another; we can also mean the various ways of conceiving it. This is a source of confusions.

I read a sentence from the middle of a story: "After he had said this, he left her as he did the day before." Do I understand the sentence? – It's not altogether easy to give an answer. It is an English sentence, and to that extent I understand it. I should know how the sentence might be used, I could invent a context for it. And yet I do not understand it in the sense in which I should understand it if I had read the story. (Compare various language-games: describing a state of affairs, making up a story, etc. What counts as a significant sentence in the several cases?)

Do we *understand* Christian Morgenstern's poems, or Lewis Carroll's poem "Jabberwocky"? In these cases it's very clear that the concept of understanding is a fluid one.

6 A sentence is given me in unfamiliar code together with the key for deciphering it. Then, in a certain sense, everything required for the understanding of the sentence has been given me. And yet if I were asked whether I understood the sentence I should reply "I must first decode it" and only when I had it in front of me decoded as an English sentence, would I say "now I understand it".

If we now raise the question "At what moment of translating into English does understanding begin?" we get a glimpse into the nature of what is called "understanding".

I say the sentence "I see a black patch there"; but the words are after all arbitrary: so I will replace them one after the other by the first six letters of the alphabet. Now it goes "a b c d e f". But now it is clear that – as one would like to say – I cannot think the sense of the above sentence straight away in the new expression. I might also put it like this: I am not used to saying "a" instead of "I", "b" instead of "see", "c" instead of "a" and so on. I don't mean that I am not used to making an immediate association between the word "I" and the sign "a"; but that I am not used to using "a" in the place of "I".

"To understand a sentence" can mean "to know what the sentence signifies"; i.e. to be able to answer the question "what does this sentence say?"

It is a prevalent notion that we can only imperfectly *exhibit* our understanding; that we can only point to it from afar or come close to it, but never lay our hands on it, and that the ultimate thing can never be said. We say: "Understanding is something *different* from the expression of understanding. *Understanding* cannot be exhibited; it is something inward and spiritual." – Or "Whatever I do to exhibit understanding, whether I repeat an explanation of a word, or carry out an order to show that I have understood it, these bits of behaviour do not *have* to be taken as proofs of understanding." Similarly, people also say "I cannot show anyone else my toothache; I cannot *prove* to anyone else that I have toothache." But the impossibility spoken of here is supposed to be a logical one. "Isn't it the case that the expression of understanding is always an incomplete expression?" That means, I suppose, an expression with something missing – but the something missing is essentially *inexpressible*, because otherwise I might find a better expression for it. And "essentially inexpressible" means that it makes no sense to talk of a more complete expression.

The psychological processes which are found by experience to accompany sentences are of no interest to us. What does interest us is the understanding that is embodied in an explanation of the sense of the sentence.

7 To understand the grammar of the word "to mean" we must ask ourselves what is the criterion for an expression's being meant *thus*. What should be regarded as a criterion of the meaning?

An answer to the question "How is that meant?" exhibits the relationship between two linguistic expressions. So the question too is a question about that relationship.

The process we call the understanding of a sentence or of a description is sometimes a process of translation from one symbolism into another; tracing a picture, copying something, or translating into another mode of representation.

In that case understanding a description means making oneself a picture of what is described. And the process is more or less like making a drawing to match a description.

We also say: "I understand the picture exactly, I could model it in clay".

8 We speak of the understanding of a sentence as a condition of being able to apply it. We say "I cannot obey an order if I do not understand it" or "I cannot obey it before I understand it".

"Must I really understand a sentence to be able to act on it? – Certainly, otherwise you wouldn't know what you had to do." – But how does this knowing help me? Isn't there in turn a jump from knowing to doing?

"But all the same I must understand an order to be able to act according to it" – here the "must" is fishy. If it is a logical must, then the sentence is a grammatical remark.

45

Here it could be asked: How long before obeying it *must* you understand the order? – But of course the proposition "I must understand the order before I can act on it" makes good sense: but not a metalogical sense. – And 'understanding' and 'meaning' are not metalogical concepts.

If "to understand a sentence" means somehow or other to act on it, then understanding cannot be a precondition for our acting on it. But of course experience may show that the specific behaviour of understanding is a precondition for obedience to an order.

"I cannot carry out the order because I don't understand what you mean. – Yes, I understand you now." – What went on when I suddenly understood him? Here there are *many* possibilities. For example: the order may have been given in a familiar language but with a wrong emphasis, and the right emphasis suddenly occurred to me. In that case perhaps I should say to a third party: "Now I understand him: he means . . ." and should repeat the order with the right emphasis. And when I grasped the familiar sentence I'd have understood the order, – I mean, I should not first have had to grasp an abstract sense. – Alternatively: I understood the order in *that* sense, so it was a correct English sentence, but it seemed preposterous. In such a case I would say: "I do not understand you: because you can't mean *that*." But then a more comprehensible interpretation occurred to me. Before I understand several interpretations, several explanations, may pass through my mind, and then I decide on one of them.

(Understanding, when an absent-minded man at the order "Right turn!" turns left, and then, clutching his forehead, says "Oh! right turn" and does a right turn.)

9 Suppose the order to square a series of numbers is written in the form of a table, thus:

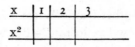

x	1	2	3
x^2			

– It seems to us as if by understanding the order we add something to it, something that fills the gap between command and execution. So that if someone said "You understand it, don't you, so it is not incomplete" we could reply "Yes, I understand it, but only because I add something to it, namely the interpretation." – But what makes you give just *this* interpretation? Is it the order? In that case it was already unambiguous, since it demanded this interpretation. Or did you attach the interpretation arbitrarily? In that case what you understood was not the command, but only what you made of it.

(While thinking philosophically we see problems in places where there are none. It is for philosophy to show that there are no problems.)

But an interpretation is something that is given in signs. It is *this* interpretation as opposed to a different one (running differently). So if one were to say "Any sentence still stands in need of an interpretation" that would mean: no sentence can be understood without a rider.

Of course sometimes I do *interpret* signs, give signs an interpretation; but that does not happen every time I understand a sign. (If someone asks me "What time is it?" there is no inner process of laborious interpretation; I simply react to what I see and hear. If someone whips out a knife at me, I do not say "I interpret that as a threat".)

10 "Understanding a word" may mean: *knowing* how it is used; *being able to* apply it.

"Can you lift this ball?" – "Yes". Then I try and fail. Then perhaps I say "*I was wrong*, I cannot". Or perhaps "I can't now, because I am too tired; but when I said I could, I really could." Similarly "I thought I could play chess, but now I have forgotten

47

how", but on the other hand "When I said 'I can play chess' I really could, but now I've lost it."– But what is the criterion for my being able at that particular time? How did I know that I could? To that question I would answer "I've always been able to lift that sort of weight", "I lifted it just a moment before", "I've played chess quite recently and my memory is good", "I'd just recited the rules" and so on. What I regard as an answer to that question will show me in what way I use the word "can".

Knowing, being able to do something, a capacity is what we would call a *state*. Let us compare with each other propositions which all in various senses describe states.

"I have had toothache since yesterday."

"I have been longing for him since yesterday."

"I have been expecting him since yesterday."

"I have known since yesterday that he is coming."

"Since yesterday I can play chess."

Can one say: "I have known continuously since yesterday that he is coming?" In which of the above sentences can one sensibly insert the word "continuously"?

If knowledge is called a "state" it must be in the sense in which we speak of the state of a body or of a physical model. So it must be in a physiological sense or in the sense used in a psychology that talks about unconscious states of a mind-model. Certainly no one would object to that; but in that case one still has to be clear that we have moved from the grammatical realm of 'conscious states' into a different grammatical realm. I can no doubt speak of unconscious toothache, if the sentence "I have unconscious toothache" means something like "I have a bad tooth that doesn't ache". But the expression "conscious state" (in its old sense) doesn't have the same grammatical relationship to the expression "unconscious state" as the expression "a chair which I see" has to "a chair which I don't see because it's behind me".

Instead of "to know something" we might say "to keep a piece of paper on which it is written".

If "to understand the meaning of a word" means to know the grammatically possible ways of applying it, then I can ask "How can I know what I mean by a word at the moment I utter it? After all, I can't have the whole mode of application of a word in my head all at once".

I can have the possible ways of applying a word in my head in the same sense as the chess player has all the rules of chess in his head, and the alphabet and the multiplication table. Knowledge is the hypothesized reservoir out of which the visible water flows.

11 So we mustn't think that when we understand or mean a word what happens is an act of instantaneous, as it were non-discursive, grasp of grammar. As if it could all be swallowed down in a single gulp.

It is as if I get tools in the toolbox of language ready for future use.

"I can use the word 'yellow' " is like "I know how to move the king in chess".

In this example of chess we can again observe the ambiguity of the word "understand". When a man who knows the game watches a game of chess, the experience he has when a move is made usually differs from that of someone else watching without understanding the game. (It differs too from that of a man who doesn't even know that it's a game.) We can also say that it's the knowledge of the rules of chess which makes the difference between the two spectators, and so too that it's the knowledge of the rules which makes the first spectator have the particular experience he has. But this experience is not the knowledge of the rules. Yet we are inclined to call them both "understanding".

The understanding of language, as of a game, seems like a background against which a particular sentence acquires meaning. – But this understanding, the knowledge of the language, isn't a conscious state that accompanies the sentences of the language. Not even if one of its consequences is such a state. It's much more like the understanding or mastery of a calculus, something like the *ability* to multiply.

12 Suppose it were asked: "When do you know how to play chess? All the time? Or just while you say that you can? Or just during a move in the game?" – How queer that knowing how to play chess should take such a short time, and a game of chess so much longer!
    (Augustine: *"When* do I measure a period of time?")

It can seem as if the rules of grammar are in a certain sense an unpacking of something we experience all at once when we use a word.

In order to get clearer about the grammar of the word "understand", let's ask: *when* do we understand a sentence? – When we've uttered the whole of it? Or while uttering it? – Is understanding, like the uttering of a sentence, an articulated process and does its articulation correspond exactly to that of the sentence? Or is it non-articulate, something accompanying the sentence in the way a pedal note accompanies a melody?

How long does it take to understand a sentence?
    And if we understand a sentence for a whole hour, are we always starting afresh?

13 Chess is characterized by its rules (by the list of rules). If I define the game (distinguish it from draughts) by its rules, then

these rules belong to the grammar of the word "chess". Does that mean that if someone uses the word "chess" intelligently he must have a definition of the word in mind? Certainly not. – He will only give one if he's asked what he means by "chess".

Suppose I now ask: "When you uttered the word, what did you mean by it?" – If he answered "I meant the game we've played so often, etc. etc." I would know that this explanation hadn't been in his mind at all when he used the word, and that he wasn't giving an answer to my question in the sense of telling me what "went on inside him" while he was uttering the word.

When someone interprets, or understands, a sign in one sense or another, what he is doing is taking a step in a calculus (like a calculation). What he *does* is roughly what he does if he gives expression to his interpretation.

"Thought" sometimes means a particular mental process which may accompany the utterance of a sentence and sometimes the sentence itself in the system of language.

"He said those words, but he didn't think any thoughts with them." – "Yes, I did think a thought while I said them". "*What* thought?" "Just what I said."

On hearing the assertion "This sentence makes sense" you cannot really ask "what sense?" Just as on hearing the assertion "this combination of words is a sentence" you cannot ask "what sentence?"

II

14 Can what the rules of grammar say about a word be described in another way by describing the process which takes place when understanding occurs?

Suppose the grammar is the geometry of negation for example, can I replace it by the description of what "lies behind" the word "not" when it is applied?

We say: "Anyone who understands negation knows that two negations yield an affirmation."

That sounds like "Carbon and oxygen yield carbonic acid". But in reality a doubled negation does not *yield* anything, it *is* something.

Something here gives us the illusion of a fact of physics. As if we saw the result of a logical process. Whereas the only result is the result of the physical process.

We would like to say: "Negation has the property that when it is doubled it yields an affirmation," But the rule doesn't give a further description of negation, it constitutes negation.

Negation has the property that it denies truly such and such a sentence.

Similarly, a circle – say one painted on a flat surface – has the property of being in such and such a position, of having the colour it has, of being bisected by a certain line (a boundary between two colours) and so on; but it doesn't have the properties that geometry seems to ascribe to it (i.e. the *ability* to have the other properties).

Likewise one doesn't have the property that when it's added to itself it makes two.

15 Geometry no more speaks about cubes than logic does about negation.

Geometry defines the form of a cube but does not describe it. If the description of a cube says that it is red and hard, then 'a description of the form of a cube' is a sentence like "This box has the form of a cube".

But if I describe how to make a cubical box, doesn't this contain a description of the form of a cube? A description only insofar as this thing is said to be cubical, and for the rest an analysis of the concept of cube.

"This paper is *not* black, and two such negations yield an affirmation".
The second clause is reminiscent of "and two such horses can pull the cart". But it contains no assertion about negation; it is a rule for the replacement of one sign by another.

"That two negations yield an affirmation must already be contained in the negation that I am using now." Here I am on the verge of inventing a mythology of symbolism.
It looks as if one could *infer* from the meaning of negation that "~ ~ p" means p. As if the rules for the negation sign *follow from* the nature of negation. So that in a certain sense there is first of all negation, and then the rules of grammar.
It also looks as if the essence of negation had a double expression in language: the one whose meaning I grasp when I understand the expression of negation in a sentence, and the consequences of this meaning in the grammar.

16 What does it mean to say that the "is" in "The rose is red" has a different meaning from the "is" in "Twice two is four"? If it is answered that it means that different rules are valid for these two words, we can say that we have only *one* word here. – And if all I am attending to is grammatical rules, these do allow the use of the word "is" in both connections. – But the rule which shews that the word "is" has different meanings in the two sentences is the one

allowing us to replace the word "is" in the second sentence by "equals" and forbidding this substitution in the first sentence.

"Is this rule then only the consequence of the *first* rule, that the word 'is' has different meanings in the two sentences? Or is it rather that this very rule is the expression of the word's having a different meaning in the two contexts?"

It looks as if a sentence with e.g. the word "ball" in it already contained the shadow of other uses of this word. That is to say, the *possibility* of forming those other sentences. To whom does it look like that? And under what circumstances?

The comparison suggests itself that the word "is" in different cases has different *meaning-bodies* behind it; that it is perhaps each time a square surface, but in one case it is the end surface of a prism and in the other the end surface of a pyramid.

Imagine the following case. Suppose we have some completely transparent glass cubes which have one face painted red. If we arrange these cubes together in space, only certain arrangements of red squares will be permitted by the shape of the glass bodies. I might then express the rule for the possible arrangements of the red squares without mentioning the cubes; but the rule would none the less contain the essence of the form of cube – Not, of course, the fact that there are glass cubes behind the red squares, but the geometry of the cube.

But suppose we *see* such a cube: are we immediately presented with the rules for the possible combinations, i.e. the geometry of the cube? Can I read off the geometry of the cube from a cube?

Thus the cube is a notation for the rule. And if we had discovered such a rule, we really wouldn't be able to find anything better than the drawing of a cube to use as a notation for it. (And it is significant that here a drawing of a cube will do instead of a cube.)

But how can the cube (or the drawing) serve as a notation for a geometrical rule? Only if it belongs, as a proposition or part of a proposition, to a system of propositions.

17 "Of course the grammatical possibilities of the negation sign reveal themselves bit by bit in the use of the signs, but I *think* negation all at once. The sign 'not' is only a pointer to the thought 'not'; it is only a stimulus to produce the right thought, only a signal."

(If I were asked what I mean by the word "and" in the sentence "pass me the bread and butter" I would answer by a gesture of gathering together; and that gesture would illustrate what I mean, in the same way as a green pattern illustrates the meaning of "green" and the T-F notation illustrates the meaning of "not", "and" etc.)

For instance, this sign for negation:

"p	"
T	F
F	W

is worth no more and no less than any other negation sign; it is a complex of lines just like the expression "not-p" and it is only made into a sign for negation by the way it *works* – I mean, the way it is used in the game.

(The same goes for the T-F schemata for tautology and contradiction.)

What I want to say is that to be a sign a thing must be dynamic, not static.

18 Here it can easily seem as if the sign contained the whole of the grammar; as if the grammar were contained in the sign like a string of pearls in a box and he had only to pull it out. (But this kind of picture is just what is misleading us). As if understanding were an instantaneous grasping of something from which later we only draw consequences which already exist in an ideal sense before they are drawn. As if the cube already contained the geometry of the cube, and I had only to unpack it. But which cube? Or is there

an ideal geometrical cube? – Often we have in mind the process of deriving geometrical propositions from a drawing, a representation (or a model). But what is the role of the model in such a case? It has the role of a sign, a sign employed in a particular game. – And it is an interesting and remarkable thing how this sign is employed, how we perhaps use the drawing of a cube again and again in different contexts. – And it is this sign, (*which has the identity proper to a sign*) that we take to be the cube in which the geometrical laws are already laid up. (They are no more laid up there than the disposition to be used in a certain way is laid up in the chessman which is the king).

In philosophy one is constantly tempted to invent a mythology of symbolism or of psychology, instead of simply saying what we know.

19 The concept of meaning I adopted in my philosophical discussions originates in a primitive philosophy of language.

The German word for "meaning" is derived from the German word for "pointing".

When Augustine talks about the learning of language he talks about how we attach names to things, or understand the names of things. *Naming* here appears as the foundation, the be all and end all of language.

Augustine does not speak of there being any difference between parts of speech and means by "names" apparently words like "tree", "table", "bread" and of course, the proper names of people; also no doubt "eat", "go", "here", "there" – all words, in fact. Certainly he's thinking first and foremost of *nouns*, and of the remaining words as something that will take care of itself. (Plato too says that a sentence consists of nouns and verbs.)[1]

1. Sophist, 261E, 262A. [I have replaced "kinds of word" which appears in the translation of the parallel passages in *Philosophical Investigations* §1 with "parts of speech", which appears to have been Wittgenstein's preferred translation. I am indebted for this information to Mr. R. Rhees. Trs.]

They describe the game as simpler than it is.

But the game Augustine describes is certainly a part of language. Imagine I want to put up a building using building stones someone else is to pass me; we might first make a convention by my pointing to a building stone and saying "that is a pillar", and to another and saying "that is called 'a block' ", "that is called 'a slab' " and so on. And then I call out the words "pillar", "slab", etc. in the order in which I need the stones.

Augustine does describe a calculus of our language, only not everything that we call language is this calculus. (And one has to say this in many cases where we are faced with the question "Is this an appropriate description or not?" The answer is: "Yes, it is appropriate, but only *here*, and not for the whole region that you were claiming to describe.") So it could be said that Augustine represents the matter too simply; but also that he represents something simpler.

It is as if someone were to say "a game consists in moving objects about on a surface according to certain rules . . ." and we replied: You must be thinking of board games, and your description is indeed applicable to them. But they are not the only games. So you can make your definitions correct by expressly restricting it to those games.

20 The way Augustine describes the learning of language can show us the way of looking at language from which the concept of the meaning of words derives.

The case of our language could be compared with a script in which the letters were used to stand for sounds, and also as signs of emphasis and perhaps as marks of punctuation. If one conceives this script as a language for describing sound-patterns, one can imagine someone misinterpreting the script as if there were simply a correspondence of letters to sounds and as if the letters had not also completely different functions.

Just as the handles in the cabin of a locomotive have different kinds of job, so do the words of language, which in one way are like handles. One is the handle of a crank, it can be moved continuously since it operates a valve; another works a switch, which has two positions; a third is the handle of a pump and only works when it is being moved up and down etc. But they all look alike, since they are all worked by hand.

A connected point: it is possible to speak perfectly intelligibly of *combinations of colours and shapes* (e.g. of the colours red and blue and the shapes square and circle) just as we speak of combinations of different shapes or spatial objects. And this is the origin of the bad expression: a fact is a complex of objects. Here the fact that a man is sick is compared with a combination of two things, one of them the man and the other the sickness.

21 A man who reads a sentence in a familiar language experiences the different parts of speech in quite different ways. (Think of the comparison with meaning-bodies.) We quite forget that the written and spoken words "not", "table" and "green" are similar to each other. It is only in a foreign language that we see clearly the uniformity of words. (Compare William James on the feelings that correspond to words like "not", "but" and so on.)

("Not" makes a gesture of rejection.
No, it *is* a gesture of rejection. To grasp negation is to understand a gesture of rejection.)

Compare the different parts of speech in a sentence with lines on a map with different functions (frontiers, roads, meridians, contours.) An uninstructed person sees a mass of lines and does not know the variety of their meanings.

Think of a line on a map crossing a sign out to show that it is void

The difference between parts of speech is comparable to the differences between chessmen, but also to the even greater difference between a chessman and the chess board.

22 We say: the essential thing in a word is its *meaning*. We can replace the word by another with the same meaning. That fixes a place for the word, and we can substitute one word for another provided we put it in the same place.

If I decide to say a new word instead of "red" (perhaps only in thought), how would it come out that it took the place of the word "red"?
Suppose it was agreed to say "non" in English instead of "not", and "not" instead of "red". In that case the word "not" would remain in the language, and one could say that "non" was now used in the way in which "not" used to be, and that "not" now had a *different* use.

Would it not be similar if I decided to alter the shape of the chess pieces, or to use a knight-shaped piece as the king? How would it be clear that the knight is the king? In this case can't I very well talk about a change of meaning?

23 I want to say the place of a word in grammar is its meaning.

But I might also say: the meaning of a word is what the explanation of its meaning explains.

"What 1 c.c. of water weighs is called '1 gram' – Well, what *does* it weigh?"

The explanation of the meaning explains the use of the word.

The use of a word in the language is its meaning.

Grammar describes the use of words in the language.
So it has somewhat the same relation to the language as the description of a game, the rules of a game, have to the game.

Meaning, in our sense, is embodied in the explanation of meaning. If, on the other hand, by the word "meaning" we mean a characteristic sensation connected with the use of a word, then the relation between the explanation of a word and its meaning is rather that of cause to effect.

24 An explanation of meaning can remove every *disagreement* with regard to a meaning. It can clear up misunderstandings.
The understanding here spoken of is a correlate of explanation.
By "explanation of the meaning of a sign" we mean rules for use but above all *definitions*. The distinction between verbal definitions and ostensive definitions gives a rough division of these types of explanation.
In order to understand the role of a definition in the calculus we must investigate the particular case.

It may seem to us as if the other grammatical rules for a word had to follow from its ostensive definition; since after all an ostensive definition, e.g. "that is called 'red'" determines the meaning of the word "red".
But this definition is only those words plus pointing to a red object, e.g. a red piece of paper. And is this definition really unambiguous? Couldn't I have used the very same one to give the word "red" the meaning of the word "paper", or "square", or "shiny", or "light", or "thin" etc. etc.?

However, suppose that instead of saying "that is called 'red'"

I had phrased my definition "that colour is called 'red' ". That certainly is unambiguous, but only because the expression "colour" settles the grammar of the word "red" up to this last point. (But here questions could arise like "do you call just *this* shade of colour red, or also other similar shades?"). Definitions might be given like this: the colour of this patch is called "red", its shape "ellipse".

I might say: one must already understand a great deal of a language in order to understand that definition. Someone who understands that definition must already know where the words ("red", "ellipse") are being put, where they belong in language.

25 The words "shape" and "colour" in the definitions determine the *kind of use* of the word, and therefore what one may call the *part of speech*. And in ordinary grammar one might well distinguish "shape words", "colour words", "sound words", "substance words" and so on as different parts of speech. (There wouldn't be the same reason for distinguishing "metal words", "poison words", "predator words". It makes sense to say "iron is a metal", "phosphorus is a poison", etc. but not "red is a colour", "a circle is a shape" and so on.)

I can ostensively define a word for a colour or a shape or a number, etc. etc. (children are given ostensive explanations of numerals and they do perfectly well); negation, too, disjunction and so on. The *same* ostension might define a numeral, or the name of a shape or the name of a colour. But in the grammar of each different part of speech the ostensive definition has a different role; and in each case it is only *one* rule.

(Consider also the grammar of definitions like: "today is called Monday", "I will call this day of the year 'the day of atonement' ").

26 But when we learn the meaning of a word, we are very often given *only* the single rule, the ostensive definition. So how does it

come about that on the strength of this definition we understand the word? Do we guess the rest of the rules?

Think also of teaching a child to understand words by showing it objects and uttering words. The child is given ostensive definitions and then it understands the words. – But what is the criterion of understanding here? Surely, that the child applies the words correctly. Does it guess rules? – Indeed we must ask ourselves whether we are to call these signs and utterances of words "definitions" at all. The language game is still very simple and the ostensive definition has not the same role in this language-game as in more developed ones. (For instance, the child cannot yet ask "What is that called?") But there is no sharp boundary between primitive forms and more complicated ones. I wouldn't know what I can and what I can't still call "definition". I can only describe language games or calculi; whether we still want to call them calculi or not doesn't matter as long as we don't let the use of the general term divert us from examining each particular case we wish to decide.

I might also say of a little child "he can use the word, he knows how it is applied." But I only see what that means if I ask "what is the criterion for this knowledge?" In this case it isn't the ability to state rules.

What's the sign of someone's understanding a game? Must he be able to recite the rules? Isn't it also a criterion that he can play the game, i.e. that he does in fact play it, even if he's baffled when asked for the rules? Is it only by being told the rules that the game is learnt and not also simply by watching it being played? Of course a man will often say to himself while watching "oh, so that's the rule"; and he might perhaps write down the rules as he observes them; but there's certainly such a thing as learning the game without explicit rules.

The grammar of a language isn't recorded and doesn't come into existence until the language has already been spoken by human beings for a *long* time. Similarly, primitive games are played without their rules being codified, and even without a single rule being formulated.

But we look at games and language under the guise of a game played according to rules. That is, we are always *comparing* language with a procedure of that kind.

27 The names I give to bodies, shapes, colours, lengths have different grammars in each case. ("A" in "A is yellow" has one grammar if A is a body and another if A is the surface of a body; for instance it makes sense to say that the body is yellow all through, but not to say that the surface is.) And one points in different sense to a body, and to its length or its colour; for example, a possible definition would be: "to point to a colour" means, to point to the body which has the colour. Just as a man who marries money doesn't marry it in the same sense as he marries the woman who owns the money.

Money, and what one buys with it. Sometimes a material object, sometimes the right to a seat in the theatre, or a title, or fast travel, or life, etc.

A name has meaning, a proposition has sense in the calculus to which it belongs. The calculus is as it were autonomous. – Language must speak for itself.

I might say: the only thing that is of interest to me is the *content* of a proposition and the content of a proposition is something internal to it. A proposition has its content as part of a calculus.

The meaning is the role of the word in the calculus.

The meaning of a name is not the thing we point to when we give an ostensive definition of the name; that is, it is not the bearer of the name. – The expression "the bearer of the name 'N' " is synonymous with the name "N". The expression can be used in place of the name. "The bearer of the name 'N' is sick" means "N is sick". We don't say: The meaning of "N" is sick.

The name doesn't lose its meaning if its bearer ceases to exist (if he dies, say).

But doesn't "Two names have a single bearer" mean the same as "two names have the same meaning?" Certainly, instead of "A = B" one can write "the bearer of the name 'A' = the bearer of the name 'B' ".

28 What does "to understand a word" mean?

We say to a child "No, no more sugar" and take it away from him. Thus he learns the meaning of the word "no". If, while saying the same words, we had given him a piece of sugar he would have learnt to understand the word differently. (In this way he has learnt to use the word, but also to associate a particular feeling with it, to experience it in a particular way.)

What constitutes the meaning of a word like "perhaps"? How does a child learn the use of the word "perhaps"? It may repeat a sentence it has heard from an adult like "*perhaps* she will come"; it may do so in the same tone of voice as the adult. (That is a kind of a game). In such a case the question is sometimes asked: Does it already understand the word "perhaps" or is it only repeating it? – What shows that it really understands the word? – Well, that it uses it in particular circumstances in a particular manner – in certain contexts and with a particular intonation.

What does it mean "to understand the word 'perhaps' "? – Do *I* understand the word "perhaps"? – And how do I judge whether I do? Well, something like this: I know how it's used, I can explain its use to somebody, say by describing it in made-up cases. I can describe the occasions of its use, its position in sentences, the intonation it has in speech. – Of course this only means that "I understand the word 'perhaps'" comes to the same as: "I know how it is used etc."; not that I try to call to mind its entire application in order to answer the question whether I understand the word. More likely I would react to this question immediately with the answer "yes", perhaps after having said the word to myself once again, and as it were convinced myself that it's familiar, or else I might think of a single application and pronounce the word with the correct intonation and a gesture of uncertainty. And so on.

This is like the case in which someone is explaining to me a calculation "that I don't quite understand", and when he has reached a particular point of his explanation, I say: "ah, now I understand; now I know how to go on". How do I know that I know how to go on? Have I run through the rest of the calculation at that moment? Of course not. Perhaps a bit of it flashed before my mind; perhaps a particular application or a diagram. If I were asked: how do you know that you can use the word "perhaps" I would perhaps simply answer "I have used it a hundred times".

29 But it might be asked: Do I *understand* the word just be describing its application? Do I understand its point? Haven't I deluded myself about something important?

At present, say, I know only how men use this word. But it might be a game, or a form of etiquette. I do not know why they behave in this way, how *language* meshes with their life.

Is meaning then really only the use of a word? Isn't it the way this use meshes with our life?

But isn't its use a part of our life?

Do I understand the word "fine" when I know how and on what occasions people use it? Is that enough to enable me to use it myself? I mean, so to say, use it with conviction.

Wouldn't it be possible for me to know the use of the word and yet follow it without understanding? (As, in a sense, we follow the singing of birds). So isn't it something else that constitutes under-standing – the feeling "in one's own breast", the living experience of the expressions? – They must mesh with *my own* life.

Well, language does connect up with my own life. And what is called "language" is something made up of heterogeneous ele-ments and the way it meshes with life is infinitely various.

30 We may say that the words "fine", "oh", and also "perhaps" are *expressions* of sensation, of feeling. But I don't call the feeling the meaning of the word. We are not interested in the relation of the words to the senesation, whatever it may be, whether they are evoked by it, or are regularly accompanied by it, or give it an outlet. We are not interested in any empirical facts about language, considered as empirical facts. We are only concerned with the description of what happens and it is not the truth but the form of the description that interests us. What happens considered as a game.

I am only *describing* language, not *explaining* anything.

For my purposes I could replace the sensation the word is said to express by the intonation and gestures with which the word is used.

I might say: in many cases understanding a word involves being able to use it on certain occasions in a special tone of voice.

You might say that certain words are only pegs to hang intona-tions on.

But instead of the intonation and the accompanying gestures, I might for my own purposes treat the word itself as a gesture. (Can't I say that the sound "ha ha" is a laugh and the sound "oh!" is a sigh?)

31 I could imagine a language that was spoken in a uniform metre, with quasi-words intercalated between the words of the sentences to maintain the metre. Suppose we talked about the meaning of these quasi-words. (The smith putting in extra taps between the real strokes in order to maintain a rhythm in striking).

Language is like a collection of very various tools. In the tool box there is a hammer, a saw, a rule, a lead, a glue pot and glue. Many of the tools are akin to each other in form and use, and the tools can be roughly divided into groups according to their relationships; but the boundaries between these groups will often be more or less arbitrary and there are various types of relationship that cut across one another.

I said that the meaning of a word is its role in the calculus of language. (I compared it to a piece in chess). Now let us think how we calculate with a word, for instance with the word "red". We are told where the colour is situated; we are told the shape and size of the coloured patch or the coloured object; we are told whether the colour is pure or mixed, light or dark, whether it remains constant or changes, etc. etc. Conclusions are drawn from the propositions, they are translated into diagrams and into behaviour, there is drawing, measurement and calculation. But think of the meaning of the word "oh!" If we were asked about it, we would say "'oh'! is a sigh; we say, for instance, things like 'Oh, it is raining again already'". And that would describe the use of the word. But what corresponds now to the calculus, the complicated game that we play with other words? In the use of the words "oh!", or "hurrah", or "hm", there is nothing comparable.

Moreover, we mustn't confuse signs with symptoms here. The sound "hm" may be called an expression of dubiousness and also, for other people, a *symptom* of dubiousness, in the way that clouds are a symptom of rain. But "hm" is not the *name* of dubiousness.

32 Suppose we want to describe *ball-games*. There are some games like football, cricket and tennis, which have a well-developed and complicated system of rules; there is a game consisting simply of everyone's throwing a ball as high as he can; and there is the game little children play of throwing a ball in any direction and then retrieving it. Or again someone throws a ball high into the air for the fun of it and catches it again without any element of competition. Perhaps one will be unwilling to call some of these ball games at all; but is it clear where the boundary is to be drawn here?

We are interested in language as a procedure according to explicit rules, because philosophical problems are misunderstandings which must be removed by clarification of the rules according to which we are inclined to use words.

We consider language from one point of view only.

We said that when we understood the use we didn't yet understand the *purpose* of the word "perhaps". And by "purpose" in this case we meant the role in human life. (This role can be called the "meaning" of the word in the sense in which one speaks of the 'meaning of an event for our life'.)

But we said that by "meaning" we meant what an explanation of meaning explains. And an explanation of meaning is not an empirical proposition and not a causal explanation, but a rule, a convention.

It might be said that the purpose of the word "hey!" in our language is to alarm the person spoken to. But what does its having this purpose amount to? What is the criterion for it? The word "purpose" like all the words of our language is used in various more or less related ways. I will mention two characteristic games. We might say that the purpose of doing something is what the person doing it would say if asked what its purpose was. On the other hand if we say that the hen clucks in order to call her chicks together we infer this purpose from the *effect* of the clucking. We wouldn't call the gathering of the chicks the purpose of the clucking if the clucking didn't have this result always, or at least commonly or in specifiable circumstances. – One may now say that the purpose, the effect of the word "hey" is the important thing about the word; but explaining the purpose or the effect is not what we call explaining the meaning.

It may be that if it is to achieve its effect a particular word cannot be replaced by any other; just as it may be that a gesture cannot be replaced by any other. (The word has a *soul* and not just a meaning.) No one would believe that a poem remained *essentially unaltered* if its words were replaced by others in accordance with an appropriate convention.

Our proposition "meaning is what an explanation of meaning explains" could also be interpreted in the following way: let's only bother about what's called the explanation of meaning, and let's not bother about meaning in any other sense.

33 But one might say something like this. The sentences that we utter have a particular purpose, they are to produce certain effects. They are parts of a mechanism, perhaps a psychological mechanism, and the words of the sentences are also parts of the mechanism (levers, cogwheels and so on). The example that seems to illustrate what we're thinking of here is an automatic music player, a pianola. It contains a roll, rollers, etc., on which the piece of music is written in some kind of notation (the position of holes, pegs and so on). It's as if these written signs gave orders which are carried out by the keys and hammers. And so shouldn't we say that the sense of the sign is its effect? – But suppose the pianola is in bad condition and the signs on the roll produce hisses and bangs instead of the notes. – Perhaps you will say that the sense of the signs is their effect on a mechanism in good condition, and corres-

pondingly that the sense of an order is its effect on an obedient man. But what is regarded as a criterion of obedience here?

You might then say that the sense of the signs is not their effect, but their purpose. But consider too, that we're tempted to think that this purpose is only a part of the larger purpose served by the pianola. – This purpose, say, is to entertain people. But it's clear that when we spoke of "the sense of the signs" we didn't mean any part of *that* purpose. We were thinking rather of the purpose of the signs *within* the mechanism of the pianola. – And so you can say that the purpose of an order is its sense, only so far as the purpose can be expressed by a rule of language. "I am saying 'go away' because I want you to leave me alone", "I am saying 'perhaps' because I am not quite sure."

An explanation of the operation of language as a psychophysical mechanism is of no interest to us. Such an explanation itself uses language to describe phenomena (association, memory etc); it is itself a linguistic act and stands outside the calculus; but we need an explanation which is *part of the calculus.*

"How is he to know what colour he is to pick out when he hears the word 'red'? – Very simple: he is to take the colour whose image occurs to him when he hears the word" – But how will he know what that means, and which colour it is "which occurs to him when he hears the word"?

Certainly there is such a procedure as choosing the colour which occurs to you when you hear that word. And the sentence "red is the colour that occurs to you when you hear the word 'red' " is a definition.

If I say, "a symbol is something which produces this effect" the question remains: how can I speak of "this effect"? And if it occurs, how do I know that it's *the one I meant*?" "Very simple", we may say "we compare it with our memory image." But this explanation does not get to the root of our dissatisfaction. For how are we given the method we're to use in making the comparison – i.e. how do we know what we're to do when we're told to compare?

In our language one of the functions of the word "red" is to call that particular colour to mind; and indeed it might be discovered that this word did so better than others, even that it alone served that purpose. But instead of the mechanism of association we might also have used a colour chart or some such apparatus; and then our calculus would have to get along with the associated, or visible, colour sample. The psychological effectiveness of a sign does not concern us. I wouldn't even scruple to invent that kind of mechanism.

Investigating whether the meaning of a word is its effect or its purpose, etc. is a grammatical investigation.

34 Why can one understand a word and not a penholder? Is it the difference between their shapes? But you will say that we could understand a penholder too, if we had given it a meaning. But then how is giving it a meaning done? – How was meaning given to the word "red"? Well, you point at something, and you say "I call that 'red'". Is that a kind of consecration of mystical formula? How does this pointing and uttering words work? It works only as part of a system containing other bits of linguistic behaviour. And so now one can understand a penholder too; but does this understanding contain the whole system of its application? Impossible. We say that we understand its meaning when we know its use, but we've also said that the word "know" doesn't denote a state of consciousness. That is: the grammar of the word "know" isn't the grammar of a "state of consciousness", but something different. And there is only one way to learn it: to watch how the word is used in practice.

A truthful answer to the question "Did you understand the

sentence (that you have just read)" is sometimes "yes" and sometimes "no". "So something different must take place when I understand it and when I don't understand it."

Right. So when I understand a sentence something happens like being able to follow a melody as a melody, unlike the case when it's so long or so developed that I have to say "I can't follow this bit". And the same thing might happen with a picture, and here I mean an ornament. First of all I see only a maze of lines; then they group themselves for me into well-known and accustomed forms and I see a plan, a familiar system. If the ornamentation contains representations of well-known objects the recognition of these will indicate a further stage of understanding. (Think in this connection of the solution of a puzzle picture.) I then say "Yes, now I see the picture rightly".

Asked "what happened when you read that sentence with understanding" I would have to say "I read it as a group of English words linked in a familiar way". I might also say that a picture came into my mind when I heard it. But then I am asked: "Is that all? After all, the understanding couldn't consist in that and nothing else!" Well, that or something like it is all that happened while I read the sentence and immediately afterwards; but what we call "understanding" is related to countless things that happen before and after the reading of *this* sentence.

What of when I don't understand a sentence? Well, it might be a sentence in a foreign language and all I see is a row of unknown words. Or what I read seemed to be an English sentence, but it contained an unfamiliar phrase and when I tried to grasp it (and that again can mean various things) I didn't succeed. (Think of what goes on when we try to understand the sense of a poem in our native language which makes use of constructions we don't yet understand.)

But I can say that I understand a sentence in a foreign language –

say a Latin one that I can only decipher by a painful effort to construe – even if I have only turned it into English bit by bit and have never succeeded in grasping the overall phrasing of the sentence.

But all the same, in order to understand a sentence I have to understand the words in it! And when I read, I understand some words and not others.

I hear a word and someone asks me "did you understand it?" and I reply truly "yes". What happened when I understood? How was the understanding different from what happens when I don't understand a word? – Suppose the word was "tree". If I am to say truly that I understood it, must the image of a tree have come before my mind? No; nor must any other image. All I can say is that when I was asked "do you understand the word tree?" I'd have answered "yes" unthinkingly and without lying. – If the other person had asked me further "and what is a tree?" I would have described one for him, or shown him one, or drawn one; or perhaps I would have answered "I know, but I don't want to explain." And it may be that when I gave my reply the image of a tree came before my mind, or perhaps I looked for something which had some similarity with a tree, or perhaps other words came into my head, etc. etc.

Let's just look how we actually use the word "understand".

The word might also have been one of which I would say "I used to know what it meant, and it will come back to me", and then later on say "now it's come back to me". What happened then? – Perhaps there came into my mind the situation in which the word was first explained to me: I saw myself in a room with others, etc. etc. (But if now I read and understand the word in a sentence that picture wouldn't have to come before my mind; perhaps no picture at all comes to mind.)

Or it was a word in a foreign language; and I had already often heard it, but never understood it. Perhaps I said to myself "what can it mean?" and tried to give it a meaning which fitted the context (again various possibilities). Perhaps now this situation comes to mind and I say "I don't understand the word". But I might also react immediately to the foreign word with the answer "I don't understand it", just as I reacted to the word "tree" with the opposite answer.

Suppose it is the word "red" and I say automatically that I understood it; then he asks again "do you really understand it?" Then I summon up a red image in my mind as a kind of check. But how do I know that it's the right colour that appears to me? And yet I say now with full conviction that I understand it. – But I might also look at a colour chart with the word "red" written beneath the colour. – I could carry on for ever describing such processes.

35 The problem that concerns us could be summed up roughly thus: "Must one see an image of the colour blue in one's mind whenever one reads the word 'blue' with understanding?" People have often asked this question and have commonly answered no; they have concluded from this answer that the characteristic process of understanding is just a different process which we've not yet grasped. – Suppose then by "understanding" we mean what makes the difference between reading with understanding and reading without understanding; what *does* happen when we understand? Well, "Understanding" is not the name of a single process accompanying reading or hearing, but of more or less interrelated processes against a background, or in a context, of facts of a particular kind, viz. the actual use of a learnt language or languages. – We say that understanding is a "psychological process", and this label is misleading, in this as in countless other cases. It compares understanding to a particular *process* like translation from one language into another, and it suggests the same conception of thinking, knowing, wishing, intending, etc. That is to say, in all these cases we see that what we would perhaps naively suggest as the hallmark of such a process is not present in

every case or even in the majority of cases. And our next step is to conclude that the essence of the process is something difficult to grasp that still awaits discovery. For we say: since I use the word "understand" in all these cases, there must be some one thing which happens in every case and which is the essence of understanding (expecting, wishing etc.). Otherwise, why should I call them by all the same name?

This argument is based on the notion that what is needed to justify characterizing a number of processes or objects by a general concept-word is something common to them all.

This notion is, in a way, *too primitive*. What a concept-word indicates is certainly a kinship between objects, but this kinship need not be the sharing of a common property or a constituent. It may connect the objects like the links of a chain, so that one is linked to another *by intermediary links*. Two neighbouring members may have common features and be *similar* to each other, while distant ones belong to the same family without any longer having anything in common. Indeed even if a feature is common to all members of the family it need not be that feature that defines the concept.

The relationship between the members of a concept may be set up by the sharing of features which show up in the family of the concept, crossing and overlapping in very complicated ways.

Thus there is probably no single characteristic which is common to all the things we call games. But it can't be said either that "game" just has several independent meanings (rather like the word "bank"). What we call "games" are procedures interrelated in various ways with many different transitions between one and another.

It might be said that the use of the concept-word or common noun is justified in this case because there are transitional steps between the members. – Then it might be objected that a transition can be made from anything to anything, and so the concept isn't bounded. To this I have to say that for the most part it isn't in fact bounded and the way to specify it is perhaps: "by 'knowledge' we mean these processes, and these, *and similar ones*". And instead of "and similar ones" I might have said "and others akin to these in many ways".

But if we wish to draw boundaries in the use of a word, in order to clear up philosophical paradoxes, then alongside the actual picture of the use (in which as it were the different colours flow into one another without sharp boundaries) we may put another picture which is in certain ways like the first but is built up of colours with clear boundaries between them.

III

36 If we look at the actual use of a word, what we see is something constantly fluctuating.

In our investigations we set over against this fluctuation something more fixed, just as one paints a stationary picture of the constantly altering face of the landscape.

When we study language we *envisage* it as a game with fixed rules. We compare it with, and measure it against, a game of that kind.

If for our purposes we wish to regulate the use of a word by definite rules, then alongside its fluctuating use we set up a different use by codifying one of its characteristic aspects.

Thus it could be said that the use of the word "good" (in an ethical sense) is a combination of a very large number of interrelated games, each of them as it were a facet of the use. What makes a single concept here is precisely the connection, the relationship, between these facets.

But this isn't like the way physics gives a simplified description of a natural phenomenon, abstracting from secondary factors. It can't be said that logic depicts an idealised reality, or that it holds strictly only for an ideal language and so on. For where do we get the concept of this ideal? The most that could be said is that we are *constructing* an ideal language which contrasts with ordinary language; but it can't be said that we are *saying* something that would hold only of an ideal language.

37 There is something else I would like to say about the understanding of a picture. Take a genre-picture: we say we understand

it if we recognise what is happening in it, what the people in it are doing. Here the criterion for this recognition is perhaps that if asked what they are doing we explain it in words or represent it in mime etc. It's possible that this recognition doesn't come easily, perhaps because we don't immediately see the figures in the picture as figures (as in puzzle pictures), perhaps because we can't make out what they are doing together, etc. In these cases there may be a period of doubt followed by a familiar process of recognition. On the other hand, it may be the kind of picture we'd say we took in at first glance, and in that case we find it difficult to say what the understanding really consists of. In the first place what happened was not that we took the painted objects for real ones. And again "I understand it" in this case doesn't mean that finally, after an effort, I understand that it is *this* picture. And nothing takes place like recognizing an old acquaintance in the street, no saying "oh, there's . . . ". If you insist on saying there is a recognition, what does this recognition consist of? Perhaps I recognize a certain part of the picture as a human face. Do I have to look at a real face, or call before my mind's eye the memory of a face I've seen before? Is what happens that I rummage in the cupboard of my memory until I find something which resembles the picture? Is the recognition just this finding? In our case there is no one thing that happens that could be called recognition, and yet if the person who sees the picture is asked "do you recognize what it is?" he may truly answer "yes", or perhaps reply "it is a face". It can indeed be said that when he sees the complex of signs as a face he sees something different from when he doesn't do so. In that case I'd like to say that I see something *familiar*[1] in front of me. But what constitutes the familiarity is not the historical fact that I've often seen objects like that etc; because the history behind the experience is certainly not present in the experience itself. Rather, the familiarity

1. Cf. p. 165f (Ed.)

lies in the fact that I immediately grasp a particular ryhthm of the picture and stay with it, fell at home with it, so to speak. For the rest it is a different experience that constitutes the familiarity in each particular case; a picture of a table carries one experience with it and a picture of a bed another.

If I say: "I understand this picture" the question arises: do I mean "I understand it *like that*"? With the "*like that*" standing for a translation of what I understand into a different expression? Or is it a sort of intransitive understanding? When I'm understanding one thing do I as it were think of another thing? Does understanding, that is, consist of thinking of something else? And if that isn't what I mean, then what's understood is as it were autonomous, and the understanding of it is comparable to the understanding of a melody.

(It is interesting to observe that the pictures which come before our minds when we read an isolated word and try to understand it correctly just like that are commonly altogether absent when we read a sentence; the picture that comes before our minds when we read a sentence with understanding is often something like a resultant of the whole sentence).

38 It is possible for a person to forget the meaning of a word (e.g. "blue"). What has he forgotten? – How is that manifested?

He may point, for instance, to a chart of different colours and say "I don't know any longer which of these is called 'blue'". Or again, he may not any longer know at all what the word means (what purpose it serves); he may know only that is it an English word.

We might say: if someone has forgotten the meaning of the word "blue" and is asked to choose a blue object from among others he feels as he looks at the objects that the connection between the word "blue" and the colour no longer holds but has been broken off. The connection will be reestablished, it might be said, if we repeat the definition of the word for him. But we might reestablish the connection in various ways: we might point to a blue object and say "that is blue", or say "remember your blue patch" or we perhaps utter the German word "blau", etc. etc. And if I now say there are these different ways in which we can establish the connection this suggests there's a single particular phenomenon I call the connection between word and colour, or the understanding of the word, a phenomenon I've produced in all these different ways, just as I can use objects of different shapes and materials as conductors to connect the ends of two wires. But there is no need for such a phenomenon of connection, no need, say, that when I hear the word a picture of the colour should occur before my inner eye. For if what is reestablished in his understanding of the word, this can manifest itself in very various processes. There isn't a further process hidden behind, which is the real understanding, accompanying and causing these manifestations in the way that toothache causes one to groan, hold one's cheek, pull faces, etc. If I am now asked if I think that there's no such thing as understanding but only manifestations of understanding, I must answer that this question is as senseless as the question whether there is a number three. I can only describe piecemeal the grammar of the word "understand" and point out that it differs from what one is inclined to portray without looking closely. We are like the little painter Klecksel who drew two eyes in a man's profile, since he knew that human beings have two eyes.

39 The effect of an explanation of the meaning of a word is like 'knowing how to go on', when you recite the beginning of a poem to someone until he says "now I know how to go on". (Tell yourself the various psychological forms this knowing how to go on may take.)

The way in which language was learnt is not *contained* in its use. (Any more than the cause is contained in the effect.)

How does an ostensive definition work? Is it put to work again every time the word is used, or is it like a vaccination which changes us once and for all?

A definition as a part of the calculus cannot act at a distance. It acts only by being applied.

40 Once more: in what cases shall we say that the man understands the word "blue"? Well, if he picks out a blue object from others on demand; or if he credibly says that he could now pick out the blue object but doesn't want to (perhaps we notice that while he says this he glances involuntarily at the blue object; perhaps we believe him simply on account of his previous behaviour). And how does *he* know that he understands the word? i.e. in what circumstances will *he* be able to say it? Sometimes after some kind of test, but sometimes also without. But in that case won't he sometimes have to say later "I was wrong, I did not understand it after all" if it turns out that he can't apply it? Can he justify himself in such cases by saying that he did indeed understand the word when he said he did, but that the meaning later slipped his memory? Well, what can he offer as a criterion (proof) that he did understand the word at the previous time? – Perhaps he says "At that time I saw the colour in my mind's eye, but now I can't remember it." Well, if that implies that he understood it, he did understand it then. – Or he says: "I can only say I've used the word a hundred times before", or "I'd used it just before, and while I was saying I understood it I was thinking of that occasion." It is what is regarded as the justification of an assertion that constitutes the sense of the assertion.

Suppose we say "he understands the word 'blue', he picked the blue ball out from the others right away" and then he says "I just picked it out by guesswork, I didn't understand the word". What sort of criterion did he have for not having understood the word? Ought we to believe him? If one asks oneself "How do I know that

I don't understand this word" it produces a very strange thought sensation. One wants to say " I don't connect anything with it", "it says nothing to me", "It's a mere noise", and in order to understand these utterances one has to call to mind what it's like "when one connects something with a word", when a definition has made the sound into a meaningful word, when one can *do* *something* with the word.

You will say: "But he certainly can't be wrong when he says that he didn't understand the word." And that is an observation about the grammar of the statement "I didn't understand the word". It is also an observation about grammar when we say, "Whether he understood, is something he knows which we cannot *know* but only guess". Moreover the statement "I didn't understand the word" doesn't describe a state at the time of hearing the word; there are many different ways in which the processes characteristic of not understanding may have taken place later.

41 We speak of understanding (a process of understanding, and also a state of understanding) and also of certain processes which are criteria for this understanding.

We are inclined to call understanding a mental process or a state of mind. This characterizes it as a *hypothetical* process etc., or rather as a process (or state) in the sense of a hypothesis. That is, we banish the word "understanding" to a particular region of grammar.

The grammar of a mental state or process is indeed in many respects similar to that of e.g. a brain-process. The principal difference is perhaps that in the case of a brain-process a direct check is admitted to be possible; the process in question may perhaps be seen by opening the skull. But there is no room for a similar "immediate perception" in the grammar of mental process. (There is no such move in this game.)

What is the criterion for our understanding the word "red"? That we pick out a red object from others on demand, or that we can give the ostensive definition of the word "red"?

We regard both things as signs of understanding. If we hear someone use the word "red" and are in doubt whether he understands it, we can check by asking: "which colour do you call red?" On the other hand, if we'd given someone the ostensive definition of the word and then wanted to see whether he'd understood it rightly, we wouldn't ask him to repeat it, but we would set him a task like picking out the red objects from a row.

Here it can be asked: "are we talking about *my* understanding or other people's understanding?"

"Only I can know whether I understand, others can only guess."

" 'He understands' is a hypothesis; 'I understand' is not."

If that's what we say, then we're conceiving "understanding" as an experience, analogous e.g. to a pain.

People say: "You cannot know whether I understand (whether I am glad), etc.; you can't look inside me." "You can't know what I think." Yes, but that's so only as long as you don't think aloud; and we aren't interested here in the difference between thinking out loud (or in writing) and thinking in the imagination.

Here you may object that thinking is after all private even if it is only the *visual* experience of writing, and that though another person can see what my physical hand is writing he cannot have my visual experience. These questions must occupy us in another place.

But for our present purpose can't we say "he is writing" and "I am writing"instead of "he understands" and "I understand?" Then we leave the question of experience *completely* out of the game. Also, for instance, the question of private understanding. For then it appears unimportant here.

What we call "understanding" is not the behaviour—whatever it may be – that shows us the understanding, but a state of which this behaviour is a sign. And that is a statement about the grammar of denoting such a state.

42 We might call the recital of the rules on its own a criterion for understanding, or alternatively tests of use on their own. Then in the one case "he understands" would mean: "if you ask him for for the rules, he will tell you them"; in the other case "if you require him to apply the rule, he will carry out your order".

Or we may regard the recital of the rules as a symptom of the man's being able to do something other than recite the rules. As when I hold a watch to my ear, hear it ticking and say: it is going. In that case I don't just expect it to go on ticking, but also to show the time.

One might say: "The recital of the rules is a criterion of understanding, if the man recites them with understanding and not purely mechanically." But here once again an intelligent intonation during the recitation can count as understanding; and so why not the recitation itself?

To understand is to grasp, to receive a particular impression from an object, to let it work on one. To let a proposition work on one; to consider consequences of the proposition, to imagine them, etc.

What we call "understanding" is a psychological phenomenon that has a special connection with the phenomena of learning and using our human language.

What happens when I remember the meaning of a word? I see before me an object of a certain colour and I say "this book is brown and I have always called this colour 'brown' ". What sort of act of remembering must take place for me to be able to say that? This question could be put in a much more general form. For instance, if someone asked me "have you ever before seen the table at which you are now sitting?" I would answer "yes, I have seen it countless times". And if I were pressed I would say "I have sat at it every day for months". – What act or acts of remembering occur in such a case? After all I don't see myself in my mind's eye "sitting at this table every day for months". And yet I say that I remember that I've done so, and I can later corroborate it in various ways. Last summer too, for example, I was living in this room. But how do I know that? Do I see it in my mind's eye? No. In this case what does the remembering consist of? If I as it were hunt for the basis of the memory, isolated pictures of my earlier sojourn surface in my mind; but even so they don't have, say, a date written into them. And even before they've surfaced and before I've called any particular evidence into my mind, I can say truly that I remember that I lived here for months and saw this table. Remembering, then, isn't at all the mental process that one imagines at first sight. If I say, rightly, "I remember it" the most *varied* things may happen; perhaps even just that I say it. And when I here say "rightly" of course I'm not laying down what the right and wrong use of the expression is; on the contrary I'm just describing the actual use.

The psychological process of understanding is in the same case as the arithmetical object Three. The word "process" in the one case, and the word "object" in the other produce a false grammatical *attitude* to the word.

43 Isn't it like this? First of all, people use an explanation, a chart, by looking it up; later they as it were look it up in the head (by calling it before the inner eye, or the like) and finally they work

without the chart, as if it had never existed. In this last case they are playing a different game. For it isn't as if the chart is still in the background, to fall back on; it is excluded from our game, and if I "fall back on it" I am like a blinded man falling back on the sense of touch. An explanation provides a chart and when I no longer use the chart it becomes mere history.

I must distinguish between the case in which I follow the table, and the case in which I behave in accordance with the table without making use of it. – The rule we learnt which makes us now behave in such and such a way is of no interest to us considered as the cause or history behind our present behaviour. – But as a general description of our manner of behaving it is a hypothesis. It is the hypothesis that the two people who sit at the chess board will behave (move) in such and such a manner. (Here even a breach of the rules falls under the hypothesis, since it says something about the behaviour of the players when they become aware of the breach). But the players might also use the rules by looking up in each particular case what is to be done; here the rule would enter into the conduct of the game itself and would not be related to it as hypothesis to confirmation. But there is a difficulty here. For a player who plays without using the list of rules, and indeed has never seen one, might nevertheless if asked give the rules of his game – not by ascertaining through repeated observation what he does in such and such a position in the game, but by superintending a move and saying "in such a case *this is how one moves*". – But, if that is so, that just shows that in certain circumstances he can enunciate the rules, not that he makes explicit use of them while playing.

It is a hypothesis that he will if asked recite a list of rules; if a disposition or capacity for this is postulated in him, it is a psychological disposition analogous to a physiological one. If it is said that this disposition characterizes the process of playing, it characterizes it as the psychological or physiological one it really is. (In our study of symbolism there is no foreground and background; it isn't a matter of a tangible sign with an accompanying intangible power or understanding.)

44 What interests *us* in the sign, the meaning which matters for us is what is embodied in the grammar of the sign.

We ask "How do you use the word, what do you do with it" – that will tell us how you understand it.

Grammar is the account books of language. They must show the actual transactions of language, everything that is not a matter of accompanying sensations.

In a certain sense one might say that we are not concerned with nuances.

(I could imagine a philosopher who thought that he must have a proposition about the essence of knowing printed in red, otherwise it would not really express what it was meant to express.)

IV

45 The interpretation of written and spoken signs by ostensive definitions is not an *application* of language, but part of the grammar. The interpretation remains at the level of generality preparatory to any application.

The ostensive definition may be regarded as a rule for translating from a gesture language into a word language. If I say "the colour of this object is called 'violet'", I must already have denoted the colour, already presented it for christening, with the words "the colour of that object" if the naming is to be able to take place. For I might also say "the name of this colour is for you to decide" and the man who gives the name would in that case already have to know what he is to name (where in the language he is stationing the name).

That one empirical proposition is true and another false is no part of grammar. What belongs to grammar are all the conditions (the method) necessary for comparing the proposition with reality. That is, all the conditions necessary for the understanding (of the sense).

In so far as the meaning of words becomes clear in the fulfilment of an expectation, in the satisfaction of a wish, in the carrying out of an order etc., it already shows itself when we put the expectation into language. It is therefore completely determined in the grammar, in what could be foreseen and spoken of already before the occurrence of the event.

46 Does our language consist of primary signs (ostensive gestures) and secondary signs (words)? One is inclined to ask, whether it isn't the case that our language *has* to have primary signs while it could get by without the secondary ones.

The false note in this question is that it expects an explanation of existing language instead of a mere description.

It sounds like a ridiculous truism to say that a man who thinks that gestures are the primitive signs underlying all others would not be able to replace an ordinary sentence by gestures.

One is inclined to make a distinction between rules of grammar that set up "a connection between language and reality" and those that do not. A rule of the first kind is "this colour is called 'red' ", – a rule of the second kind is " $\sim \sim p = p$". With regard to this distinction there is a common error; language is not something that is first given a structure and then fitted on to reality.

One might wish to ask: So is it an accident that in order to define signs and complete the sign-system I have to go outside the written and spoken signs? When I do that don't I go right into the realm where what is to be described occurs? – But in that case isn't it strange that I can do anything at all with the written signs? – We say perhaps that the written signs are mere representatives of the things the ostensive definition points to. – But how then is this representing possible? I can't after all make just anything stand in for anything else. – It is indeed important that such representing is possible; for the representative must, in certain cases at least, do the job as well as the principal.

47 We say that something like a red label is the primary sign for the colour red, and the word is a secondary sign, because the meaning of the word "red" is explained if I point, etc. to a red label, but not if I say "red" means the same as "rouge". But don't I explain the meaning of the word "red" to a Frenchman in just this way? "Yes, but only because he has learnt the meaning of 'rouge' by *ostensive* definition". But if he understands my explanation "red =

rouge" does he have to have this definition – or a red image – present to his mind? If not, it is mere history. Must he have such a picture present whenever we would say he was using the word "rouge" with understanding? (Think of the order: "Imagine a round red patch.")

48 Are the signs one wants to call 'primary' incapable of being misinterpreted?

Can one perhaps say, they don't really any longer need to be *understood*? – If that means that they don't have to be further *interpreted*, that goes for words too; if it means, they *cannot* be further interpreted, then it's false. (Think of the explanation of gestures by words and vice versa).

Is it correct, and if so in what sense, to say that the ostensive definition is like the verbal definition in replacing one sign by another – the pointing by the word?

49 Suppose I lay down a method of designation. Suppose, for example, I want to give names to shades of colours for my private use. I may do so by means of a chart; and of course I won't write a name beside a wrong colour (beside a colour I don't want to give that name to). But why not? Why shouldn't "red" go beside the green label and "green" beside the red, etc.? If the ostensive definition merely replaces one sign by another, that shouldn't make any difference. – Here there are at any rate two different possibilities. It may be that the table with green beside "red" is used in such a way that a man who 'looks it up' goes diagonally from the word "red" to the red label, and from the word "green" to the green one and so on. We would then say that though the table was arranged differently (had a different spatial scheme) it connected the signs in the same way as the usual one. – But it might also be that the person using the table looks from one side horizontally to another, and in some sentences uses a green label instead of the word "red", and yet obeys an order like "give me a

red book" not by bringing a green book, but perfectly correctly by bringing a red one (i.e. one that we too would call "red"). Such a man would have used the table in a different way from the first, but still in such a way that the word "red" means the same colour for him as it does for us.

Now it is the second case which interests us, and the question is: can a green label be a *sample* of red? –

I can imagine an arrangement according to which a man to whom I show a green label with the words "paint me this colour" is to paint me red and if I show him blue with the same words, is to paint me yellow (always the complementary colour). And someone might interpret my order in that way even without such a convention. The convention might also have been "if I say, 'paint this colour', then always paint one slightly darker", and again we could imagine the order being thus interpreted even without this prearrangement. – But can it be said that when someone is painting a certain shade of green he is *copying* the red of the label – as he may copy a geometrical figure according to various methods of projection, copying it in different but equally exact ways? – Can I compare colours with shapes? Can a green label be used both as the name of a particular shade of red, and also as a sample of it just as a circle can serve as the name of a particular elliptical shape, and also as a sample for it?

It is clear that a sample is not used like a word (a name). And an ostensive definition, a table, which leads us from words to samples, is used differently from a table which replaces one name by another.

50 However, the word "copy" has different meanings in different cases and what I mean by "pattern" changes correspondingly. What does "to copy a figure exactly" mean? Does it mean copy it exactly with the unaided eye? Or with measuring instruments, and if so which? What shall we be willing to call the same colour as that of the pattern? Think of various methods of comparison. How far is the rule to copy darker comparable to a rule to copy a figure

on a larger, or small scale?

Imagine a man who claimed to be able to copy shades of red into green, who fixed his eye on a red sample and with every outward sign of exact copying mixed a shade of green. For us he would be on a par with someone who listened carefully and mixed colours in accordance with notes on a violin. In such a case we'd say "I don't know *how* he does it"; not because we didn't understand the processes in his brain or in his muscles, but because we don't understand what is meant by "this shade of colour is a copy of this note on the violin". Unless that means that as a matter of experience a man associates a particular shade of colour with a particular note (sees it in his mind's eye, paints it etc). The difference between the meanings of "associate" and "copy" shows itself in the fact that it doesn't make sense to speak of a projection-method (rule of translation) for association. We say: "you haven't copied correctly", but not "you haven't associated correctly".

On the other hand it is certainly conceivable that human beings might agree so exactly with each other in associating colours with violin notes that one might say to another: "No, you haven't represented that violin note correctly, it was yellower than you painted it" and the other would answer something like "you're right, the same thought occurred to me".

51 If the table connects the word with a sample, then it isn't indifferent which label the word is linked with when the table is consulted – "So then there are signs that are arbitrary and signs that are not!" Compare the giving of information by maps and drawings, with the giving of information by sentences. The sentences are no more arbitrary than the drawings are; only the words are arbitrary. On the other hand the projection of the maps is arbitrary; and how would you decide which of the two is the more arbitrary?

Certainly I can compare deciding on the meanings of words with deciding on a method of projection, such as that for the representation of spatial forms ("the proposition is a picture"). That is a good comparison, but it doesn't exempt us from investigating the way words signify, which has its own rules. We can of course say – that is, it accords with usage – that we communicate by signs whether we use words or patterns, but the game of acting in accordance with words is not the same game as acting in accordance with patterns. (Words are not essential to what we call "language", and neither are samples). Word-language is only one of many possible kinds of language, and there are transitions between one kind and another. (Think of two ways of writing the proposition "I see a red circle": it might be done by writing a circle and giving it the appropriate colour (red), or by writing a circle with a red patch beside it. Consider what corresponds in a map to the form of expression of a word-language.)

5 2 "I won't insist that the red pattern in the explanatory chart must be horizontally opposite the word 'red', but there must be some sort of law for reading the table or it will lose its sense." But is there no law if the chart is read in the way indicated by the arrows of the following schema?

"But in that case *mustn't* this schema of arrows be given in advance?" – Well, must you give this schema before we follow the normal use?

"But in that case mustn't there at least be a regularity through time in the use of the table? Would it work if we were to use the table in accordance with different schemata at different times? *How would one know* in that case how the table was to be used?" Well, how does one know *anyway*? Explanations of signs come to an end somewhere.

Of course if I showed someone the way by pointing my finger not in the direction in which he was to go, but in the opposite direction, in the absence of a special arrangement I should cause a misunderstanding. It is part of human nature to understand pointing with the finger in the way we do. (As it is also part of human nature to play board games and to use sign languages that consist of written signs on a flat surface.)

The chart doesn't guarantee that I shall pass from one part of it to another in a uniform manner. It doesn't compel me to use it always in the same way. It's there, like a field, with paths leading through it: but I can also cut across. – Each time I apply the chart I make a fresh transition. The transitions aren't made as it were once for all the chart (the chart merely suggests to me that I make them).

(What kind of propositions are these? – They are like the observation that explanations of signs come to an end somewhere. And that is rather like saying "How does it help you to postulate a creator, it only pushes back the problem of the beginning of the word." This observation brings out an aspect of my explanation that I perhaps hadn't noticed. One might also say: "Look at your explanation in *this* way – now are you still satisfied with it?")

53 Is the word "red" enough to enable one to look for something red? Does one need a memory image to do so?

Can one say that the word "red" needs a supplement in memory in order to be a usable sign?

If I use the words "there is a red book in front of me" to describe an experience, is the justification of the choice of these words, apart from the experience described, the fact that I remember that I've always used the word "red" for this colour? Does that *have to* be the justification?

In order to be able to obey a spoken order do we need something like a memory picture of what we did when we last obeyed it?

So is the real order "Do now what you remember doing then"? This order too might be given. But does that mean that in order to obey it, I need a memory image of searching my memory?

The order "do now what you remember doing then" tells me that I am to look in a particular place for a picture that will tell me what I am to do. So the order is very similar to "Do what is written on the piece of paper in this drawer". If there is nothing on the piece of paper then the order lacks sense.

If the use of the word "red" depends on the picture that my memory automatically reproduces at the sound of this word, then I am as much at mercy of this reproduction as if I had decided to settle the meaning by looking up a chart in such a way that I would surrender unconditionally to whatever I found there.

If the sample I am to work with appears darker than I remember it being yesterday, I need not agree with the memory and in fact I do not always do so. And I might very well speak of a darkening of my memory.

54 If I tell someone "paint from memory the colour of the door of your room" that doesn't settle what he is to do any more un-ambiguously than the order "paint the green you see on this chart". Here too it is imaginable that the first of the sentences might be understand in the way one would normally understand a sentence

like "paint a colour somewhat lighter than the one you remember seeing there". On the other hand the man ordered to paint the shade of colour in accordance with the sample will usually be in no doubt about the method of projection.

If I'm told: "look for a red flower in this meadow and bring it to me" and then I find one – do I compare it with my memory picture of the colour red? – And must I consult yet another picture to see whether the first is still correct? – In that case why should I need the first one? – I see the colour of the flower and recognize *it*. (It would naturally be *conceivable* that someone should hallucinate a colour sample and compare it, like a real sample, with the object he was looking for.)

But if I say "no, this colour isn't the right one, it's brighter than the colour I saw there" that doesn't mean that I see the colour in my mind's eye and go through a process of comparing two simultaneously given shades of colour. Again, it isn't as if when the right colour is found a bell rings somewhere in my mind and I carry round a picture of this ringing, so as to be able to judge when it rings.

Searching with a sample which one places beside objects to test whether the colours match is one game; acting in accordance with the words of a word-language without a sample is another. Think of reading aloud from a written text (or writing to dictation). We might of course imagine a kind of table that might guide us in this; but in fact there isn't one, there's no act of memory, or anything else, which acts as an intermediary between the written sign and the sound.

55 Suppose I am now asked "why do you choose *this* colour when given this order; how do you justify the choice?" In the one case I can answer "because *this* colour is opposite the word 'red' in my chart." In the other case there is no answer to the question and the question makes no sense. But in the first game there is no sense in *this* question: "why do you call 'red' the colour in the chart

opposite the word 'red'"? A *reason* can only be given *within* a game. The links of the chain of reasons come to an end, at the boundary of the game. (Reason and cause.)

If one calls to mind "that the chart does not compel us" to use it in a particular way, or even always to use it in the same way, it becomes clear to everyone that our use of the words "rule" and "game" is a fluctuating one (blurred at the edges).

The connection between "language and reality" is made by definitions of words, and these belong to grammar, so that language remains self-contained and autonomous.

56 Imagine a gesture language used to communicate with people who have no word-language in common with us. Do we feel there too the need to go outside the language to explain its signs?

"The connection between words and things is set up by the teaching of language." What kind or sort of connection is this? A mechanical, electrical, psychological connection is something which may or may not function. *Mechanism* and *Calculus*.

The correlation between objects and names is simply the one set up by a chart, by ostensive gestures and simultaneous uttering of the name etc. It is a part of the symbolism. Giving an object a name is essentially the same kind of thing as hanging a label on it.

It gives the wrong idea if you say that the connection between name and object is a psychological one.

57 Imagine someone copying a figure on the scale of 1 to 10. Is the understanding of the general rule of such mapping contained in the process of copying? – The pencil in my hand was free from

presuppositions, so to speak, and was guided (influenced) only by the length of the lines in the pattern. – I would say that if the pattern had been longer, I should have drawn my pencil further and if it had been shorter, not so far. But is the mind which thus expresses itself already contained in the copying of the line?

Suppose I want to meet someone on the street. I can decide "I will go on until I find N" – and then go along the street and stop when I meet him at a particular point. Did the process of walking, or some other simultaneous process, include acting in accordance with the general rule I intended? Or was what I did only *in agreement* with that rule, but also in agreement with other rules?

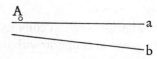

I give someone the order to draw from A a line parallel to a. He tries (intends) to do it, but with the result that the line is parallel to b. Was what happened when he copied the same as if he had intended to draw a line parallel to b and carried out his intention?

If I *succeed* in reproducing a paradigm in accordance with a prescribed rule, is it possible to use a different general rule to describe the process of copying, the way it took place? Or can I reject such a description with the words "No, I was guided by *this* rule, and not by the other, though admittedly in this case the other would have given the same result"?

58 One is inclined to say: If I intentionally copy a shape, then the process of copying has the shape in common with the pattern. The form is a facet of the process of copying; a facet which fits the copied object and coincides with it there.

Even if my pencil doesn't do justice to the model, my intention always does.

If I intend to play the piano from written music, it is experience that will show which notes I actually play and the description of what is played need not have anything in common with the written notes. But if I want to describe my *intention*, the description must be that I wanted to reproduce *these* written notes in sounds. – That alone can be the expression of the fact that intention reaches up to the paradigm and contains a general rule.

An expression of intention describes the model to be copied; describing the copy does not.

59 For the purposes of our studies it can never be essential that a symbolic phenomenon occurs in the mind and not on paper so that others can see it. One is constantly tempted to explain a symbolic process by a special psychological process; as if the mind "could do much more in these matters" than signs can.

We are misled by the idea of a mechanism that works in special media and so can explain special movements. As when we say: this movement can't be explained by any arrangement of levers.

A *description* of what is psychological must be something which can itself be used as a symbol.

A connected point is that an explanation of a sign can replace the sign itself. This gives an important insight into the nature of the explanation of signs, and brings out a contrast between the idea of this sort of explanation and that of causal explanation.

60 It could be said that it can't be decided by outward observation whether I am *reading* or merely producing sounds while a text runs before my eyes. But what is of interest to us in reading can't be essentially something *internal*. Deriving a translation from the

original may also be a visible process. For instance, it must be possible to regard as a derivation what takes place on paper when the terms of the series 100, 121, 144, 169 are derived from the terms of the series 10, 11, 12, 13 by the following calculations

$$\frac{\begin{array}{c} 10 \times 10 \\ 00 \end{array}}{100}, \quad \frac{\begin{array}{c} 11 \times 11 \\ 11 \end{array}}{121}. \quad \frac{\begin{array}{c} 12 \times 12 \\ 24 \end{array}}{144}, \quad \frac{\begin{array}{c} 13 \times 13 \\ 39 \end{array}}{169}$$

(The distinction between "inner" and "outer" does not interest us.)

Every such more or less behaviourist account leaves one with the feeling that it is crude and heavy handed; but this is misleading – we are tempted to look for a "better" account, but there isn't one. One is as good as the other and in each case what represents is the *system* in which a sign is used. – ("Representation is dynamic, not static.").

(Even a psychological process cannot "leave anything open" in any way essentially different from the way in which an empty bracket in the symbolism leaves open an argument place.)

One may not ask "What sort of thing are mental processes, since they can be true and false, and non-mental ones cannot?" For, if the 'mental' ones can, then the others must be able to do as well and vice versa. – For, if the mental processes can, their descriptions must be able to as well. For how this is possible must show itself in their descriptions.

If one says that thought is a mental activity, or an activity of the mind, one thinks of the mind as a cloudy gaseous medium in which many things can happen which cannot occur in a different sphere, and from which many things can be expected that are otherwise not possible.

(The process of thinking in the human mind, and the process of digestion).

61 Every case of copying (acting *in obedience to*, not just in accordance with, particular rules), every case of *deriving* an action from a command or justifying an action by a command, is the same kind of thing as writing down the steps that lead to the answer of a sum, or pointing to signs standing beside each other in a table.

x	1	2	3	4
x^2				16
x^3				64

"I write the number '16' here *because* it says 'x^2' there, and '64' here because it says x^3 there." That is what every justification looks like. In a certain sense it takes us no further. But indeed it can't take us *further* i.e. into the realm of metalogic.

(The difficulty here is: in not trying to justify what admits of no justification.)

Suppose, though, I said "I write a '+' here because it says 'x^2' there? You would ask "Do you always write a '+' where it says "x^2"? – that is, you would look for a general rule; otherwise the "because" in my sentence makes no sense. Or you might ask "So how do you know that *that* is why you wrote it?"

In that case you've taken the "because" as introducing a statement of the cause, instead of the reason.

If I write "16" under "4" in accordance with the rule, it might appear that some causality was operating that was not a matter of hypothesis, but something immediately perceived (experienced).

(Confusion between 'reason' and 'cause'.)

What connection do I mean in the sentence "I am going out, *because* he's telling me to"? And how is this sentence related to "I am going out, *although* he told me to". (Or "I am going out, but not because he told me to" "I am going out, because he told me not to".)

V

62 "That's *him*" (this picture represents *him*) – that contains the whole problem of representation.

What is the criterion, how is it to be verified, that this picture is the portrait of that object, i.e. that it is *meant* to represent it? It is not similarity that makes the picture a portrait (it might be a striking resemblance of one person, and yet be a portrait of someone else it resembles less).

How can I know that someone means the picture as a portrait of N? – Well, perhaps because he says so, or writes it underneath.

What is the connection between the portrait of N and N himself? Perhaps, that the name written underneath is the name used to address him.

When I remember my friend and see him "in my mind's eye", what is the connection between the memory image and its subject? The likeness between them?

Well, the image, *qua picture,* can't do more than resemble him.

The image of him is an unpainted portrait.

In the case of the image too, I have to write his name under the picture to make it the image of him.

I have the intention of carrying out a particular task and I make a plan. The plan in my mind is supposed to consist in my seeing myself acting thus and so. But how do I know, that it is myself that I'm seeing? Well, it isn't myself, but a kind of a picture. But why do I call it the picture of *me*?

"How do I know that it's myself?": the question makes sense if it means, for example, "how do I know that I'm the one I see there". And the answer mentions characteristics by which I can be recognized.

But it is my own decision that makes my image represent myself. And I might as well ask "how do I know that the word 'I' stands for myself?" For my shape in the picture was only another word "I".

"I can imagine your being about to go out of the door." We suffer from a strange delusion that in the proposition, the thought, the objects do what the proposition states about them. It's as though the command contained a shadow of the execution. But a shadow of just *this* execution. It is *you* in the command who go to such and such a place. – Otherwise it would be just a *different* command.

This identity is indeed the identity contrasted with the diversity of two different commands.

"I thought Napoleon was crowned in the year 1805." – What has your thought got to do with Napoleon? – What connection is there between your thought and Napoleon? – It may be, for example, that the word "Napoleon" occurs in the expression of my thought, plus the connection that word had with its bearer; e.g. that was the way he signed his name, that was how he was spoken to and so on.

"But when you utter the word 'Napoleon' you designate that man and no other" – "How then does this act of designating work, in your view? Is it instantaneous? Or does it take time?" – "But after all if someone asks you 'did you mean the very man who won the battle of Austerlitz' you will say 'yes'. So you meant that man *when you uttered the sentence.*" – Yes, but only in the kind of way that I then knew also that $6 \times 6 = 36$.

The answer "I meant the victor of Austerlitz" is a new step in our calculus. The past tense is deceptive, because it looks as if it was giving a description of what went on "inside me" while I was uttering the sentence.

("But I meant *him*". A strange process, this meaning! Can you mean in Europe someone who's in America? Even if he no longer exists?)

63 Misled by our grammar, we are tempted to ask "*How* does one think a proposition, *how* does one expect such and such to happen? (how does one do that?)"

"How does thought work, how does it use its expression?" – This question looks like "How does a Jacquard loom work, how does it use the cards".

In the proposition "I believe that p is the case " we feel that the essential thing, the real process of belief, isn't expressed but only hinted at; we feel it must be possible to replace this hint by a description of the mechanism of belief, a description in which the series of words "p" would occur as the cards occur in the description of the loom. This description, we feel, would be at last the full expression of the thought.

Let's compare belief with the utterance of a sentence; there too very complicated processes take place in the larynx, the speech muscles, the nerves, etc. These are *accompaniments* of the spoken sentence. And the sentence itself remains the only thing that interests us – not as part of a mechanism, but as part of a calculus.

"How does thought manage to represent?" – the answer might be "Don't you really know? You certainly see it when you think." For nothing is concealed.
How does a sentence do it? Nothing is hidden.

But given this answer "But you know how sentences do it, for nothing is concealed" one would like to say "yes, but it all goes by so quick, and I should like to see it as it were laid open to view".

We feel that thoughts are like a landscape that we have seen and are supposed to describe, but don't remember exactly enough to describe how all the parts fitted together. Similarly, we think, we can't describe thought after the event because then the many delicate processes have been lost sight of. We would like as it were to see these intricacies under the magnifying glass. (Think of the proposition "Everything is in flux".)

We ask: "What is a thought? What kind of thing must something be to perform the function of thought?" This question is like: "What is a sewing machine, how does it work? – And the answer which would be like ours would be "Look at the stitch it is meant to sew; you can see from that what is essential in the machine, everything else is optional."

So what is the function, that makes thought what it is? –

If it is its *effect*, then we are not interested in it.

We are not in the realm of causal explanations, and every such explanation sounds trivial for our purposes.

64 If one thinks of thought as something specifically human and organic, one is inclined to ask "could there be a prosthetic apparatus for thinking, an inorganic substitute for thought?" But if thinking consists only in writing or speaking, why shouldn't a machine do it? "Yes, but the machine doesn't know anything." Certainly it is senseless to talk of a prosthetic substitute for seeing and hearing. We do talk of artificial feet, but not of artificial pains in the foot.

"But could a machine think?" – Could it be in pain? – Here the important thing is what one means by something *being in* pain. I can look on another person – another person's *body* – as a machine which is in pain. And so, of course, I can in the case of my own body. On the other hand, the phenomenon of pain which I describe when I say something like "I have toothache" doesn't presuppose a physical body. (I can have toothache without teeth.) And in this case there is no room for the machine. – It is clear that the machine can only replace a physical body. And in the sense in which we can say of such a body that it is in pain, we can say it of a machine as well. Or again, what we can compare with machines and call machines is the *bodies* we say are in pain.

In the consideration of our problems one of the most dangerous ideas is the idea that we think *with*, or *in, our heads*.

The idea of a process in the head, in a completely enclosed space, makes thinking something occult.[1]

"Thinking takes place in the head" really means only "the head is connected with thinking". – Of course one says also "I think with my pen" and this localisation is at least as good.

It is a travesty of the truth to say "Thinking is an activity of our mind, as writing is an activity of the hand". (Love in the heart. The head and the heart as loci of the soul).

65 We may say "Thinking is operating with symbols". But 'thinking' is a fluid concept, and what 'operating with symbols' is must be looked at separately in each individual case.

I might also say "Thinking is operating with language" but 'language' is a fluid concept.

It is correct to say "Thinking is a mental process" only if we also call seeing a written sentence or hearing a spoken one a mental process. In the sense, that is, in which pain is called a mental state. In that case the expression "mental process" is intended to distinguish 'experience' from 'physical processes'. – On the other hand, of course, the expression "mental process" suggests that we are concerned with imperfectly understood processes in an inaccessible sphere.

Psychology too talks of 'unconscious thought' and here "thought" means a process in a mind-model. ('Model' in the sense in which one speaks of a mechanical model of electrical processes).

By contrast, when Frege speaks of the thought a sentence expresses the word "thought" is more or less equivalent to the expression "sense of the sentence".

1. The parallel passage in *Zettel* 606 is translated in a way that does not fit this context (Trs.)

It might be said: in every case what is meant by "thought" is the *living* element in the sentence, without which it is dead, a mere succession of sounds or series of written shapes.

But if I talked in the same way about a something that gives meaning to an arrangement of chessmen, something that makes it different from an arbitrary collection of bits of wood, I might mean almost anything! I might mean the rules that make the arrangement of chessmen a position in a game, or the special experiences we connect with positions in the game or the use of the game.

It is the same if we speak of a something that makes the difference between paper money and mere printed bits of paper, something that gives it its meaning, its life.

Though we speak of a thought and its expression, the thought is not a kind of condition that the sentence produces as a potion might. And communication by language is not a process by which I use a drug to produce in others the same pains as I have myself.

(What sort of process might be called "thought-transference" or "thought-reading"?)

66 A French politician once said it was a special characteristic of the French language that in French sentences words occurred in the sequence in which one thinks them.

The idea that one language in contrast to others has a word order which corresponds to the order of thinking arises from the notion that thought is an essentially different process going on independently of the expression of the thoughts.

(No one would ask whether the written multiplication of two numbers in the decimal system runs parallel with the thought of the multiplication.)

"I meant something definite by it, when I said . . ."

– "Did you mean something different when you said each word, or did you mean the same thing throughout the whole sentence?"

It is strange, though: you can mean something by each word and the combination of them can still be nonsense!

"At the time when you said the sentence, did you think of the fact that . . ."

"I thought only what I said."

(It perplexes us that there is no moment at which the thought of a sentence is completely present. Here we see that we are comparing the thought with a thing that we manufacture and possess as a whole; but in fact as soon as one part comes into being another disappears. This leaves us in some way unsatisfied, since we are misled by a plausible simile into expecting something different.)

Does the child learn only to talk, or also to think? Does it learn the sense of multiplication *before* or *after* it learns multiplication?

Is it, as it were, a contamination of the sense that we express it in a particular language which has accidental features, and not as it were bodiless and pure?

Do I really not play chess itself because the chessmen might have had a different shape?

(Is a mathematical proof in the general theory of irrational numbers less general or rigorous because we go through it using the decimal notation for those numbers? Does it impair the rigour and purity of the proposition $25 \times 25 = 625$ that it is written down in a particular number system?)

Thought can only be something common-or-garden and *ordinary*. (We are accustomed to thinking of it as something ethereal and unexplored, as if we were dealing with something whose exterior alone is known to us, and whose interior is yet unknown like our brain.) One is inclined to say: "Thought, what a strange thing!" But when I say that thought is something quite common-or-garden, I mean that we are affected by this concept as we are by a concept like that of the number one. There seems to be something mysterious about it, because we misunderstand its grammar and feel the lack of a tangible substance to correspond to the substantive. (It is almost like hearing a human voice coming from in front of us, and seeing nobody there.)

67 What does man think for? What use is it? Why does he *calculate* the thickness of the walls of a boiler and not leave it to chance or whim to decide? After all it is a mere fact of experience that boilers do not explode so often if made according to calculations. But just as having once been burnt he would do anything rather than put his hand into the fire, so he would do anything rather than not calculate for a boiler. – Since we are not interested in causes, we might say: human beings do in fact think: this, for instance, is how they proceed when they make a boiler. – Now, can't a boiler produced in this way explode? Certainly it can.

We think over our actions before we do them. We make pictures of them – but why? After all, there is no such thing as a "thought-experiment".

We expect something, and act in accordance with the expectation; must the expectation come true? No. Then why do we act in accordance with the expectation? Because we are impelled to, as we are impelled to get out of the way of a car, to sit down when we are tired, to jump up if we have sat on a thorn.

What the thought of the uniformity of nature amounts to can perhaps be seen most clearly when we fear the event we expect. Nothing could induce me to put my hand into a flame – although after all it is *only in the past* that I have burnt myself.

The belief that fire will burn me is of the same nature as the fear that it will burn me.

Here I see also what "it is certain" means.

If someone pushed me into the fire, I would struggle and go on resisting; and similarly I would cry out "it will burn me!" and not "perhaps it will be quite agreeable".

"But after all you do believe that more boilers would explode if people did not calculate when making boilers!" Yes, I believe it; – but what does that mean? Does it follow that there will in fact be fewer explosions? – Then what is the foundation of this belief?

68 I assume that his house in which I am writing won't collapse during the next half hour. – When do I assume this? The whole time? And what sort of an activity is this assuming?

Perhaps what is meant is a psychological disposition; or perhaps the thinking and expressing of particular thoughts. In the second case perhaps I utter a sentence which is part of a train of thought (a calculation). Now someone says: you must surely have a reason to assume that, otherwise the assumption is unsupported and worthless. – (Remember that we stand on the earth, but the earth doesn't stand on anything else; children think it'll have to fall if it's not supported). Well, I do have reasons for my assumption. Perhaps that the house has already stood for years, but not so long that it may already be rickety, etc. etc. – *What* counts as a reason for an assumption can be given *a priori* and determines a calculus, a system of transitions. But if we are asked now for a reason for the calculus itself, we see that there is none.

So is the calculus something we adopt arbitrarily? No more so than the fear of fire, or the fear of a raging man coming at us.

"Surely the rules of grammar by which we act and operate are not arbitrary!" Very well; why then does a man think in the way he does, why does he go through these activities of thought? (This question of course asks for reasons, not for causes.) Well, reasons can be given within the calculus, and at the very end one is tempted to say "it just is very probable, that things will behave in this case as they always have" – or something similar. A turn of phrase which masks the beginning of the chain of reasons. (The creator as the explanation at the beginning of the world).[1]

The thing that's so difficult to understand can be expressed like this. *As long as* we remain in the province of the true-false games a change in the grammar can only lead us from *one* such game to another, and never from something true to something false. On the other hand if we go outside the province of these games, we don't any longer call it 'language' and 'grammar', and once again we don't come into contradiction with reality.

1. Cf. p. 94

VI

69 What is a proposition? – What am I distinguishing a proposition from? What do I want to distinguish it from? From things which are only parts of propositions in the same grammatical system (like the parts of an equation)? Or from everything we don't call propositions, including this chair and my watch, etc. etc?

The question "how is the general concept of proposition bounded?" must be countered with another: "Well, do we have a *single* concept of proposition?"

"But surely I have a definite concept of what I mean by 'proposition'." Well, and how would I explain it to another or to myself? This explanation will make clear what my concept is (I am not concerned with a feeling accompanying the word 'proposition'). I would explain the concept by means of examples. – So my concept goes as far as the examples. – But after all they're only examples, and their range is capable of extension. – All right, but in that case you must tell me what "capable of extension" means here. The grammar of this word must have definite boundaries.

"But I know a proposition when I see one, so I must also be able to draw the boundaries of the concept precisely." But is it really the case that no doubt is possible? – Imagine a language in which all sentences are commands to go in a particular direction. (This language might be used by a primitive kind of human beings exclusively in war. Remember how restricted the use of written language once was.) Well, we would still call the commands "come here", "go there", "sentences".[1] But suppose now the language consisted only in pointing the finger in one direction or the other. – Would this sign still be a proposition? – And what about a language like the early speech of children whose signs expressed only desire for particular objects, a language which consisted simply of signs for these objects (of nouns, as it were)? Or consider

1. The same German word corresponds to "sentence" as to "proposition" (Tr.)

a system consisting of two signs, one expressing acceptance and the other rejection of proferred objects. Is this a language, does it consist of propositions?

And on the other hand: does everything that sounds like a sentence in English fall under our concept of proposition? "I am tired", "$2 \times 2 = 4$", "time passes", "there is only one zero"?

The word "proposition" does not signify a sharply bounded concept. If we want to put a concept with sharp boundaries beside our use of this word, we are free to define it, just as we are free to narrow down the meaning of the primitive measure of length "a pace" to 75 cm.

70 "What happens when a *new* proposition is taken into the language: what is the criterion for its being a *proposition*?" Let us imagine such a case. We become aquainted with a new experience, say the tingling of an electric shock, and we say it's unpleasant. What right have I to call this newly formed statement a "proposition"? Well, what right did I have to speak of a new "experience", or a new "muscular sensation"? Surely I did so by analogy with my earlier use of these words. But, on the other hand, did I *have* to use the word "experience" and the word "proposition" in the new case? Do I already assert something about the sensation of the electric shock when I call it an experience? And what difference would it make if I excluded the statement "the tingling is unpleasant" from the concept of proposition, because I had already drawn its boundaries once and for all?

Compare the concept of proposition with the concept 'number' and then with the concept of cardinal number. We count as numbers cardinal numbers, rational numbers, irrational numbers, complex numbers; whether we call other constructions numbers because of their similarities with these, or draw a definitive boundary here or elsewhere, depends on us. In this respect the concept of number is like the concept of proposition. On the other hand the concept of cardinal number [1, ξ, ξ + 1] can be called a rigorously circumscribed concept, that's to say it's a concept in a different sense of the word.

71 How did I come by the concept 'proposition' or the concept 'language'? Only through the languages I've learnt. – But in a certain sense they seem to have led me beyond themselves, since I'm now able to construct a new language, for instance to invent words. – So this construction too belongs to the concept of language. But only if I so stipulate. The sense of my "etc." is constantly given limits by its grammar.

That's also what I meant when I said "there are surprises in reality but not in grammar."

"But language can expand" – Certainly; but if this word "expand" has a sense here, then I know *already* what I mean by it. I must be able to specify how I imagine such an expansion. And what I can't think, I can't now express or even hint at. And in *this* case the word "now" means: "in this calculus" or "if the words are used according to *these* grammatical rules".

But here we also have this nagging problem: how is it possible even to *think* of the existence of things when we always see only images, copies of them? – We ask: "Then how did I come by this concept at all?" It would be quite correct to add in thought the rider: "It is not as if I was able to transcend my own thought", "It is not as if I could sensibly transcend what has sense for me." We feel that there is no way of smuggling in by the back door a thought I am barred from thinking directly.

No sign leads us beyond itself, and no argument either.

What does a man do when he constructs (invents) a new language; on what principle does he operate? For this principle is the concept of 'language'. Does every newly constructed language broaden (alter) the concept of language? – Consider its relationship to the earlier concept: that depends on how the earlier concept was established. – Think of the relation of complex numbers to the earlier concept of number; and again of the relation of a *new* multiplication to the general concept of the multiplication of cardinal numbers, when two particular (perhaps very large) cardinal numbers are written down for the first time and multiplied together.

72 In logic one cannot employ generality in a void. If I determine the grammar of my generality, then there are no more surprises in logic. And if I do not determine it, then I am no longer in the realm of an exact grammar.

That's to say, the indeterminacy of generality is not a logical indeterminacy. Generality is a freedom of movement, not an indeterminacy of geometry.

But if the general concept of language dissolves in this way, doesn't philosophy dissolve as well? No, for the task of philosophy is not to create a new, ideal language, but to clarify the use of our language, the existing language. Its aim is to remove particular misunderstandings; not to produce a real understanding for the first time.

If a man points out that a word is used with several different meanings, or that a certain misleading picture comes to mind when we use a certain expression, if he sets out (tabulates) rules according to which certain words are used, he hasn't committed himself to giving an explanation (definition) of the words "rule", "proposition", "word", etc.

I'm allowed to use the word "rule" without first tabulating the rules for the use of the word. And those rules are not super-rules.

Philosophy is concerned with calculi in the same sense as it is concerned with thoughts, sentences and languages. But if it was really concerned with the concept of calculus, and thus with the concept of the calculus of all calculi, there would be such a thing as metaphilosophy. (But there is not. We might so present all that we have to say that this would appear as a leading principle.)

73 How do we use the word "rule", say when we are talking of games? In contrast to what? – We say for instance "that follows from this rule", but in that case we could cite the rule in question and thus avoid the word "rule". Or we speak of "all the rules of a game" and in that case either we've listed them (in which case we have a repetition of the first case) or we're speaking of the rules as a group of expressions produced in a certain way from given basic rules, and then the word "rule" stands for the expression of *those* basic rules and operations. Or we say "*this* is a rule and *that* isn't" – if the second, say, is only an individual word or a sentence which is incomplete by the standards of English grammar, or the illustration of a position of pieces in a game. (Or "No, according to the new convention that too is a rule"). If we had to write down the list of rules of the game, something like that might be said and then it would mean "*this* belongs in it and *that* doesn't". But this isn't on the strength of a particular property, the property of being a rule, like the case when one wants to pack only apples in a box and says, "no, that shouldn't go in there, that's a pear".

Yes, but there are many things we call games and many we don't, many things we call rules and many we don't! – But it's never a question of drawing a boundary between everything we call games and everything else. For us games are *the* games of which we have heard, the games we can list, and perhaps some others newly devised by analogy; and if someone wrote a book on games, he wouldn't really need to use the word "game" in the title of the book, he could use as a title a list of the names of the individual games.

If he's asked "but what's *common* to all these things that makes you collect them together?" he might say: I can't give it straight off – but surely you may see many analogies. Anyway the question seems to me idle, because proceeding by analogy, I can also come by imperceptible steps to things that no one in ordinary life would any longer call "games". Hence I call games things on this list, and whatever is similar to these games up to a certain point that I don't further specify. Moreover, I reserve the right to decide in every new case whether I will count something as a game or not.

The case is the same with the concepts 'rule', 'proposition', 'language', etc. It is only in special cases (i.e. not every time we use the word "rule") that it is a question of drawing a boundary between rules and what are not rules, and in all cases it is easy to give the distinguishing mark. We use the word "rule" in contrast to "word", "projection" and some other words and these demarcations can be clearly drawn. On the other hand we commonly do not draw boundaries where we do not need them. (Just as in certain games a single line is drawn in the middle of the field to separate the sides, but the field is not otherwise bounded since it is unnecessary.)

We are able to use the word "plant" in a way that gives rise to no misunderstanding, yet countless borderline cases can be constructed in which no one has yet decided whether something still falls under the concept 'plant'. Does this mean that the meaning of the word "plant" in all other cases is infected by uncertainty, so that it might be said we use the word without understanding it? Would a definition which bounded this concept on several sides make the meaning of the word clearer to us in *all* sentences? Would we understand better all the sentences in which it occurs?

74 How did we learn to understand the word "plant", then? Perhaps we learnt a definition of the concept, say in botany, but I leave out that of account since it only has a role in botany. Apart

from that, it is clear that we learnt the meaning of the word by example; and if we disregard hypothetical dispositions, these examples stand only for themselves. Hypotheses about learning and using language and causal connections don't interest us. So we don't assume that the examples produce something in the learner, that they set before his mind an essence, the meaning of the concept-word, the concept 'plant'. If the examples should have an effect, say they produce a particular visual picture in the learner, the causal connection between the examples and this picture does not concern us, and for us they are merely *coincidental*. So we can perhaps disregard the examples altogether and look on the picture alone as a symbol of the concept; or the picture and the examples together.

If someone says "we understand the word 'chair', since we know what is common to all chairs" – what does it mean to say we *know* that? That we are ready to say it (like "we know that 6 × 6 is 36")? What is it that is common, then? Isn't it only because we can apply the word "chair" that we say here we know what is common? Suppose I explained the word "red" by pointing to a red wall, a red book, and a red cloth and in accordance with this explanation someone produced a sample of the colour red by exhibiting a red label. One might say in this case that he had shown that he had grasped the common element in all the examples I gave him. Isn't it an analogy like this that misleads us in the case of "chair"?

The grammatical place of the words "game", "rule", etc. is given by examples in rather the way in which the place of a meeting is specified by saying that it will take place *beside* such and such a tree.

75 One imagines the meaning as something which *comes before* our minds when we hear a word.

What comes before our minds when we hear a word is certainly something characteristic of the meaning. But what comes before my mind is an example, an application of the word. And this coming to mind doesn't really consist in a particular image's being present whenever I utter or hear the word, but in fact that when I'm asked the meaning of the word, applications of the word *occur* to me.

Someone says to me: "Shew the children a game" I teach them gaming with a dice, and the other says "I didn't mean that sort of game". Must the exclusion of the game with dice have come before his mind when he gave me the order?

Suppose someone said: "No. I didn't mean that sort of game; I used 'game' in the narrower sense." How does it come out, that he used the word in the narrower sense?

But can't one also use the word "game" in its broadest sense? But which is that? No boundaries have been drawn unless we fix some on purpose.

If we found a sentence like "The Assyrians knew various games" in a history book without further qualifications, it would strike us as very curious; for we wouldn't be certain that we could give an example that even roughly corresponded to the meaning of the word "game" in this case.

Someone wants to include in the list of rules of a game the proposition that the game was invented in such and such a year. I say "No, that doesn't belong to the list of rules, that's not a rule." So I'm excluding historical propositions from the rules. And similarly I would exclude from the rules, as an empirical proposition, a proposition like "this game can only be learnt by long practice". But it could easily be misleading to say boundaries had thereby been drawn around the area of rules.

76 If I try to make clear to someone by characteristic examples

the use of a word like "wish", it is quite likely that the other will adduce as an objection to the examples I offered another one that suggests a different type of use. My answer then is that the new example may be useful in discussion, but isn't an objection to my examples. For I didn't want to say that those examples gave the essence of what one calls "wishing". At most they present different essences which are all signified by this word because of certain inter-relationships. The error is to suppose that we wanted the examples to illustrate the essence of wishing, and that the counter examples showed that this essence hadn't yet been correctly grasped. That is, as if our aim were to give a theory of wishing, which would have to explain every single case of wishing.

But for this reason, the examples given are only useful if they are clearly worked out and not just vaguely hinted at.

The use of the words "proposition", "language", etc. has the haziness of the normal use of concept-words in our language. To think this makes them unusable, or ill-adapted to their purpose, would be like wanting to say "the warmth this stove gives is no use, because you can't feel where it begins and where it ends".

If I wish to draw sharp boundaries to clear up or avoid misunderstandings in the area of a particular use of language, these will be related to the fluctuating boundaries of the natural use of language in the same way as sharp contours in a pen-and-ink sketch are related to the gradual transitions between patches of colour in the reality depicted.

Socrates pulls up the pupil who when asked what knowledge is enumerates cases of knowledge. And Socrates doesn't regard that as even a preliminary step to answering the question.

But our answer consists in giving such an emuneration and a

few analogies. (In a certain sense we are always making things easier and easier for ourselves in philosophy.)

77 The philosophy of logic speaks of sentences and words in exactly the sense in which we speak of them in ordinary life when we say "Here is a Chinese sentence", or "No, that only looks like writing; it is actually just an ornament" and so on.

We are talking about the spatial and temporal phenomenon of language, not about some non-spatial, non-temporal phantasm. But we talk about it as we do about the pieces in chess when we are stating the rules of the game, not describing their physical properties.

The question "what is a word?" is analogous to "What is a piece in chess (say the king)?"

In reflecting on language and meaning we can easily get into a position where we think that in philosophy we are not talking of words and sentences in a quite common-or-garden sense, but in a sublimated and abstract sense. – As if a particular proposition wasn't really the thing that some person utters, but an ideal entity (the "class of all synonymous sentences" or the like). But is the chess king that the rules of chess deal with such an ideal and abstract entity too?

(We are not justified in having any more scruples about our language than the chess player has about chess, namely none.)

Again, we cannot achieve any greater generality in philosophy than in what we say in life and in science. Here too (as in mathematics) we leave everything as it is.

When I talk about language (words, sentences, etc.) I must speak the language of every day. Is this language somehow too coarse and material for what we want to say? Then how is another one to be constructed? – And how strange that we should be able to do anything at all with the one we have!

In giving philosophical explanations about language I already have to use language full-blown (not some sort of preparatory, provisional one); this by itself shows that I can adduce only exterior facts about language.

"Yes, but then how can these explanations satisfy us?" – Well, your very questions were framed in this language! – And your scruples are misunderstandings. Your questions refer to words, so I have to talk about words.

You say: the point isn't the word, but its meaning, and you think of the meaning as a thing of the same kind as the word, though also different from the word. Here the word, there the meaning. The money, and the cow that you can buy with it. (But contrast: money, and its use).

78 If we ask about the general form of proposition – bear in mind that in normal language sentences have a particular rhythm and sound but we don't call everything 'that sounds like a sentence' a sentence. – Hence we speak also of significant and non-significant "sentences".

On the other hand, sounding like a sentence in this way isn't essential to what we call a proposition in logic. The expression "sugar good" doesn't sound like an English sentence, but it may very well replace the proposition "sugar tastes good". And not e.g. in such a way that we should have to add in thought something that is missing. (Rather, all that matters is the system of expressions to which the expression "sugar good" belongs.)

So the question arises whether if we disregard this misleading business of sounding like a sentence we still have a general concept of proposition.

Imagine the English language altered in such a way that the order of the words in a sentence is the reverse of the present one. The result would be the series of words which we get if we read sentences of an English book from right to left. It's clear that the multiplicity of possible ways of expression in this language must be exactly the same as in English; but if a longish sentence were read thus we could understand it only with great difficulty and we'd perhaps never learn "to think in this language". (The example of such a language can make clear a lot about the nature of what we call "thought".)

79 The definition "A proposition is whatever can be true or false" fixes the concept of proposition in a particular language system as what in that system can be an argument of a truth-function.

And if we speak of what makes a proposition a proposition, we are inclined to mean the truth-functions.

"A proposition is whatever can be true or false" means the same as "a proposition is whatever can be denied".

"p" is true = p
"p" is false = ~p
What he says is true = Things are as he says.

One might say: the words "true" and "false" are only items in a particular notation for truth-functions.

So is it correct to write " 'p' is true", " 'p' is false"; mustn't it be "p is true" (or false)? The ink mark is after all not *true*; in the way in which it's black and curved.

Does " 'p' is true" state anything about the sign "p" then? "Yes, it says that 'p' agrees with reality." Instead of a sentence of our word language consider a drawing that can be compared with reality according to exact projection-rules. This surely must show as clearly as possible what " 'p' is true" states about the picture "p". The proposition " 'p' is true" can thus be compared with the proposition "this object is as long as this metre rule" and "p" to the proposition "this object is one metre long". But the comparison is incorrect, because "this metre rule" is a description, whereas "metre rule" is the determination of a concept. On the other hand in " 'p' is true" the ruler enters immediately into the proposition. "p" represents here simply the length and not the metre rule. For the representing drawing is also not 'true' except in accordance with a particular method of projection which makes the ruler a purely geometrical appendage of the measured line.

It can also be put thus: The proposition " 'p' is true" can only be understood if one understands the grammar of the sign "p" as a propositional sign; not if "p" is simply the name of the shape of a particular ink mark. In the end one can say that the quotation marks in the sentence " 'p' is true" are simply superfluous.

If one explains: "(x).fx" is true, if "f( )" gives true sentences for all substitutions – we must reflect that the sentence "(x).fx" follows from the proposition " 'f( )' gives true sentences for all substitutions", and *vice versa*. So the two propositions say the same.
So that explanation does not assemble the mechanism of generality from its parts.

One can't of course say that a proposition is whatever one can predicate "true" or "false" of, as if one could put symbols together with the words "true" and "false" by way of experiment to see whether the result makes sense. For something could only be decided by this experiment if "true" and "false" already have definite meanings, and they can only have that if the contexts in which they can occur are already settled. – (Think also of identifying parts of speech by questions. "Who or what . . . ?")

80 In the schema "This is how things stand" the "how things stand" is really a handle for the truth-functions.
"Things stand", then, is an expression from a notation for truth-functions. An expression which shows us what part of grammar comes into play here.

If I let "that is how things stand" count as the general form of proposition, then I must count "$2 + 2 = 4$" as a proposition. Further rules are needed if we are to exclude the propositions of arithmetic.

Can one give the *general form of a proposition*? – Why not? In the same way as one might give the general form of a number, for example by the sign "$|0, \xi, \xi +1|$". I am free to restrict the name "number" to *that*, and in the same way I can give an analogous formula for the construction of propositions or laws and use the word "proposition" or "law" as equivalent to that formula. – If someone objects and says that this will only demarcate certain laws from others, I reply: of course you can't draw a boundary if you've decided in advance not to recognize one. But of course the question remains: how do you use the word "proposition"? In contrast to what?

("Can a proposition treat of all propositions, or all propositional functions?" What is meant by that? Are you thinking of a proposition of logic? – What does the proof of such a proposition look like?)

A general propositional form determines a proposition as part of a calculus.

81 Are the rules that say that such and such a combination of words yields no sense comparable to the stipulations in chess that the game does not allow two pieces to stand on the same square, for instance, or a piece to stand on a line between two squares? Those propositions in their turn are like certain actions; like e.g. cutting a chess board out of a larger sheet of squared paper. They draw a boundary.

So what does it mean to say "this combination of words has no sense"? One can say of a name (of a succession of sounds): "I haven't given anyone this name"; and name-giving is a definite action (attaching a label). Think of the representation of an explorer's route by a line drawn in each of the two hemispheres projected on the page: we may say that a bit of line going outside the circles on the page makes no sense in this projection. We might also express it thus: no stipulation has been made about it.

"How do I manage always to use a word significantly? Do I always look up the grammar? No, the fact that I mean something, – what I mean prevents me from talking nonsense." – But what do I mean? – I would like to say: I speak of bits of an apple, but not bits of the colour red, because in connection with the words "bits of an apple", unlike the expression "bits of the colour red", I can imagine something, picture something, want something. It would be more correct to say that I *do* imagine, picture, or want something in connection with the words "bits of an apple" but not in connecttion with the expression "bits of the colour red".

But the expression "I'm cutting red into bits" can have a sense (e.g. the sense of the proposition "I'm cutting something red into bits"). – Suppose I asked: which word is it, which mistake, that makes the expression senseless? This shows that this expression, in spite of its senselessness, makes us think of a quite definite grammatical system. That's why we also say "red can't be cut into bits" and so give an answer; whereas one wouldn't make any answer to a combination of words like "is has good". But if one is thinking of a particular system, a language game plus its application, then what is meant by " 'I'm cutting red into bits' is senseless" is first and foremost that this expression doesn't belong to the particular game its appearance makes it seem to belong to.

If we do give a sense to the set of words "I'm cutting red into bits" how do we do it? – We can indeed turn it into quite different things; an empirical proposition, a proposition of arithmetic (like $2 + 2 = 4$), an unproved theorem of mathematics (like Goldbach's conjecture), an exclamation, and other things. So I've a free choice: how is it bounded? That's hard to say – by various types of utility, and by the expression's formal similarity to certain primitive forms of proposition; and all these boundaries are blurred.

"How do I know that the colour red can't be cut into bits?" That isn't a question either.

I would like to say: "I must *begin* with the distinction between sense and nonsense. Nothing is possible prior to that. I can't give it a foundation."

82 Can one ask: "How must we make the grammatical rules for words if they are to give a sentence sense"?

I say, for instance: There isn't a book here, but there could be one; on the other hand it's nonsensical to say that the colours green and red could be in a single place at the same time. But if what gives a proposition sense is its agreement with grammatical rules then let's make just this rule, to permit the sentence "red and green are both at this point at the same time". Very well; but that doesn't fix the grammar of the expression. Further stipulations have yet to be made about how such a sentence is to be used; e.g. how it is to be verified.

If a proposition is conceived as a picture of the state of affairs it describes and a proposition is said to show just how things stand if it's true, and thus to show the possibility of the asserted state of affairs, still the most that the proposition can do is what a painting or relief does: and so it can at any rate not set forth what is just not the case. So it depends wholly on our grammar what will be called possible and what not, i.e. what that grammar permits. But surely that is arbitrary! Certainly; but the grammatical constructions we call empirical propositions (e.g. ones which describe a visible distribution of objects in space and could be replaced by a representational drawing) have a particular application, a particular use. And a construction may have a superficial resemblance to such an empirical proposition and play a somewhat similar role in a calculus without having an analogous application; and if it hasn't we won't be inclined to call it a proposition.

"Possible" here means the same as "conceivable"; but "conceivable" may mean "capable of being painted", "capable of being modelled", "capable of being imagined"; i.e. representable in a particular system of propositions. What matters is the system. – For example someone asks: "is it conceivable that a row of trees might go on forever in the same direction without coming to an end?" Why shouldn't it be 'conceivable'? After all it's expressible in a grammatical system. But if so what's the application of the proposition? How is it verified? What is the relation between its verification and the verification of a proposition like "this row of trees ends at the hundredth tree"? That will tell us how much this conceivability is worth, so to speak.

Chemically possible $\begin{array}{c} \text{O—O—H} \\ | \\ \text{O—H} \end{array}$[1]

"I haven't ever in fact seen a black line gradually getting lighter until it was white, and then more reddish until it was red: but I know that it is possible, because I can imagine it." The form of expression "I know that it is possible, because . . . " is taken from cases like "I know that it is possible to unlock the door with this key, because I once did so". So am I making *that* sort of conjecture: that the colour transition will be possible since I can imagine it? – Isn't this rather the way it is: here "the colour transition is possible" has the same meaning as "I can imagine it?" What about *this*: "The alphabet *can* be said aloud, *because* I can recite it in my mind"?

"I can imagine the colour transition" isn't an assertion here about a particular power of my own imagination, in the way that "I can lift this stone" is about the power of my own muscles. The sentence "I can imagine the transition", like "this state of affairs can be drawn", connects the linguistic representation with another form of representation; it is to be understood as a proposition of grammar.

83 It looks as if we could say: Word-language allows of senseless combination of words, but the language of imagining does not

1. Cf. *Philosophical Investigations* § 521 (Ed.)

allow us to imagine anything senseless. Hence too the language of drawing doesn't allow of senseless drawings. – But that isn't how it is: for a drawing can be senseless in the same way as a proposition. Think of a blueprint from which a turner is to work; here it is very easy to represent an exact analogy with a senseless pseudo-proposition. Remember too the example of drawing a route on a projection of the globe.

When one wants to show the senselessness of metaphysical turns of phrase, one often says "I couldn't imagine the opposite of that", or "What would it be like if it were otherwise?" (When, for instance, someone has said that my images are private, that only I alone can know if I am feeling pain, etc.) Well, if I can't imagine how it might be otherwise, I equally can't imagine that it is *so*. For here "I can't imagine" doesn't indicate a lack of imaginative power. I can't even *try* to imagine it; it makes no sense to say "I imagine it". And that means, no connection has been made between this sentence and the method of representation by imagination (or by drawing).

But why does one say "I can't imagine how it could be *otherwise*" and not "I can't imagine the thing itself"? One regards the sense-less sentence (e.g. "this rod has a length") as a tautology as opposed to a contradiction. One says as it were: "Yes, it has a length; but how could it be otherwise; and why say so?" To the proposition "This rod has a length" we respond not "Nonsense!" but "Of course!" We might also put it thus: when we hear the two proposi-tions, "This rod has a length" and its negation "This rod has no length", we take sides and favour the first sentence, instead of declaring them both nonsense. But this partiality is based on a confusion: we regard the first proposition as verified (and the second as falsified) by the fact "that the rod has a length of 4 metres". "After all, 4 metres is a length" – but one forgets that this is a grammatical proposition.

It is often possible to show that a proposition is meant metaphysically by asking "Is what you affirm meant to be an empirical proposition? Can you conceive (imagine) its being otherwise?" – Do you mean that substance has never yet been destroyed, or that it is *inconceivable* that it should be destroyed? Do you mean that experience shows that human beings always prefer the pleasant to the unpleasant?

How strange that one should be able to say that such and such a state of affairs is inconceivable! If we regard thought as essentially an accompaniment going with an expression, the words in the statement that specify the inconceivable state of affairs must be unaccompanied. So what sort of sense is it to have? Unless it says these words are senseless. But it isn't as it were their sense that is senseless; they are excluded from our language like some arbitrary noise, and the reason for their *explicit* exclusion can only be that *we are tempted* to confuse them with a sentence of our language.

84 The role of a sentence in the calculus is its sense.

A *method* of measurement – of length, for example – has exactly the same relation to the correctness of a statement of length as the sense of a sentence has to its truth or falsehood.

What does "discovering that an assertion doesn't make sense" mean? – and what does it mean to say: "If I mean something by it, surely it must make sense to say it"? "If I mean something by it" – if I mean *what* by it? –

One wants to say: a significant sentence is one which one can not merely say, but also think. But that would be like saying: a significant picture is one that can not merely be drawn but also represented plastically. And saying this would make sense. But the thinking of a sentence is not an activity which one does from the words (like singing from a score). The following example shews this.

Does it make sense to say "The number of my friends is equal to a root of the equation $x^2 + 2x - 3 = 0$?" Here, one might think, we have a notation whose grammar doesn't settle by itself whether a sentence makes sense or not, so that it wasn't determined in advance. That is a fine example of what is meant by understanding a proposition.

If the expression "the root of the equation ..." were a Russellian description, then the proposition "I have n apples and $2 + n = 6$" would have a different sense from the proposition "I have 4 apples".

The sense of a proposition (or a thought) isn't anything spiritual; it's what is given as an answer to a request for an explanation of the sense. Or: one sense differs from another in the same way as the explanation of the one differs from the explanation of the other. So also: the sense of one proposition differs from the sense of another in the same way as the one proposition differs from the other.

The sense of a proposition is not a soul.

It is only in a language that something is a proposition. To understand a proposition is to understand a language.

A proposition is a sign in a system of signs. It is *one* combination of signs among a number of possible ones, and as opposed to other possible ones. As it were *one* position of an indicator as opposed to other possible ones.

"Go in the direction the arrow points."
"Go a hundred times as far as the arrow is long."
"Go as many paces as I draw arrows."
"Draw a copy of this arrow."
"Come at the time shown by this arrow considered as the hour hand of a clock."
For all of these commands the same arrow might do.

↑ in contrast to ↗ is a different sign from ↑ in contrast to ↑.

VII

85 Symbols appear to be of their nature unsatisfied.

Wishes, conjectures, beliefs, commands appear to be something unsatisfied, something in need of completion. Thus I would like to characterize my feeling of grasping a command as a feeling of an innervation. But the innervation in itself isn't anything unsatisfied, it doesn't leave anything open, or stand in need of completion.

And I want to say: "A wish is unsatisfied because it's a wish *for something*; opinion is unsatisfied, because it's the opinion that something is the case, something real, something outside the process of opining."

I would like to say: "my expectation is so made that whatever happens has to accord with it or not".

The proposition seems set over us as a judge and we feel answerable to it. – It seems to demand that reality be compared with it.

I said that a proposition was laid against reality like a ruler. And a ruler – like all logical comparisons for a proposition – is itself in a particular case a propositional sign. Now one would like to say: "Put the ruler against a body: it does not say that the body is of such-and-such a length. Rather it is in itself dead and achieves nothing of what thought achieves." It is as if we had imagined that the essential thing about a living being was the outward form. Then we made a lump of wood in that form, and were abashed to see the stupid block, which hasn't even any similarity to life.

86 I want to say: "if someone could see the process of expectation, he would necessarily be seeing what was expected." – But that is the case: if you see the expression of an expectation you see what is being expected. And in what other way, in what other sense would it be possible to see it?

When we give an order, it can look as if the ultimate thing sought by the order had to remain unexpressed, as there is always a gulf between an order and its execution. Say I want someone to make a particular movement, say to raise his arm. To make it quite clear, I do the movement. This picture seems unambiguous till we ask: how does he know that *he is to make that movement*? – How does he know at all what use he is to make of the signs I give him, whatever they are? Perhaps I shall now try to supplement the order by means of further signs, by pointing from myself to him, making encouraging gestures etc. Here it looks as if the order were beginning to stammer.

Suppose I wanted to tell someone to square the number 4, and did so by means of the schema:

$$
\begin{array}{c|c}
x & 4 \\
\hline
x^2 & ? \\
\end{array}
$$

Now I'm tempted to say that the question mark only hints at something it doesn't express.

As if the sign were precariously trying to produce understanding in us. But if we now understand it, by what token do we understand?

The appearance of the awkwardness of the sign in getting its meaning across, like a dumb person who uses all sorts of suggestive gestures – this disappears when we remember that the sign does its job only in a grammatical system.

(In logic what is unnecessary is also *useless*.)

87 In what sense can one call wishes as such, beliefs, expectations etc. 'unsatisfied'? What is the prototype of nonsatisfaction from which we take our concept? Is it a hollow space? And would one call that unsatisfied? Wouldn't this be a metaphor too? Isn't what we call nonsatisfaction a feeling – say hunger?

In a particular system of expressions we can describe an object by means of the words "satisfied" and "unsatisfied". For example, if we lay it down that we call a hollow cylinder an "unsatisfied cylinder" and the solid cylinder that fills it its "satisfaction".

It seems as if the expectation and the fact satisfying the expectation fitted together somehow. Now one would like to describe an expectation and a fact which fit together, so as to see what this agreement consists in. Here one thinks at once of the fitting of a solid into a corresponding hollow. But when one wants to describe these two one sees that, to the extent that they fit, a *single* description holds for both. (On the other hand compare the meaning of: "These trousers don't go with this jacket"!)

Expectation is not related to its satisfaction in the same way as hunger is related to its satisfaction. I can describe the hunger, and describe what takes it away, and say that it takes it away. And it isn't like this either: I have a wish for an apple, and so I will call 'an apple' whatever takes away the wish.

88 The strange thing is expressed in the fact that if this is the event I expected, it isn't distinct from the one I expected.

I say: "that's just how I imagined it"; and someone says something like "That's impossible, because the one was an image and the other isn't. Did you take your image for reality?"

I see someone pointing a gun and say "I expect a report". The shot is fired. – Well, that was what you expected, so did that bang somehow already exist in your expectation? Or is it just that there is some other kind of agreement between your expectation and what occurred; that that noise was not contained in your expectation and merely accidentally supervened when the expectation was being fulfilled? But no, if the noise had not occurred, my expectation would not have been fulfilled; the noise fulfilled it; it was not an accompaniment of the fulfilment like a second guest accompanying the one I expected. – Was the thing about the event that was not in the expectation too an accident, an extra provided by fate? – But then what was *not* an extra? Did something of the shot already occur in my expectation? – Then what was extra? for wasn't I expecting the whole shot?

"The report was not so loud as I had expected." "Then was there a louder bang in your expectation?"

"The red which you imagine is surely not the same (the same thing) as the red which you see in front of you; so how can you say that it is what you imagined?" – But haven't we an analogous case with the propositions "Here is a red patch" and "Here there isn't a red patch"? The word "red" occurs in both; so this word cannot indicate the presence of something red. The word "red" does its job only in the propositional context. Doesn't the misunderstanding consist in taking the meaning of the word "red" as being the sense of a sentence saying that something is red?

The possibility of this misunderstanding is also contained in the ambiguity of expressions like "the colour red as the common element of two states of affairs" – This may mean that in each something *is* red, has the colour red; or else that both propositions are about the colour red.

What is common in the latter case is the harmony between reality and thought to which indeed a form of our language corresponds.

89 If we say to someone "imagine the colour red" he is to imagine a patch or something that is red, not one that is green, since that is *not red*.

(Could one define the word "red" by pointing to something that was *not red*? That would be as if one were supposed to explain the word "modest" to someone whose English was weak, and one pointed to an arrogant man and said "That man is *not* modest". That it is ambiguous is no argument against such a method of definition. Any definition can be misunderstood. But it might well be asked: are we still to call this "definition"? – For, of course, even if it has the same practical consequences, the same *effect* on the learner, it plays a different part in the calculus from what we ordinarily call "ostensive definition" of the word "red".)

It would be odd to say: "A process looks different when it happens from when it doesn't happen." Or "a red patch looks different when it is there from when it isn't there; but language abstracts from this *difference*, for it speaks of a red patch whether it is there or not."

Reality is not a property still missing in what is expected and which accedes to it when one's expectation is fulfilled. – Nor is reality like the daylight that things need to acquire colour, when they are already there, as it were colourless, in the dark.

"How do you know that you are expecting a *red* patch; that is, how do you know that a red patch is the fulfilment of your expectation?" But I might just as well ask: "how do you know that that *is* a red patch?"

How do you know that what you did really was to recite the alphabet in your head? – But how do you know that what you are reciting aloud really *is* the alphabet?

Of course that is the same question as "How do you know that what you call 'red' is really the same as what another calls 'red'?" And in its metaphysical use the one question makes no more sense than the other.

In these examples, I would like to say, you see how the words are really used.

90 One might think: What a remarkable process willing must be,

if I can now will the very thing I won't be doing until five minutes hence!

How can I expect the event, when it isn't yet there at all?

"Socrates: so if someone has an idea of what is not, he has an idea of nothing? – Theaetetus: It seems so. Socrates: But surely if he has an idea of nothing, then he hasn't any idea at all? – Theaetetus: That seems plain."[1]

If we put the word "kill", say, in place of "have an idea of" in this argument, then there is a rule for the use of this word: it makes no sense to say "I am killing something that does not exist". I can imagine a stag that is not there, in this meadow, but not kill one that is not there. And "to imagine a stag in this meadow" means to imagine *that* a stag is there. But to kill a stag does not mean to kill *that* . . . But if someone says "in order for me to be able to imagine a stag it must after all exist in some sense", the answer is: no, it does not have to *exist* in any sense. And if it should be replied: "But the colour brown at any rate must exist, for me to be able to have an idea of it" – then we can say 'the colour brown exists' means nothing at all; except that it exists here or there as the colouring of an object, and that is not necessary in order for me to be able to imagine a brown stag.

We say that the expression of expectation 'describes' the expected fact and think of an object or complex which makes its appearance as fulfilment of the expectation. – But it is not the expected thing that is the fulfilment, but rather: its coming about.

The mistake is deeply rooted in our language: we say "I expect him" and "I expect his arrival".

It is difficult for us to shake off this comparison: a man makes his appearance – an event makes its appearance. As if an event even now stood in readiness before the door of reality and were then to make its appearance in reality – like coming into a room.

---

1. Plato: Theaetetus 189A. (I have translated Wittgenstein's German rather than the Greek original. Trs.)

91 I can look for him when he is not there, but not hang him when he is not there.

One might want to say: "But he must be somewhere there if I am looking for him." – Then he must be somewhere there too if I don't find him and even if he doesn't exist at all.

A search for a particular thing (e.g. my stick) is a particular kind of search, and differs from a search for something else because of what one does (says, thinks) while searching, not because of what one finds.

Suppose while I am searching I carry with me a picture or an image – very well. If I say that the picture is a picture of what I am looking for, that merely tells the place of the picture in the process of searching. And if I find it and say "There it is! *That's* what I was looking for" those words aren't a kind of definition of the name of the object of the search (e.g. of the words "my stick"), a definition that couldn't have been given until the object had been found.

"You were looking for *him*? You can't even have known if he was there!" (Contrast looking for the trisection of the angle.)

One may say of the bearer of a name that he does not exist; and of course that is not an activity, although one may compare it with one and say: he must be there all the same, if he does not exist. (And this has certainly already been written some time by a philosopher.)

The idea that it takes finding to show what we were looking for, and fulfilment of a wish to show what we wanted, means one is judging the process like the symptoms of expectation or search in someone else. I see him uneasily pacing up and down his room; then someone comes in at the door and he relaxes and gives signs of satisfaction. And I say "obviously he was expecting this person."

The symptoms of expectation are not the expression of expectation.

One may have the feeling that in the sentence "I expect he is coming" one is using the words "he is coming" in a different sense from the one they have in the assertion "he is coming". But if it were so, how could I say that my expectation had been fulfilled? And the words "he is coming" mean the same in the expression of expectation as in the description of its fulfilment, because if I wanted to explain the words "he" and "is coming", say by means of ostensive definitions, the same definitions of these words would go for both sentences.

But it might now be asked: what's it like for him to come? – The door opens, someone walks in, and so on. – What's it like for me to expect him to come? – I walk up and down the room, look at the clock now and then, and so on. But the one set of events has not the smallest similarity to the other! So how can one use the same words in describing them? What has become now of the hollow space and the corresponding solid?

But perhaps I say as I walk up and down: "I expect he'll come in." Now there is a similarity somewhere. But of what kind?!

But of course I might walk up and down in my room and look at the clock and so without expecting him to come. I wouldn't describe doing that by saying "I expect he is coming". So what made it e.g. the expectation precisely of *him*?

I may indeed say: to walk restlessly up and down in my room, to look at the door, to listen for a noise is: to expect N. – That is simply a definition of the expression "to expect N". Of course it isn't a definition of the word "expect", because it doesn't explain what e.g. "to expect M" means. Well, we can take care of that; we say something like: to expect X means to act as described and to utter the name "X" while doing so. On this definition the person expected is the person whose name is uttered. Or I may give as a definition: to expect a person X is to do what I described in the second example, and to make a drawing of a person. In that case, the person expected is the bearer of the name X, the person who corresponds to the drawing. – That of course wouldn't explain what "to expect N to *go*" means, and I would have to give either an independent definition of that, or a general definition including going and coming. And even that wouldn't explain say what "to expect a storm" means; etc. etc.

What characterizes all these cases is, that the definition can be used to read off the object of the expectation from the expectant behaviour. It isn't a later experience that decides *what* we are expecting.

And I may say: it is in language that expectation and its fulfilment make contact.

So *in this case* the behaviour of the expectant person is behaviour which can be translated in accordance with given rules into the proposition "He is expecting it to happen that p". And so the simplest typical example to illustrate this use of the word "expect" is that the expectation of its happening that p should consist in the expectant person *saying* "I expect it to happen that p". Hence in so many cases it clarifies the grammatical situation to say: let us put the expression of expectation in place of the expectation, the expression of the thought in place of the thought.

93 One can conceive expectation as expectant, preparatory behaviour. Expectation is like a player in a ball game holding his hands in the right position to catch the ball. The expectation of the player might consist in his holding out his hands in a particular way and looking at the ball.

Some will perhaps want to say: "An expectation is a thought". Obviously, that corresponds to one use of the word "expect". And we need to remember that the process of thinking may be *very various*.[1]

And if expectation is the thought "I am expecting it to happen that p" it is senseless to say that I won't perhaps know until later what I expected.

1. A line has dropped out of the translation of the corresponding passage in *Zettel* (§63).

Something analogous might be said of wishing, fear and hope. (Plato called hope "a speech"[1]).

But it is different if *hunger* is called "a wish", say the body's wish for food to satisfy it. For it is a hypothesis that just that will satisfy the wish; there's room for conjecture and doubt on the topic.

Similarly if what I call "expectation" is a feeling, say a feeling of disquiet or dissatisfaction. But of course these feelings are not thoughts in an amorphous form.

The idea of thought as an unexplained process in the human mind makes it possible to imagine it turned into a persistent amorphous condition.

If I say " I have been expecting him all day", "expect" here doesn't mean a persistent condition including as ingredients the person expected and his arrival, in the way that a dough may contain flour, sugar and eggs mixed into a paste. What constitutes expectation is a series of actions, thoughts and feelings.

94 When I expect someone, – what happens? I perhaps look at my calendar and see his name against today's date and the note "5 p.m." I say to someone else "I can't come to see you today, because I'm expecting N". I make preparations to receive a guest. I wonder "Does N smoke?", I remember having seen him smoke and put out cigarettes. Towards 5 p.m. I say to myself "Now he'll come soon", and as I do so I imagine a man looking like N; then I imagine him coming into the room and my greeting him and calling him by his name. This and many other more or less *similar* trains of events are called "expecting N to come".

1. Philebus, 40A. (The Greek word in the context means rather "a word", "a proposition". Tr.)

But perhaps I'm also prepared to say "I have been expecting N" in a case where the only thing that connects him with my expectant activity is for instance that on a particular day I prepare a meal for myself and one other person, and that N. has announced his intention of taking that meal with me.

What does the process or state of wanting an apple consist in? Perhaps I experience hunger or thirst or both, and meanwhile imagine an apple, or remember that I enjoyed one yesterday; perhaps I say "I would like to eat an apple"; perhaps I go and look in a cupboard where apples are normally kept. Perhaps all these states and activities are combined among themselves and with others.

95 The same sort of thing must be said of intention. If a mechanism is *meant* to act as a brake, but for some reason does not slow down the motion of the machine, then the purpose of the mechanism cannot be found out *immediately* from it and from its effect. If you were to say "that is a brake, but it doesn't work" you would be talking about intention. But now suppose that whenever the mechanism didn't work as a brake a particular person became angry. Wouldn't the intention of the mechanism now be expressed in its effect? No, for now it could be said that the lever sometimes triggers the brake and sometimes triggers the anger. For how does it come out that the man is angry *because* the lever doesn't operate the brake? "Being annoyed that the apparatus does not function" is itself something like "wishing that it did function in that way". – Here we have the old problem, which we would like to express in the following way: "the thought that p is the case doesn't presuppose that it is the case; yet on the other hand there must be something in the fact that is a presupposition even of having the thought (I can't think that something is red, if the colour red does not exist)". It is the problem of the harmony between world and thought. – To this it may be replied that thoughts are in the same

space as the things that admit of doubt; they are laid against them in the same way as a ruler is laid against what is to be measured.

What I really want to say is this: the wish that he should come is the wish that really *he* should really *come*. If a further explanation of this assurance is wanted, I would go on to say "and by 'he' I mean that man there, and by 'come' I mean doing this . . ." But these are just grammatical explanations, explanations which *create* language.

It is *in language* that it's all done.

"I couldn't think that something is red if red didn't exist." What that proposition really means is the image of something red, or the existence of a red sample *as part of our language*. But of course one can't say that our language *has to* contain such a sample; if it didn't contain it, it would just be another, a different language. But one can say, and emphasize, that it does contain it.

96 It's beginning to look somehow as if intention could never be recognized as *intention* from outside; as if one must be doing the meaning of it oneself in order to understand it as meaning. That would amount to considering it not as a phenomenon or fact but as something intentional which has a direction given to it. What this direction is, we do not know; it is something which is absent from the phenomenon as such.

Here, of course, our earlier problem returns, because the point is that one has to read off from a thought that it is the thought that such and such is the case. If one can't read it off (as one can't read off the cause of a stomach-ache) then it is of no logical interest.

My idea seems nonsensical if it is expressed like *this*. It's supposed to be possible to see what someone is thinking of by opening up his head. But how is that possible? The objects he's thinking about are certainly not in his head – any more than in his thoughts!

If we consider them 'from outside' we have to understand thoughts as thoughts, intentions as intentions and so on, *without* getting any information about something's meaning. For it is with the phenomenon of thinking that meaning belongs.

If a thought is observed there can be no further question of an understanding; for if the thought is seen it must be recognized as a thought with a certain content; it doesn't need to be interpreted! – That really is how it is; when we are thinking, there isn't any interpretation going on.

97 If I said "but that would mean considering intention as something other than a phenomenon" that would make intention reminiscent of the will as conceived by Schopenhauer. Every phenomenon seems dead in comparison with the living thought.

"Intention seen from outside" is connected with the question whether a machine could think. "Whatever phenomenon we saw, it couldn't ever be intention; for that has to contain the very thing that is intended, and any phenomenon would be something complete in itself and unconcerned with anything outside itself, something merely dead if considered by itself."

This is like when we say: "The will can't be a phenomenon, for whatever phenomenon you take is something that *simply happens,* something we undergo, not something we *do*. The will isn't *something* I see happen, it's more like my being involved in my actions, my *being* my actions." Look at your arm and move it and you will experience this very vividly: "You aren't observing it moving itself, you aren't having an experience – not just an experience, anyway – you're *doing* something." You may tell yourself that you could also imagine exactly the same thing happening to your hand, but merely observed and not willed by you. But shut your eyes, and move your arm so that you have, among other things, a certain experience: now ask yourself whether you still can imagine that you were having the same experience but without willing it.

If someone wants to express the distinction between voluntary and involuntary movements by saying that voluntary movements of the arm, for example, are differentiated from involuntary ones by a feeling of innervation, you feel an urge to say "But I don't *undergo* this experience, I *do* it – " But *can* one speak of a distinction between undergoing and doing in the case of an experience of innervation? I would like to say: "If I will, then there isn't anything that happens to me, neither the movement nor a feeling; I am the agent." Very well; but there's no doubt that you *also* have experiences when you voluntarily move your arm; because you *see* (and feel) it moving whether or not you take up the attitude of an *observer*. So just for once try to distinguish between *all the experiences* of acting plus the doing (which is not an experience) and *all* those experiences without the element of doing. Think over whether you still need this element, or whether it is beginning to appear redundant. – Of course you can say correctly that when you do something, there isn't anything happening to you, because the phenomena of doing *are* different from the phenomena of observing something like a reflex movement. But this doesn't become clear until one considers the very different sorts of things that people call voluntary activities and that people call unintentional or involuntary processes in our life. (More about this in another place.)

98 By "intention" I mean here what uses a sign in a thought. The intention seems to interpret, to give the final interpretation; which is not a further sign or picture, but something else, the thing that cannot be further interpreted. But what we have reached is a psychological, not a logical terminus.

Think of a sign language, an 'abstract' one, I mean one that is strange to us, in which we do not feel at home, in which, as we should say, we do not *think* (we used a similar example once before), and let us imagine this language interpreted by a translation into – as we should like to say – an unambiguous picture-language, a language consisting of pictures painted in perspective. It is quite clear that it is much easier to imagine different *interpretations* of the written language than of a picture painted in the usual way depicting say a room with normal furniture. Here we shall also be inclined to think that there is no further possibility of interpretation.

Here we might also say we didn't enter into the sign-language, but did enter into the painted picture.

(This is connected with the fact that what we call a 'picture by similarity' is not a picture in accordance with some established method of projection. In this case the "likeness" between two objects means something like the possibility of mistaking one for the other.)

"Only the intended picture reaches up to reality like a yardstick. Looked at from outside, there it is, lifeless and isolated." – It is as if at first we looked at a picture so as to enter into it and the objects in it surrounded us like real ones; and then we stepped back, and were now outside it; we saw the frame, and the picture was a painted surface. In this way, when we intend, we are surrounded by our intention's pictures and we are inside them. But when we step outside intention, they are mere patches on a canvas, without life and of no interest to us. When we intend, we exist among the pictures (shadows) of intention, as well as with real things. Let us imagine we are sitting in a darkened cinema and entering into the happenings in the film. Now the lights are turned on, though the film continues on the screen. But suddenly we see it "from outside" as movements of light and dark patches on a screen.

(In dreams it sometimes happens that we first read a story and then are ourselves participants in it. And after waking up after a dream it is sometimes as if we had stepped back out of the dream and now see it before us as an alien picture.) And it also means something to speak of "living in the pages of a book". That is connected with the fact that our body is not at all essential for the occurrence of our experience. (Cf. eye and visual field.)

(Compare also the remark: if we understand a sentence, it has a certain depth for us.)

99 What happens is not that this symbol cannot be further interpreted, but: I do no interpreting. I do not interpret because I feel natural in the present picture. When I interpret, I step from one level of my thought to another.

If I see the thought symbol "from outside", I become conscious that it *could* be interpreted thus or thus; if it is a step in the course of my thoughts, then it is a stopping-place that is natural to me, and its further interpretability does not occupy (or trouble) me. As I have a railway time-table and use it without being concerned with the fact that a table can be interpreted in various ways.

When I said that my image wouldn't be a portrait unless it bore the name of its subject, I didn't mean that I have to imagine it and his name at the same time. Suppose I say something like: "What I see in my mind isn't just a picture which is like N (and perhaps like others too). No, I know that it is him, that he is the person it portrays." I might then ask: *when* do I know that and what does knowing it amount to? There's no need for anything to take place during the imagining that could be called "knowing" in this way. Something of that sort may happen after the imagining; I may go on from the picture to the name, or perhaps say that I imagined N, even though at the time of the imagining there wasn't anything, except a kind of similarity, to characterize the image as N's. Or again there might be something preceding the image that made the connection with N. And so the interpretation isn't something that accompanies the image; what gives the image its interpretation is the *path* on which it lies.

That all becomes clearer if one imagines images replaced by

drawings, if one imagines people who go in for drawing instead of imagining.

100 If I try to describe the process of intention, I feel first and foremost that it can do what it is supposed to only by containing an extremely faithful picture of what it intends. But further, that that too does not go far enough, because a picture, whatever it may be, can be variously interpreted; hence this picture too in its turn stands isolated. When one has the picture in view by itself it is suddenly dead, and it is as if something had been taken away from it, which had given it life before. It is not a thought, not an intention; whatever accompaniments we imagine for it, articulate or inarticulate processes, or any feeling whatsoever, it remains isolated, it does not point outside itself to a reality beyond.

Now one says: "Of course it is not the picture that intends, but we who use it to intend." But if this intending, this meaning, is something that is done with the picture, then I cannot see why that has to involve a human being. The process of digestion can also be studied as a chemical process, independently of whether it takes place in a living being. We want to say "Meaning is surely essentially a mental process, a process of consciousness and life, not of dead matter." But what will give such a thing the specific character of what goes on? – so long as we speak of it as a process. And now it seems to us as if intending could not be any process at all, of any kind whatever. – For what we are dissatisfied with here is the grammar of *process*, not the specific kind of process. – It could be said: we should call any process 'dead' in this sense.

Let's say the wish for this table to be a little higher is the act of my holding my hand above the table at the height I wish it to be. Now comes the objection: "The hand above the table can't be the wish: it doesn't express that the table is to be higher; it is where it is and the table is where it is. And *whatever other* gesture I made it wouldn't make any difference."

(It might almost be said: "Meaning *moves,* whereas a process stands still.")

101 However, if I imagine the expression of a wish as the act of wishing, the problem appears solved, because the system of language seems to provide me with a medium in which the proposition is no longer dead.

If we imagine the expression of a wish as the wish, it is rather as if we were led by a train of thought to imagine something like a network of lines spread over the earth, and living beings who moved only along the lines.

But now someone will say: even if the *expression* of the wish is the wish, still the whole language isn't present during this expression, yet surely the wish is!
So how does language help? Well, it just isn't necessary that anything should be *present* except the expression.

102 You might as it were locate (look up) all of the connections in the grammar of the language. There you can see the whole network to which the sentence belongs.

Suppose we're asked "When we're thinking, meaning and so on why don't we come upon the bare picture?" We must tell ourselves that when we're thinking we don't wonder whether the picture is the thought or the meaning, we simply *use* pictures, sentences and so on and discard them one after the other.

But of course if you call the picture the wish (e.g. that this table were higher) then what you're doing is comparing the picture with an expression of our language, and certainly it doesn't correspond to such an expression unless it's part of a system translatable into our language.

One says: how can this way of holding the hand, this picture be the wish that such and such were the case? It is nothing more than a hand over a table, and there it is, alone and without a *sense*. Like a single bit of scenery from the production of a play which has been left by itself. It had life only in the play.

In the gesture we don't see the real shadow of the fulfilment, the unambiguous shadow that admits of no further interpretation.

We ask: "does the hand above a table wish?" Does anything, spiritual or material, that we might add, wish? Is there any such situation or process that really contains what is wished? – And what is our paradigm of such containing? Isn't it our language? Where are we to find what makes the wish *this* wish, even though it's only a wish? Nowhere but in the expressed wish.

"After all, the wish must show *what* is wished, it must prefigure in the realm of wishes that which is wished." But what actual process do you have in mind here as the prefiguring? (What is the mirror in which you think you saw what was wished?)

"The gesture *tries* to prefigure" one wants to say "but it can't".

103 Can one say that *while I'm wishing* my wish seems to prefigure the fulfilment? While I'm wishing it doesn't *seem* to do anything; I notice nothing odd about it. It's only considering the linguistic manifestation of the wish that produces this appearance.

We are considering an event that we might call an instance of the wish that this table were higher. But this event *doesn't even seem* to contain the fulfilment. Now someone says: "But this event does have to be a shadow of the very state of affairs that is wished, and these actions aren't that." But why do you say that's what a wish has to be? "Well, because it's the wish that just that were the case". Precisely: that's the only answer you can give to the question. So after all that event is the shadow, insofar as it corresponds within a system to the expression of the wish in the word-language. (It is in language that wish and fulfilment meet.) Remember that the expression of a wish can be the wish, and that the expression doesn't derive its sense from the presence of some extraordinary spirit.

Think also of a case very similar to the present one: "This table isn't 80 cm high". Must the fact that it is 90 cm, and so *not* 80 cm, high contain the shadow of the fact of its being 80 cm high? What gives this impression? When I see a table which is 90 cm high does it give a shadowy impression of having a height it doesn't have?

This is rather as if we misunderstood the assertion "⊢ ∼ p" in such a way as to think that it contained the assertion "⊢ p", rather as "⊢ p.q" contains in its sense "⊢ p".

Someone describes to me what went on when he, as he says, had the wish that the table were 10 cm higher. He says that he held his hand 10 cm above the table. I reply "But how do you know that you weren't just wishing that the table were higher, since in that case too you would have held your hand at some height above the table." He says "After all, I must know what I wished" I reply "Very well, but I want to know *by what token* you remember when you remember your wish. What *happened* when you wished, and what makes you say you wished just that?" He says "I know that I *intentionally* held my hand just 10 cm above." I say "But what constituted just *that* intention?" – I might also ask "Is it certain that when you were wishing you were using the scale 1 : 1? How do you know that?"

If he had described the process of wishing by saying "I said 'I would like to have the table 10 cm higher'", then the question how he could know what he wished wouldn't have arisen. (Unless someone had gone on to ask: "And did you *mean* those words in the way they are usually meant?".)

What it always comes to in the end is that without any further *meaning* he *calls* what happened the wish that that should happen. [Manifestation, not description.]

"How do I know it's *him* I'm remembering, if the remembering is a picture?" To what extent *do* I know it? ("When two men look perfectly alike, how can I remember one of them in particular?")

104 We say "A proposition isn't just a series of sounds, it is something more". We think of the way a Chinese sentence is a mere series of sounds for us, which just means that we don't understand it, and we say this is because we don't have any thoughts in connection with the Chinese sentence (e.g. the Chinese word for "red" doesn't call up any image in us). "So what distinguishes a significant sentence from mere sounds is the thoughts it evokes." The sentence is like a key-bit whose indentations are constructed to move levers in the soul in a particular way. The sentence, as it were, plays a melody (the thought) on the instrument of the soul. But why should I now hypothesize, in addition to the orderly series of words, another series of mental elements running parallel? That simply duplicates language with something else of the same kind.

Suppose the sentence is: "This afternoon N went into the Senate House." The sentence isn't a mere noise for me, it evokes an image of a man in the vicinity of the Senate House, or something similar. But the sentence and the image aren't just a noise plus a faint image; calling up the image, and having certain other consequences, is something as it were internal to the sentence; *that* is what its sense is. The image seems only a faint copy of the sense, or shall we say, only a single view of the sense. – But what do I mean by this? Don't I just see the sentence as part of a system of consequences?

Let us suppose that proposition evoked in me a very clear picture of N on the way to the Senate House and that in the picture there could also be seen the setting sun ("evening") and a calendar with today's date. Suppose that instead of letting the sentence call up this picture, I actually painted it and showed it to someone else as a means of communication in place of the sentence. He might say of this too that it expressed a thought but needed to be understood; what he would think of as an act of understanding would probably be a translation into word languages.

"I arrive in Vienna on the 24th of December." They aren't mere words! Of course not: when I read them various things happen inside me in addition to the perception of the words: maybe I feel joy, I have images, and so on. – But I don't just mean that various more or less inessential concomitant phenomena occur in conjunction with the sentence; I mean that the sentence has a definite sense and I perceive it. But then what is this definite sense? Well, that this particular person, whom I know, arrives at such and such a place etc. Precisely: when you are giving the sense, you are moving around in the grammatical background of the sentence. You're looking at the various transformations and consequences of the sentence as laid out in advance; and so they are, in so far as they are embodied in a grammar. (You are simply looking at the sentence as a move in a given game.)

I said that it is the *system* of language that makes the sentence a thought and makes it a thought *for us*.

That doesn't mean that it is while we are using a sentence that the system of language makes it into a thought for us, because the system isn't present then and there isn't any need for anything to make the sentence alive for us, since the question of being alive doesn't arise. But if we ask: "why doesn't a sentence strike us as isolated and dead when we are reflecting on its essence, its sense, the thought etc." it can be said that we are continuing to move in the system of language.

To match the words "I grasp the sense" or "I am thinking the thought of this sentence" you hypothesize a process which unlike the bare propositional sign contains these consequences.

105   "This queer thing, thought": but it does not strike us as queer while we are thinking *it*. It strikes us as queer when we tell ourselves that it connects objects in the mind, because it is the very thought that *this* person *is doing that*; or that it isn't a sign or a picture, because I would still have to know how they were meant in their turn; or that thought isn't something dead, because *for me* what I think *really* happens.

What is the source of this odd way of looking at things?

What makes us think that a thought, or a proposition we think, contains the reality? It's that we're all ready to pass from it to the reality, and we feel this transition as something already potentially contained in it (when, that is, we reflect on it), because we say "that word *meant him*". We feel this transition as something just as legitimate as a permitted move in a game.

Thought does not strike us as mysterious while we are thinking, but only when we say, as it were retrospectively: "How was that possible?" How was it possible for thought to deal with the very person *himself*? But here I am merely being astonished by my own linguistic expression and momentarily misunderstanding it.

Thought strikes us as mysterious. But not while we think. And we don't mean that it's psychologically remarkable. It isn't only that we see it as an extraordinary way of producing pictures and signs, we actually feel as if by means of it we had caught reality in our net.

It isn't while we're *looking at* it that it seems a strange process; but when we let ourselves be guided by language, when we look at what we say about it.

We mistakenly locate this mystery in the nature of the process.

(We interpret the enigma created by our misunderstanding as the enigma of an incomprehensible process.)

106 "Thought is a remarkable process, because when I think of what will happen tomorrow, I am mentally already in the future." If one doesn't understand the grammar of the proposition "I am mentally in the future" one will believe that here the future is in some strange way caught in the sense of a sentence, in the meaning of words. Similarly people think that the endless series of cardinal numbers is somehow before our mind's eye, whenever we can use that expression significantly.

"For me this portrait is *him*"? What does that mean? I have the same attitude to the portrait, as to the man himself. For I do of course distinguish between him and his picture.

A thought experiment comes to much the same as an experiment which is sketched or painted or described instead of being carried out. And so the result of a thought experiment is the fictitious result of a fictitious experiment.

"The sense of this proposition was present to me." What was it that happened?

"Only someone who is *convinced* can say that". – How does the conviction help him when he says it? – Is it somewhere at hand by the side of the spoken expression? (Or is it masked by it, as a soft sound by a loud one, so that it can, as it were, no longer be heard when one expresses it out loud?) What if someone were to say "In order to be able to sing a tune from memory one has to hear it in one's mind and sing from that"?

Try the following experiment: Say a sentence, perhaps "The weather is very fine today"; right, and now think the thought of the sentence, but unadulterated, without the sentence.

107 "It looks as if intention could never be recognized as intention "from outside", as if one must be doing the meaning of it oneself in order to understand it as meaning."[1]

Can one recognize stomach-ache as such "from outside"? What are stomach-aches "from outside"? Here there is no outside or inside! Of course, in so far as meaning is a specific experience, one wouldn't call any other experience "meaning". Only it isn't any remarkable feature of the sensation which explains the directionality of meaning. And if we say "from outside intention cannot be recognised as intention etc." we don't want to say that meaning is a special experience, but that it isn't anything which happens, or happens to us, but something that we do, otherwise it would be just dead. (The subject – we want to say – does not here drop out of the experience but is so much involved in it that the experience cannot be described.)

It is almost as if one said: we can't see ourselves going hither and thither, because it is we who are doing the going (and so we can't stand still and watch). But here, as so very often, we are suffering from an inadequate form of expression, which we are using at the very time we want to shake it off. *We* clothe the protest against our form of expression in an apparently factual proposition expressed in that very form. For if we say "we see ourselves going thither" we mean simply that we see what someone sees when he is going himself and not what he sees if someone else is going. And one does indeed have a particular visual experience if one is doing the going oneself.

That is to say, what we are speaking of is a case in which contrary to experience the subject is linked like an element in a chemical compound. But where do we get this idea from? The concept of living activity in contrast with dead phenomena.

1. p. 143 above.

Imagine someone now saying: "going somewhere oneself isn't an experience".

We want to say: "When we mean something, there isn't a dead picture (of any kind); it's as if we went up to someone. We go up to what we mean."

But here we're constructing a false contrast between experience and something else, as if experience consisted of sitting still and letting pictures pass in front of one.

"When one means, it is oneself doing the meaning"; similarly, it is oneself that does the moving. One rushes forward oneself, and one can't simultaneously observe the rushing. Of course not.

Yes, meaning something is like going up to someone.

108 Fulfilment of expectation doesn't consist in this: a third thing happens which can be described otherwise than as "the fulfilment of this expectation", i.e. as a feeling of satisfaction or joy or whatever it may be. The expectation that something will be the case is the same as the expectation of the fulfilment of that expectation.

Could the justification of an action as fulfilment of an order run like this: "You said 'bring me a yellow flower', upon which this one gave me a feeling of satisfaction; that is why I have brought it"? Wouldn't one have to reply: "But I didn't set you to bring me the flower which should give you that sort of feeling after what I said!"

(I go to look for the yellow flower. Suppose that while I am looking a picture comes before my mind, – even so, do I need it when I see the yellow flower – or another flower? If I say: "as soon as I see a yellow flower, something as it were clicks into place in my memory" – rather like a lever into a cog in the striking mechanism of a clock – can I foresee, or expect, this clicking into place any better than the yellow flower? Even if in a particular case it really is true that what I'm expecting isn't what I am looking for, but some other (indirect) criterion, that certainly isn't an explanation of expectation.)

But isn't the occurrence of what is expected always accompanied by a phenomenon of agreement (or satisfaction?). Is this phenomenon something different from the occurrence of what is expected? If so, then I don't know whether fulfilment is always accompanied by such a phenomenon.

If I say: the person whose expectation is fulfilled doesn't have to shout out "yes, that is it" or the like – I may be told: "Certainly, but he must *know* that the expectation is fulfilled." Yes, if the knowledge is part of its *being* fulfilled. "Yes, but when someone has his expectation fulfilled, there's always a relaxation of tension!" – How do you know that?

VIII

109 A description of language must achieve the same result as language itself. "For in that case I really can learn from the proposition, from the description of reality, how things are in reality." – Of course it's only *this* that is called description, or "learning how things are". And that is all that is ever said when we say that we learn from the description how things are in reality.

"From the order you get the knowledge of what you have to do. And yet the order only gives you itself, and its effect is neither here nor there." But here we are simply misled by the form of expression of our language, when it says "the knowledge of *what* you have to do" or "the knowledge of the action". For then it looks as if this something, the action, is a thing which is to come into existence when the order is carried out, and as if the order made us acquainted with this very thing by showing it us in such a way that it already in a certain sense brought it into existence. (How can a command – an expectation – show us a man before he has come into the room?)

Suppose someone says that one can infer from an order the action that obeys it, and from a proposition the fact which verifies it. What on earth can one infer from a proposition apart from *itself*? How can one pull the action out of the order before it takes place? Unless what is meant is a different form of description of the action, such as say making a drawing, in accordance with the order, of what I'm to do. But even this further description isn't there until I have drawn it; it doesn't have a shadowy existence in the order itself.

Being able to do something seems like a shadow of the actual doing, just as the sense of a sentence seems like the shadow of a fact, and the understanding of an order the shadow of its execution.

In the order the fact as it were "casts its shadow before it"! But this shadow, whatever it may be, is not the event.

The shadowy anticipation of the fact consists in our being able already to think that *that very thing* will happen, which *hasn't yet* happened. Or, as it is misleadingly put, in our being now able to think of (or about) *what hasn't yet* happened.

110 Thinking plus its application proceeds step by step like a calculus. – However many intermediate steps I insert between the thought and its application, each intermediate step always follows the previous one without any intermediate link, and so too the application follows the last intermediate step. It is the same as when we want to insert intermediate links between decision and action.

The ambiguity of our ways of expressing ourselves: If an order were given us in code with the key for translating in into English, we might call the procedure of constructing the English form of the order "derivation of what we have to do from the code" or "derivation of what executing the order is". If on the other hand we act according to the order, obey it, here too in certain cases one may speak of a derivation of the execution.

We can't cross the bridge to the execution until we are there.

111 It is as a calculus that thinking has an interest for us; not as an activity of the human imagination.

It is the *calculus* of thought that connects with extra-mental reality.

From expectation to fulfilment is a step in a calculation. Indeed, the relation between the calculation

$$\frac{25 \times 25}{\begin{array}{r} 50 \\ \hline 125 \end{array}}$$

and its result 625 is exactly the same as that between expectation and its fulfilment. Expectation is a picture of its fulfilment to exactly the same degree as this calculation is a picture of its result, and the fulfilment is determined by the expectation to exactly the same degree as the result is determined by the calculation.

112 When I think in language, there aren't meanings going through my mind in addition to the verbal expressions; the language is itself the vehicle of thought.

In what sense does an order anticipate its execution? By ordering *just that* which later on is carried out? But one would have to say "which later on is carried out, or again is not carried out". And that is to say nothing.

"But even if my wish does not determine what is going to be the case, still it does so to speak determine the theme of a fact, whether the fact fulfils the wish or not." We are – as it were – surprised, not at anyone's knowing the future, but at his being able to prophesy at all (right or wrong).

As if the mere prophecy, no matter whether true or false, fore-shadowed the future; whereas it knows nothing of the future and cannot know less than nothing.

Suppose you now ask: then are facts defined one way or another by an expectation – that is, is it defined for whatever event may occur whether it fulfils the expectation or not? The answer has to be: Yes, unless the expression of the expectation is indefinite, e.g. by containing a disjunction of different possibilities.

"The proposition determines in advance what will make it true." Certainly, the proposition "p" determines that p must be the case in order to make it true; and that means:

(the proposition p) = (the proposition that the fact p makes true). And the statement that the wish for it to be the case that p is satis-fied by the event p, merely enunciates a rule for signs:

(the wish for it to be the case that p) = (the wish that is satisfied by the event p).

Like everything metaphysical the harmony between thought and reality is to be found in the grammar of the language.

IX

113 Here instead of harmony or agreement of thought and reality one might say: the pictorial character of thought. But is this pictorial character an agreement? In the *Tractatus* I had said something like: it is an agreement of form. But that is misleading.

Anything can be a picture of anything, if we extend the concept of picture sufficiently. If not, we have to explain what we call a picture of something, and what we want to call the agreement of the pictorial character, the agreement of the forms.

For what I said really boils down to this: that every projection must have something in common with what is projected no matter what is the method of projection. But that only means that I am here extending the concept of 'having in common' and am making it equivalent to the general concept of projection. So I am only drawing attention to a possibility of generalization (which of course can be very important).

The agreement of thought and reality consists in this: if I say falsely that something is *red*, then, for all that, it isn't *red*. And when I want to explain the word "red" to someone, in the sentence "That is not red", I do it by pointing to something red.

In what sense can I say that a proposition is a picture? When I think about it, I want to say: it must be a picture if it is to show me what I am to do, if I am to be able to act in accordance with it. But in that case all you want to say is that you act in accordance with a proposition in the same sense as you act in accordance with a picture.

To say that a proposition is a picture gives prominence to certain features of the grammar of the word "proposition".

Thinking is quite comparable to the drawing of pictures.

But one can also say that what looks like an analogue of a proposition is actually a particular case of our general concept. When I compared the proposition with a ruler, strictly speaking what I did was to take the use of a ruler in making a statement of length as an example for all propositions.

114 The sense of a proposition and the sense of a picture. If we compare a proposition with a picture, we must think whether we are comparing it to a portrait (a historical representation) or to a genre-picture. And both comparisons have point.

Sentences in fiction correspond to genre-pictures.

"When I look at a genre-picture, it 'tells' me something even though I don't believe (imagine) for a moment that the people I see in it really exist, or that there have really been people in that situation."

Think of the quite different grammar of the expressions:

"This picture shows people in a village inn."

"This picture shows the coronation of Napoleon."

(Socrates: "And if you have an idea must it not be an idea of *something*?" -- Theaetetus: "Necessarily." – Socrates: "And if you have an idea of something, mustn't it be of something real?" – Theaetetus: "It seems so").[1]

Does the picture tell me, for instance, "two people are sitting in an inn drinking wine?" Only if this proposition somehow enters into the process of understanding *outside the picture,* say if I say which I look at the picture "here two people are sitting etc." If the picture tells me something in this sense, it tells me *words*. But how far does it declare itself in these words? After all, if reality is declaring itself via language, it is taking a long way round.

So for the picture to tell me something it isn't essential that words should occur to me while I look at it; because the picture was supposed to be the more direct language.

Here it is important to realise that instead of a picture one might have considered a slice of material reality. For although our

1. Theaetetus, 189A (immediately before the passage quoted in §90).

attitude to a painted table derives historically from our attitude to real tables, the latter is not a part of the former.

115 So what the picture tells me is itself.

Its telling me something will consist in my recognizing in it objects in some sort of characteristic arrangement. (If I say: "I see a table in this picture" then what I say characterizes the picture – as I said – in a manner which has nothing to do with the existence of a 'real' table. "The picture shows me a cube" can e.g. mean: It contains the form ⬡.)

Asked "Did you recognize your desk when you entered your room this morning?" – I should no doubt say "Certainly!" and yet it would be misleading to call what took place "a recognition". Certainly the desk was not strange to me; I was not surprised to see it, as I should have been if another one had been standing there, or some unfamiliar kind of object.

"Something is familiar if I know what it is."

"What does it mean: 'this object is familiar to me'?" – "Well, I know that it's a table." But that can mean any number of things, such as "I know how it's used", "I know it looks like a table when it's opened out", "I know that it's what people call 'a table'."

What kind of thing is "familiarity"? What constitutes a view's being familiar to me? (The question itself is peculiar; it does not sound like a grammatical question.)

I would like to say: "I see what I see". And the familiarity can only consist in my being at home in what I see.

116 "I see what I see": I say that because I don't want to give a name to what I see. I don't want to say "I see a flower" because that

presupposes a linguistic convention, and I want a form of expression that makes no reference to the history of the impression.

The familiarity consists in my recognizing that what I see is a flower. I may say: the utterance of the words "that is a flower" is a recognition reaction; but the criterion for recognition isn't that I name the object correctly, but that when I look at it I utter a series of sounds and have a certain experience. For that the sounds are the correct English word, or that they are a word at all in any existent language, isn't part of my experience during the utterance.

I want to exclude from my consideration of familiarity every-thing that is 'historical'. When that's been done what remains is impressions (experiences, reactions). Even where language does enter into our experience, we don't consider it as an existing institution.

So the multiplicity of familiarity, as I understand it, is that of feeling at home in what I see. It might consist in such facts as these: my glance doesn't move restlessly (inquiringly) around the object. I don't keep changing the way I look at it, but immediately fix on one and hold it steady.

I see the picture of a heavy coat and have a feeling of warmth and cosiness; I see the picture of a winter landscape and shiver. These reactions, it might be said, are justified by earlier experience. But we aren't concerned *now* about the history of our experiences or about any such justification.

No one will say that every time I enter a room, my long familiar surroundings, there is enacted a recognition of all that I see and have seen hundreds of times before.

117 If we think of our understanding of a picture, of a genre

picture say, we are perhaps inclined to assume that there is a particular phenomenon of recognition and that we recognize the painted people as people, the painted trees as trees and so on.

But when I look at a genre picture do I compare the painted people with real people etc.?

So should I say that I recognize the painted people as painted people? And similarly real people as real people?

Of course there is a phenomenon of recognition in a case where it takes some sort of investigation to recognize a drawing as a representation of a human being; but when I see a drawing immediately as the representation of a human being, nothing of that kind happens.

A picture of a human face is a no less familiar object than the human face itself. But there is no question of recognition here.

118 It is easy to have a false concept of the processes called "recognizing"; as if recognizing always consisted in comparing two impressions with one another. It is as if I carried a picture of an object with me and used it to perform an identification of an object as the one represented by the picture. Our memory seems to us to be the agent of such a comparison, by preserving a picture of what has been seen before, or by allowing us to look into the past (as if down a spy-glass).

In most cases of recognition no such process takes place.

Someone meets me in the street and my eyes are drawn to his face; perhaps I ask myself "who is that?"; suddenly the face begins to look different in a particular way, "it becomes familiar to me"; I smile, go up to him and greet him by name; then we talk of the past and while we do so perhaps a memory image of him comes before my mind, and I see him in a particular situation.

Perhaps someone will say: if I hadn't kept his image in my memory, I couldn't have recognized him. But here he is either using a metaphor, or expressing a hypothesis.

One might say: "What I saw was memory-laden."

We say: "we couldn't use words at all, if we didn't recognize them and the objects they denote." If (because of a faulty memory) we didn't recognize the colour green for what it is then we couldn't use the word "green". But have we any sort of check on this recognition, so that we know that it is really a recognition? If we speak of recognition, we mean that we recognize something as what, in accordance with other criteria, it is. "To recognize" means "to recognize what *is*".

119 Familiarity gives confirmation to what we see, but not by comparing it with anything else. It gives it a stamp, as it were.

On the other hand I would like to say: "what I see here in front of me is not *any old* shape seen in a particular manner: what I see is my shoes, which I know, and not anything else". But here it is just that two forms of expression fight against each other.

This shape that I see – I want to say – is not simply *a* shape; it is one of the shapes I know; it is a shape marked out in advance. It is one of those shapes of which I already had a pattern in me; and only because it corresponds to such a pattern is it this familiar shape. (I as it were carry a catalogue of such shapes around with me, and the objects portrayed in it *are* the familiar ones.)

But my already carrying the pattern round with me would be only a causal explanation of the present impression. It is like saying: this movement is made as easily as if it had been practised.

And it is not so much as if I were comparing the object with a picture set beside it, but as if the object *coincided* with the picture. So I see only one thing, not two.

120 We say: "This face has a quite *particular* expression", and look perhaps for words to characterise it.

Here it is easy to get into that dead-end in philosophy, where one believes that the difficulty of the task consists in this: our having to describe phenomena that are hard to get hold of, the present experience that slips quickly by, or something of the kind. Where we find ordinary language too crude, and it looks as if we were having to do, not with the phenomena of every-day, but with ones that "easily elude us, and in their coming to be and passing away, produce those others as an average effect".

And here one must remember that all the phenomena that now strike us as so remarkable are the very familiar phenomena that don't surprise us in the least when they happen. They don't strike us as remarkable until we put them in a strange light by philosophizing.

121 "What the picture tells me is itself" is what I want to say. That is, its telling me something consists in its own structure, in *its own* forms and colours.

It is as if, e.g. "it tells me something" or "it is a picture" meant: it shows a certain combination of cubes and cylinders.

"It tells me something" can mean: it narrates something to me, it is a story.

It tells me itself, just as a proposition, a story tells me itself.

The concept of a narrative picture is surely like that of a genre picture (or a battle scene). If I wanted to explain what a battle scene is, I wouldn't need to refer to any reality outside the picture, I would only have to talk about painted men, painted horses, painted cannon and so on.

"The picture tells me something": it uses *words*, so to speak: here are eyes, mouth, nose, hands etc. I am comparing the picture to a combination of linguistic forms.

The system of language, however, is not in the category of experience. The experiences characteristic of using the system are not the system. (Compare: the meaning of the word "or" and the or-feeling).

"Now, that series of signs tells me something; earlier, before I learnt the language, it said nothing to me". Let us suppose what we mean by that is that the sentence is now read with a particular experience. Certainly, before I learnt the language, that series of signs used not to make the same impression on me. Of course, if we disregard the causal element, the impression is quite independent of the system of language. – And there is something in me that is reluctant to say: the sentence's telling me something is constituted by its making this impression on me.
"It's only in a language that something is a proposition" is what I want to say.

122 'Language' is only languages, plus things I invent by analogy with existing languages. Languages *are* systems.

"A proposition belongs to a language." But that just means: it is units of languages that I call "propositions".

But we must pay attention to the *use* of the expression "English language", otherwise we shall ask questions like "What is the language? Is it all the sentences which have so far been spoken? Or the set of rules and words? etc. etc." What is the system? Where is it? What is chess? All the games that have been played? The list of rules?

"A *proposition* is a unit of language." "After all, what constitutes propositions is the combination of words which might be otherwise combined." But that means: what constitutes propositions *for me*. That is the way I regard language.

What *we* want to attend to is the system of language.

123 Certainly I read a story and don't give a hang about any system of language. I simply read, have impressions, see pictures in my mind's eye, etc. I make the story pass before me like pictures, like a cartoon story. (Of course I do not mean by this that every sentence summons up one or more visual images, and that that is, say, the purpose of a sentence.)

Let us imagine a picture story in schematic pictures, and thus more like the narrative in a language than a series of realistic pictures. Using such a picture-language we might in particular e.g. keep our hold on the course of battles. (Language-game.) And a sentence of our word-language approximates to a picture in this picture language much more closely than we think.

Let us remember too that we don't have to translate such pictures into realistic ones in order to 'understand' them, any more than we ever translate photographs or film pictures into coloured pictures, although black-and-white men or plants in reality would strike us as unspeakably strange and frightful.

Suppose we were to say at this point: "Something is a picture only in a picture-language"?

A sentence in a story gives us the same satisfaction as a picture.

124 We can on the other hand imagine a language in whose use the impression made on us by the signs played no part; in which there was no question of an understanding, in the sense of such an impression. The signs are e.g. written and transmitted to us and we are able to *take notice of them*. (That is to say, the only impression that comes in here is the pattern of the sign.) If the sign is an order,

we translate it into action by means of rules, tables. It does not get as far as an impression like that of a picture; nor are stories written in this language. But there is perhaps a kind of reading for entertainment which consists in certain series of signs being translated into bodily movements to make a kind of dance. (Compare the remark about translation and code.)

In this case one really might say "the series of signs is *dead* without the system".

We could of course also imagine that we had to use rules and translate a verbal sentence into a drawing in order to get an *impression* from it. (That only the picture had a soul.)

(I might say to my pupils: When you have been through these exercises you will think differently.)

But even in our normal speech we may often quite disregard the impression made by a sentence so that all that is important is how we operate with the sentence (Frege's conception of logic).

"There is no such thing as an isolated proposition." For what I call a "proposition" is a position in the game of language.

Isn't what misleads us the fact that I can look ever so closely at a position in a game without discovering that it is *a position in a game*? What misleads us here is something in the grammar of the expression "position in a game".

Thinking is an activity, like calculating. No one would call calculating, or playing chess, a state.

125 Let us imagine a kind of puzzle picture: there is not *one* particular object to find; at first glance it appears to us as a jumble

of meaningless lines, and only after some effort do we see it as, say, a picture of a landscape. – What makes the difference between the look of the picture before and after the solution? It is clear that we see it differently the two times. But what does it amount to to say that after the solution the picture means something to us, whereas it meant nothing before?

We can also put this question like this: What is the general mark of the solution's having been found?

I will assume that as soon as it is solved I make the solution obvious by strongly tracing certain lines in the puzzle picture and perhaps putting in some shadows. Why do you call the picture you have sketched in a solution?

a) Because it is the clear representation of a group of spatial objects.

b) Because it is the representation of a regular solid.

c) Because it is a symmetrical figure.

d) Because it is a shape that makes an ornamental impression on me.

e) Because it is the representation of a body I am familiar with.

f) Because there is a list of solutions and this shape (this body) is on the list.

g) Because it represents a kind of object that I am very familiar with; for it gives me an instantaneous impression of familiarity, I instantly have all sorts of associations in connexion with it; I know what it is called; I know I have often seen it; I know what it is used for etc.

h) Because it represents a face which strikes me as familiar.

i) Because it represents a face which I recognize: α) it is the face of my friend so and so; β) it is a face which I have often seen pictures of.

k) Because it represents an object which I remember having seen at some time.

l) Because it is an ornament that I know well (though I don't remember where I have seen it).

m) Because it is an ornament that I know well; I know its name, I know where I have seen it.

n) Because it represents part of the furniture of my room.

o) Because I instinctively traced out those lines and now feel easy.

p) Because I remember that this object has been described.

q) Because I seem to be familiar with the object, a word occurs to me at once as its name (although the word does not belong to any existent language); I tell myself "of course, that is an α such as I have often seen in β; one γs δ's with it until they ϵ." Something of the kind occurs e.g. in dreams.

And so on.

(Anyone who does not understand why we talk about these things must feel what we say to be mere trifling.)

126 The impression is one thing, and the impression's being determinate is another thing.

What I call the impression of familiarity is as multifarious as being determinate is.

When we look into a human face that we know very well, we need not have any impression, our wits may be completely dull, so to speak; and between that case and a strong impression there are any number of stages.

Suppose the sight of a face has a strong effect on us, inspiring us say with fear. Am I to say: first of all there must occur an impression of familiarity, the form of the human face as such must make an impression of familiarity on me, and only then is the impression of fear added to that impression? – Isn't it like this, that what I call the impression of specific familiarity is a characteristic of every strong impression that a face makes on me? – The characteristic, say of determinacy. I did indeed say that the impression of familiarity consists in things like our feeling at home in what we see, in our not changing our way of looking and the like.

127 Can I think away the impression of individual familiarity where it exists; and think it into a situation where it does not? And what does that mean? I see e.g. the face of a friend and ask myself: what does this face look like if I see it as an unfamiliar face (as if I were seeing it now for the first time)? What remains, as it were, of the look of this face, if I think away, subtract, the impression of familiarity from it? Here I am inclined to say: "It is *very difficult* to separate the familiarity from the impression of the face." But I also feel that this is a misleading way of putting things. For I have no notion how I should so much as try to separate these two things. The expression "to separate them" does not have any clear sense for me.

I know what *this means*: "Imagine this table black instead of brown"; it means something like: "paint a picture of this table, but black instead of brown"; or similarly: "draw this man but with longer legs than he has".

Suppose someone were to say "Imagine this butterfly exactly as it is, but ugly instead of beautiful"?!

"It is very difficult to think away . . .": here it looks as if it was a matter of a psychological difficulty, a difficulty of introspection or the like. (That is true of a large range of philosophical problems: think of the problem of the exact reproduction or description of what is seen in the visual field; of the description of the perpetual flux of phenomena; also of "how many raindrops do you see, if you look at the rain?")

Compare: "It is difficult *to will* that table to move from a distance."

In this case *we* have not *determined* what thinking the familiarity away is to mean.

It might mean, say, to recall the impression which I had when I saw the face for the first time. And here again one must know what it means to "*try*" to remember the impression. For that has several meanings. Let us ask ourselves what activities we call "trying to remember something". What do we do if we want to remember what we had for lunch yesterday? Is that method available for the early memories of an adult? Can one *try* to remember one's own birth?

I tell myself: I want to try to look at a printed English word and see it as if I hadn't learnt to read, as if the black shapes on the paper were strange drawings whose purpose I couldn't imagine or guess. And then what happens is that I can't look at the printed word without the sound of the word or of the letter I'm actually looking at coming before my mind.

For someone who has no knowledge of such things a diagram representing the inside of a radio receiver will be a jumble of meaningless lines. But if he is acquainted with the apparatus and its function, that drawing will be a significant picture for him.

Given some solid figure (say in a picture) that means nothing to me at present – can I at will imagine it as meaningful? That's as if I were asked: Can I imagine a body of any old shape as an appliance? But for what sort of use?

Well, at any rate one class of corporeal shapes can readily be imagined as dwellings for beasts or men. Another class as weapons. Another as models of landscapes. Etc. etc. So here I know how I can ascribe meaning to a meaningless shape.

128 If I say that this face has an expression of gentleness, or kindness, or cowardice, I don't seem just to mean that we associate such and such feelings with the look of the face, I'm tempted to say that the face is itself one aspect of the cowardice, kindness, etc. (Compare e.g. Weininger). It is possible to say: I see cowardice in this face (and might see it in another too) but at all events it doesn't seem to be merely associated, outwardly connected, with the face;

the fear has the multiplicity of the facial features. And if, for example, the features change slightly, we can speak of a corresponding change in the fear. If we were asked "Can you think of this face as an expression of courage too?" – we should, as it were, not know how to lodge courage in these features. Then perhaps I say "I don't know what it would mean if this is a courageous face." [This sentence cannot be corrected by saying "for this to be a courageous face" instead of "if this is a courageous face"].[1] But what would an answer to such a question be like? Perhaps one says: "Yes, now I understand: the face as it were shews indifference to the outer world." So we have somehow read courage into the face. Now once more, one might say, courage *fits* this face. But *what* fits *what* here?

There is a related case (though perhaps it will not seem so) when for example we (Germans) are surprised that the French do not simply say "the man is good" but put an attributive adjective where there should be a predicative one; and when we solve the problem for ourselves by saying: they mean: "the man is *a good one*".

Couldn't different interpretations of a facial expression consist in my imagining each time a different kind of sequel? Certainly that's often how it is. I see a picture which represents a smiling face. What do I do if I take the smile now as a kind one, now as malicious? Don't I imagine it with a spatial and temporal context which I call kind or malicious? Thus I might supply the picture with the fancy that the smiler was smiling down at a child at play, or again on the suffering of an enemy.

This is in no way altered by the fact that I can also take the at first sight gracious situation and interpret it differently by putting it into a wider context. – If no special circumstances reverse my interpretation I shall conceive a particular smile as kind, call it a "kind" one, react correspondingly.

1. Cf. *Philosophical Investigations*, I, §537 (Trs.)

That is connected with the contrast between *saying* and *meaning*.

"Any expression can lie": but you must think what you mean by "lie". How do you imagine a lie? Aren't you contrasting one expression with another? At any rate, you are contrasting with the expression some other process which might very well be an expression.

129 What does it mean: "to *read* kindness *into* the smile"? Perhaps it means: I make a face which is coordinated with the smiling face in a particular way. I coordinate my face to the other one in some such way as to exaggerate one or other of its features.

A friendly mouth, friendly eyes. How would one think of a friendly hand? Probably open and not as a fist. – And could one think of the colour of a man's hair as an expression of friendliness or the opposite? Put like that the question seems to ask whether we can *manage* to. The question ought to run: Do we want to call anything a friendly or unfriendly hair-colour? If we wanted to give such words a sense, we should perhaps imagine a man whose hair darkened when he got angry. The reading of an angry expression into dark hair, however, would work *via* a previously existent conception.

It may be said: the friendly eyes, the friendly mouth, the wagging of a dog's tail, are among the primary and mutually independent symbols of friendliness; I mean: They are parts of the phenomena that are called friendliness. If one wants to imagine further appearances as expressions of friendliness, one reads these symbols into them. We say: "He has a black look", perhaps because the eyes are more strongly shadowed by the eyebrows; and now we transfer the idea of darkness to the colour of the hair. He has glowering hair. If I were asked whether I could imagine a chair with a friendly expression, it would be above all a friendly *facial expression* I would want to imagine it with; I would want to read a friendly *face* into it.

I say "I can think of this face (which *at first* gives an impression of timidity) as courageous too." We *do not mean* by this that I can imagine someone with this face perhaps saving someone's life (that, of course, is imaginable in connexion with any face). I am speaking rather of an aspect of the face itself. Nor do I mean that I can imagine that this man's face might change so that, in the ordinary sense, it looked courageous; though I may very well mean that there is quite a definite way in which it can change into a courageous face. The reinterpretation of a facial expression can be compared with the reinterpretation of a chord in music, when we hear it as a modulation first into this, then into that key. (Compare also the distinction between mixed colours and intermediary colours).

Suppose we ask ourselves "what proper name would suit the character of this man" – and portray it in sound? The method of projection we use for the portrayal is something which as it were stands firm. (A writer might ask himself what name he wants to give to a person.) But sometimes we project the character into the name that has been given. Thus it appears to us that the great masters have names which uniquely fit the character of their works.

Experience of the real size. Suppose we saw a picture showing a chair-shape; we are told it represents a construction the size of a house. Now we see it differently.

What happens when we learn to feel the ending of a church mode as an ending?

Think of the multifariousness of what we call "language". Word-language, picture-language, gesture-language, sound-language.

130 " 'This object is familiar to me' is like saying 'this object is portrayed in my catalogue'." In that case it would consist in the fact that it was a picture filed with others in a particular folder, in *this* drawer. But if that really is what I imagine – if I think I simply

compare the seen object with pictures in my catalogue and find it to agree with one of them – it is something quite unlike the phenomenon of familiarity. That is, we are making the assumption that the picture in our catalogue is itself familiar. If it were something strange, then the fact that it was in this folder, in this drawer, would mean nothing to us.

When I speak of a pattern in my mental catalogue, or of a sheath into which an object fits if it is familiar, what I would like to say is that the sheath in my mind is, as it were, the "form of imagining", so that it isn't possible for me to say of a pattern that it is in my mind unless it really is there. – The pattern as it were retires into my mind, so that it is no longer presented to it as an object. But that only means: it didn't make sense to talk of a pattern at all. (The spatial spectacles we can't take off.)

If we represent familiarity as an object's fitting into a sheath, that's not quite the same as our *comparing* what is seen with a copy. What we really have in mind is the feeling when the object slips smoothly into the contour of the sheath. But that is a feeling we might have even if there were no such perfectly fitting sheath there at all.

We might also imagine that every object had an invisible sheath; that alters nothing in our experience, it is an empty form of representation.

It shouldn't really be "Yes, I recognize it, it's a face" but "I recognize it, I see a face". (Here the word face might mean for me the mere ornament ☻ and have no reference to the human face; it might be on a level with any other familiar figure, e.g. a swastika.) For the question is: "*What* do I recognize *as what*?" For "to recognize a thing as itself" is meaningless.

131 The comparison between memory and a notebook. On the one hand this comparison serves as a picture of the conscious phenomena, and on the other hand it provides a psychological model. (And the word "conscious" is a reference to a chapter of the grammar and is not one side of the psychological contrast between "conscious" and "unconscious".)

Many very different things happen when we remember.

"Have you been in your room?" "Yes". "Are you sure?" "I would know if I hadn't been here yesterday!" For this I don't need to see myself, even for a moment, in memory in my room. But let's assume that when I said that I saw myself standing at the window in my room; how does the picture show me that it was yesterday? Of course, the picture could show that as well, if for instance I saw in it a wall-calendar with yesterday's date. But if that wasn't the case, how did I read off from the memory image, or from the memory, that I stood thus at the window *yesterday*? How do I translate the experience of remembering into words? – But did I translate an experience into words? Didn't I just utter the words in a particular tone of voice with other experiences of certainty? But wasn't that the experience of remembering? (The experience of translating is the same kind of thing as the experience of the tone of voice.) But what made you so certain when you spoke those words? Nothing *made* me certain; I *was* certain.

Of course, I have other ways of checking – as one might say – what I then uttered. That is: I can now try to remember particular things that happened yesterday and to call up pictures before my mind's eye etc. But certainly that didn't *have* to have happened before I answered.

When we narrate a set of events from memory we do sometimes see memory pictures in our mind; but commonly they are only scattered through the memory like illustrations in a story book.

Someone says to me "Imagine a patch of the colour called 'red' on this white wall". I do so – shall I now say that I *remembered* which colour is called 'red'? When I talk about this table, do I remember that this object is called a 'table'?

Mightn't someone object: "So if a man has not learned a language is he unable to have certain memories?" Of course – he cannot have verbal memories, verbal wishes and so on. And memories etc. in language are not mere threadbare representations of the real experiences; for is what is linguistic not an experience? (Words are deeds.)

Some men recall a musical theme by having an image of the score rise before them, and reading it off.

It could be imagined that what we call "memory" in some man consisted in his seeing himself looking things up in a notebook in spirit, and that what he read in that book was what he remembered. (How do I *react* to a memory?)

Incidentally, when I treat the objects around me as familiar, do I think of that comparison? Of course not. I only do so when I look at the act of recognition (individual recognition) after the event; and not so much when I look at it to see what actually happened, as when I look at it through a preconceived schema. (The flux of time.)[1]

132 If one takes it as obvious that a man takes pleasure in his own fantasies, let it be remembered that fantasy does not correspond to a painted picture, to a sculpture or a film, but to a complicated formation out of heterogeneous components – words, pictures, etc. Then one will not contrast operating with written and spoken

---

1. [Earlier draft of the parenthesis]. (Something very similar to this is the problem of the nature and flow of time).

signs with operating with "imagination-pictures" of events.

(The ugliness of a human being can repel in a picture, in a painting, as in reality, but so it can too in a description, in words.)

Attitude to a picture (to a thought). The way we experience a picture makes it real for us, that is, connects it with reality; it establishes a continuity with reality.

(Fear connects a picture with the terrors of reality.)

X

133 Can an ostensive definition come into collision with the other rules for the use of a word? – It might appear so; but rules can't collide, unless they contradict each other. That aside, it is they that determine a meaning; there isn't a meaning that they are answerable to and could contradict.

Grammar is not accountable to any reality. It is grammatical rules that determine meaning (constitute it) and so they themselves are not answerable to any meaning and to that extent are arbitrary.

There cannot be a question whether these or other rules are the correct ones for the use of "not" (that is, whether they accord with its meaning). For without these rules the word has as yet no meaning; and if we change the rules, it now has another meaning (or none), and in that case we may just as well change the word too.

"The only correlate in language to an intrinsic necessity is an arbitrary rule. It is the only thing which one can milk out of this intrinsic necessity into a proposition."[1]

Why don't I call cookery rules arbitrary, and why am I tempted to call the rules of grammar arbitrary? Because I think of the concept "cookery" as defined by the end of cookery, and I don't think of the concept "language" as defined by the end of language. You cook badly if you are guided in your cooking by rules other than the right ones; but if you follow other rules than those of chess you are playing another game; and if you follow grammatical

1. In pencil in the MS: [Perhaps apropos of the paradox that mathematics consists of rules.]

184

rules other than such and such ones, that does not mean you say something wrong, no, you are speaking of something else.

If I want to carve a block of wood into a particular shape any cut that gives it the right shape is a good one. But I don't call an argument a good argument just because it has the consequences I want (Pragmatism). I may call a calculation wrong even if the actions based on its result have led to the desired end. (Compare the joke "I've hit the jackpot and he wants to give me lessons!"[1]) That shows that the justifications in the two cases are different, and also that "justification" means something different in each case. In the one case one can say "Just wait, you will soon see that it will come out right (i.e. as desired)". In the other case that is no justification.

The connection between the rules of cookery and the grammar of the word "cook" is not the same as that between the rules of chess and the expression "play chess" or that between the rules of multiplication and the grammar of the word "multiply".

The rules of grammar are arbitrary in the same sense as the choice of a unit of measurement. But that means no more than that the choice is independent of the length of the objects to be measured and that the choice of one unit is not 'true' and of another 'false' in the way that a statement of length is true or false. Of course that is only a remark on the grammar of the word "unit of length".

134 One is tempted to justify rules of grammar by sentences like "But there are really four primary colours". And if we say that the

---

1. A tells B that he has hit the jackpot in the lottery; he saw a box lying in the street with the numbers 5 and 7 on it. He worked out that $5 \times 7 = 64$ – and took the number 64.
B: But 5×7 isn't 64!
A: I've hit the jackpot and he wants to give me lessons!

rules of grammar are arbitrary, that is directed against the possibility of this justification. Yet can't it after all be said that the grammar of colour words characterizes the world as it actually is? One would like to say: May I not really look in vain for a fifth primary colour? (And if looking is possible, then finding is conceivable.) Doesn't grammar put the primary colours together because there is a kind of similarity between them? Or colours, anway, in contrast to shapes or notes? Or, when I set this up as the right way of dividing up the world, have I a preconceived idea in my head as a paradigm? Of which in that case I can say: "Yes, that is the way we look at things" or "We just do want to form this sort of picture." For if I say "there is a particular similarity among the primary colours" – whence do I derive the idea of this similarity? Just as the idea 'primary colour' is nothing else but 'blue or red or green or yellow' is not the idea of that similarity too given simply by the four colours? Indeed, aren't these concepts the same? (For here it can be said: "what would it be like if these colours did not have this similarity?") (Think of a group containing the four primary colours plus black and white, or the visible colours plus ultraviolet and infrared.)

I do not call rules of representation conventions if they can be justified by the fact that a representation made in accordance with them will agree with reality. For instance the rule "paint the sky brighter than anything that receives its light from it" is not a convention.

The rules of grammar cannot be justified by shewing that their application makes a representation agree with reality. For this justification would itself have to describe what is represented. And if something can be said in the justification and is permitted by its grammar – why shouldn't it also be permitted by the grammar that I am trying to justify? Why shouldn't both forms of expression have the same freedom? And how could what the one says restrict what the other can say?

But can't the justification simply *point* to reality?

How far is such pointing a justification? Does it have the multiplicity of a justification? Of course it may be the cause of our saying one sentence rather than another. But does it give a reason for it? Is *that* what we call a justification?

No one will deny that studying the nature of the rules of games must be useful for the study of grammatical rules, since it is beyond doubt there is some sort of similarity between them. – The right thing is to let the certain instinct that there is a kinship lead one to look at the rules of games without any preconceived judgement or prejudice about the analogy between games and grammar. And here again one should simply report what one sees and not be afraid that one is undermining a significant and correct intuition, or, on the other hand, wasting one's time with something super-fluous.

135 One can of course consider language as part of a psychological mechanism. The simplest case is if one uses a restricted concept of language in which language consists only of commands.

One can then consider how a foreman directs the work of a group of people by shouting.

One can imagine a man inventing language, imagine him dis-covering how to train other human beings to work in his place, training them through reward and punishment to perform certain tasks when he shouts. This discovery would be like the invention of a machine.

Can one say that grammar describes language? If we consider language as part of the psycho-physical mechanism which we use when we utter words – like pressing keys on a keyboard – to make a human machine work for us, then we can say that grammar describes that part of the machine. In that case a correct language would be one which would stimulate the desired activities.

Cleárly I can establish by experience that a human being (or animal) reacts to one sign as I want him to, and to another not. That e.g. a human being goes to the right at the sign " → "and goes to the left at the sign " ← "; but that he does not react to the sign "◇—|"as to "← ".

I do not even need to fabricate a case, I have only to consider what is in fact the case; namely, that I can direct a man who has learned only German, only by using the German language. (For here I am looking at learning German as adjusting (conditioning) a mechanism to respond to a certain kind of influence; and it may be all one to us whether someone else has learned the language, or was perhaps from birth constituted to react to sentences in German like a normal person who has learned it.)

Suppose I now made the discovery that someone would bring me sugar at a sign plus the cry "Su", and would bring me milk at a sign and the cry "Mi", and would not do so in response to other words. Should I say that this shows that "Su" is the correct (the only correct) sign for sugar, "Mi" the correct sign for milk?

Well, if I say that, I am not using the expression "sign for sugar" in the way it is ordinarily used or in the way I intended to use it.

I do not use "that is the sign for sugar" in the same way as the sentence "if I press this button, I get a piece of sugar".

136 All the same, let us compare grammar with a system of buttons, a keyboard which I can use to direct a man or a machine by pressing

different combinations of keys. What corresponds in this case to the grammar of language?

It is easy to construct such a keyboard, for giving different "commands" to the machine. Let's look at a very simple one: it consists of two keys, the one marked "go" and the other "come". Now one might think it must obviously be a rule of the grammar that the two keys shouldn't be depressed simultaneously (that would give rise to a contradiction). But what does happen if we press them both at the same time? Am I assuming that this has an effect? Or that it has no effect? In each case I can designate the effect, or the absence of an effect, as the point and sense of the simultaneous depression of both keys.

Or: When I say that the orders "Bring me sugar" and "Bring me milk" make sense, but not the combination "Milk me sugar", that does not mean that the utterance of this combination of words has no effect. And if its effect is that the other person stares at me and gapes, I don't on that account call it the order to stare and gape, even if *that* was precisely the effect that I wanted to produce.

"This combination of words makes no sense" does not mean it has no effect.

Not even "it does not have the desired effect".

137 To say "This combination of words makes no sense" excludes it from the sphere of language and thereby bounds the domain of language. But when one draws a boundary it may be for various kinds of reasons. If I surround an area with a fence or a line or otherwise, the purpose may be to prevent someone from getting in or out; but it may also be part of a game, and the players be supposed, say, to jump over the boundary; or it may show where A's property ends and B's begins; and so on. So if I draw a boundary line that is not yet to say what I am drawing it for.

Language is not defined for us as an arrangement fulfilling a definite purpose. Rather "language" is for me a name for a collection and I understand it as including German, English, and so on, and further various systems of signs which have more or less affinity with these languages.

Language is of interest to me as a phenomenon and not as a means to a particular end.

138 Grammar consists of conventions. An example of such conventions be one saying "the word 'red' means this colour". Such a convention may be included say in a chart. – Well, now, how could a convention find a place in a mechanism (like the works of a pianola?) Well, it is quite possible that there is a part of the mechanism which resembles a chart, and is inserted between the language-like part of the mechanism and the rest of it.

Of course an ostensive definition of a word sets up a connection between a word and 'a thing', and the purpose of this connection may be that the mechanism of which our language is a part should function in a certain way. So the definition can make it work properly, like the connection between the keys and the hammers in a piano; but the connection doesn't consist in the hearing of the words now having *this* effect, since the effect may actually be caused by the making of the convention. And it is the connection and not the effect which determines the meaning.

When someone is taught language, does he learn at the same time what is sense and nonsense? When he uses language to what extent does he employ grammar, and in particular the distinction between sense and nonsense?

When someone learns musical notation, he is supplied with a kind of grammar. This is to say: this note corresponds to this key on the piano, the sign ♯ sharpens a note, the sign ♮ cancels the ♯ etc. etc. If the pupil asked whether there was a distinction between

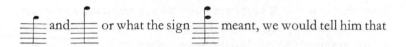 and ⎯⎯ or what the sign ⎯⎯ meant, we would tell him that

the distance between the top of the note and the stave didn't mean anything, and so on. One can view this instruction as part of the preparation that makes the pupil into a playing-machine.

So he can speak of a grammar in the case where a language is taught to a person by a mere drill? It is clear that if I want to use the word "grammar" here I can do so only in a "degenerate" sense, because it is only in a degenerate sense that I can speak of "explanation", or of "convention".

And a trained child or animal is not acquainted with any problems of philosophy.

139 When I said that for us a language was not something that achieved a particular end, but a concept defined by certain systems we call "languages" and such systems as are constructed by analogy with them – I could also have expressed the same thing in the following way: causal connections in the mechanism of language are things that I don't scruple to *invent*.

Imagine that someone were to explain "Language is whatever one can use to communicate". What constitutes communication? To complete the explantation we should have to describe what happens when one communicates; and in the process certain causal connections and empirical regularities would come out. But these are just the things that wouldn't interest me; they are the kinds of connection I wouldn't hesitate to make up. I wouldn't call just anything that opened the door a "key-bit", but only something with a particular form and structure.

"Language" is a word like "keyboard". There are machines which have keyboards. For some reason or other I might be interested in forms of keyboard (both ones in actual use and others merely devised by myself). And to invent a keyboard might mean to invent something that had the desired effect; or else to devise new forms which were similar to the old ones in various ways.

"It is always for living beings that signs exist, so that must be something essential to a sign." Yes, but how is a "living" being defined? It appears that here I am prepared to use its capacity to use a sign-language as a defining mark of a living being.

And the concept of a living being really has an indeterminacy very similar to that of the concept "language".

140   To invent a language could mean to invent an instrument for a particular purpose on the basis of the laws of nature (or consistently with them); but it also has the other sense, analogous to that in which we speak of the invention of a game.

Here I am stating something about the grammar of the word "language" by connecting it with the grammar of the word "invent".

Are the rules of chess arbitrary? Imagine that it turned out that only chess entertained and satisfied people. Then the rules aren't arbitrary if the purpose of the game is to be achieved.

"The rules of a game are arbitrary" means: the concept 'game' is not defined by the effect the game is supposed to have on us.

There is an analogous sense in which it is arbitrary which unit of measurement we use to express a length, and another sense in which the choice of units is limited or determined.

For us language is a calculus; it is characterized by *linguistic activities*.

Where does language get its significance? Can we say "Without language we couldn't communicate with one another"? No. It's not like "without the telephone we couldn't speak from Europe to America". We can indeed say "without a mouth human beings couldn't communicate with each other". But the concept of language *is contained in* the concept of communication.

141 Is philosophy a creation of word-language? Is word-language a necessary condition for the existence of philosophy? It would be more proper to ask: is there anything like philosophy outside the region of our word-languages? For philosophy isn't anything except philosophical problems, the particular individual worries that we call "philosophical problems". Their common element extends as far as the common element in different regions of our language.

Let us consider a particular philosophical problem, such as "How is it possible to measure a period of time, since the past and the future aren't present and the present is only a point?" The characteristic feature of this is that a confusion is expressed in the form of a question that doesn't acknowledge the confusion, and that what *releases* the questioner from his problem is a particular alteration of his method of expression.

I could imagine an organ whose stops were to be operated by keys distributed among the keys of the manual which looked exactly like them. There might then arise a philosophical problem: "How are silent notes possible?" And the problem would be solved by someone having the idea of replacing the stop-keys by stops which had no similarity with the note-keys.

A problem or worry like a philosophical one might arise because someone *played* on all the keys of the manual, and the result didn't sound like music, and yet he was tempted to think that it must be music etc.

(Something that at first sight looks like a sentence and is not one.)

The following design for the construction of a steam roller was shown to me and seems to be of philosophical interest. The inventor's mistake is akin to a philosophical mistake. The invention consists of a motor inside a hollow roller. The crank-shaft runs through the middle of the roller and is connected at both ends by spokes with the wall of the roller. The cylinder of the petrol-engine is fixed onto the inside of the roller. At first glance this construction looks like a machine. But it is a rigid system and the piston cannot move to and fro in the cylinder. Unwittingly we have deprived it of all possibility of movement.

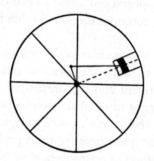

142 "Could a language consist simply of independent signals?" Instead of this we might ask: Are we willing to call a series of independent signals "a language"? To the question "can such a language achieve the same as one which consists of sentences, or combinations of signs?" one would have to answer: it is *experience*

that will show us whether e.g. these signals have the same effect on human beings as sentences. But the effect is of no interest to us; we are looking at the phenomenon, the calculus of language.

Imagine something like a diary kept with signals. One side is divided into sections for the hours of the day, like a timetable. The sign "A" means: I am sleeping; "B" means "I am working"; "C" I am eating, etc. etc. But now the question is: are explanations like this given, so that the signals are connected to another language? Is the signal-language supplemented with ostensive definitions of the signals? Or is the language really only to consist of the signs A, B, C etc.?

Suppose someone asked: "how do you know, that you are now doing the same as you were an hour ago?", and I answered: "I wrote it down, yes, here there's a 'C'" – Can one ask whether the sign "A" always means the same? In what circumstances can this question be answered one way or the other? (One can imagine a language in which the words, the names of the colours, say, changed their meanings with the day of the week; this colour is called "red" on Monday, "blue" on Tuesday. "A = A" might say that in the language to which this rule applies there is no change in the meaning of the sign "A".)

Imagine again a language consisting of commands. It is to be used to direct the movements of a human being; a command specifies the distance, and adds one of the words "forwards", "backwards", "right" and "left" and one of the words "fast" and "slowly". Now of course all the commands which will actually be used to direct the movements of a human being; a command such signals in the first place as abbreviations of the sentences of the first language, perhaps translating them back into it before obeying them, and then later on act immediately in response to the signals. – In that case we might speak of two languages and say the first was more pictorial than the second. That is, we wouldn't say that a series of such signals by itself would enable me to *derive* a picture of the movement of a man obeying them unless in addition to the signal there is something that might be called a general rule for translating into drawing. We wouldn't say: from the sign a b b c d you can *derive* the figure

but we would say that you can derive it from a b b c d plus the table

a	↑
b	→
c	↓
d	←

We can say: the grammar *explains* the meaning of the signs and thus makes the language pictorial.

I can justify the choice of a word by a grammar. But that doesn't mean that I do, or have to, use definitions to justify the words I use in a description or something similar.

A comparable case is when ordinary grammar completes an elliptical sentence, and so takes a particular construction as an abbreviated *sentence*.

Appendix

I
Complex and Fact

The use of the words 'fact' and 'act' –'That was a noble act.'
– 'But, that never happened.' –

It is natural to want to use the word 'act' so that it only corresponds to a *true* proposition. So that we then don't talk of an act
which was never performed. But the proposition 'That was a
noble act' must still have a sense even if I am mistaken in thinking
that what I call an act occurred. And that of itself contains all that
matters, and I can only make the stipulation that I will only use the
words 'fact', 'act' (perhaps also 'event') in a proposition which,
when complete, asserts that this fact obtains.

It would be better to drop the restriction on the use of these
words, since it only leads to confusion, and say quite happily:
'This act was never performed', 'This fact does not obtain',
'This event did not occur'.

Complex is not like fact. For I can, e.g., say of a complex that it
moves from one place to another, but not of a fact.
But that this complex is now situated here is a fact.

'This complex of buildings is coming down' is tantamount to:
'The buildings thus grouped together are coming down'.

I call a flower, a house, a constellation, complexes: moreover,
complexes of petals, bricks, stars etc.
That this constellation is located here, can of course be described
by a proposition in which only its stars are mentioned and neither
the word 'constellation' nor its name occurs.

But that is all there is to say about the relation between complex and fact. And a complex is a spatial object, composed of spatial objects. (The concept 'spatial' admitting of a certain extension.)

A complex is composed of its parts, the things of a kind which go to make it up. (This is of course a grammatical proposition concerning the words 'complex', 'part' and 'compose'.)

To say that a red circle is *composed* of redness and circularity, or is a complex with these component parts, is a misuse of these words and is misleading. (Frege was aware of this and told me.)

It is just as misleading to say the fact that this circle is red (that I am tired) is a complex whose component parts are a circle and redness (myself and tiredness).

Neither is a house a complex of bricks and their spatial relations. i.e. that too goes against the correct use of the word.

Now, you can of course point at a constellation and say: this constellation is composed entirely of objects with which I am already acquainted; but you can't 'point at a fact' and say this.

'To describe a fact', or 'the description of a fact', is also a misleading expression for the assertion stating that the fact obtains, since it sounds like: 'describing the animal that I saw'.

Of course we also say: 'to point out a fact', but that always means; 'to point out the fact that . . .'. Whereas 'to point at (or point out) a flower' doesn't mean to point out that this blossom is on this stalk; for we needn't be talking about this blossom and this stalk at all.

It's just as impossible for it to mean: to point out the fact that this flower is situated there.
To point out a fact means to assert something, to state something. 'To point out a flower' doesn't mean this.

A chain, too, is composed of its links, not of these and their spatial relations.

The fact that these links are so concatenated, isn't '*composed*' of anything at all.

The root of this muddle is the confusing use of the word 'object'.

The part is smaller than the whole: applied to fact and component part (constituent), that would yield an absurdity.

The schema: thing-property. We say that actions have properties, like swiftness, or goodness.

2

Concept and Object, Property and Substrate

When Frege and Russell talk of concept and object they really mean property and thing; and here I'm thinking in particular of a spatial body and its colour. Or one can say: concept and object are the same as predicate and subject. The subject-predicate form is one of the forms of expression that occur in human languages. It is the form "x is y" ("x ∈ y"): "My brother is tall", "The storm is nearby", "This circle is red", "Augustus is strong", "2 is a number", "This thing is a piece of coal".

The concept of a material point in physics is an abstraction from the material objects of experience; in the same way the subject-predicate form of logic is an abstraction from the subject-predicate form of our languages. The pure subject-predicate form is supposed to be a ∈ f(x), where "a" is the name of an object. Now let's look for an application of this schema. The first things that come to mind as "names of objects" are the names of persons and of other spatial objects (the Koh-i-Noor). Such names are given by ostensive definitions ("that ↗ is called 'N' "). Such a definition might be conceived as a rule substituting the word "N" for a gesture pointing to the object, with the proviso that the gesture can always be used in place of the name. Thus, I may have explained "this man is called 'N' ", and I go on to say " 'N' is a mathematician", "N is lazy", and in each of these sentences I might have said "this man" (with the ostensive gesture) instead of "N". (In that case, incidentally it would have been better to phrase the ostensive definition "this man is called 'N' "[1] or "I want to call this man 'N' ", because the version above is also the proposition that this man bears this name).

However, this isn't the normal way of using a name; it is an essential feature of the normal use that I can't fall back on to a sign of the gesture language in place of the name. That's to say, in the way in which we use the name "N", if N goes out of the room and later a man comes into the room it makes sense to ask whether

1. There appears to be something wrong with the German text here. Possibly Wittgenstein meant to write "let this man be called 'N' " and inadvertently wrote a version which is the same as the one he is correcting. (Trs.)

this man is N, whether he is the same man as the one who left the room earlier. And the sentence "N has come back into the room" only makes sense if I can decide the question. And its sense will vary with the criterion for this being the object that I earlier called 'N'. Different kinds of criteria will make different rules hold for the sign 'N', will make it a 'name' in a different sense of the word. Thus the word 'name' and the corresponding word 'object' are each headings to countless different lists of rules.

If we give names to spatial objects, our use of such names depends on a criterion of identity which presupposes the impenetrability of bodies and the continuity of their movement. So if I could treat two bodies A and B as I can treat their shadows on the wall, making two into one and one into two again, it would be senseless to ask which of the two after the division is A and which is B, unless I go on to introduce a totally new criterion of identity e.g. the direction of their movements. (There is a rule for the name of a river arising from the confluence of two rivers, thus:

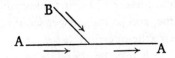

The resulting river takes the name of that source in whose approximate direction it flows onward.)

Think of the possible criteria of identity for things like colour patches in my visual field (or figures on a cinema screen) and of the different kinds of use of names given to such patches or figures.

If we turn to the form of expression "($\exists$x).fx" it's clear that this is a sublimation of the form of expression in our language: "There are human beings on this island" "There are stars that we do not see". To every proposition of the form "($\exists$x).fx" there is supposed to correspond a proposition "fa", and "a" is supposed to be a name. So one must be able to say "($\exists$x).fx, namely a and b",

("There are some values of x, which satisfy fx, namely a and b"), or "(∃x).fx, e.g. a", etc. And this is indeed possible in a case like "There are human beings on this island, namely Messrs A, B, C, D." But then is it essential to the sense of the sentence "There are men on this island" that we should be able to name them, and fix a particular criterion for their identification? That is only so in the case where the proposition "(∃x).fx" is defined as a disjunction of propositions of the form "f(x)", if e.g. it is laid down that "There are men on this island" means "Either Mr. A or Mr. B or Mr. C or Mr. D. or Mr. E is on this island" – if, that is, one determines the concept "man" extensionally (which of course is quite contrary to the normal use of this word.) (On the other hand the concept "primary colour" really is determined extensionally.)

So it doesn't always make sense when presented with a proposition "(∃x).fx" to ask "*Which* xs satisfy f?" "Which red circle a centimetre across is in the middle of this square"? – One mustn't confuse the question "which object satisfies f?" with the question "*what sort of* object . . .etc.?" The first question would have to be answered by a name, and so the answer would have to be able to take the form "f(a)"; the question "*what sort of* . . .?" is answered by "(∃x).fx.φx". So it may be senseless to ask "which red spot do you see?" and yet make sense to ask "what kind of a red spot do you see (a round one, a square one, etc.)?"

I would like to say: the old logic contains more convention and physics than has been realised. If a noun is the name of a *body*, a verb is to denote a movement, and an adjective to denote a property of a body, it is easy to see how much that logic presupposes; and it is reasonable to conjecture that those original presuppositions go still deeper into the application of the words, and the logic of propositions.

(Suppose we were set the task of projecting figures of various shapes on a given plane I into a plane II. We could then fix a method of projection (say orthogonal projection) and carry out the mapping in accordance with it. We could also easily make inferences from the representations on plane II about the figures on plane I. But we could also adopt another procedure: we might decide that the representations in the second plane should all be circles, no matter what the copied figures in the first plane might be. (Perhaps this is the most convenient form of representation for us.) That is, different figures on I are mapped onto II by different methods of projection. In order in this case to construe the circles in II as representations of the figures in I, I shall have to give the method of projection for each circle; the mere fact that a figure in I is represented as a circle in II[1] by itself tells us nothing about the shape of the figure copied. That an image in II is a circle is just the established norm of our mapping. – Well, the same thing happens when we depict reality in our language in accordance with the subject-predicate form. The subject-predicate form serves as a projection of countless different logical forms.

Frege's "Concept and Object" is the same as subject and predicate.

If a table is painted brown, then it's easy to think of the wood as bearer of the property brown and you can imagine what remains the same when the colour changes. Even in the case of *one* particular circle which appears now red, now blue. It is thus easy to imagine *what* is red, but difficult to imagine what is circular. What *remains* in this case if form and colour alter? For position is part of the form and it is arbitrary for me to lay down that the centre should stay fixed and the only changes in form be changes in the radius.

We must once more adhere to ordinary language and say that a *patch* is circular.

It is clear that here the phrase "bearer of a property" in this context conveys a completely wrong – an impossible – picture. If I have a lump of clay, I can consider it as the bearer of a form, and that, roughly, is where this picture comes from.

1. I have here corrected an inadvertent transposition of "I" and "II" in Wittgenstein's German. (Trs.)

"The patch changes its form" and "the lump of clay changes its form" are different forms of propositions.

You can say "Measure whether *that* is a circle" or "See whether *that* over there is a hat". You can also say "Measure whether that is a circle or an ellipse", but not ". . . whether that is a circle or a hat"; nor "See whether that is a hat or red".

If I point to a curve and say "That is a circle" then someone can object that if it were not a circle it would no longer be *that*. That is to say, what I mean by the word "that" must be independent of what I assert about it.

("Was *that* thunder, or gunfire?" Here you could not ask "Was that a noise?")

How are two circles of the same size distinguished? This question makes it sound as if they were pretty nearly one circle and only distinguished by a nicety.

In the technique of representation by equations what is common is expressed by the form of the equation, and the difference by the difference in the coordinates of the centres.

So it is as if what corresponds with the objects falling under the concept were here the coordinates of the centres.

Couldn't you then say, instead of "This is a circle", "This point is the centre of a circle"? For to be the centre of a circle is an external property of the point.

What is necessary to a description that – say – a book is in a certain position? The internal description of the book, i.e. of the concept, and a description of its place which it would be possible to give by giving the co-ordinates of three points. The proposition "Such a book is *here*" would mean that it had *these* three co-ordinates. For the specification of the "here" must not prejudge *what* is here.

But doesn't it come to the same thing whether I say "*This* is a book" or "Here is a book"? The proposition would then amount to saying, "These are three corners of such a book".

Similarly you can also say "This circle is the projection of a sphere" or "This is a man's appearance".

All that I am saying comes to this, that $\Phi(x)$ must be an *external* description of x.

If in this sense I now say in three-dimensional space "Here is a circle" and on another occasion "Here is a sphere" are the two "here's" of the same type? I want to ask: can one significantly say of the same 'object': it is a circle, and: it is a sphere? Is the subject of each of these predicates of the same type? Both could be the three coordinates of the relevant centre-point. But the position of the circle in three-dimensional space is not fixed by the coordinates of its centre.

On the other hand you can of course say "It's not the noise, but the colour that makes me nervous" and here it might look as if a variable assumed a colour and a noise as values. ("Sounds and colours can be used as vehicles of communication".) It is clear that this proposition is of the same kind as "if you hear a shot, or see me wave, run". For this is the kind of co-ordination on the basis of which a heard or seen language functions.

"Is it conceivable that two things have all their properties in common?" – If it isn't conceivable, then neither is its opposite.

We do indeed talk about a circle, its diameter, etc. etc., as if we were describing a concept in complete abstraction from the objects falling under it. – But in that case 'circle' is not a predicate in the original sense. And in general geometry is the place where concepts from the most different regions get mixed up together.

3
Objects

"In a certain sense, an object cannot be described." (So too Plato: "You can't give an account of one but only name it.") Here "object" means "reference of a not further definable word", and "description" or "explanation" really means: "definition". For of course it isn't denied that the object can be "described from outside", that properties can be ascribed to it and so on.

So when we use the proposition above we are thinking of a calculus with signs or names that are indefinable – or, more accurately, undefined – and we are saying that no account can be given of them.

"What a word means a proposition cannot tell."

What is the distinction, then, between blue and red?
We aren't of the opinion that one colour has one property and the other another. In any case, the properties of blue and red are that this body (or place) is blue, and that other is red.

When asked "what is the distinction between blue and red?" we feel like answering: one is blue and the other red. But of course that means nothing and in reality what we're thinking of is the distinction between the surfaces or places that have these colours. For otherwise the question makes no sense at all.

Compare the different question: "What is the distinction between orange and pink?" One is a mixture of yellow and red, the other a mixture of white and red. And we may say accordingly: blue comes from purple when it gets more bluish, and red comes from purple when that gets more and more reddish.

So what I am saying means: red can't be described. But can't we represent it in painting by painting something red?

No, that isn't a representation in painting of the meaning of the word 'red' (there's no such thing).
The portrait of red.

Still, it's no accident that in order to define the meaning of the word "red" the natural thing is to point to a red object.

(What is natural about it is portrayed in that sentence by the double occurrence of the word 'red').

To say that blue is on the bluish side of blue-red and red on the reddish side is a grammatical sentence and therefore akin to a definition. And indeed one can also say: more bluish = more like blue.

"If you call the colour green an object, you must be saying that it is an object that occurs in the symbolism. Otherwise the sense of the symbolism, and thus its very existence as a symbolism, would not be guaranteed."
But what does that assert about green, or the word "green"? ((That sentence is connected with a particular conception of the meaning-relation and a particular formulation of the problem the relation raises)).

4
Elementary Propositions
A[1]

Can a logical product be hidden in a proposition? And if so, how does one tell, and what methods do we have of bringing the hidden element of a proposition to light? If we haven't yet got a method, then we can't speak of something being hidden or possibly hidden. And if we do have a method of discovery then the only way in which something like a logical product can be hidden in a proposition is the way in which a quotient like 753/3 is hidden until the division has been carried out.

The question whether a logical product is hidden in a sentence is a mathematical problem.

So an elementary proposition is a proposition which, in the calculus as I am now using it, is not represented as a truth-function of other sentences.

The idea of constructing elementary propositions (as e.g. Carnap has tried to do) rests on a false notion of logical analysis. It is not the task of that analysis to discover a *theory* of elementary propositions, like discovering principles of mechanics.

My notion in the *Tractatus Logico-Philosophicus* was wrong: 1) because I wasn't clear about the sense of the words "a logical product is *hidden* in a sentence" (and suchlike), 2) because I too thought that logical analysis had to bring to light what was hidden (as chemical and physical analysis does).

The proposition "this place is now red" (or "this circle is now red") can be called an elementary proposition if this means that it is

---

1. From the 1932(?) typescript where it appears as a chapter by itself.

neither a truth-function of other propositions nor defined as such. (Here I am disregarding combinations such as p . : qv ~ q and the like.)

But from "a is now red" there follows "a is now not green" and so elementary propositions in this sense aren't independent of each other like the elementary propositions in the calculus I once described – a calculus to which, misled as I was by a false notion of reduction, I thought that the whole use of propositions must be reducible.

B[1]

If you want to use the appellation "elementary proposition" as I did in the *Tractatus Logico-Philosophicus,* and as Russell used "atomic proposition", you may call the sentence "Here there is a red rose" an elementary proposition. That is to say, it doesn't contain a truth-function and it isn't defined by an expression which contains one. But if we're to say that a proposition isn't an elementary proposition unless its complete logical analysis shows that it isn't built out of other propositions by truth-functions, we are presupposing that we have an idea of what such an 'analysis' would be. Formerly, I myself spoke of a 'complete analysis', and I used to believe that philosophy had to give a definitive dissection of propositions so as to set out clearly all their connections and remove all possibilities of misunderstanding. I spoke as if there was a calculus in which such a dissection would be possible. I vaguely had in mind something like the definition that Russell had given for the definite article, and I used to think that in a similar way one would be able to use visual impressions etc. to define the concept say of a sphere, and thus exhibit once for all the connections between the concepts and lay bare the source of all misunderstandings, etc. At the root of all this there was a false and idealized picture of the use of language. Of course, in particular cases one can

---

1. From a later MS note book, probably written in summer 1936, some two years after the main text of this volume.

clarify by definitions the connections between the different types of use of expressions. Such a definition may be useful in the case of the connection between 'visual impression' and 'sphere'. But for this purpose it is not a definition of the concept of a physical sphere that we need; instead we must describe a language game related to our own, or rather a whole series of related language games, and it will be in these that such definitions may occur. Such a contrast destroys grammatical prejudices and makes it possible for us to see the use of a word as it really is, instead of *inventing* the use for the word.

There could perhaps be a calculus for dissecting propositions; it isn't hard to imagine one. Then it becomes a problem of calculation to discover whether a proposition is or is not an elementary proposition.

The question whether e.g. a logical product is hidden in a sentence is a mathematical problem. – What "hidden" means here is defined by the method of discovery (or, as it might be, by the lack of a method).

. . . .

What gives us the idea that there is a kind of agreement between thought and reality? – Instead of "agreement" here one might say with a clear conscience "pictorial character".[1]

But is this pictorial character an agreement? In the *Tractatus Logico-Philosophicus* I said something like: it is an agreement of form. But that is an error.

First of all, "picture" here is ambiguous. One wants to say that an order is the picture of the action which was carried out on the order; but also, a picture of the action which *is to be* carried out as an order.

1. Cf. p. 163.

We may say: a blueprint *serves as a picture* of the object which the workman is to make from it.

And here we might call the way in which the workman turns such a drawing into an artefact "the method of projection". We might now express ourselves thus: the method of projection mediates between the drawing and the object, it reaches from the drawing to the artefact. Here we are comparing the method of projection with projection lines which go from one figure to another. – But if the method of projection is a bridge, it is a bridge which isn't built until the application is made. – This comparison conceals the fact that the picture *plus* the projection lines leaves open various methods of application; it makes it look as if what is depicted, even if it does not exist in fact, is determined by the picture and the projection lines in an ethereal manner; every bit as determined, that is to say, as if it did exist. (It is 'determined give or take a yes or no.') In that case what we may call 'picture' is the blueprint plus the method of its application. And we now imagine the method as something which is attached to the blueprint whether or not it is used. (One can *"describe"* an application even if it doesn't exist).

Now I would like to ask "How can the blueprint be used as a representation, unless there is already an agreement with what is to be made?" – But what does that mean? Well, perhaps this: how could I play the notes in the score on the piano if they didn't already have a relationship to particular types of movement of the hand? Of course such a relationship *sometimes* consists in a certain agreement, but sometimes not in any agreement, but merely in our having learnt to apply the signs in a particular way. What the comparison between the method of projection and the projection lines connecting the picture with the object does is to make all these cases alike – because *that* is what attracts us. You may say: I count the projection lines as part of the picture – but not the method of projection.

1. Cf. Tractatus 2. 1513 (Editor).

You may of course also say: I count a *description* of a method of projection as part of the picture.

So I am imagining that the difference between proposition and reality is ironed out by the lines of projection belonging to the picture, the thought, and that no further room is left for a method of application, but only for agreement and disagreement.

5
Is time essential to propositions?
Comparison between time and truth-functions

If we had grammar set out in the form of a book, it wouldn't be a series of chapters side by side, it would have quite a different structure. And it is here, if I am right, that we would have to see the distinction between phenomenological and non-phenomenological. There would be, say, a chapter about colours, setting out the rules for the use of colour-words; but there would be nothing comparable in what the grammar had to say about the words "not", "or", etc. (the "logical constants").

It would, for instance, be a consequence of the rules, that these latter words unlike the colour words were usable in every proposition; and the generality belonging to this "every" would not be the kind that is discovered by experience, but the generality of a supreme rule of the game admitting of no appeal.

How does the temporal character of facts manifest itself? How does it express itself, if not by certain expressions having to occur in our sentences? That means: how does the temporal character of facts express itself, if not grammatically? "Temporal character" – that doesn't mean that I come at 5 o'clock, but that I come at some time or other, i.e. that my proposition has the structure it has.

We are inclined to say that negation and disjunction are connected with the nature of the proposition, but that time is connected with its content rather than with its nature.

But if two things are equally universal, how can it show itself in grammar that one of them is connected with the nature of the proposition and the other is not?

Or should I have said that time is not equally universal since mathematical propositions can be negated and occur in disjunctions, without being temporal? There is indeed a connection here, though this form of portraying the matter is misleading.

But that shows what I mean by "proposition." or "nature of the proposition".

Why – I want to ask – is the temporal character of propositions so universal?

Might one also put the question thus: "How does it happen that every fact of experience can be brought into a relationship with what is shown by a clock?"

Having two kinds of generality in the way I spoke of would be as strange as if there were two equally exceptionless rules of a game and one of them were pronounced to be more fundamental. As if one could ask whether in chess the king or the chess board was more important; which of the two was more essential, and which more accidental.

There's at least one question that seems in order: suppose I had written up the grammar, and the different chapters on the colour words, etc. etc. were there one after the other, like rules for each of the chess pieces, how would I know that those were *all* the chapters? If there turns out to be a common property in all the chapters so far in existence, we seem to have encountered a logical generality that is not an essential, i.e. *a priori* generality. But we can't say that the fact that chess is played with 16 pieces is any less essential to it than its being played on a chessboard.

Since time and the truth-functions taste so different, and since they manifest their nature only and wholly in grammar, it is grammar that must explain the different taste.
One tastes like content, the other like form of representation.
They taste as different as a plan and a line through a plan.

It appears to me that the present, as it occurs in the proposition "the sky is blue" (if this proposition isn't meant as a hypothesis), is not a form of time, so that the present in *this* sense is atemporal.

Does time enter into a landscape picture? or into a still life?
Literature consisting of descriptions of landscapes.

It is noteworthy that the time of which I am here speaking is not time in a physical sense. We are not concerned with measuring time. It is fishy that something which is unconnected with measurement is supposed to have a role in propositions like that of physical time in the hypotheses of physics.

Discuss:
The distinction between the logic of the content and the logic of the propositional form in general. The former seems, so to speak, brightly coloured, and the latter plain; the former seems to be concerned with what the picture represents, the latter to be a characteristic of the pictorial form like a frame.

By comparison with the way in which the truth-functions are applicable to all propositions, it seems to us accidental that all propositions contain time in some way or other.
The former seems to be connected with their nature as propositions, the latter with the nature of the reality we encounter.

((Added later in the margins))
A sentence can contain time in very different senses.
You are hurting me.
The weather is marvellous outside.
The Inn flows into the Danube.
Water freezes at 0°.
I often make slips of the pen
Some time ago . . .
I hope he will come.
At 5 o'clock.

This kind of steel is excellent.
The earth was once a ball of gas.

6

The Nature of Hypotheses

You could obviously explain an hypothesis by means of pictures. I mean, you could e.g. explain the hypothesis "there is a book lying here" with pictures showing the book in plan, elevation and various cross-sections.

Such a representation gives a *law*. Just as the equation of a curve gives a law, by means of which you may discover the ordinates, if you cut at different abscissae.

In which case the verifications of particular cases correspond to cuts that have actually been made.

If our experiences yield points lying on a straight line, the proposition that these experiences are various views of a straight line is an hypothesis.

The hypothesis is a way of representing this reality, for a new experience may tally with it or not, or possibly make it necessary to modify the hypothesis.

If for instance we use a system of coordinates and the equation for a sphere to express the proposition that a sphere is located at a certain distance from our eyes, this description has a greater multiplicity than that of a verification by eye. The first multiplicity corresponds not to *one* verification but to a *law* obeyed by verifications.

An hypothesis is a law for forming propositions.

You could also say: an hypothesis is a law for forming expectations.

A proposition is, so to speak, a particular cross-section of an hypothesis.

According to my principle two suppositions must have the same sense if every *possible* experience that confirms the one also confirms the other, if, that is, no decision between the two is conceivable on the basis of experience.

The representation of a curve as a straight line with deviations. The equation of the curve includes a parameter whose course expresses the deviations from a straight line. It isn't essential that these deviations should be "slight". They can be so large that the curve doesn't look like a straight line at all. "Straight line with deviations" is only one form of description. It makes it easier for me to eliminate, or neglect, a particular component of the description if I so wish. (The form "rule with exceptions").

What does it mean, to be certain that one has toothache? (If one *can't* be certain, then grammar doesn't allow the use of the word "certain" in this connection.)
The grammar of the expression "to be certain".

We say "If I say that I see a chair there, I am saying more than I know for certain". And commonly that means "But all the same, there's *one* thing that I do know for certain." But if we now try to say what it is, we find ourselves in a certain embarrassment.
"I see something *brown* – that is certain." That's meant to say that the brown colour is seen and not perhaps merely conjectured from other symptoms. And we do indeed say quite simply: "I *see* something brown."

If someone tells me "Look into this telescope, and make me a sketch of what you see", the sketch I make is the expression of a proposition, not of a hypothesis.

If I say "Here there is a chair", I mean more – people say – than the mere description of what I perceive. This can only mean that that proposition doesn't have to be true, even though the description fits what is seen. Well, in what circumstances would I say that that proposition wasn't true? Apparently, if certain other propositions aren't true that were implicit in the first. But it isn't as if the first turns out to have been a logical product all along.

The best comparison for every hypothesis, – something that is itself an example of an hypothesis – is a body in relation to a systematic series of views of it from different angles.

Making a discovery in a scientific investigation (say in experimental physics) is of course not the same thing as making a discovery in ordinary life outside the laboratory; but the two are *similar* and a comparison with the former can throw light on the latter.

There is an essential distinction between propositions like "That is a lion", "The sun is larger than the earth", and propositions like "Men have two hands". Propositions like the first pair contain a "this", "now", "here" and thus connect immediately with reality. But if there happened to be no men around, how would I go about checking the third proposition?

It is always single faces of hypotheses that are verified.

Perhaps this is how it is: what an hypothesis explains is itself only expressible by an hypothesis. Of course, this amounts to asking whether there are any primary propositions that are definitively verifiable and not merely facets of an hypothesis. (That is rather like asking: are there surfaces that aren't surfaces of bodies?)

At all events, there can't be any distinction between an hypothesis used as an expression of an immediate experience and a proposition in the stricter sense.

There is a distinction between a proposition like "Here there is a sphere in front of me" and "It looks as if there is a sphere in front of me". The same thing shows itself also thus: one can say "There seems to be a sphere in front of me", but it is senseless to say "It looks as if there seems to be a sphere here". So too one can say

"Here there is probably a sphere", but not "Here there probably appears to be a sphere". In such a case people would say "After all, you must know whether there *appears* to be".

There is nothing hypothetical in what connects the proposition with the given fact.

It's clear that reality – I mean immediate experience – will sometimes give an hypothesis the answer yes, and sometimes the answer no (here of course the "yes" and "no" express only confirmation and lack of confirmation); and it's clear that these affirmations and denials can be given expression.

The hypothesis, if *that* face of it is laid against reality, becomes a proposition.

It may be doubtful whether the body I see is a sphere, but it can't be doubtful that from here it looks to be something like a sphere. – The mechanism of hypothesis would not function if appearance too were doubtful so that one couldn't verify beyond doubt even a facet of the hypothesis. If there were a doubt here, what could take the doubt away? If this connection too were loose, there would be no such thing as confirming an hypothesis and it would hang entirely in the air, quite pointless (and therefore senseless).

If I say "I saw a chair", that (in *one* sense) isn't contradicted by the proposition "there wasn't one there". For I could use the first proposition in the description of a dream and then nobody would use the second to contradict me. But the description of the dream throws a light on the sense of the words "*I saw*".

Again, in the proposition "there wasn't one there", the word "there" may have more than one meaning.

I am in agreement with the opinions of contemporary physicists when they say that the signs in their equations no longer have any "meanings" and that physics cannot attain to any such meanings, but must stay put at the signs. But they don't see that the signs have meaning in as much as – and only in as much as – observable phenomena do or do not correspond to them, in however circuitous a manner.

Let us imagine that chess had been invented not as a board game, but as a game to be played with numbers and letters on paper, so that no one had ever imagined a board with 64 squares in connection with it. And now suppose someone made the discovery that the game corresponded exactly to a game which could be played on a board in such and such a way. This discovery would have been a great simplification of the game (people who would earlier have found it too difficult could now play it). But it is clear that this new illustration of the rules of the game would be nothing more than a new, more easily surveyable symbolism, which in other respects would be on the same level as the written game. Compare with this the talk about physics nowadays not working with mechanical models but "only with symbols".

The probability of an hypothesis has its measure in how much evidence is needed to make it profitable to throw it out.

It's only in this sense that we can say that repeated uniform experience in the past renders the continuation of this uniformity in the future probable.

If, in this sense, I now say: I assume the sun will rise again tomorrow, because the opposite is so unlikely, I here mean by "likely" and "unlikely" something completely different from what I mean by these words in the proposition "It's equally likely that I'll throw heads or tails". The two meanings of the word "likely" are, to be sure, connected in certain ways, but they aren't identical.

We only give up an hypothesis for an ever higher gain.

Induction is a process based on a principle of economy.

The question how simple a representation is yielded by assuming a particular hypothesis is directly connected, I believe, with the question of probability.

We may compare a part of an hypothesis with the movement of a part of a gear, a movement that can be stipulated without prejudicing the intended motion. But then of course you have to make appropriate adjustments to the rest of the gear if it is to produce the desired motion. I'm thinking of a differential gear. – Once I've decided that there is to be no deviation from a certain part of my hypothesis no matter what the experience to be described may be, I have stipulated a mode of representation and this part of my hypothesis is now a postulate.

A postulate must be such that no conceivable experience can refute it, even though it may be extremely inconvenient to cling to the postulate. To the extent to which we can talk here of greater or slighter convenience, there is a greater or slighter probability of the postulate.

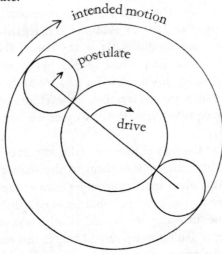

It's senseless to talk of a measure for this probability at this juncture. The situation here is like that in the case of two kinds of numbers where we can with a certain justice say that the one is more like the other (is closer to it) than a third, but there isn't any numerical measure of the similarity. Of course you could imagine a measure being constructed in such cases, too, say by counting the postulates or axioms common to the two systems, etc. etc.

I give someone the following piece of information, and no more: at such and such a time you will see a point of light appear in the interval AB.

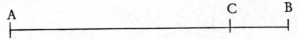

Does the question now makes sense "Is it more likely that this point will appear in the interval AC than in CB"? I believe, obviously not. – I can of course decide that the probability of the event's happening in CB is to be in the ratio CB/AC to the probability of its happening in AC; however, that's a decision I can have empirical grounds for making, but about which there is nothing to be said *a priori*. It is possible for the observed distribution of events not to lead to this assumption. The probability, where infinitely many possibilities come into consideration, must of course be treated as a limit. That is, if I divide the stretch AB into arbitrarily many parts of arbitrary lengths and regard it as equally likely that the event should occur in any one of these parts, we immediately have the simple case of dice before us. And now I can – arbitrarily – lay down a law for constructing parts of equal likelihood. For instance, the law that, if the lengths of the parts are equal, they are equally likely. But any other law is just as permissible.

Couldn't I, in the case of dice too, take, say, five faces together as one possibility, and oppose them to the sixth as the second possibility? And what, apart from experience, is there to prevent me from regarding these two possibilities as equally likely?

Let's imagine throwing, say, a red ball with just one very small green patch on it. Isn't it much more likely in this case for the red area to strike the ground than for the green? – But how would we support this proposition? Presumably by showing that when we throw the ball, the red strikes the ground much more often than the green. But that's got nothing to do with logic. – We may always project the red and green surfaces and what befalls them onto a surface in such a way that the projection of the green surface is greater than or equal to the red; so that the events, as seen in this projection, appear to have a quite different probability ratio from the one they had on the original surface. If, e.g. I reflect the events in a suitably curved mirror and now imagine what I would have held to be the more probable event if I had only seen the image in the mirror.

The one thing the mirror can't alter is the number of clearly demarcated possibilities. So that if I have n coloured patches on my ball, the mirror will also show n, and if I have *decided* that these are to be regarded as equally likely, then I can stick to this decision for the mirror image too.

To make myself even clearer: if I carry out the experiment with a concave mirror, i.e. make the *observations* in a concave mirror, it will perhaps then look as if the ball falls more often on the small surface than on the much larger one; and it's clear that neither experiment – in the mirror or outside it – has a claim to precedence.

We may apply our old principle to propositions expressing a probability and say, we shall discover their sense by considering what verifies them.

If I say "That will probably occur", is this proposition verified by the occurrence or falsified by its non-occurrence? In my opinion, obviously not. In that case it doesn't say anything about either. For if a dispute were to arise as to whether it is probable or not, it would always be arguments from the past that would be adduced. And this would be so even when what actually happened was already known.

Causality depends on an observed uniformity. This does not mean that a uniformity so far observed will always continue, but what cannot be altered is that the events so far have been uniform; *that* can't be the uncertain result of an empirical series which in its turn isn't something given but something dependent on another uncertain one and so on *ad infinitum*.

When people say that the proposition "it is probable that p will occur" says something about the event p, they forget that the probability remains even when the event p does *not* occur.

The proposition "p will probably occur" does indeed say something about the future, but not something "about the event p", as the grammatical form of the statement makes us believe.

If I ask for the grounds of an assertion, the answer to the question holds not only for this person and for *this* action (assertion), but quite *generally*.

If I say "the weather looks like rain" do I say anything about future weather? No; I say something about the present weather, by means of a law connecting weather at any given time with weather at an earlier time. This law must already be in existence, and we are using it to construct certain statements about our experience. –

We might say the same of historical statements too. But I was too quick to say that the proposition "the weather looks like rain" says nothing about future weather. It all depends what is meant by "saying something about something". The sentence says just what it says.

The sentence "p will probably occur" says something about the future only in a sense in which its truth and falsehood are completely independent of what will happen in the future.

If we say: "the gun is now aiming at the point p" we aren't saying anything about where the shot will hit. Giving the point at which it is aiming is a *geometrical* means of assigning its direction. That this is the means we use is certainly connected with certain observations (projectile parabolas, etc.) but these observations don't enter into our present description of the direction.

Parabola

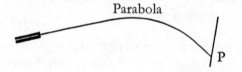

A Galtonian photograph is the picture of a probability.

The law of probability is the natural law you see when you screw up your eyes.

"On average, the points yielded by the experiment lie on a straight line". "If I throw with a good die, then on average I throw a one every six throws". What does that mean? Is the proposition compatible with *any* experience I may have? If so, it says nothing. Have I decided in advance which experiences are incompatible with it and what is the limit beyond which exceptions may not go without upsetting the rule? No. But couldn't I have set such a limit? Of course. – Suppose that the limit had been set thus: if 4 out of 6 successive throws turn out the same, then it's a bad die. Now someone says: "But if that happens only very seldom, mayn't it be a good one after all?" – To that the answer is as follows. If I permit the turning up of 4 similar throws among 6 successive ones to occur within a certain number of throws, then I am replacing the first limit with a *different* one. But if I say "any number of similar successive throws is allowed, as long as it happens sufficiently rarely", then strictly speaking I've defined the goodness of the die in a way that makes it independent of the result of the throws; unless by the goodness of a die I do not mean a property of the die, but a property of a particular game played with it. In that case I can certainly say: in any game I call the die good provided that among the N throws of the game there occur not more than log N similar successive throws. However, that doesn't give a test for the checking of dice, but a criterion for judging a particular game.

We say that if the die is quite regular and isn't interfered with then the distribution of the numbers 1, 2, 3, 4, 5, 6 among the throws must be uniform, since *there is no reason* why one number should occur more often than another.

But now let's represent the throws by the values of the function $(x - 3)^2$ for the arguments 1 to 6, i.e. by the numbers 0, 1, 4, 9 instead of by the numbers 1 to 6. Is there a reason why one of *these* numbers should turn up in the new results more often than another? This shows us that the *a priori* law of probability, like the minimum-principles of mechanics etc., is a form that laws may take. If it had been discovered by experiment that the distribution of the throws 1 to 6 with a regular die was such that the distribution of the values of $(x - 3)^2$ was uniform, it would have been *this* regularity that was defined as the *a priori* regularity.

We do the same thing in the kinetic theory of gases: we represent the distribution of molecular movements in the form of some sort of uniform distribution; but we make the choice of *what* is uniformly distributed – and in the other case of *what* is reduced to a minimum – in such a way that our theory agrees with experience.

"The molecules move purely according to the laws of probability" is supposed to mean: physics gets out of the way, and now the molecules move as it were purely according to laws of logic. This idea is similar to the idea that the law of inertia is an *a priori* proposition: there too one speaks of what a body does when it isn't interfered with. But what is the criterion for its not being interfered with? Is it ultimately that it moves uniformly in a straight line? Or is it something different? If the latter, then it's a matter of experience whether the law of inertia holds; if the former, then it wasn't a law at all but a definition. So too with the proposition, "if the particles aren't interfered with, then the distribution of their motions is such and such". What is the criterion for their not being interfered with? etc.

To say that the points yielded in this experiment lie roughly on this line, e.g. a straight line, means something like: "seen for this distance, they seem to lie on a straight line".

I may say that a stretch gives the general impression of a straight line; but I cannot say: "This bit of line looks straight, for it could be a bit of a line that as a whole gives me the impression of being straight." (Mountains on the earth and moon. The earth a ball.)

An experiment with dice lasts a certain time, and our expectations about future throws can only be based on tendencies we observe in what happens during this experiment. That is to say, the experiment can only give grounds for expecting that things will go in *in the way* shown by the experiment; but we can't expect that the experiment, if continued, will now yield results that tally better with a preconceived idea of its course than did those of the experiment we have actually performed. So if, for instance, I toss a coin and find no tendency in the results of the experiment itself for the number of heads and tails to approximate to each other more closely, then the experiment gives me no reason to suppose that if it were continued such an approximation would emerge. Indeed, the expectation of such an approximation must *itself* refer to a definite point in time, since we can't say we're expecting something to happen *eventually,* in the infinite future.

Any "reasonable expectation" is an expectation that a rule we have observed up to now will continue to hold.
(But the rule must have been observed and can't, for its part too, be merely expected.)

The logic of probability is only concerned with the state of expectation in the sense in which logic in general is concerned with thinking.

A ray is emitted from the light source S striking the surface AB to form a point of light there, and then striking the surface AB'. We have no reason to suppose that the point on AB lies to the left or to the right of M, and equally none for supposing that the

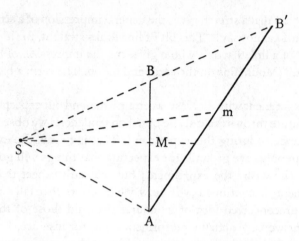

point on AB' lies on one side or the other of m. This yields therefore
incompatible probabilities. But if I make an assumption about the
probability of the point on AB lying in AM, how is this assumption
verified? Surely, we think, by a frequency experiment. Supposing
this confirms the view that the probabilities of AM and BM are
equal (and so the probabilities of Am and B'm differ), then it is
recognized as the right one and thus shows itself to be an hypothesis belonging to physics. The geometrical construction merely
shows that the fact that AM = MB was *no* ground for assuming
equal likelihood.

Suppose that measurement shows the die to be accurate and
regular, that the numbers on its sides don't influence the throws,
and that it is thrown by a hand whose movements follow no
definite rules: does it follow that the distribution among the
throws of each of the throws from 1 to 6 will be uniform on
average? Where is the uniform distribution supposed to come
from? The accuracy and regularity of the die can't establish that the
distribution of throws will be *uniform on average*. (It would be, as it
were, a monochrome premise with a mottle conclusion.) And we

haven't made any suppositions about the movements while throwing. (Making the bundles of hay equal gives reason to believe that the donkey will starve to death between them; it doesn't give reason to believe that he will eat from each with roughly equal frequency.) – It is perfectly compatible with our assumptions for one hundred ones to be thrown in succession, if friction, hand-movements and air-resistance coincide appropriately. The experimental fact that this never happens is a fact about those factors, and the hypothesis that the throws will be uniformly distributed is an hypothesis about the operation of those factors.

Suppose someone says that a lever with arms of equal length must remain at rest under the influence of equal and opposite forces, since there is no cause to make it move to one side rather than to the other. That only means that if the lever moves to one side after we have ascertained the equality of the arms and the equal and opposite nature of the forces, then we can't explain this on the basis of the preconditions we know or have assumed. (The form that we call "explanation" must be asymmetrical: like the operation which makes "2a + 3b" out of "a + b"). But on the basis of our presuppositions we can indeed explain the lever's continuance at rest. – Could we also explain a swing to left and right with roughly equal frequency? No, because once again the swing involves asymmetry; we would only explain the symmetry in this asymmetry. If the lever had rotated to the right with a uniform motion, one could similarly have said: given the symmetry of the conditions I can explain the uniformity of the motion, but not its direction.

A lack of uniformity in the distribution of the throws is *not* to be explained by the symmetry of the die. It is only to this extent that the symmetry explains the uniformity of the distribution. – For one can of course say: if the numbers on the sides of the die have no effect, then the difference between them cannot explain an irregularity in the distribution; and of course similar circumstances can't explain differences; and so to that extent one might infer a regularity. But in that case why is there any difference at all between different throws? Whatever explains that must also explain their approximate regularity. It's just that the regularity of the die doesn't interfere with that regularity.

Suppose that a man throwing dice every day threw nothing but ones for a week, using dice that proved good by every other method of testing and that gave the usual results when thrown by others. Has he grounds, now, for supposing that there is a law of nature that he will always throw ones? Has he grounds for believing that it will go on like this, or has he grounds for believing that this regularity can't last much longer? Has he reason to abandon the game since it has become clear that he can only throw ones, or reason to play on since in these circumstances it is all the more probable that he will throw a higher number at the next throw? In actual fact, he will refuse to accept the regularity as a natural law: at least, it will have to go on for a long time before he will entertain the possibility. But why? I believe it is because so much of his previous experience in life speaks against there being a law of nature of such a sort, and we have – so to speak – to surmount all that experience, before embracing a totally new way of looking at things.

If we infer from the relative frequency of an event its relative frequency in the future, we can of course only do that from the frequency which has in fact been so far observed. And not from one we have derived from observation by some process or other for calculating probabilities. For the probability we calculate is compatible with *any* frequency *whatever* that we actually observe, since it leaves the time open.

When a gambler or insurance company is guided by probability, they aren't guided by the probability calculus, since one can't be guided by this on its own, because *anything* that happens can be reconciled with it: no, the insurance company is guided by a

frequency actually observed. And that, of course, is an absolute
frequency.

The concept "about"
Problem of the "heap"

"He came from about there →."
"About *there* is the brightest point of the horizon".
"Make the plank about 2 m long".
In order to say this, must I know of limits which determine the margin of tolerance of this length? Obviously not. Isn't it enough e.g. to say "A margin of ±1 cm is perfectly permissible; 2 would be too much"? – Indeed it's an essential part of the sense of my proposition that I'm not in a position to give "precise" bounds to the margin. Isn't that obviously because the space in which I am working here doesn't have the same metric as the Euclidean one?

Suppose one wanted to fix the margin of tolerance exactly by experiment, by altering the length, approaching the limits of the margin and asking in each case whether such a length would do or not. After a few shortenings one would get contradictory results: at one time a point would be described as being within the limits, and at another time a point closer in would be described as impermissible, each time perhaps with the remark that the answers were no longer quite certain.

It is the same sort of uncertainty as occurs in giving the highest point of a curve. We just aren't in Euclidean space and here there isn't a highest point in the Euclidean sense. The answer will mean "The highest point is about *there*" and the grammar of the word "about" – in this context – is part of the geometry of our space.

Surely it is like the way the butcher weighs things only to the nearest ounce, though that is arbitrary and depends on what are the customary counterweights. Here it is enough to know: it doesn't weigh more than P_1 and it doesn't weigh less than P_2. One might say: in principle giving the weight thus isn't giving a number, but an interval, and the intervals make up a discontinuous series.

Yet one might say: "at all events keep *within* ± 1 cm", thus setting an arbitrary limit. – If someone now said "Right, but that isn't the real limit of the permissible tolerance; so what is?" the answer would be e.g. "I don't know of any; I only know that ±2 is too much".

Imagine the following psychological experiment.

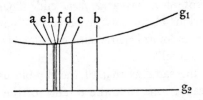

The subject is shown curves g_1 g_2 with a straight line A drawn across them. I will call the section of this line between g_1 and g_2 a. Parallel to a we now draw b at an arbitrary distance and ask the subject whether he sees the section b as bigger than a, or cannot any longer distinguish between the two lengths. He replies that b seems bigger than a. Next we move closer to a, measuring half the distance from a to b and drawing c. "Do you see c as bigger than a?" "Yes." – We halve the distance c-a and draw d. "Do you see d as bigger than a?" "Yes." We halve a-d. "Do you see e as bigger than a?" – "No." – So we halve e-d. "Do you see f as bigger than e?" – "Yes." – So we halve e-f and draw h. We might approach the line a from the left hand side as well and then say that what corresponds in Euclidean space to a seen length a is not a single length but an interval of lengths, and in a similar way what corresponds to a single seen position of a line (say the pointer of an instrument) is an interval of positions in Euclidean space; but this interval has no precise limits. That means: it is bounded not by points, but by converging intervals which do not converge upon a point. (Like the series of binary fractions that we get by throwing heads and tails.) The special thing about two intervals which are bounded in this *blurred* way instead of by points is that in certain cases the answer to the question whether they overlap or are quite distinct is "undecided"; and the question whether they touch, whether they have an end-point in common, is always a senseless one since they don't have end-points at all. But one might say "they have *de facto* end-points", in the sense in which the development of π has a *de facto* end. There is of course nothing mysterious about this property of "blurred" intervals; the somewhat paradoxical character is explained by the double use of the word "interval".

The case is the same as that of the double use of the word "chess" to mean at one time the totality of the currently valid chess rules, and at another time the game invented in Persia by N. N. which developed in such and such a way. In one case it is nonsensical to talk of a development of the rules of chess and in another not. What we mean by "the length of a measured section" may be either what results from a particular measurement which I carry out today at 5 o'clock – in that case there is no "± etc." for this assignment of length – or, something to which measurements approximate, etc.; in the two cases the word "length" is used with quite different grammars. So too the word "interval" if what I mean by an interval is at one time something fixed and at another time something in flux.

But we must not be surprised that an interval should have such a strange property; for we're now just using the word "interval" in a sense different from the usual one. And we can't say that we have discovered new properties of certain intervals, any more than we would discover new properties of the king in chess if we altered the rules of the game while keeping the designation "chess" and "king". (On the other hand cf. Brouwer on the law of excluded middle.)

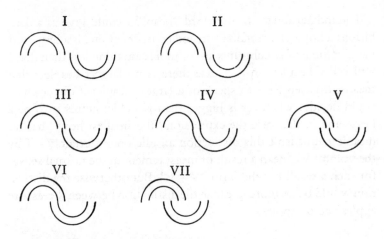

I)   the intervals are separate
II)   they are separate with a *de facto* contact
III) undecided
IV)   undecided
V)   undecided
VI)   they overlap
VII) they overlap

So basically that experiment gives what we have called a "blurred" interval; on the other hand of course we could conceive experiments which would give a sharp interval instead. Suppose we moved a straight-edge from the starting position b, in the direction of a, keeping it parallel to b, until our subject began to display a particular reaction; in that case we could call the point at which the reaction first occurs the limit of our strip. Likewise we might of course call the result of a weighing "the weight of a body" and in that sense there would be an absolutely exact weighing, that is, one whose result did not have the form "W ± w". We would thus have altered the form of our expression, and we would have to say that the weight of bodies varied according to a law that was unknown to us. (The distinction between "absolutely exact" weighing and "essentially inexact weighing" is a grammatical distinction connected with two different meanings of the expression "result of weighing").

The indeterminacy of the word "heap". I could give as a definition: a body of a certain form and consistency etc. is a heap, if it has a volume of K cubic metres, or more; anything less than that I will call a heaplet. In that case there is no largest heaplet; that means, it is senseless to speak of a largest heaplet. Conversely, I could decide: whatever is bigger than K cubic metres is to be a heap, and in that case the expression "the smallest heap" has no meaning. But isn't this distinction an idle one? Certainly – if by the volume we mean a result of measurement in the normal sense; for such a result has the form "V ± v". But otherwise the distinction would be no more idle than the distinction between threescore apples and 61 apples.

About the problem of the "heap": Here, as in similar cases, one might think that there is an official concept like the official length of a pace; say "A heap is anything that is bigger than half a cubic metre". But this would still not be the concept we normally use. For that there exists no delimitation (and if we fix one, we are altering the concept); it is just that there are cases that we count as within the extension of the concept, and cases that we no longer count as within the extension of the concept.

"Make me a heap of sand here." – "Fine, that is certainly something he would call a heap." I was able to obey the command, so it was in order. But what about this command "Make me the smallest heap you would still call a heap"? I would say: that is nonsense; I can only determine a *de facto* upper and lower limit.

Part II
On Logic and Mathematics

Is it because we understand the propositions that we know that q entails p?
Does a sense give rise to the entailment?

p.q. = .p means "q follows from p".

p	q	p ∨ q	q	q $\\|$ (p ∨ q).q	$(p ∨ q)$ $\\|$ (p ∨ q) ∨q
T	T	T	T	T	T
T	F	T	F	F	T
F	T	T	T	T	T
F	F	F	F	F	F

(∃x).fx ∨ fa. = .(∃x).fx, (∃x).fx.fa. = .fa. How do I know that?
(Because for the equation above I gave a kind of proof). One might
say something like: "I just understand '(∃x).fx' ". (An excellent
example of what "understand" means).

But I might equally ask "How do I know that (∃x).fx follows
from fa?" and answer "because I understand '(∃x).fx'."

But really how do I know that it follows? – Because that is the
way I calculate.

How do I know that (∃x).fx follows from fa? Is it that I as it were
see behind the sign "(∃x).fx", that I see the sense lying behind it and
see from that that it follows from fa? Is *that* what understanding
is?

No, what that equation expresses is a part of the understanding
(that is thus unpacked before my eyes).

Compare the idea that understanding is first of all grasping
in a flash something which then has to be unpacked like that.

If I say "I know that (∃x).fx follows, because I understand it"
that would mean, that when I understand it, I see something
different from the sign I'm given, a kind of definition of the sign
which gives rise to the entailment.

Isn't it rather that the connection is set up and prescribed by the equations? For there is no such thing as a hidden connection.

$(\exists x).fx$	fa
T	T
T	F
~~F~~	~~T~~
F	F

But, I used to think, mustn't $(\exists x).fx$ be a truth function of fa for that to be possible, for that connection to be possible?

For doesn't $(\exists x).Fx \lor Fa = (\exists x).fx$ simply say that fa is already contained in $(\exists x).fx$? Doesn't it show the connection between the fa and the $(\exists x).fx$? Not unless $(\exists x).fx$ is *defined* as a logical sum (with fa as one of the terms of the sum). – If that is the case, then $(\exists x).fx$ is merely an abbreviation.

In logic there is no such thing as a hidden connection.

You can't get behind the rules, because there isn't any behind.

$fE.fa. = fa$. Can one say: that is only possible if fE follows from fa? Or must one say: that settles that fE is to follow from fa?

If the former, it must be the structure that makes it follow, say because fE is so defined as to have the appropriate structure. But can the entailment really be a kind of result of the visible structure of the signs, in the way that a physical reaction is the result of a physical property? Doesn't it rather always depend on stipulations like the equation $fE.fa. = .fa$? Can it be read off from $p \lor q$ that it follows from p, or only from the rules Russell gives for the truth-functions?

And why should the rule fE.fa. = .fa be an effect of another rule rather than being itself the primary rule?

For what is "fE must somehow contain fa" supposed to mean? It doesn't contain it, in so far as we can work with fE without mentioning fa; but it does in so far as the rule fE.fa = .fa holds.

But the idea is that fE.fa. = fa can only hold in virtue of a definition of fE.

That is, I think, because otherwise it looks, wrongly, as if a further stipulation had been made about fE after it had already been introduced into the language. But in fact there isn't any stipulation left for future experience to make.

And the definition of fE in terms of "all particular cases" is *no less* impossible than the enumeration of *all* rules of the form fE.fx. = fx.

Indeed the individual equations fE.fx. = fx are just precisely an expression of this impossibility.

If we are asked: but is it now really certain that it isn't a different calculus being used, we can only say: if that means "don't we use other calculi too in our real language?" I can only answer "I don't know any others at present". (Similarly, if someone asked "are these all the calculi of contemporary mathematics?" I might say "I don't remember any others, but I can read it up and find out more exactly"). But the question cannot mean "can no other calculus be used?" For how is the answer to that question to be discovered?

A calculus exists when one describes it.

Can one say 'calculus' is not a mathematical concept?

If I were to say "whether p follows from q must result from p and q alone": it would have to mean this: that p follows from q is a stipulation that determines the sense of p and q, not some extra truth that can be asserted about the sense of both of them. Hence one can indeed give rules of inference, but in doing so one is giving for the use of the written signs rules which determine their as yet undetermined sense; and that means simply that the rules must be laid down arbitrarily, i.e. are not to be read off from reality like a description. For when I say that the rules are arbitrary, I mean that they are not determined by reality in the way the description of reality is. And that means: it is nonsense to say that they agree with reality, e.g. that the rules for the words "blue" and "red" agree with the facts about those colours etc.

What the equation $p.q = p$ really shows is the connection between entailment and the truth-functions.

1. Cf. Tractatus 5. 132 (Ed.).

2

"If p follows from q, then thinking that q must involve thinking that p."

Remember that a general proposition might entail a logical sum of a hundred or so terms, which we certainly didn't think of when we uttered the general proposition. Yet can't we say that it follows from it?

"What follows from a thought must be involved in thinking it. For there is nothing in a thought that we aren't aware of while we are thinking it. It isn't a machine which might be explored with unexpected results, a machine which might achieve something that couldn't be read off from it. That is, the way it works is *logical*, it's quite different from the way a machine works. *Qua* thought, it contains nothing more than was put into it. As a machine functioning causally, it might be believed capable of anything; but in logic we get out of it only what we meant by it."

If I say that the square is entirely white, I don't think of ten smaller rectangles contained in it which are white, and I can't think of "*all*" rectangles or patches contained in it. Similarly in the proposition "he is in the room" I don't think of a hundred possible positions he might be in and certainly not of *all* possible positions.

"Wherever you hit the target you've won. You've hit it in the upper right hand section, so . . . "

At first sight there seem to be two kinds of deduction: in one of them the premise mentions everything the conclusion does and in the other not. An instance of the first kind is the inference from p.q to q; an instance of the second is the inference; the whole stick is white, so the middle third of it is white too. This conclusion mentions boundaries that are not mentioned in the first proposition. (That is dubious.) Again, if I say "If you hit the target anywhere in this circle you will win the prize . . . " and then "You have hit it here, so . . . " the place mentioned in the second proposition was not prescribed in the first. The target after the shot stands in a certain internal relation to the target as I saw it before, and that

247

relation consists in the shot's falling within the bounds of the general possibility that we foresaw. But the shot was not in itself foreseen and did not occur, or at least need not have occurred, in the first picture. For even supposing that at the time I thought of a thousand definite possibilities, it was at least possible for the one that was later realised to have been omitted. And if the foreseeing of that possibility really had been essential, the overlooking of this single case would have given the premise the wrong sense and the conclusion wouldn't any longer follow from it.

On the other hand you don't add anything to the proposition "Wherever you hit this circle . . ." by saying "Wherever you hit this circle, and in particular if you hit the black dot . . ." If the black dot was already there when the first proposition was uttered, then of course it was meant too; and if it wasn't there, then the actual sense of the proposition has been altered by it.

But what is it supposed to mean to say "If one proposition follows from another, thinking the second must involve thinking the first", since in the proposition "I am 170 cm tall" it isn't necessary to think of even a single one of the negative statements of height that follow from it?

"The cross is situated thus on the straight line: $|\!\!-\!\!-\!\!-\!\!-\!\!\times\!\!-\!\!|$"– "*So* it is between the strokes".

"It is $16\frac{1}{2}°$ here" – "So it is certainly more than $15°$"

Incidentally, if you are surprised that one proposition can follow from another even though one doesn't think of the former while thinking of the latter, you should consider that p $\mathbf{v}$ q follows from p, and I certainly don't think all propositions of the form p $\mathbf{v}$ ξ while I am thinking p.

The whole idea that a proposition has to be thought along with any proposition that entails it rests on a false, psychologising notion. We must concern ourselves only with what is contained in the signs and the rules.

If the criterion for p's following from q consists in "thinking of p being involved in thinking of q" then while thinking of the proposition "in this box there are 10^5 grains of sand", you are thinking also of the 10^5 sentences "In this box there is one grain of sand" ". . . 2 grains of sand", etc. etc. What's the criterion here for the thought of one proposition's being involved in the thought of another?

And what about a proposition like "There is a patch (F) between the limits AA"?

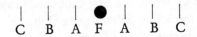

Doesn't it follow from that that F is also between BB and CC and so on? Don't infinitely many propositions follow from a single one? Does that make it infinitely significant? – From the proposition "There is a patch between the limits AA" there follow as many propositions of the type "there is a patch between the limits BB" as I write out – and no more than I write out. Similarly, from p there follow as many propositions of the form p ∨ ξ as I write out (or utter etc.).

(A proof by induction proves as many propositions of the form . . . as I write out.)

3

The case of infinitely many propositions following from a single one

Is it impossible that infinitely many propositions should follow from a single one – in the sense, that is, that we might go on ad infinitum constructing new propositions from a single one according to a rule?

Suppose that we wrote the first thousand propositions of the series in conjunction. Wouldn't the sense of this product necessarily approximate more closely to the sense of our first proposition than the product of the first hundred propositions? Wouldn't we obtain an ever closer approximation to the first proposition the further we extended the product? And wouldn't that show that it can't be the case that from one proposition infinitely many others follow, since I can't understand even the product with 10^{10} terms and yet I understood the proposition to which the product with 10^{100} terms is a closer approximation than the one with 10^{10} terms?

We imagine, perhaps, that the general proposition is an abbreviated expression of the product. But what is there in the product to abbreviate? It doesn't contain anything superfluous.

If we need an example of infinitely many propositions following from a single one, perhaps the simplest is the way in which "a is red" entails the negation of all propositions that ascribe a different colour to a. The negative propositions are certainly not contained in the thought of the single positive one. Of course we might say that we don't distinguish infinitely many shades of colour; but the question is whether the number of shades of colour we distinguish has anything at all to do with the complexity of the first sentence: is it more or less complex the more or fewer colours we distinguish?

Wouldn't this be what we'd have to say: it's only when a proposition exists that it follows from it. It's only when we have constructed ten propositions following from the first one that ten propositions do follow from it.

I want to say that one proposition doesn't follow from another until it is confronted with it. The "etc ad infinitum" indicates only the possiblity of constructing propositions following from the first; it doesn't yield a definite number of such propositions.

So mightn't I simply say: it is *because* it is impossible to write out infinitely many propositions (i.e. to say that is a piece of nonsense) that infinitely many propositions don't follow from a single proposition.

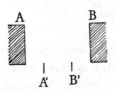

What about the proposition "the surface is white from A to B"? It does follow from it that the surface is white from A' to B'. It needn't be a seen patch of white that is in question; and certainly the inference from the first proposition to the second is often drawn. Someone says to me "I have painted the patch white from A to B" and then I say "so it's certainly painted white from A' to B'".

It must be possible to say a priori that F(A'B') *would* follow from F(AB).

If the lines A' and B' exist, then the second proposition certainly does follow from the first (in that case the compositeness is already there in the first proposition); but in that case it is only as many propositions as correspond to its compositeness that follow from the first proposition (and so never infinitely many).

"The whole is white, therefore a part bounded by such and such a line is white." "The whole *was* white, so that part of it also *was* white even if I didn't then perceive it bounded within it."

"A surface seen as undivided has no parts."
But let's imagine a ruler laid against the surface, so that the

appearance we are presented with is first ⬜⬜⬜⬜⬜ and then ⬜⬜⬜⬜ and then ⬜⬜⬜⬜⬜ . It doesn't at all follow from the first strip's being entirely white that in the second and the third everything except the graduating lines is white.

"If you hit the target anywhere within the circle, you have won."
"I think you will hit the target somewhere within the circle."
Someone might ask about the first proposition: how do you know? Have you tried *all* possible places? And the answer would have to be: that isn't a proposition at all, it is a general *stipulation*.

The inference doesn't go like this: "If the shot hits the target anywhere, you have won. You have hit the target *there*, so you have won". For where is this *there*? Is it marked out in any way other than by the shot – say by a circle? And was that already there on the target beforehand? If not, then the target has changed; if so, it must have been foreseen as a possible place to hit. We should rather say: "You have hit the target, so . . . "

The place on the target does not necessarily have to be given by a mark on the target, like a circle. For there are always descriptions like "nearer the centre", "nearer the edge", "on the right side at the top", etc. Wherever the target is hit such descriptions *must* always be possible. (But there are not "infinitely many" such descriptions.)

Does it make sense to say: "But if you hit the target, you must hit it *somewhere*" or "Wherever he hits the surface it won't be a surprise, we won't have to say 'I didn't expect that. I didn't know there was such a place'?" What that means is that it can't be a geometrical surprise.

What sort of proposition is: "On this strip you may see all shades of grey between black and white"? Here it looks at first glance as if we're talking about infinitely many shades.

Indeed, we are apparently confronted here by the paradox that we can, of course, only distinguish a finite number of shades, and naturally the distinction between them isn't infinitely slight, and yet we see a continuous transition.

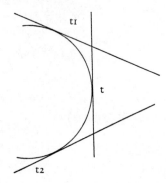

It is just as impossible to conceive of a particular grey as being one of the infinitely many greys between black and white as it is to conceive of a tangent t as being one of the infinitely many transitional stages in going from t_1 to t_2. If I see a ruler roll around the circle from t_1 to t_2 I see – if its motion is continuous – none of the intermediate positions in the sense in which I see t when the tangent is at rest; or else I see only a finite number of such positions. But if in such a case I appear to infer a particular case from a general proposition, then the general proposition is never derived from experience, and the proposition isn't a real proposition.

If, e.g., I say "I saw the ruler move from t_1 to t_2 *therefore* I must have seen it at t" this doesn't give us a valid logical inference. That is, if what I mean is that the ruler must have *appeared* to me at t and so, if I'm talking about the position in visual space, then it doesn't in the least follow from the premise. But if I'm talking about the physical ruler, then of course it's possible for the ruler to have skipped over position t and yet for the phenomenon in visual space to have remained continuous.

4

Can an experience show that one proposition follows from another?

The only essential point is that we cannot say that it was through experience we were made aware of an extra application of grammar. For in making that statement we would have to describe the application, and even if this is the first time I have realised that the description is true I must have been able to understand it even before the experience.

It is the old question: how far can one now speak of an experience that one is not now having?

What I cannot foresee I can not foresee.

And what I can now speak of, I can now speak of independently of what I *can't* now speak of.

Logic just is always complex.

"How can I know everything that's going to follow?" What I can know then, I can also know now.

But are there general rules of grammar, or only rules for general signs?

What kind of thing in chess (or some other game) would count as a general rule or a particular rule? Every rule is general.

Still, there is one kind of generality in the rule that p **v** q follows from p and a different kind in the rule that every proposition of the form p, $\sim\sim$ p, $\sim\sim\sim\sim$ p . . . follows from p.q. But isn't the generality of the rule for the knight's move different from the generality of the rule for the beginning of a game?

Is the word "rule" altogether ambiguous? So should we talk only about particular cases of rules, and stop talking about rules in general, and indeed about languages in general?

"If $F_1(a)$ [= a has the colour F_1] entails $\sim F_2(a)$ then the possibility of the second proposition must have been provided for in the grammar of the first (otherwise how could we call F_1 and F_2 colours?)

"If the second proposition as it were turned up without being expected by the first it couldn't possibly follow from it."

"The first proposition must acknowledge the second as its consequence. Or rather they must be united in a single grammar which remains the same before and after the inference."

(Here it is very difficult not to tell fairy tales about symbolic processes, just as elsewhere it is hard not to tell fairy tales about psychological processes. But everything is simple and familiar (there is nothing new to be discovered). That is the terrible thing about logic, that its extraordinary difficulty lies in the fact that nothing must be constructed, and everything is already present familiar.)

"No proposition is a consequence of p unless p acknowledges it as its consequence."

Whether a proposition entails another proposition must be clear from the grammar of the proposition and from that alone. It cannot be the result of any insight into a new sense: only of an insight into the old sense. It is not possible to construct a new proposition that follows from the old one which could not have been constructed (perhaps without knowing whether it was true or false) when the old one was constructed. If a new sense were discovered and followed from the first proposition, wouldn't that mean that that proposition had altered its sense?

II GENERALITY

The proposition "The circle is in the square" is in a certain sense inde-pendent of the assignment of a particular position. (In a certain sense it is totally unconnected.)

I would like to say: a general picture like | o | does not have the same metric as a particular one.

In the general sign "|o|" the distances play no greater part than they do in the sign "aRb".

The drawing | o | can be looked on as a representation of the "general case". It is as if it were not in a measurable space: the distances between the circle and the lines are of no consequence. The picture, taken thus, is not seen as occurring in the same system as when one sees it as the representation of a particular position of the circle between the lines. Or rather, taken thus, it is a part of a different calculus. The rules that govern variables are not the same as those that govern their particular values.

"How do you know he is in the room?" "Because I put him in and there is no way he can get out." Then your knowledge of the general fact that he is somewhere in the room has the same multi-plicity as that reason.

Let us take the particular case of the general state of affairs of the cross being between the end-lines.

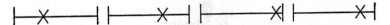

Each of these cases, for instance, has its own individuality. Is there any way in which this individuality enters into the sense of the general sentence? Obviously not.

'Being between the lines, or the walls' seems something simple and the particular positions (both the visual appearances and the positions established by measurement) seem quite independent of it.

That is, when we talk about the individual (seen) positions we appear to be talking about something quite different from the topic of the general proposition.

There is one calculus containing our general characterization and another containing the disjunction. If we say that the cross is between the lines we don't have any disjunction ready to take the place of the general proposition.

If we consider a general proposition like "the circle is in the square" it appears time and again that the assignment of a position in the square is not (at least so far as visual space is concerned) a more precise specification of the statement that the circle is *in the square* any more than a statement of the colour of a material is a more precise specification of a statement of its hardness. – Rather, "in the square" appears a complete specification which in itself does not admit of any more precise description. Now of course the statements about the circle are not related to each other like the statements about colour and hardness, and yet that feeling is not baseless.

The grammatical rules for the terms of the general proposition must contain the multiplicity of possible particular cases provided for by the proposition. What isn't contained in the rules isn't provided for.

All these patterns might be the same state of affairs distorted. (Imagine the two white strips and the middle black strip as elastic.)

Does fa's following from (x).fx mean that a is mentioned in

(x).fx? Yes, if the general proposition is meant in such a way that its verification consists in an enumeration.

If I say "there is a black circle in the square", it always seems to me that here again I have something simple in mind, and don't have to think of different possible positions or sizes of the circle. And yet one may say: if there is a circle in the square, it must be somewhere and have some size. But in any case there cannot be any question of my thinking in advance of *all* the possible positions and sizes. – It is rather that in the first proposition I seem to put them through a kind of sieve so that "circle in a square" corresponds to a single impression, which doesn't take any account of the *where* etc., as if it were (against all appearance) something only physically, and not logically, connected with the first state of affairs.

The point of the expression "sieve" is this. If I look at a landscape or something similar through a glass which transmits only the distinction between brightness and darkness and not the distinctions between colours, such a glass can be called a sieve; and if one thinks of the square as being looked at through a glass which transmits only the distinction "circle in the square or not in the square" and no distinction between positions or sizes of the circle, here too we might speak of a sieve.

I would like to say that in the proposition "there is a circle in the square" the particular positions are not mentioned at all. In the picture I don't see the position, I disregard it, as if the distances from the sides of the square were elastic and their lengths of no account.

Indeed, can't the patch actually be moving in the square? Isn't that just a special case of being in the square? So in that case it wouldn't be true that the patch has to be in a particular position in the square if it is there at all.

I want to say that the patch seems to have a relation to the edge that is independent of its distance. – Almost as if I were using a geometry in which there is no such thing as distance, but only inside and outside. Looked at in this way, there is no doubt that the two pictures and are the same.

By itself the proposition "The patch is in the square" does no more than hold the patch in the square, as it were; it is only in this way that it limits the patch's freedom; within the square it allows it complete freedom. The proposition constructs a frame that limits the freedom of the patch but within the frame it leaves it free, that is, it *has nothing to do* with its position. For that to be so the proposition must have the logical nature of the frame (like a box enclosing the patch). And so it has, because I could explain the proposition to someone and set out the possibilities, quite independently of whether such a proposition is true or not, independently of a fact.

"Wherever the patch is in the square . . ." means "as long as it is in the square . . ." and here all that is meant is the freedom (lack of restraint) in the square, not a set of positions.

Of course between this freedom and the totality of possibilities, there is a logical similarity (formal analogy), and that is why the same words are often used in the two cases ("all", "every", etc.).

"No degrees of brightness below this one hurt my eyes." Test the type of generality.

"All points on this surface are white." How do you verify that? – then I will know what it means.

6

The proposition "The circle is in the square" is not a disjunction of cases.

If I say the patch is in the square, I know – and must know – that it may have various possible positions. I know too that I couldn't give a definite number of all such positions. I do not know in advance how many positions "I could distinguish". – And trying it out won't tell me what I want to know here either.

The darkness veiling the possible positions etc. is the current logical situation, just as dim lighting is a particular sort of lighting.

Here it always seems as if we can't quite get an overall view of a logical form because we don't know how many or what possible positions there are for the patch in the square. But on the other hand we do know, because we aren't surprised by any of them when they turn up.

Of course "position of the circle in this square" isn't a concept which particular positions fall under as objects. You couldn't discover objects and ascertain that they were positions of the circle in the square which you didn't know about beforehand.

Incidentally, the centre and other special positions in the circle are quite analogous to the primary colours on the colour scale. (This comparison might be pursued with profit.)

Space is as it were a single possibility; it doesn't consist of several possibilities.

So if I hear that the book is somewhere on the table, and then find it in a particular position, it isn't possible for me to be surprised and say "oh, I didn't know that there was this position"; and yet I hadn't foreseen this particular position i.e. envisaged it in advance as a particular possibility. It is physical, not logical possibilities that take me by surprise!

But what is the difference between "the book is somewhere on the table" and "the event will occur sometime in the future?" Obviously the difference is that in the one case we have a sure method of verifying whether the book is on the table, while in the other case there is no such method. If a particular event were supposed to occur at one of the infinitely many bisections of a line, or better, if it were supposed to occur when we cut the line at a single point, not further specified, and then waited a minute at that point, that statement would be as senseless as the one about the infinite future.

Suppose I stated a disjunction of so many positions that it was impossible for me to see a single position as distinct from all those given; would *that* disjunction be the general proposition $(\exists x).fx$? Wouldn't it be a kind of pedantry to continue to refuse to recognize the disjunction as the general proposition? Or is there an essential distinction, and is the disjunction totally unlike the general proposition?

What so strikes us is that the one proposition is so complicated and the other so simple. Or is the simple one only an abbreviation for the more complicated one?

What then is the criterion for the general proposition, for the circle's being in the square? Either, nothing that has anything to do with a set of positions (or sizes) or something that deals with a finite number of such positions.

If one says that the patch A is somewhere between the limits B and C, isn't it obviously possible to describe or portray a number of positions of A between B and C in such a way that I see the succession of all the positions as a continuous transition? And in that case isn't the disjunction of all those N positions the very proposition that A is somewhere between B and C?

But what are these N pictures really like? It is clear that a picture must not be visually discernible from its immediate successor, or the transition will be discontinuous.

The positions whose succession I see as a continuous transition are positions which are not in visual space.

How is the extension of the concept "lying between" determined? Because it has to be laid down in advance what possibilities belong to this concept. As I say, it cannot be a surprise that I call *that* too "lying between". Or: how can the rules for the expression "lie between" be given when I can't enumerate the cases of lying between? Of course that itself must be a characteristic of the meaning of the expression.

Indeed if we wanted to explain the word to someone we wouldn't try to do so by indicating *all particular instances*, but by showing him one or two such instances and intimating in some way that it wasn't a question of the particular case.

It is not only that the enumeration of positions is unnecessary: in the nature of things there can be no question of such an enumeration here.

Saying "The circle is either between the two lines or *here*" (where "here" is a place between the lines) obviously means no more than "The circle is between the two lines", and the rider "or here" is superfluous. You will say: the "here" is already included in the "somewhere". But that is strange, since it isn't mentioned in it.

There is a particular difficulty when the signs don't appear to say what the thought grasps, or the words don't say what the thought appears to grasp.

As when we say "this theorem holds of all numbers" and think that in our thought we have comprehended all numbers like apples in a box.

But now it might be asked: how can I know in advance which propositions entail this general proposition, if I can't specify the propositions?

But can one say "We can't say which propositions entail this proposition"? That sounds like: we don't know. But of course that isn't how it is. I can indeed say, and say in advance, propositions that entail it. "Only not *all* of them." But that just has no meaning.

There is just the general proposition and particular propositions (not *the* particular propositions). But the general proposition does not enumerate particular propositions. In that case what characterizes it as general, and what shows that it doesn't simply comprise the particular propositions we are speaking of in this particular case?

It cannot be characterized by its instantiations, because however many we enumerate, it could still be mistaken for the product of the cited cases. Its generality, therefore, lies in a property (a grammatical property) of the variables.

7

The inadequacy of the Frege-Russell notation for generality

The real difficulty lies in the concept of "(∃n)" and in general of "(∃x)". The original source of this notation is the expression of our word-language: "There is a . . . with such and such properties". And here what replaces the dots is something like "book from my library" or "thing (body) in this room", "word in this letter", etc. We think of objects that we can go through one after the other. As so often happens a process of sublimation turned this form into "there is an object such that . . ." and here too people imagined originally the objects of the world as like 'objects' in the room (the tables, chairs, books, etc.), although it is clear that in many cases the grammar of this "(∃x), etc." is not at all the same as the grammar of the primitive case which serves as a paradigm. The discrepancy between the original picture and the one to which the notation is now applied becomes particularly palpable when a proposition like "there are two circles in this square" is rendered as "there is no object that has the property of being a circle in this square without being the circle a or the circle b" or "there are not three objects that have the property of being a circle in this square". The proposition "there are only two things that are circles in this square" (construed on the model of the proposition "there are only two men who have climbed this mountain") sounds crazy, with good reason. That is to say, nothing is gained by forcing the proposition "there are two circles in this square" into that form; it only helps to conceal that we haven't cleared up the grammar of the proposition. But at the same time the Russellian notation here gives an appearance of exactitude which makes people believe the problems are solved by putting the proposition into the Russellian form. (This is no less dangerous than using the word "probably" without further investigation into the use of the word in this particular case. For understandable reasons the word "probably", too, is connected with an idea of exactitude.)

"One of the four legs of this table doesn't hold","There are Englishmen with black hair", "There is a speck on this wall" "The two pots have the same weight", "There are the same number of words on each of the two pages". In all these cases in the Russellian notation the "(∃...)..." is used, and each time with a different grammar. The point I want to make is that nothing much is gained by translating such a sentence from word-language into Russellian notation.

It makes sense to say "write down any cardinal number" but not "write down all cardinal numbers". "There is a circle in the square" [(∃x).fx)] makes sense, but not ~∃x. ~ fx: "all circles are in the square." "There is a red circle on a background of a different colour" makes sense, but not "there isn't a background-colour other than red that doesn't have a red circle on it."

"In this square there is a black circle". If this proposition has the form "(∃x).x is a black circle in a square" what sort of thing is it that has the property of being a black circle (and so can also have the property of not being a black circle)? Is it a place in the square? But then there is no proposition "(x).x is a black . . ." On the other hand the proposition could mean "There is a speck in the square that is a black circle". How is that proposition verified? Well, we take the different specks in the square in turn and investigate whether they are quite black and circular. But what kind of proposition is "There isn't a speck in the square"? For if in the former case the 'x' in '(∃x)' meant 'speck in the square', then though "(∃x).fx" is a possible proposition both "(∃x)" and "~(∃x)" are not. Or again, I might ask: what sort of thing is it that has (or does not have) the property of being a speck in the square?

And if we can say "There is a speck in the square" does it then also make sense to say "All specks are in the square"? All *which*?

Ordinary language says "In this square there is a red circle"; the Russellian notation says "There is an object which is a red circle in this square". That form of expression is obviously modelled on "There is a substance which shines in the dark" "There is a circle in this square which is red". – Perhaps even the expression "there is" is misleading. "There is" really means the same as "Among these circles there is one . . ." or ". . . there exists one . . .".

So if we go as far as we can in the direction of the Russellian mode of expression and say "In this square there is a place where there is a red circle", that really means, among these places there is one where . . . etc.

(In logic the most difficult standpoint is that of sound common sense. For in order to justify its view it demands the whole truth; it will not help by the slightest concession or construction.)

The correct expression of this sort of generality is therefore the expression of ordinary language "There is a circle in the square", which simply leaves the position of the circle *open* (leaves it *undecided*). ("Undecided" is a correct expression, since there just *has not been* any decision.)

8

Criticism of my former view of generality

My view about general propositions was that $(\exists x) . \varphi x$ is a logical sum and that though its terms aren't enumerated *here*, they are capable of being enumerated (from the dictionary and the grammar of language).

For if they can't be enumerated we don't have a logical sum. (A rule, perhaps, for the construction of logical sums).

Of course, the explanation of $(\exists x) . \varphi x$ as a logical sum and of $(x) . \varphi x$ as a logical product is indefensible. It went with an incorrect notion of logical analysis in that I thought that some day the logical product for a particular $(x) . \varphi x$ would be found. – Of course it is correct that $(\exists x) . \varphi x$ behaves in some ways like a logical sum and $(x) . \varphi x$ like a product; indeed for *one* use of words "all" and "some" my old explanation is correct, – for instance for "all the primary colours occur in this picture" or "all the notes of the C major scale occur in this theme". But for cases like "all men die before they are 200 years old" my explanation is not correct. The way in which $(\exists x) . \varphi x$ behaves like a logical sum is expressed by its following from φa and from $\varphi a \mathbf{v} \varphi b$, i.e. in the rules

$$(\exists x) . \varphi x : \varphi a . = . \varphi a \qquad \text{and}$$
$$(\exists x) . \varphi x : \varphi a \ \mathbf{v} \ \varphi b . = . \varphi a \ \mathbf{v} \ \varphi b$$

From these rules Russell's fundamental laws follow as tautologies:

$$\varphi x . \supset . (\exists z) . \varphi z$$
$$\varphi x \ \mathbf{v} \ \varphi y . \supset . (\exists z) . \varphi z$$

For $(\exists x) . \varphi x$ we need also the rules:

$$(\exists x) . \varphi x \ \mathbf{v} \ \psi x . = . (\exists x) . \varphi x . \mathbf{v} . (\exists x) . \psi x$$
$$(\exists x,y) \ \varphi x . \psi y . \mathbf{v} . (\exists x) . \varphi x . \psi x . = . (\exists x) . \varphi x : (\exists x) . \psi x .$$

Every such rule is an expression of the analogy between $(\exists x) . \varphi x$ and a logical sum.

Incidentally, we really could introduce a notation for $(\exists x).\varphi x$ in which it was replaced by a sign "$\varphi r \vee \varphi s \vee \varphi t \ldots$" which could then be used in calculation like a logical sum; but we would have to provide rules for reconverting this notation at any time into the "$(\exists x).\varphi x$" notation and thus distinguishing the sign "$\varphi a \vee \varphi b \vee \varphi c \ldots$" from the sign for a logical sum. The point of this notation could simply be to enable us to calculate more easily with $(\exists x).\varphi x$ in certain cases.

If I am right, there is no concept "pure colour"; the proposition "A's colour is a pure colour" simply means "A is red, or yellow, or blue, or green". "This hat belongs either to A or B or C" is not the same proposition as "This hat belongs to a person in this room" even when in fact only A, B and C are in the room, for that itself is something that has to be added. – "On this surface there are two pure colours" *means*: on this surface there is red and yellow, or red and green, or . . . etc.

If this means I can't say "there are 4 pure colours", still the pure colours and the number 4 are somehow connected with each other and that must express itself in some way. – For instance, I may say "on this surface I see 4 colours: yellow, blue, red, green".

The generality notation of our ordinary language grasps the logical form even more superficially than I earlier believed. In this respect it is comparable with the subject-predicate form.

Generality is as ambiguous as the subject-predicate form.

There are as many different "alls" as there are different "ones".

So it is no use using the word "all" for clarification unless we know its grammar in this particular case.

9

The explanation of generality by examples

Let us think how we explain the concept plant. We show someone several objects and say they are plants; then he points to
another object and asks "is that a plant too?" and we reply "yes,
that too" etc. I would once have said that he has now seen in
what he has been shown the concept 'plant' – the common element – and that he does not see the examples used in the explanation in the same way when he sees the concept in them as when he
views them just as representatives of a particular shape and colour
or the like. (Just as I also used to say that when he understands
variables as variables he sees something in them which he doesn't
see in the sign for the particular case). But the notion of "seeing in"
is taken from the case in which I see a figure like |||| differently
"phrased". In that case, I really do see different figures, but in a
different sense; and what these have in common, apart from their
similarity, is their being caused by the same physical pattern.

But this explanation cannot be applied without further ado to
the case of the understanding of a variable or of the examples
illustrating the concept "plant". For suppose we really had seen
something in them that we don't see in plants that are shown only
for their own sake, the question remains whether this, or any other,
picture can entitle us to apply them as variables. I might have
shown someone the plants by way of explanation and given him
in addition a drug causing him to see the examples in the special
way. (Just as it would be possible that a drunken man might
always see a group like |||| as ||| |). And this would give the ex-
planation of the concept in an unambiguous manner, and the
specimens exhibited and the accompanying gestures would
communicate to anyone who understood just *this* picture. But
that is not the way it is. – It may well be true that someone who
sees a sign like |||||| as a numeral for 6 sees it differently (sees
something different in it) from someone who views it only as a

sign for "some", since he fixes his attention on something different; but what matters is the system of rules governing the signs, and it isn't seeing the signs in a particular manner that is the essence of understanding.

It would be possible to say "now I don't see it as a rose, but as a plant".
Or "now I see it only as a rose, and no longer as *this* rose".
"I see the patch merely in the square and no longer in a specific position."

The mental process of understanding is of no interest to us (any more than the mental process of an intuition).

"Still, there's no doubt that someone who understands the examples as arbitrary cases chosen to illustrate the concept doesn't understand the same as a man who regards them as a definitely bounded enumeration." Quite right, but *what* does the first man understand that the second doesn't? Well, in the things he is shown he sees only *examples* to illustrate certain features; he doesn't think that I am showing him the things for their own sake as well. –

I would like to call the one class "logically bounded" and the other "logically unbounded".

Yes, but is it really true that he sees only these features in the things? In a leaf, say, does he see only what is common to all leaves? That would be as if he saw everything else blank like an uncompleted form with the essential features ready printed. (But the function "f(. . .)" is just such a form.)

But what sort of a process is it when someone shows me several different things as examples of a concept to get me to see what is common to them, and when I look for it and then actually see it? He may *draw my attention* to what is common. – But by doing this does he make me *see* the object differently? Perhaps so; for surely I may take a special look at one of the parts, when otherwise I would have seen the whole with equal clarity. But this seeing is not the understanding of the concept. For what we see isn't something with an *empty* argument place.

One might also ask: Does a man who regards the sign "||| . . ." as a sign for the concept of number (in contrast with "||||" to denote 3) see the first group of lines differently from the second? Even if he does see it differently (perhaps, as it were, more blurred) does he *see* there anything like the essence of the concept of number? Wouldn't that mean that he would actually have to be unable to distinguish "||| . . ." and "|||| . . ." from each other? (As indeed he would, if I had given him some drug that made him see the *concept*.)

For if I say: by giving us a few examples he makes us see the common element in them and disregard the rest, that really means that the rest falls into the background, as it were becomes paler (or altogether disappears – why not?) and "the common element", say the oval shape, remains alone in the foreground.

But that isn't the way it is. Apart from anything else, the multiplicity of examples would be no more than a mechanical device, and once I had seen what I was supposed to, I could see it in a single example too. (As indeed '$(\exists x).fx$' itself contains only *one* example.)

So it is the rules governing the example that make it an example.

But by now at any rate, if someone says to me something like "make an egg shape" the bare concept word without any illustration suffices to make itself understood (and the past history of this understanding is of no interest to us): and I do not want to say that when I understand the command (and the word "egg") I see the concept of an egg before my mind's eye.

When I make an application of the concept "egg" or "plant" there certainly isn't some general picture in front of my mind before I do so, and when I hear the word "plant" it isn't that there comes before my mind a picture of a certain object which I then describe as a plant. No, I make the application as it were spontaneously. Still, in the case of certain applications I might say "No, I didn't mean that by 'plant' ", or, "Yes, I meant that too". But does that mean that these pictures came before my mind and that mentally I expressly rejected and admitted them? – And yet that is what it looks like, when I say: "Yes, I meant all those things, but not *that*." But one might then ask: "But did you foresee all those cases?" and then the answer might be "yes" or "no, but I imagined there must be something between this form and that one" or the like. But commonly at that moment I did not draw any bounds, and they can only be produced in a roundabout way after reflection. For instance, I say "Bring me a flower about so big"; he brings one and I say: Yes, that is the size I meant. Perhaps I do remember a picture which came before my mind, but it isn't that that makes the flower that has been brought acceptable. What I am doing is making an application of the picture, and the application was not anticipated.

The only thing of interest to us is the *exact* relationship between the example and the behaviour that accords with it.

The example is the point of departure for further calculation.

Examples are decent signs, not rubbish or hocus-pocus.

The only thing that interests us is the geometry of the mechanism. (That means, the grammar of its description.)

But how does it come out in our rules, that the instances of fx we are dealing with are not essentially closed classes? – Only indeed in the generality of the general rule. – How does it come out that they don't have the same significance for the calculus as a closed group of primitive signs (like the names of the 6 basic colours)? How else could it come out except in the rules given for them? – Suppose that in some game I am allowed to help myself to as many pieces as I like of a certain kind, while only a limited number of another kind is available; or suppose a game is unbounded in time but spatially bounded, or something similar. The case is exactly the same. The distinction between the two different types of piece in the game must be laid down in the rules; they will say about the one type that you can take as many pieces as you want of that kind. And I mustn't look for another more restrictive expression of that rule.

That means that the expression for the unboundedness of the particular instances in question will be a general expression; there cannot be some other expression in which the other unconsidered instances appear in some shadowy way.

It is clear that I do not recognize any logical sum as a definition of the proposition "the cross is between the lines". And that says everything that is to be said.

There is one thing I always want to say to clarify the distinction between instances that are offered as examples for a concept and instances that make up a definite closed group in the grammar. Suppose, after explaining "a, b, c, d are books", someone says "Now bring me a book". If the person brings a book which isn't one of the ones shown him he can still be said to have acted correctly in accordance with the rule given. But if what had been said was "a, b, c, d, are my books. – Bring me one of my books", it would have been incorrect to bring a different one and he would have been told "I told you that a, b, c, d are my books". In the first case it isn't against the rule to bring an object other than those named, in the second case it is. But if in the order you named only a, b, c, and d, and yet you regarded the behaviour f(e) as obeying the order, doesn't that mean that by F(a, b, c, d, . . .) you meant F(a, b, c, d, e) after all? Again, how are these orders distinct from each other if the same thing obeys both of them? – But f(g) too would have been in accordance with the order and not only f(e). Right, then your first order must have meant F(a, b, c, d, e, g) etc. Whatever you bring me is something I could have included in a disjunction. So if we construct the disjunction of all the cases we actually use, how would it differ syntactically from the general proposition? For we can't say: by the fact that the general proposition is also made true by r (which doesn't occur in the disjunction), because that doesn't distinguish the general proposition from a disjunction which contains r. (And every other similar answer too is impossible.) But it will make sense to say: F(a, b, c, d, e) is the disjunction of all the cases we have actually used, but there are also other cases (we won't of course, mention any) that make true the general proposition "F(a, b, c, d, . . .)". And here of course we can't put the general proposition in place of F(a, b, c, d, e,).

It is, by the way, a very important fact that the parenthesis in the previous paragraph "and every other similar answer too is impossible" is senseless, because though you can give as instances of a generalization different particular cases, you can't give different variables because the variables r, s, t don't differ in their meaning.

Of course one couldn't say that when we do f(d) we don't obey f(∃) in the same way as we obey a disjunction containing f(d), because f(∃) = f(∃) ∨ f(d). If you give someone the order "bring me some plant or other, or this one" (giving him a picture of it), he will simply discard the picture and say to himself "since any one will do, the picture doesn't matter". By contrast, we won't simply discard the picture if we are given it plus five others and the order to bring one of these six plants. (So what matters is *which* disjunction contains the particular command.) And you wouldn't be guided in the same way by the order "f(a) **v** f(b) **v** f(c)" as by the order "f(∃)" (= f(∃) **v** f(c)), even if in each case you do f(c). – The picture f(c) sinks into f(∃). (It is no good sitting in a boat, if you and it are under water and sinking). Someone may be inclined to say: "Suppose you do f(c) on the command f(∃); in that case f(c) might have been expressly permitted and then how would the general command have differed from a disjunction?" – But if the permission had occurred in a disjunction with the general sentence, you couldn't have *appealed* to it.

So is this how it is: "bring me a flower" can never be replaced by an order of the form "bring me a or b or c", but must always be "bring me a or b or c *or some other flower*"?

But why does the general sentence behave so indeterminately when every case which actually occurs is something I could have described in advance?

But even that seems to me not to get to the heart of the matter; because what matters, I believe, isn't really the infinity of the possibilities, but a kind of indeterminacy. Indeed, if I were asked how many possibilities a circle in the visual field has of being within a particular square, I could neither name a finite number, nor say that there were infinitely many (as in a Euclidean plane). Here, although we don't ever come to an end, the series isn't endless in the way in which | 1, ξ, ξ + 1 | is.

Rather, no end to which we come is really the end; that is, I could always say: I don't understand why these should be all the possibilities. – And doesn't that just mean that it is senseless to speak of "all the possibilities"? So enumeration *doesn't touch* the concepts "plant" and "egg" at all.

And although we say that we could always have forseen f(a) as a possible particular execution of the order, still we didn't in fact ever do so. – But even if I do foresee the possibility f(a) and expressly include it in my order, it gets lost beside the general proposition, because I can see from the general proposition itself that this particular case is permitted; it isn't just from its being expressly permitted in the order that I see this. If the general proposition is there, the addition of the particular case isn't any extra use to me (that is, it doesn't make the command more explicit). Indeed it was only the general proposition that gave me the justification for placing this particular case beside it. What my whole argument is aiming at, is that someone might believe that the addition of the particular case supersedes the – as it were blurred – generality of the proposition, that you could say "we don't need it any more, now we have the particular case." Yes, but say I admit that the reason I put in the particular case is that it agrees with the general proposition! Or suppose I admit that I recognize that f(a) is a particular case of f(∃)! For I can't say: that just means that f(∃) is a disjunction with f(a) as one of its terms; for if that is so, the disjunction must be capable of being stated, and f(∃) must be defined as a disjunction. There would be no difficulty in giving such a definition, but it wouldn't correspond to the use of f(∃) that we have in mind. It isn't that the disjunction always leaves something over; it is that it just doesn't touch the essential thing in generality, and even if it is added to it it depends on the general proposition for its justification.

First I command f(∃); he obeys the order and does f(a). Then I think that I could just as well have given him the command "f(∃) ∨ f(a)". (For I knew in advance that f(a) obeyed the order f(∃) and to command him f(∃) ∨ f(a) would come to the same.) In that case when he obeyed the order he would have been acting on the disjunction "do something or f(a)". And if he obeys the order by doing f(a) isn't it immaterial what else is disjoined with f(a)? If he does f(a) in any case, the order is obeyed whatever the alternative is.

I would also like to say: in grammar nothing is supplementary, no stipulations come *after* others, everything is there simultaneously.

Thus I can't even say that I first gave the command f(∃) and only later realised that f(a) was a case of f(∃); at all events my order was and remained f(∃) and I added f(a) to it in the knowledge that f(a) was in accordance with f(∃). And the stipulation that f(a) is in accordance with f(∃) presupposes the sense that belongs to the proposition f(∃) if it is taken as an independent unit and not defined as replaceable by a disjunction. And my proposition "at all events my order was and remained f(∃) etc." only means that I didn't replace the general order by a disjunction.

Suppose I give the order p **v** f(a), and the addressee doesn't clearly understand the first part of the order but does understand that the order goes " . . . **v** f(a)". He might then do f(a) and say "I know for certain that I've obeyed the command, even though I didn't understand the first part". And that too is how I imagine it when I say that the other alternative doesn't matter. But in that case he didn't obey the order *that was given*, but simply treated it as "f(a)!" One might ask: if someone does f(a) at the command "f(∃) **v** f(a)" is he obeying the order because (i.e. in so far as) the order is of the form ξ **v** f(a), or because f(∃) **v** f(a) = f(∃)? If you understand f(∃) and therefore know that f(∃) **v** f(a) = f(∃), then by doing f(a) you are obeying f(∃) even if I write it "f(∃) **v** f(a)" because you can see *none the less* that f(a) is a case of f(∃). And now someone might object: if you see that Fa is a case of F(∃) that just means that f(a) is contained disjunctively in f(∃), and therefore that f(∃) is defined *by means of* f(a). The remaining parts of the disjunction – he will have to say – don't concern me because the terms I see are the only ones I now need. – By explaining 'that f(a) is an instance of f(∃)' you have said no more than that f(a) occurs in f(∃) alongside certain other terms." – But that is precisely what we don't mean. It isn't as if our stipulation was an *incomplete definition* of f(∃);

for that would mean that a complete definition was *possible*. That would be the disjunction which would make the addition "∨ f(∃)" as it were ridiculous, since it would only be the enumerated instances which concerned us. But according to our idea of f(∃), the stipulation that f(a) is a case of f(∃) is not an incomplete definition of f(∃); it is not a definition of f(∃) at all. That means that I don't approximate to the sense of f(∃) by multiplying the number of cases in the disjunction; though the disjunction of the cases ∨ f(∃) is equivalent to f(∃), it is never equivalent to the disjunction of the cases alone; it is a totally different proposition.

What is said about an enumeration of individual cases cannot ever be a roundabout explanation of generality.

But can I give the rules of entailment that hold in this case? How do I know that (∃x).fx does follow from fa? After all I can't give *all* the propositions from which it follows. – But that isn't necessary; if (∃x).fx follows from fa, *that* at any rate was something that could be known in advance of any particular experience, and stated in the grammar.

I said "in advance of any experience it was possible to know and to state in the grammar that (∃x).fx follows from fa". But it should have been: '(∃x).fx follows from fa' is not a proposition (empirical proposition) of the language to which '(∃x).fx' and 'fa' belong; it is a rule laid down in their grammar.

We can of course set up a rule for the use of the variables, and the fact that in order to do so we need the same kind of variable does not make it pleonastic. For if we didn't use it, then the variable would be defined by the rules, and we don't assume that it can be defined, or that it must be defined (for sooner or later definitions come to an end).

This means only that – e.g. – the variable "x^2" is not an abbreviation (say for a logical sum), and that in our thought too there is only a sign for this multiplicity.

For suppose I had enumerated 7 particular instances and said "but their logical sum isn't the general proposition" that still wouldn't be enough; and I want to say further that no other number of instances yields the general proposition either. But in this rider once again I seem to go through an enumeration, in a kind of shadowy manner if not in actuality. But that is not the way it is, because the words that occur in the rider are quite different from the numerals.

"But how can I forbid a particular numeral to be inserted in such and such a place? I surely can't foresee what number someone will want to insert, so that I can forbid it". You can forbid it when it comes. – But here we are already speaking of the general concept of number!

But what makes a sign an expression of infinity? What gives the peculiar character that belongs to what we call infinite? I believe that it is like the case of a sign for an enormous number. For the characteristic of the infinite, conceived in this way, is its enormous size.

But there isn't anything that is an enumeration and yet not an enumeration; a generality that enumerates in a cloudy kind of way without really enumerating or enumerating to a determined limit.

The dots in "$1 + 1 + 1 + 1 \ldots$" are just the four dots: a sign, for which it must be possible to give certain rules. (The same rules, in fact, as for the sign "and so on ad inf.".) This sign does in a manner ape enumeration, but it isn't an enumeration. And that means that the rules governing it don't totally agree with those which govern an enumeration; they agree only up to a point.

There is no third thing between the particular enumeration and the general sign.

Of course the natural numbers have only been written down up to a certain highest point, let's say 10^{10}. Now what constitutes the *possibility* of writing down numbers that have not yet been written down? How odd is this feeling that they are all somewhere already in existence! (Frege said that before it was drawn a construction line was in a certain sense already there.)

The difficulty here is to fight off the thought that possibility is a kind of shadowy reality.

In the rules for the variable a a variable b may occur and so may particular numerals; but not any totality of numbers.

But now it seems as if this involved *denying the existence* of something in logic: perhaps generality itself, or what the dots indicate; whatever is incomplete (loose, capable of further extension) in the number series. And of course we may not and cannot deny the existence of anything. So how does this indeterminacy find expression? Roughly thus: if we introduce numbers substitutible for the variable a, we don't say of any of them that it is the last, or the highest.

But suppose someone asked us after the explanation of a form of calculation "and is 103 the last sign I can use?" What are we to answer? "No, it isn't the last" or "there isn't a last?" Mustn't I ask him in turn "If it isn't the last, what would come next?" And if he then says "104" I should say "Quite right, you can continue the series yourself".

Of an end to the possibility, I cannot speak at all.

(In philosophy the one thing we must guard against is waffle. A rule that can be applied in practice is always in order.)

It is clear that we can follow a rule like $|a, \xi, \xi + 1|$. I mean by really following the rule for constructing it without previously being able to write down the series. In that case it's the same as if I were to begin a series with a number like 1 and then say "now add 7, multiply by 5, take the square root of the result, and always apply this complex operation once again to the result". (That would be the rule $|1, \xi, \sqrt{(\xi + 7) \cdot 5}|$.)

The expression "and so on" is nothing but the *expression "and so on"* (nothing, that is, but a sign in a calculus which can't do more than have meaning via the rules that hold of it; which can't say more than it shows).
That is, the expression "and so on" does not harbour a secret power by which the series is continued without being continued.

Of course it doesn't contain *that*, you'll say, but still it contains the meaning of infinite continuation.

But we might ask: how does it happen that someone who now applies the general rule to a further number is still following *this* rule? How does it happen that no further rule was necessary to allow him to apply the general rule to this case in spite of the fact that this case was not mentioned in the general rule?

And so we are puzzled that we can't bridge over this abyss between the individual numbers and the general proposition.

"Can one imagine an empty space?" (Surprisingly, this is where this question belongs.)

It is one of the most deep rooted mistakes of philosophy to see possibility as a shadow of reality.

But on the other hand it can't be an error; not even if one calls the proposition such a shadow.

Here again, of course, there is a danger of falling into a *positivism*, of a kind which deserves a special name, and hence of course must be an error. For we must avoid accepting party lines or particular views of things; we must not disown anything that anyone has ever said on the topic, except where he himself had a particular view or theory.

For the sign "and so on", or some sign corresponding to it, is essential if we are to indicate endlessness – through the rules, of course, that govern such a sign. That is to say, we can distinguish the limited series "1, 1 + 1, 1 + 1 + 1" from the series "1, 1 + 1, 1 + 1 + 1 and so on". And this last sign and its use is no less essential for the calculus than any other.

What troubles me is that the "and so on" apparently has to occur also in the rules for the sign "and so on". For instance, 1, 1 + 1 and so on . = . 1, 1 + 1, 1 + 1 + 1 and so on, *and so on.*

But then isn't this simply the old point that we can describe language only from the outside? So that we can't expect by describing language to penetrate to depths deeper than language itself reveals: for it is by means of language that we describe language.

We might say: there's no occasion to be afraid of our using the expression "and so on" in a way that transcends the finite.

Moreover, the distinctive part of the grammar of "and so on" can't consist in rules connecting "and so on" with particular numerals (not "*the* particular numerals") – for these rules in turn mention some bit of a series – but in rules connecting "and so on" with "and so on".

The possibility of introducing further numbers. The difficulty seems to be that the numbers I've in fact introduced aren't a group that is essential and yet there is nothing to indicate that they are an *arbitrary* collection: *Out of all numbers just those numbers that happen to have been written down.*
(As if I had all the pieces of a game in a box and a chance selection from the box on the table beside it.
Or, as if one lot of numerals was traced in ink, while all of them are as it were drawn faintly in advance.)
But apart from the ones we happen to have used we have only the general form.
Isn't it here, by the way, – odd as it may sound – that the distinction between numerals and numbers comes?

Suppose, for example, I say "By 'cardinal number' I mean whatever results from 1 by continued addition of 1". The word "continued" doesn't represent a nebulous continuation of $1, 1 + 1$, $1 + 1 + 1$; on the contrary the sign "$1, 1 + 1, 1 + 1 + 1 \ldots$" is to be taken as perfectly exact; governed by definite rules which are different from those for "$1, 1 + 1, 1 + 1 + 1$", and not a substitute for a series "which cannot be written down".

In other words: we calculate with the sign "1, 1 + 1, 1 + 1 + 1 . . . " just as with the numerals, but in accordance with different rules.

But what is it then that we imagine? What is the mistake we make? What kind of thing do we take the sign "1, 1 + 1 . . ." to be? That is: where does what we think we see in this sign *really* occur? Something like when I say "he counted 1, 2, 3, 4 and so on up to 1000", where it would also be possible really to write down all the numbers.

What do we *see* "1, 1 + 1, 1 + 1 + 1 . . .." as?
As an inexact form of expression. The dots are like extra numerals indistinctly visible. It is as if we stopped writing numerals, because after all we can't write them all down, but as if they are there all right in a kind of box. Again, it is something like when I sing only the first notes of a melody distinctly, and then merely hint at the rest and let it taper off into nothing. (Or when in writing one writes only a few letters of a word distinctly and ends with an unarticulated line.) *In all such cases the 'indistinctly' has a 'distinctly' corresponding to it.*

I once said that there couldn't be both numbers *and* and the concept of number. And that is quite correct, if it means that a variable doesn't have the same relation to a number as the concept apple has to an apple (or the concept sword to Nothung).
On the other hand, *a number-variable is not a numeral.*

But I also wanted to say that the concept of number couldn't be given independently of the numbers, and that isn't true. A number-variable is independent of particular numbers in the sense that there does exist a calculus with a class of our numerals and without the general number-variable. In that calculus, of course, not all the rules which hold of our numerals will be valid, but those numerals will correspond to ours in the way that the draughtsmen in draughts correspond to those in losing draughts.

What I am opposing is the view that the infinite number series is something given concerning which there are both particular number theorems and also general theorems about all numbers of the series; so that the arithmetical calculus wouldn't be complete if it didn't contain the general theorems about cardinal numbers, i.e. general equations of the form $a + (b + c) = (a + b) + c$. Whereas even $1/3 = 0\cdot\dot{3}$ belongs to a different calculus from $1/3 = 0\cdot3$. And similarly a general sign-rule (e.g. a recursive definition) that holds for $1,(1) + 1,((1) + 1) + 1,(((1) + 1) + 1) + 1$, and so on is something different from a particular definition. The general rule adds to the number calculus something extra, without which it would have been no less complete than the arithmetic of the number series $1, 2, 3, 4, 5$.

The question also arises: where is the concept of number (or of cardinal number) indispensable? Number, in contrast to what? $\| 1, \xi, \xi + 1 \|$, perhaps, in contrast to $| 5, \xi\sqrt{\xi} |$ etc. – For if I really do introduce such a sign (like $| 1, \xi, \xi + 1 |$) and don't just take it along as a luxury, then I must do something with it, i.e. use it in a calculus, and then it loses its solitary splendour and occurs in a system of signs coordinated with it.

You will perhaps say: but surely "cardinal number" is contrasted with "rational number", "real number", etc. But this distinction is a distinction between the rules (the rules of the appropriate game) – not a distinction between positions on the chessboard – not a distinction demanding different coordinated words in the same calculus.

We say "this theorem is proved for all cardinal numbers". But let us just see how the concept of cardinal numbers enters into the proof. Only because 1 and the operation $\xi + 1$ are spoken of in the proof – not in contrast to anything the rational numbers have. So if we use the concept-word "cardinal number" to describe the proof in prose, we see – don't we? – that no *concept* corresponds to that word.

The expressions "the cardinal numbers", "the real numbers", are extraordinarily misleading except where they are used to help specify particular numbers, as in "the cardinal numbers from 1 to 100", etc. There is no such thing as "the cardinal numbers", but only "cardinal numbers" and the concept, the form "cardinal number". Now we say "the number of the cardinal numbers is smaller than the number of the real numbers" and we imagine that we could perhaps write the two series side by side (if only we weren't weak humans) and then the one series would end in endlessness, whereas the other would go on beyond it into the actual infinite. But this is all nonsense. If we can talk of a relationship which can be called by analogy "greater" and "smaller", it can only be a relationship between the forms "cardinal number" and "real number". I learn what a series is by having it explained to me and only to the extent that it is explained to me. A finite series is explained to me by examples of the type 1, 2, 3, 4, and infinite one by signs of the type "1, 2, 3, 4, and so on" or "1, 2, 3, 4 . . ."

It is important that I can understand (see) the rule of projection without having it in front of me in a general notation. I can detect a general rule in the series $\frac{1}{1}$, $\frac{2}{4}$, $\frac{3}{9}$, $\frac{4}{16}$ – of course I can detect any number of others too, *but still I can detect a particular one,* and that means that this series was somehow for me the expression of that one rule.

If you have "intuitively" understood the law of a series, e.g. the series m, so that you are able to construct an arbitrary term m(n), then you've completely understood the law, just as well as anything like an algebraic formulation could convey it. That is, no such formulation can now make you understand it better, and therefore to that extent no such formulation is any more rigorous, although it may of course be easier to take in.

We are inclined to believe that the notation that gives a series by writing down a few terms plus the sign "and so on" is essentially inexact, by contrast with the specification of the general term.

Here we forget that the general term is specified by reference to a basic series which cannot in turn be described by a general term. Thus $2n + 1$ is the general term of the odd numbers, *if* n ranges over the cardinal numbers, but it would be nonsense to say that n was the general term of the series of cardinal numbers. If you want to define that series, you can't do it by specifying "the general term n", but of course only by a definition like "$1, 1 + 1, 1 + 1 + 1$ and so on". And of course there is no essential difference between that series and "$1, 1 + 1 + 1, 1 + 1 + 1 + 1 + 1$ and so on", which I could just as well have taken as the basic series (so that then the general term of the cardinal number series would have been $\frac{1}{2}(n - 1)$.)

$$(\exists x).\varphi x: \sim (\exists x, y).\varphi x.\varphi y$$
$$(\exists x, y).\varphi x.\varphi y: \sim (\exists x, y, z).\varphi x.\varphi y.\varphi z$$
$$(\exists x, y, z).\varphi x.\varphi y.\varphi z: \sim (\exists x, y, z, u).\varphi x.\varphi y.\varphi z.\varphi u$$

"How would we now go about writing the general form of such propositions? The question manifestly has a good sense. For if I write down only a few such propositions as examples, you understand what the *essential element* in these propositions is meant to be."

Well, in that case the row of examples is already a notation: for understanding the series consists in our applying the symbol, and distinguishing it from others in the same system, e.g. from

$$(\exists x).\varphi x$$
$$(\exists x, y, z).\varphi x.\varphi y.\varphi z.$$
$$(\exists x, y, z, u, v).\varphi x.\varphi y.\varphi z.\varphi u.\varphi v$$

But why shouldn't we write the general term of the first series thus:

$$(\exists x_1, \ldots x_n).\Pi_{x_1}^{x_n} \varphi x :(\exists x_1 \ldots x_{n+1}).\Pi_{x_1}^{x_{n+1}} \varphi x ?[1]$$

Is this notation inexact? It isn't supposed by itself to make anything graphic; all that matters are the rules for its use, the system in which it is used. The scruples attaching to it date from a train of thought which was concerned with the number of primitive signs in the calculus of *Principia Mathematica*.

[1]. Perhaps Wittgenstein inadvertently omitted a negation sign before the second quantifier. (Trs.)

III FOUNDATIONS OF MATHEMATICS

11

The comparison between mathematics and a game

What are we taking away from mathematics when we say it is only a game (or: it is a game)?

A game, in contrast to what? – What are we awarding to mathematics if we say it isn't a game, its propositions have a sense?

The sense outside the proposition.
What concern is it of ours? Where does it manifest itself and what can we do with it? (To the question "what is the sense of this proposition?" the answer is a proposition.)
("But a mathematical proposition does express a thought." – What thought? –.)

Can it be expressed by another proposition? Or only by *this* proposition? – Or not at all? In that case it is no concern of ours.

Do you simply want to distinguish mathematical propositions from other constructions, such as hypotheses? You are right to do so: there is no doubt that there is a distinction.

If you want to say that mathematics is played like chess or patience, and the point of it is like winning or coming out, that is manifestly incorrect.

If you say that the mental processes accompanying the use of mathematical symbols are different from those accompanying chess, I wouldn't know what to say about that.

In chess there are some positions that are impossible although each individual piece is in a permissible position. (E.g. if all the pawns are still in their initial position, but a bishop is already in play.) But one could imagine a game in which a record was kept of the number of moves from the beginning of the game and then there would be certain positions which could not occur after n moves and yet one could not read off from a position by itself whether or not it was a possible nth position.

What we do in games must correspond to what we do in calculating. (I mean: it's there that the correspondence must be, or again, that's the way that the two must be correlated with each other.)

Is mathematics about signs on paper? No more than chess is about wooden pieces.

When we talk about the sense of mathematical propositions, or what they are about, we are using a false picture. Here too, I mean, it looks as if there are inessential, arbitrary signs which have an essential element in common, namely the sense.

Since mathematics is a calculus and hence isn't really *about* anything, there isn't any metamathematics.

What is the relation between a chess problem and a game of chess? – It is clear that chess problems correspond to arithmetical problems, indeed that they are arithmetical problems.

The following would be an example of an arithmetical game: We write down a four-figure number at random, e.g. 7368; we are to get as near to this number as possible by multiplying the numbers 7, 3, 6, 8 with each other in any order. The players calculate with pencil and paper, and the person who comes nearest to the number 7368 in the smallest number of steps wins. (Many mathematical puzzles, incidentally, can be turned into games of this kind.)

Suppose a human being had been taught arithmetic only for use in an arithmetical game: would he have learnt something different from a person who learns arithmetic for its ordinary use? If he multiplies 21 by 8 in the game and gets 168, does he do something different from a person who wanted to find out how many 21×8 is?

It will be said: the one wanted to find out a truth, but the other did not want to do anything of the sort.

Well, we might want to compare this with a game like tennis. In tennis the player makes a particular movement which causes the ball to travel in a particular way, and we can view his hitting the ball either as an experiment, leading to the discovery of a particular truth, or else as a stroke with the sole purpose of winning the game.

But this comparison wouldn't fit, because we don't regard a move in chess as an experiment (though that too we might do); we regard it as a step in a calculation.

Someone might perhaps say: In the arithmetical game we do indeed do the multiplication 21×8,

$$168$$

but the equation $21 \times 8 = 168$ doesn't occur in the game. But isn't that a superficial distinction? And why shouldn't we multiply (and of course divide) in such a way that the equations were written down as equations?

So one can only object that in the game the equation is not a proposition. But what does that mean? How does it become a proposition? What must be added to it to make it a proposition? – Isn't it a matter of the use of the equation (or of the multiplication)? – And it is certainly a piece of mathematics when it is used in the transition from one proposition to another. And thus the specific difference between mathematics and a game gets linked up with the concept of proposition (not 'mathematical proposition') and thereby loses its actuality for us.

But one could say that the real distinction lay in the fact that in the game there is no room for affirmation and negation. For instance, there is multiplication and $21 \times 8 = 148$ would be a false move, but "$(21 \times 8 = 148)$", which is a correct arithmetical proposition, would have no business in our game.

(Here we may remind ourselves that in elementary schools they never work with inequations. The children are only asked to carry out multiplications correctly and never – or hardly ever – asked to prove an inequation.)

When I work out 21×8 in our game the steps in the calculation, at least, are the same as when I do it in order to solve a practical problem (and we could make room in a game for inequations also). But my attitude to the sum in other respects differs in the two cases.

Now the question is: can we say of someone playing the game who reaches the position "$21 \times 8 = 168$" that he has found out that 21×8 is 168? What does he lack? I think the only thing missing is an application for the sum.

Calling arithmetic a game is no more and no less wrong than calling moving chessmen according to chess-rules a game; for that might be a calculation too.

So we should say: No, the word "arithmetic" is not the name of a game. (That too of course is trivial) – But the meaning of the word "arithmetic" can be clarified by bringing out the relationship between arithmetic and an arithmetical game, or between a chess problem and the game of chess.

But in doing so it is *essential* to recognize that the relationship is not the same as that between a tennis problem and the game of tennis.

By "tennis problem" I mean something like the problem of returning a ball in a particular direction in given circumstances. (A billiard problem would perhaps be a clearer case.) A billiard problem isn't a mathematical problem (although its solution may be an application of mathematics). A billiard problem is a physical problem and therefore a "problem" in the sense of physics; a chess problem is a mathematical problem and so a "problem" in a different sense, a mathematical sense.

In the debate between "formalism" and "contentful mathematics" what does each side assert? This dispute is so like the one between realism and idealism in that it will soon have become obsolete, for example, and in that both parties make unjust assertions at variance with their day-to-day practice.

Arithmetic *isn't* a game, it wouldn't occur to anyone to include arithmetic in a list of games played by human beings.

What constitutes winning and losing in a game (or success in patience)? It isn't of course, just the winning position. A special rule is needed to lay down who is the winner. ("Draughts" and "losing draughts" differ only in this rule.)

Now is the rule which says "The one who first has his pieces in the other one's half is the winner" a statement? How would it be verified? How do I know if someone has won? Because he is pleased, or something of the kind? Really what the rule says is: you must try to get your pieces as soon as possible, etc.

In this form the rule connects the game with life. And we could imagine that in an elementary school in which one of the subjects taught was chess the teacher would react to a pupil's bad moves in exactly the same way as to a sum worked out wrongly.

I would almost like to say: It is true that in the game there isn't any "true" and "false" but then in arithmetic there isn't any "winning" and "losing".

I once said that is was imaginable that wars might be fought on a kind of huge chessboard according to the rules of chess. But if everything really went simply according to the rules of chess, then you wouldn't need a battlefield for the war, it could be played on an ordinary board; and then it wouldn't be a war in the ordinary sense. But you really could imagine a battle conducted in accordance with the rules of chess – if, say, the "bishop" could fight with the "queen" only when his position in relation to her was such that he would be allowed to "take" her in chess.

Could we imagine a game of chess being played (i.e. a complete set of chess moves being carried out) in such *different surroundings* that what happened wasn't something we could call the playing of a game?

Certainly, it might be a case of the two participants collaborating to solve a *problem*. (And we could easily construct a case on these lines in which such a task would have a utility).

The rule about winning and losing really just makes a distinction between two poles. It is not concerned with what later happens to the winner (or loser) – whether, for instance, the loser has to pay anything.

(And similarly, the thought occurs, with "right" and "wrong" in sums.)

In logic the same thing keeps happening as happened in the dispute about the nature of definition. If someone says that a definition is concerned only with signs and does no more than substitute one sign for another, people resist and say that that isn't *all* a definition does, or that there are different kinds of definition and the interesting and important ones aren't the mere "verbal definitions".

They think, that is, that if you make definition out to be a mere substitution rule for signs you take away its significance and importance. But the *significance* of a definition lies in its application, in its importance for life. The same thing is happening today in the dispute between formalism and intuitionism, etc. People cannot separate the importance, the consequences, the application of a fact from the fact itself; they can't separate the description of a thing from the description of its importance.

We are always being told that a mathematician works by instinct (or that he doesn't proceed mechanically like a chessplayer or the like), but we aren't told what that's supposed to have to do with the nature of mathematics. If such a psychological phenomenon does play a part in mathematics we need to know how far we can speak about mathematics with complete exactitude, and how far we can only speak with the indeterminacy we must use in speaking of instincts etc.

Time and again I would like to say: What *I* check is the *account books* of mathematicians; their mental processes, joys, depressions and instincts as they go about their business may be important in other connections, but they are no concern of mine.

12

There is no metamathematics.

No calculus can decide a philosophical problem.

A calculus cannot give us information about the foundations of mathematics.

So there can't be any "leading problems" of mathematical logic, if those are supposed to be problems whose solution would at long last give us the right to do arithmetic as we do.

We can't wait for the lucky chance of the solution of a mathematical problem.

I said earlier "calculus is not a mathematical concept"; in other words, the word "calculus" is not a chesspiece that belongs to mathematics.

There is no need for it to occur in mathematics. – If it is used in a calculus nonetheless, that doesn't make the calculus into a metacalculus; in such a case the word is just a chessman like all the others.

Logic isn't metamathematics either; that is, work within the logical calculus can't bring to light essential truths *about* mathematics. Cf. here the "decision problem" and similar topics in modern mathematical logic.

(Through Russell and Whitehead, especially Whitehead, there entered philosophy a false exactitude that is the worst enemy of real exactitude. At the bottom of this there lies the erroneous opinion that a calculus could be the mathematical foundation of mathematics.)

Number is not at all a "fundamental mathematical concept"[1].

1. According to Dr. C. Lewy Wittgenstein wrote in the margin of F. P. Ramsey's copy of the *Tractatus* at 6.02: "Number is *the* fundamental idea of calculus and must be introduced as such." This was, Lewy thinks, in the year 1923. See *Mind*, July 1967, p. 422.

There are so many calculations in which numbers aren't mentioned.

So far as concerns arithmetic, what we are willing to call numbers is more or less arbitrary. For the rest, what we have to do is to describe the calculus – say of cardinal numbers – that is, we must give its rules and by doing so we lay the foundations of arithmetic.

Teach it to us, and then you have laid its foundations.

(Hilbert sets up rules of a particular calculus as rules of meta-mathematics.)

A system's being *based on* first principles is not the same as its being developed from them. It makes a difference whether it is like a house resting on its lowest walls or like a celestial body floating free in space which we have begun to build beneath although we might have built anywhere else.

Logic and mathematics are not *based on* axioms, any more than a group is based on the elements and operations that define it. The idea that they are involves the error of treating the intuitiveness, the self-evidence, of the fundamental propositions as a criterion for correctness in logic.

A foundation that stands on nothing is a bad foundation.

$(p.q) \lor (p. \sim q) \lor (\sim p.q) \lor (\sim p. \sim q.)$: That is my tautology, and then I go on to say that every "proposition of logic" can be brought into this form in accordance with specified rules. But that means the same as: can be derived from it. This would take us as far as the Russellian method of demonstration and all we add to it is that this initial form is not itself an independent proposition, and that like all other "laws of logic" it has the property that $p \cdot \text{Log} = p$, $p \vee \text{Log} = \text{Log}$.

It is indeed the essence of a "logical law" that when it is conjoined with any proposition it yields that proposition. We might even begin Russell's calculus with definitions like

$$p \supset p : q . = . q$$
$$p : p \vee q . = . p, \text{ etc.}$$

13

Proofs of Relevance

If we prove that a problem can be solved, the concept "solution" must occur somewhere in the proof. (There must be something in the mechanism corresponding to the concept.) But the concept cannot have an external description as its proxy; it must be genuinely spelt out.

The only proof of the provability of a proposition is a proof of the proposition itself. But there is something we might call a proof of relevance: an example would be a proof convincing me that I *can* verify the equation $17 \times 38 = 456$ before I have actually done so. Well, how is it that I know that I can check $17 \times 38 = 456$, whereas I perhaps wouldn't know, merely by looking, whether I could check an expression in the integral calculus? Obviously, it is because I know that the equation is constructed in accordance with a definite rule and because I know the kind of connection between the rule for the solution of the sum and the way in which the proposition is put together. In that case a proof of relevance would be something like a formulation of the general method of doing things like multiplication sums, enabling us to recognize the general form of the propositions it makes it possible to check. In that case I can say I recognise that this method will verify the equation without having actually carried out the verification.

When we speak of proofs of relevance (and other similar mathematical entities) it always looks as if in addition to the particular series of operations called proofs of relevance, we had a quite definite inclusive concept of such proofs or of mathematical proof in general; but in fact the word is applied with many different, more or less related, meanings. (Like words such as "people", "king", "religion", etc.; cf Spengler.) Just think of the role of examples in the explanation of such words. If I want to explain what I mean by "proof", I will have to point to examples of proofs, just as when explaining the word "apple" I point to apples. The definition of the word "proof" is in the same case as the definition of the word "number". I can define the expression "cardinal number" by pointing to examples of cardinal numbers; indeed instead of the expression I can actually use the sign "1, 2, 3, 4, and so on ad inf". I can define the word "number" too by pointing to various kinds of number; but when I do so I am not circumscribing the concept "number" as definitely as I previously circumscribed the concept cardinal number, unless I want to say that it is only the things at present called numbers that constitute the concept "number", in which case we can't say of any new construction that it constructs a kind of number. But the way we want to use the word "proof" in is one in which it isn't simply defined by a disjunction of proofs currently in use; we want to use it in cases of which at present we "can't have any idea". To the extent that the concept of proof is *sharply* circumscribed, it is only through particular proofs, or through series of proofs (like the number series), and we must keep that in mind if we want to speak absolutely precisely about proofs of relevance, of consistency etc.

We can say: A proof of relevance *alters* the calculus containing the proposition to which it refers. It cannot *justify* a calculus containing the proposition, in the sense in which carrying out the multiplication 17×23 justifies the writing down of the equation $17 \times 23 = 391$. Not, that is, unless we expressly give the word "justify" that meaning. But in that case we mustn't believe that if mathematics lacks this justification, it is in some more general and widely established sense illegitimate or suspicious. (That would be like someone wanting to say: "the use of the expression 'pile of stones' is fundamentally illegitimate, until we have laid down officially how many stones make a pile." Such a stipulation would modify the use of the word "pile" but it wouldn't "justify" it in any generally recognized sense; and if such an official definition were given, it wouldn't mean that the use earlier made of the word would be stigmatized as incorrect.)

The proof of the verifiability of $17 \times 23 = 391$ is not a "proof" in the same sense of the word as the proof of the equation itself. (A cobbler heels, a doctor heals: both . . .) We grasp the verifiability of the equation from its proof somewhat as we grasp the verifiability of the proposition "the points A and B are not separated by a turn of the spiral" from the figure. And we see that the proposition stating verifiability isn't a "proposition" in the same sense as the one whose verifiability is asserted. Here again, one can only say: look at the proof, and you will see *what* is proved here, what gets called "the proposition proved".

Can one say that at each step of a proof we need a new insight? (The individuality of numbers.) Something of the following sort: if I am given a general (variable) rule, I must recognize each time afresh that this rule may be applied *here* too (that it holds for *this* case too). No act of foresight can absolve me from this act of *insight*. Since the form in which the rule is applied is in fact a new one at every step. But it is not a matter of an act of *insight*, but of an act of *decision*.

What I called a proof of relevance does not climb the ladder to its proposition – since that *requires* that you pass every rung – but only shows that the ladder leads in the direction of that proposition. (There are no surrogates in logic). Neither is an arrow that points the direction a surrogate for going through all the stages towards a particular goal.

14

Consistency proofs

Something tells me that a contradiction in the axioms of a system can't really do any harm until it is revealed. We think of a hidden contradiction as like a hidden illness which does harm even though (and perhaps precisely because) it doesn't show itself in an obvious way. But two rules in a game which in a particular instance contradict each other are perfectly in order until the case turns up, and it's only then that it becomes necessary to make a decision between them by a further rule.

Mathematicians nowadays make so much fuss about proofs of the consistency of axioms. I have the feeling that if there were a contradiction in the axioms of a system it wouldn't be such a great misfortune. Nothing easier than to remove it.

"We may not use a system of axioms before its consistency has been proved."
"In the rules of the game no contradictions may occur."
Why not? "Because then one wouldn't know how to play."
But how does it happen that our reaction to a contradiction is a doubt?
We don't have any reaction to a contradiction. We can only say: if it's really meant like that (if the contradiction is *supposed* to be there) I don't understand it. Or: it isn't something I've learnt. I don't understand the sign. I haven't learnt what I am to do with it, whether it is a command, etc.

Suppose someone wanted to add to the usual axioms of arithmetic the equation $2 \times 2 = 5$. Of course that would mean that the sign of equality had changed its meaning, i.e. that there would now be different rules for the equals-sign.

If I inferred "I cannot use it as a substitution sign" that would mean that its grammar no longer fitted the grammar of the word "substitute" ("substitution sign", etc.). For the word "can" in that proposition doesn't indicate a physical (physiological, psychological) possibility.

"The rules many not contradict each other" is like "negation, when doubled, may not yield a negation". That is, it is part of the grammar of the word "rule" that if "p" is a rule, "p . ∼ p" is not a rule.

That means we could also say: the rules may contradict each other, if the rules for the use of the word "rule" are different – if the word "rule" has a different meaning.

Here too we cannot give any foundation (except a biological or historical one or something of the kind); all we can do is to establish the agreement, or disagreement between the rules for certain words, and say that these words are used with these rules.

It cannot be shown, proved, that these rules *can* be used as the rules of this activity.
Except by showing that the grammar of the description of the activity fits the rules.

"In the rules there *mustn't* be a contradiction" looks like an instruction: "In a clock the hand mustn't be loose on the shaft." We expect a reason: because otherwise . . . But in the first case the reason would have to be: because otherwise it wouldn't be a set of rules. Once again we have a grammatical structure that cannot be given a logical foundation.

In the indirect proof that a straight line can have only *one* continuation through a certain point we make the supposition that a straight line could have two continuations. – If we make that supposition, then the supposition must make sense. – But what does it mean to make that supposition? It isn't making a supposition that goes against natural history, like the supposition that a lion has two tails. – It isn't making a supposition that goes against an ascertained fact. What it means is supposing a rule; and there's nothing against that except that it contradicts another rule, and for that reason I drop it.

Suppose that in the proof there occurs the following drawing ⎯⎯⎯⎯⎯⎯⎯ to represent a straight line bifurcating. There is nothing absurd (contradictory) in that unless we have made some stipulation that it contradicts.

If a contradiction is found later on, that means that hitherto the rules have not been clear and unambiguous. So the contradiction doesn't matter, because we can now get rid of it by enunciating a rule.

In a system with a clearly set out grammar there are no hidden contradictions, because such a system must include the rule which makes the contradiction is discernible. A contradiction can only be hidden in the sense that it is in the higgledy-piggledy zone of the rules, in the unorganized part of the grammar; and there it doesn't matter since it can be removed by organizing the grammar.

Why may not the rules contradict one another? Because otherwise they wouldn't be rules.

15
Justifying arithmetic and preparing it for its applications
(Russell, Ramsey)

One always has an aversion to giving arithmetic a foundation by saying something about its application. It appears firmly enough grounded in itself. And that of course derives from the fact that arithmetic is its own application.

You could say: why bother to limit the application of arithmetic, that takes care of itself. (I can make a knife without bothering about what kinds of materials I will have cut with it; that will show soon enough.)

What speaks against our demarcating a region of application is the feeling that we can understand arithmetic without having any such region in mind. Or put it like this: our instinct rebels against anything that isn't restricted to an analysis of the thoughts already before us.

You could say arithmetic is a kind of geometry; i.e. what in geometry are constructions on paper in arithmetic are calculations (on paper). You could say, it is a more general kind of geometry.

It is always a question of whether and how far it's possible to represent the most general form of the application of arithmetic. And here the strange thing is that in a certain sense it doesn't seem to be needed. And if in fact it isn't needed, then it's also impossible.

The general form of its application seems to be represented by the fact that nothing is said about it. (And if that's a possible representation, then it is also *the* right one.)

The point of the remark that arithmetic is a kind of geometry is simply that arithmetical constructions are autonomous like geometrical ones and hence so to speak themselves guarantee their applicability.

For it must be possible to say of geometry too that it is its own application.

(In the sense in which we can speak of lines which are possible and lines which are actually drawn we can also speak of possible and actually represented numbers.)

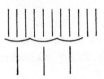

That is an arithmetical construction, and in a *somewhat* extended sense also a geometrical one.

Suppose I wish to use this calculation to solve the following problem: if I have 11 apples and want to share them among some people in such a way that each is given 3 apples how many people can there be? The calculation supplies me with the answer 3. Now suppose I were to go through the whole process of sharing and at the end 4 people each had 3 apples in their hands. Would I then say that the computation gave a wrong result? Of course not. And that of course means only that the computation was not an experiment.

It might look as though the mathematical computation entitled us to make a prediction, say, that I could give three people their share and there will be two apples left over. But that isn't so. What justifies us in making this prediction is an hypothesis of physics, which lies outside the calculation. The calculation is only a study of logical forms, of structures, and of itself can't yield anything new.

If 3 strokes on the paper are the sign for the number 3, then you can say the number 3 is to be applied in our language in the way in which the 3 strokes can be applied.

I said "One difficulty in the Fregean theory is the generality of the words 'Concept' and 'Object'. For, even if you can count tables, tones, vibrations and thoughts, it is difficult to bracket them all together."[1] But what does "you *can* count them" mean? What it means is that it *makes sense* to apply the cardinal numbers to them. But if we know that, if we know *these* grammatical rules, why do we need to rack our brains about the other grammatical rules when we are only concerned to justify the application of cardinal arithmetic? It isn't difficult "to bracket them all together"; so far as is necessary for the present purpose they are already bracketed together.

But (as we all know well) arithmetic isn't at all concerned about this application. Its applicability takes care of itself.

Hence so far as the foundations of arithmetic are concerned all the anxious searching for distinctions between subject-predicate forms, and constructing functions 'in extension' (Ramsey) is a waste of time.

The equation 4 apples + 4 apples = 8 apples is a substitution rule which I use if instead of substituting the sign "8" for the sign "4 + 4", I substitute the sign "8 apples" for the sign "4 + 4 apples."

But we must beware of thinking that "4 apples + 4 apples = 8 apples" is the concrete equation and 4 + 4 = 8 the abstract proposition of which the former is only a special case, so that the arithmetic of apples, though much less general than the truly general arithmetic, is valid in its own restricted domain (for apples). There isn't any "arithmetic of apples", because the equation 4 apples + 4 apples = 8 apples is not a proposition about apples. We may say that in this equation the word "apples" has no reference. (And we can always say this about a sign in a rule which helps to determine its meaning.)

1. *Philosophical Remarks,* p. 119.

How can we make preparations for the reception of something that may happen to exist – in the sense in which Russell and Ramsey always wanted to do this? We get logic ready for the existence of many-placed relations, or for the existence of an infinite number of objects, or the like.

Well, we can make preparations for the existence of a thing: e.g. I may make a casket for jewellery which may be made some time or other – But in this case I can say what the situation must be – what the situation is – for which I am preparing. It is no more difficult to describe the situation now than after it has already occurred; even, if it never occurs at all. (Solution of mathematical problems). But what Russell and Ramsey are making preparations for is a possible grammar.

On the one hand we think that the nature of the functions and of the arguments that are counted in mathematics is part of its business. But we don't want to let ourselves be tied down to the functions now known to us, and we don't know whether people will ever discover a function with 100 argument places; and so we have to make preparations and construct a function to get everything ready for a 100-place relation in case one turns up. – But what does "a 100-place relation turns up (or exists)" mean at all? What concept do we have of one? Or of a 2-place relation for that matter? – As an example of a 2-place relation we give something like the relation between father and son. But what is the significance of this example for the further logical treatment of 2-place relations? Instead of every "aRb" are we now to imagine "a is the father of b"? – If not, is this example or any example essential? Doesn't this example have the same role as an example in arithmetic, when I use 3 rows of 6 apples to explain $3 \times 6 = 18$ to somebody?

Here it is a matter of our concept of *application*. – We have an image of an engine which first runs idle, and then works a machine.

But what does the application add to the calculation? Does it introduce a new calculus? In that case it isn't any longer *the same* calculation. Or does it give it substance in some sense which is essential to mathematics (logic)? If so, how can we abstract from the application at all, even only temporarily?

No, calculation with apples is essentially the same as calculation with lines or numbers. A machine is an extension of an engine, an application is not in the same sense an extension of a calculation.

Suppose that, in order to give an example, I say "love is a 2-place relation" – am I saying anything about love? Of course not. I am giving a rule for the use of the word "love" and I mean perhaps that we use *this* word in such and such a way.

Yet we do have the feeling that when we allude to the 2-place relation 'love' we put meaning into the husk of the calculus of relations. – Imagine a geometrical demonstration carried out using the cylinder of a lamp instead of a drawing or analytical symbols. How far is this an application of geometry? Does the use of the glass cylinder in the lamp enter into the geometrical thought? And does the use of word "love" in a declaration of love enter into my discussions of 2-place relations?

We are concerned with different uses or meanings of the word "application". "Division is an application of multiplication"; "the lamp is an application of the glass cylinder"; "the calculation is applied to these apples".

At this point we can say: arithmetic is its own application. The calculus is its own application.

In arithmetic we cannot make preparations for a grammatical application. For if arithmetic is only a game, its application too is only a game, and either the same game (in which case it takes us no further) or a different game – and in that case we could play it in pure arithmetic also.

So if the logician says that he has made preparations in arithmetic for the possible existence of 6-place relations, we may ask him: when what you have prepared finds its application, what will be added to it? A new calculus? – but that's something you haven't provided. Or something which doesn't affect the calculus? – then it doesn't interest us, and the calculus you have shown us is application enough.

What is incorrect is the idea that the application of a calculus in the grammar of real language correlates it to a reality or gives it a reality that it did not have before.

Here as so often in this area the mistake lies not in believing something false, but in looking in the direction of a misleading analogy.

So what happens when the 6-place relation is found? Is it like the discovery of a metal that has the desired (and previously described) properties (the right specific weight, strength, etc.)? No; what is discovered is a word that we in fact use in our language as we used, say, the letter R. "Yes, but this word has meaning, and 'R' has none. So now we see that something can correspond to 'R'." But the meaning of the word does not consist in something's corresponding to it, except in a case like that of a name and what it names; but in our case the bearer of the name is merely an extension of the calculus, of the language. And it is *not* like saying "this story really happened, it was not pure fiction".

This is all connected with the false concept of logical analysis that Russell, Ramsey and I used to have, according to which we are writing for an ultimate logical analysis of facts, like a chemical analysis of compounds – an analysis which will enable us really to discover a 7-place relation, like an element that really has the specific weight 7.

Grammar is for us a pure calculus (not the application of a calculus to reality).

"How can we make preparations for something which may or may not exist?" means: how can we hope to make an *a priori* construction to cope with all possible results while basing arithmetic upon a logic in which we are still waiting for the results of an analysis of our propositions in particular cases? – One wants to say: "we don't know whether it may not turn out that there are no functions with 4 argument places, or that there are only 100 arguments that can significantly be inserted into functions of *one* variable. Suppose, for example (the supposition does appear possible) that there is only *one* four-place function F and 4 arguments a, b, c, d; does it make sense in that case to say '2 + 2 = 4' since there aren't any functions to accomplish the division into 2 and 2?" So now, one says to oneself, we will make provision for all possible cases. But of course that has no meaning. On the one hand the calculus doesn't make provision for possible existence; it constructs for itself all the existence that it needs. On the other hand what look like hypothetical assumptions about the logical elements (the logical structure) of the world are merely specifications of elements in a calculus; and of course you can make these in such a way that the calculus does not contain any 2 + 2.

Suppose we make preparations for the existence of 100 objects by introducing 100 names and a calculus to go with them. Then let us suppose 100 objects are really discovered. What happens now that the names have objects correlated with them which weren't correlated with them before? Does the calculus change? – What has the correlation got to do with it at all? Does it make it acquire more reality? Or did the calculus previously belong only to mathematics, and now to logic as well? – What sort of questions are "are there 3-place relations", "are there 1000 objects"? How is it to be decided? – But surely it is a fact that we can specify a 2-place relation, say love, and a 3-place one, say jealousy, but perhaps not a 27-place one! – But what does "to specify a 2-place relation" mean? It sounds as if we could point to a thing and say "you see, that is the kind of thing" (the kind of thing we described earlier). But nothing of that kind takes place (the comparison with pointing is altogether wrong). "The relation of jealousy cannot be reduced to 2-place relationships" sounds like "alcohol cannot be decomposed into water plus a solid substance". Is that something that is part of the nature of jealousy? (Let's not forget: the proposition "A is jealous of B because of C" is no more and no less reducible than the proposition "A is not jealous of B because of C".) What is pointed to is, say, the group of people A, B and C. – "But suppose that living beings at first knew only plane surfaces, but none the less developed a 3-dimensional geometry, and that they suddenly became acquainted with 3-dimensional space!" Would this alter their geometry, would it become richer in content? – "Isn't this the way it is? Suppose at some time I had made arbitrary rules for myself prohibiting me from moving in my room in certain directions where there were no physical hindrances to get in my way; and then suppose the physical conditions changed, say furniture was put in the room, in such a way as to force me to move in accordance with the rules which I had originally imposed on myself arbitrarily. Thus, while the 3-dimensional calculus was only a game, there weren't yet three dimensions in reality because the x, y, z belonged to the rules only because I had so decided; but now that we have linked them up to the real 3 dimensions, no other movements are *possible* for them." But that is pure fiction. There isn't any question here of a connection with reality which keeps grammar on the rails. The "connection of language with reality", by means of ostensive definitions and the like, doesn't make the grammar inevitable or provide a justification for the grammar. The grammar remains a free-floating calculus which can only be extended and never supported. The "connection with reality" merely extends language, it doesn't force anything on it. We speak of discovering a 27-place relation but on the one hand no discovery can force me to use the sign or the calculus for a 27-place relation, and on the other hand I can describe the operation of the calculus itself simply by using this notation.

When it looks in logic as if we are discussing several different universes (as with Ramsey), in reality we are considering different games. The definition of a "universe" in a case like Ramsey's would simply be a definition like

$$(\exists x) . \varphi x \stackrel{\mathrm{Def}}{=} \varphi a \lor \varphi b \lor \varphi c \lor \varphi d.$$

Ramsey's theory of identity makes the mistake that would be made by someone who said that you could use a painting as a mirror as well, even if only for a single posture. If we say this we overlook that what is essential to a mirror is precisely that you can infer from it the posture of a body in front of it, whereas in the case of the painting you have to know that the postures tally before you can construe the picture as a mirror image.

If Dirichlet's conception of function has a strict sense, it must be expressed in a *definition* that uses the table to define the function-signs as equivalent.

Ramsey defines[1] $x = y$ as

$$(\varphi_e) . \varphi_e x \equiv \varphi_e y$$

But according to the explanations he gives of his function-sign "φ_e"

$(\varphi_e) . \varphi_e x \equiv \varphi_e x$ is the statement: "every sentence is equivalent to itself."

$(\varphi_e) . \varphi_e x \equiv \varphi_e y$ is the statement: "every sentence is equivalent to every sentence."

So all he has achieved by his definition is what is laid down by the two definitions

$$x = x . \overset{\text{Def}}{=} . \text{ Tautology}$$
$$x = y . \overset{\text{Def}}{=} . \text{ Contradiction}$$

(Here the word "tautology" can be replaced by any arbitrary tautology, and similarly with "contradiction"). So far all that has happened is that definitions have been given of the two distinct signs $x = x$ and $x = y$. These definitions could of course be replaced by two sets of definitions, e.g.

$$\left. \begin{array}{l} a = a \\ b = b \\ c = c \end{array} \right\} = \text{Taut.} \qquad \left. \begin{array}{l} a = b \\ b = c \\ c = a \end{array} \right\} = \text{Contr.}$$

1. F. P. Ramsey, *The Foundations of Mathematics*, London 1931, p. 53.

But then Ramsey writes:

"$(\exists x, y) . x \neq y$",   i.e.   "$(\exists x, y) . \sim (x = y)$" –

but he has no right to: for what does the "$x = y$" mean in this expression? It is neither the sign "$x = y$" used in the definition above, nor of course the "$x = x$" in the preceding definition. So it is a sign that is still unexplained. Moreover to see the futility of these definitions, you should read them (as an unbiased person would) as follows: I permit the sign "Taut", whose use we know, to be replaced by the sign "$a = a$" or "$b = b$", etc.; and the sign "Contr." ("$\sim$Taut.") to be replaced by the sign "$a = b$" or "$a = c$", etc. From which, incidentally, it follows that $(a = b) = (c = d) = (a \neq a) = $ etc.!

It goes without saying that an identity sign defined like that has no resemblance to the one we use to express a substitution rule.

Of course I can go on to define "$(\exists x, y) . x \neq y$", say as $a \neq a . \textbf{v} . a \neq b . \textbf{v} . b \neq c . \textbf{v} . a \neq c$; but this definition is pure humbug and I should have written straightaway $(\exists x, y) . x \neq y . \overset{\text{Def}}{=} . \text{Taut}$. (That is, I would be given the sign on the left side as a new – unnecessary – sign for "Taut.") For we mustn't forget that according to the definitions "$a = a$", "$a = b$", etc. are independent signs, no more connected with each other than the signs "Taut." and "Contr." themselves.

What is in question here is whether functions in extension are any use; because Ramsey's explanation of the identity sign is just such a specification by extension. Now what exactly is the specification of a function by its extension? Obviously, it is a group of definitions, e.g.

$$fa = p \quad \text{Def.}$$
$$fb = q \quad \text{Def.}$$
$$fc = r \quad \text{Def.}$$

These definitions permit us to substitute for the known propositions "p", "q", "r" the signs "fa" "fb" "fc". To say that these three definitions determine the function $f(\xi)$ is either to say nothing, or to say the same as the three definitions say.

For the signs "fa" "fb" "fc" are no more function and argument than the words "Co(rn)", "Co(al)" and "Co(lt)" are. (Here it makes no difference whether or not the "arguments" "rn", "al", "lt" are used elsewhere as words).

(So it is hard to see what purpose the definitions can have except to mislead us.)

To begin with, the sign "$(\exists x).fx$" has no meaning; because here the rules for functions in the old sense of the word don't hold at all. According to them a definition like $fa = \ldots$ would be nonsense. If no explicit definition is given for it, the sign "$(\exists x).fx$" can only be understood as a rebus in which the signs have some kind of spurious meaning.

Each of the signs "$a = a$", "$a = c$", etc. in the definitions $(a = a). \overset{\text{Def}}{=} .\text{Taut. etc.}$ is a *word*.

Moreover, the purpose of the introduction of functions in extension was to analyse propositions about infinite extensions, and it fails of this purpose when a function in extension is introduced by a list of definitions.

There is a temptation to regard the form of an equation as the form of tautologies and contradictions, because it looks as if one can say that $x = x$ is self-evidently true and $x = y$ self-evidently false. The comparison between $x = x$ and a tautology is of course better than that between $x = y$ and a contradiction, because all correct (and "significant") equations of mathematics are actually of the form $x = y$. We might call $x = x$ a degenerate equation (Ramsey quite correctly called tautologies and contradictions degenerate propositions) and indeed a correct degenerate equation (the limiting case of an equation). For we use expressions of the form $x = x$ like correct equations, and when we do so we are fully conscious that we are dealing with degenerate equations. In geometrical proofs there are propositions in the same case, such as "the angle α is equal to the angle β, the angle γ is equal to itself . . ."

At this point the objection might be made that correct equations of the form $x = y$ must be tautologies, and incorrect ones contradictions, because it must be possible to prove a correct equation by transforming each side of it until an identity of the form x = x is reached. But although the original equation is shown to be correct by this process, and to that extent the identity x = x is the goal of the transformation, it is not its goal in the sense that the purpose of the transformation is to give the equation its correct form – like bending a crooked object straight; it is not that the equation at long last achieves its perfect form in the identity. So we can't say: a correct equation is *really* an identity. It just *isn't* an identity.

17

The concept of the application of arithmetic[1] (mathematics)

If we say "it must be essential to mathematics that it can be applied" we mean that its applic*ability* isn't the kind of thing I mean of a piece of wood when I say "I will be able to find many applications for it".

Geometry isn't the science (natural science) of geometric planes, lines and points, as opposed to some other science of gross physical lines, stripes and surfaces and *their* properties. The relation between geometry and propositions of practical life, about stripes, colour boundaries, edges and corners, etc. isn't that the things geometry speaks of, though *ideal* edges and corners, resemble those spoken of in practical propositions; it is the relation between those propositions and their grammar. Applied geometry is the grammar of statements about spatial objects. The relation between what is called a geometrical line and a boundary between two colours isn't like the relation between something fine and something coarse, but like the relation between possibility and actuality. (Think of the notion of possibility as a shadow of actuality.)

You can describe a circular surface divided diametrically into 8 congruent parts, but it is senseless to give such a description of an elliptical surface. And that contains all that geometry says in this connexion about circular and elliptical surfaces.

(A proposition based on a wrong calculation (such as "he cut a 3-metre board into 4 one metre parts") is nonsensical, and that throws light on what is meant by "making sense" and "meaning something by a proposition".)

---

1. The section does not mention arithmetic. It may be conjectured that it was never completed. (Ed.)

What about the proposition "the sum of the angles of a triangle is 180 degrees"? At all events you can't tell by looking at it that it is a proposition of syntax.

The proposition "corresponding angles are equal" means that if they don't appear equal when they are measured I will treat the measurement as incorrect; and "the sum of the angles of a triangle is 180 degrees" means that if it doesn't appear to be 180 degrees when they are measured I will assume there has been a mistake in the measurement. So the proposition is a postulate about the method of describing facts, and therefore a proposition of syntax.

IV ON CARDINAL NUMBERS

18
Kinds of cardinal number

What are numbers? – What numerals signify; an investigation of what they signify is an investigation of the grammar of numerals.

What we are looking for is not a definition of the concept of number, but an exposition of the grammar of the word "number" and of the numerals.

The reason why there are infinitely many cardinal numbers, is that *we* construct this infinite system and call it the system of cardinal numbers. There is also a number system "1, 2, 3, 4, 5, many" and even a system "1, 2, 3, 4, 5". Why shouldn't I call that too a system of cardinal numbers (a finite one)?

It is clear that the axiom of infinity is not what Russell took it for; it is neither a proposition of logic, nor – as it stands – a proposition of physics. Perhaps the calculus to which it belongs, transplanted into quite different surroundings (with a quite different "interpretation"), might somewhere find a practical application; I do not know.

One might say of logical concepts (e.g. of the, or a, concept of infinity) that their essence proves their existence.

(Frege would still have said: "perhaps there are people who have not got beyond the first five in their acquaintance with the series of cardinal numbers (and see the rest of the series only in an indeterminate form or something of the kind), but this series exists independently of us". Does chess exist independently of us, or not? –)

Here is a very interesting question about the position of the concept of number in logic: what happens to the concept of number if a society has no numerals, but for counting, calculating, etc. uses *exclusively* an abacus like a Russian abacus?

(Nothing would be more interesting than to investigate the arithmetic of such people; it would make one really understand that here there is no distinction between 20 and 21.)

Could we also imagine, in contrast with the cardinal numbers, a kind of number consisting of a series like the cardinal numbers without the 5? Certainly; but this kind of number couldn't be used for *any* of the things for which we use the cardinal numbers. The way in which these numbers are missing a five is not like the way in which an apple may have been taken out of a box of apples and can be put back again; it is of their essence to lack a 5; they do not *know* the 5 (in the way that the cardinal numbers do not know the number $\frac{1}{2}$). So these numbers (if you want to call them that) would be used in cases where the cardinal numbers (with the 5) couldn't meaningfully be used.

(Doesn't the nonsensicality of the talk of the "basic intuition" show itself here?)

When the intuitionists speak of the "basic intuition" – is this a psychological process? If so, how does it come into mathematics? Isn't what they mean only a primitive sign (in Frege's sense); an element of a calculus?

Strange as it sounds, it is possible to know the prime numbers – let's say – only up to 7 and thus to have a finite system of prime numbers. And what we call the discovery that there are infinitely many primes is in truth the discovery of a new system with no greater rights than the other.

If you close your eyes and see countless glimmering spots of light coming and going, as we might say, it doesn't make sense to speak of a 'number' of simultaneously seen dots. And you can't say "there is always a definite number of spots of light there, we just don't know what it is"; that would correspond to a rule applied in a case where you can speak of checking the number.

(It makes sense to say: I divide many among many. But the proposition "I couldn't divide the many nuts among the many people" can't mean that it was logically impossible. Also you can't say "in some cases it is possible to divide many among many and in others not"; for in that case I ask: in *which* cases is this possible and in which impossible? And to that no further answer can be given in the many-system.)

To say of a part of my visual field that it has no colour is nonsense; and of course it is equally nonsense to say that it has colour (or a colour). On the other hand it makes sense to say it has only *one* colour (is monochrome, or *uniform* in colour) or that it has at least two colours, only two colours, etc.

So in the sentence "this square in my visual field has at least two colours" I cannot substitute "one" for "two". Or again: "the square has only one colour" does not mean – on the analogy of $(\exists x) . \varphi x . \sim (\exists x, y) . \varphi x . \varphi y$ – "the square has one colour but not two colours".

I am speaking here of the case in which it is senseless to say "that part of space has no colour". If I am counting the uniformly coloured (monochrome) patches in the square, it does incidentally make sense to say that there aren't any there at all, if the colour of the square is continually changing. In that case of course it also makes sense to say that there are one or more uniformly coloured patches in the square and also that the square has one colour and not two. – But for the moment I am disregarding that use of the sentence "the square has no colour" and am speaking of a system in which it would be called a matter of course that an area of a surface had a colour, a system, therefore, in which strictly speaking there is no such proposition. If you call the proposition self-evident you really mean something that is expressed by a grammatical rule giving the form of propositions about visual space, for instance. If you now begin the series of statements giving the number of colours in the square with the proposition "there is one colour in the square", then of course that mustn't be the proposition of grammar about the "colouredness" of space.

What do you mean if you say "space is coloured"? (And, a very interesting question: what kind of question is this?) Well, perhaps you look around for confirmation and look at the different colours around you and feel the inclination to say: "wherever I look there is a colour", or "it's all coloured, all as it were painted." Here you are imagining colours in contrast to a kind of colourlessness, which on closer inspection turns into a colour itself. Incidentally, when you look around for confirmation you look first and foremost at static and monochromatic parts of space, rather than at unstable unclearly coloured parts (flowing water, shadows, etc.) If you then have to admit that you call just everything that you see colour, what you want to say is that being coloured is a property of space in itself, not of the parts of space. But that comes to the same as saying of chess that it is chess; and at best it can't amount to more than a description of the game. So what we must do is describe spatial propositions; but we can't justify them, as if we had to bring them into agreement with an independent reality.

In order to confirm the proposition "the visual field is coloured" one looks round and says "that there is black, and black is a colour; that is white, and white is a colour", etc. And one regards "black is a colour" as like "iron is a metal" (or perhaps better, "gypsum is a sulphur compound").

If I make it senseless to say that a part of the visual field has a colour, then asking for the analysis of a statement assigning the number of colours in a part of the visual space becomes very like asking for the analysis of a statement of the number of parts of a rectangle that I divide up into parts by lines.

Here too I can regard it as senseless to say that the rectangle "consists of no parts". Hence, one cannot say that it consists of one or more parts, or that it has at least *one* part. Imagine the special case of a rectangle divided by parallel lines. It doesn't matter that this is a very special case, since we don't regard a game as less remarkable just because it has only a very limited application. Here I can if I want count the parts in the usual manner, and then it is meaningless to say there are o parts. But I could also imagine a way of counting which so to say regards the first part as a matter of course and doesn't count it or counts it as o, and counts only the parts which are added to this by division. Again, one could imagine a custom according to which, say, soldiers in rank and file were always counted by giving the number of soldiers in a line over and above the first soldier (perhaps because we wanted the number of possible combinations of the fugleman with another soldier of the rank.). But a custom might also exist of always giving the number of soldiers as 1 greater than the real one. Perhaps this happened originally in order to deceive a particular officer about the real number, and later came into general use as a way of counting soldiers. (The academic quarter).[1] The number of different colours on a surface might also be given by the number of their possible combinations in pairs and in that case the only numbers that would count would be numbers of the form $\frac{n}{2}(n-1)$; it would be as senseless then to talk of the 2 or 4 colours of a surface as it now is to talk of the $\sqrt{2}$ or i colours. I want to say that it is not the case that the cardinal numbers are essentially primary and what we might call the combination numbers – 1, 2, 6, 10 etc. – are secondary. We might construct an arithmetic of the combination numbers and it would be as self-contained as the arithmetic of the cardinal numbers. But equally of course there might be an arithmetic of the even numbers or of the numbers 1, 3, 4, 5, 6, 7 . . . Of course the decimal system is ill-adapted for the writing of these kinds of number.

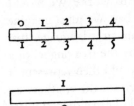

Imagine a calculating machine that calculates not with beads but with colours on a strip of paper. Just as we now use our fingers, or the beads on an abacus, to count the colours on a strip

1. This is an allusion to the German academic custom of announcing a lecture for, say, 11.15 by scheduling it "11.00 c.t." (Trs.)

so then we would use the colours on a strip to count the beads on a bar or the fingers on our hand. But how would this colour-calculating machine have to be made in order to work? We would need a sign for there being no bead on the bar. We must imagine the abacus as a practical tool and as an instrument in language. Just as we can now represent a number like 5 by the five fingers of a hand (imagine a gesture language) so we would then represent it by a strip with five colours. But I need a sign for the o, otherwise I do not have the necessary multiplicity. Well, I can either stipulate that a black surface is to denote the o (this is of course arbitrary and a monochromatic red surface would do just as well): or that any one-coloured surface is to denote zero, a two-coloured surface 1, etc. It is immaterial which method of denotation I choose. Here we see how the multiplicity of the beads is projected onto the multiplicity of the colours on a surface.

It makes no sense to speak of a black two-sided figure in a white circle; this is analogous to its being senseless to say that the rectangle consists of o parts (no part). Here we have something like a lower limit of counting before we reach the number one.

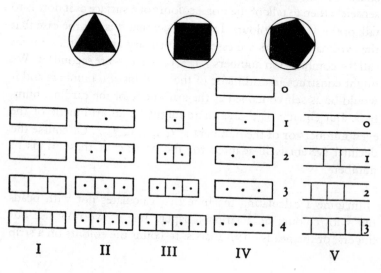

Is counting parts in I the same as counting points in IV? What makes the difference? We may regard counting the parts in I as counting rectangles; but in that case one can also say: "in this row there is *no* rectangle"; and then one isn't counting *parts*. We are disturbed both by the analogy between counting the points and counting the parts, and by the breakdown of the analogy.

There is something odd in counting the undivided surface as "one"; on the other hand we find no difficulty in seeing the surface after a single division as a picture of 2. Here we would much prefer to count "0, 2, 3", etc. And this corresponds to the series of propositions "the rectangle is undivided", "the rectangle is divided into 2 parts", etc.

If it's a question of different colours, you can imagine a way of thinking in which you don't say that here we have two colours, but that here we have a distinction between colours; a style of thought which does not see 3 at all in red, green and yellow; which does indeed recognise as a series a series like: red; blue, green; yellow, black, white; etc., but doesn't connect it with the series |; ||; |||; etc., or not in such a way as to correlate | with the term red.

From the point of view from which it is 'odd' to count the undivided surface as one, it is also natural to count the singly divided one as two. That is what one does if one regards it as two rectangles, and that would mean looking at it from the standpoint from which the undivided one might well be counted as one rectangle. But if one regards the first rectangle in I as the undivided surface, then the second appears as a whole with one division (one distinction) and division here does not necessarily mean dividing line. What I am paying attention to is the distinctions, and here there is a series of an increasing number of distinctions. In that case I will count the rectangles in I "0, 1, 2, etc."

This is all right where the colours on a strip border on each other, as in the schema

red	green	white

But it is different if the arrangement is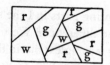

or 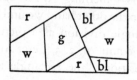 Of course I might also correlate each of these two schemata with the schema `w | g | r`

and correlate schemata like 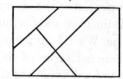 with

the schema `w | g | r | bl` , etc. And that way of thinking though certainly unnatural is perfectly correct.

The most natural thing is to conceive the series of schemata as

A
A B
A B C
A B C D

etc. And here we may denote the first schema by 'o', the second by '1', but the third say with '3', if we think of all possible distinctions, and the fourth by '6' Or we may call the third schema '2' (if we are concerned simply with *an* arrangement) and the fourth '3'.

We can describe the way a rectangle is divided by saying: it is divided into five parts, or: 4 parts have been cut off it, or: its division-schema is ABCDE, or: you can reach every part by crossing four boundaries or: the rectangle is divided (i.e. into 2 parts), one part is divided again, and both parts of *this* part divided, etc. I want to show that there isn't only *one* method of describing the way it is divided.

But perhaps we might refrain altogether from using a number to denote the distinction and keep solely to the schemata A, AB, ABC, etc.; or we might describe it like this: 1, 12, 123 etc., or, what comes to the same, 0, 01, 012 etc.

We may very well call these too numerals.

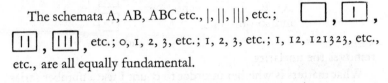

The schemata A, AB, ABC etc., |, ||, |||, etc.; □, |□|, |□□|, |□□□|, etc.; 0, 1, 2, 3, etc.; 1, 2, 3, etc.; 1, 12, 121323, etc., etc., are all equally fundamental.

We are surprised that the number-schema by which we count soldiers in a barracks isn't supposed also to hold for the parts of a rectangle. But the schema for the soldiers in the barracks is □, ⊡, ⊡⊡, etc., the one for the parts of the rectangle is □, □□, □□□, etc. Neither is primary in comparison with the other.

I can compare the series of division-schemata with the series 1, 2, 3, etc. as well as with the series 0, 1, 2, 3, etc.

If I count the parts, then there is no 0 in my number series because the series

$$A$$
$$A \quad B$$
$$A \quad B \quad C$$

etc. begins with *one* letter whereas the series □, ⊡, ⊡⊡, etc. does not begin with *one* dot. On the other hand, I can represent any fact about the division by this series too, only in that case "I'm not counting the parts".

A way of expressing the problem which, though incorrect, is natural is: why can one say "there are 2 colours on this surface" but not "there is *one* colour on this surface?" Or: how must I express the grammatical rule so that it is obvious and so that I'm not any longer tempted to talk nonsense? Where is the false thought, the false analogy by which I am misled into misusing language? How must I set out the grammar so that this temptation ceases? I think that setting it out by means of the series

A
A B
A B C
and so on   and

and so on

removes the unclarity.

What matters is whether in order to count I use a number series that begins with o or one that begins with 1.

It is the same if I am counting the lengths of sticks or the size of hats.

If I counted with strokes, I might write them thus $|$, $\vee$, $\vee\!\!\!\!/$, $\angle\!\!\!/$, in order to show that what matters is the *distinction* between the directions and that a simple stroke corresponds to o (i.e. is the beginning).

Here incidentally there is a certain difficulty about the numerals (1), ((1) + 1), etc.: beyond a certain length we cannot distinguish them any further without counting the strokes, and so without translating the signs into different ones. "||||||||||" and "|||||||||||" cannot be distinguished in the same sense as 10 and 11, and so they aren't in the same sense distinct signs. The same thing could also happen incidentally in the decimal system (think of the numbers 1111111111 and 11111111111), and that is not without significance.

Imagine someone giving us a sum to do in a stroke-notation, say |||||||||| + |||||||||||, and, while we are calculating, amusing himself by removing and adding strokes without our noticing. He would keep on saying: "but the sum isn't right", and we would keep going through it again, fooled every time. – Indeed, strictly speaking, we wouldn't have any concept of a criterion for the correctness of the calculation.

Here one might raise questions like: is it only *very probable* that $464 + 272 = 736$? And in that case isn't $2 + 3 = 5$ also only very probable? And where is the objective truth which this probability approaches? That is, how do we get a concept of $2 + 3$'s really *being* a certain number, apart from what it *seems* to us to be?

For if it were asked: what is the criterion in the stroke-notation for our having the same numeral in front of us twice? – the answer might be: "if it looks the same both times" or "if it contains the same number of lines both times". Or should it be: if a one-one correlation etc. is possible?

How can I know that |||||||||| and |||||||||| are the *same* sign? After all it is not enough that they look *alike*. For having roughly the same gestalt can't be what is to constitute the identity of the signs, but just their being the same in number.

(The problem of the distinction between $1 + 1 + 1 + 1 + 1 + 1 + 1$ and $1 + 1 + 1 + 1 + 1 + 1 + 1 + 1$ is much more fundamental than appears at first sight. It is a matter of the distinction between physical and visual number.)

19

$$2 + 2 = 4$$

A cardinal number is an internal property of a list. Are numbers essentially concerned with concepts? I believe this amounts to asking whether it makes sense to ascribe a number to objects that haven't been brought under a concept. Does it, for example, make sense to say "a, b and c are three objects"? – Admittedly we have a feeling: why talk about concepts, the number of course depends only on the *extension* of the concept, and once that has been determined the concept may drop out of the picture. The concept is only a method for determining an extension, but the extension is autonomous and, in its essence, independent of the concept; for it's quite immaterial which concept we have used to determine the extension. That is the argument for the extensional viewpoint. The immediate objection to it is: if a concept is really only an expedient for aiming at an extension, then there is no place for concepts in arithmetic; in that case we must simply divorce a class completely from the concept which happens to be associated with it. But if it isn't like that, then an extension independent of the concept is just a chimaera, and in that case it's better not to speak of it at all, but only of the concept.

The sign for the extension of a concept is a list. We might say, as an approximation, that a number is an external property of a concept and an internal property of its extension (the list of objects that fall under it). A number is a schema for the extension of a concept. That is, as Frege said, a statement of number is a statement about a concept (a predicate). It's not about the extension of a concept, i.e. a list that may be something like the extension of a concept. But a number-statement about a concept has a similarity to a proposition saying that a determinate list is the extension of the concept. I use such a list when I say "a, b, c, d, fall under the concept F(x)": "a, b, c, d," is the list. Of course this proposition says the same as Fa.Fb.Fc.Fd; but the use of the list in writing the proposition shows its relationship to "$(\exists x, y, z, u).\,Fx.Fy.Fz.Fu$" which we can abbreviate as "$(\exists||||x).\,F(x)$."

What arithmetic is concerned with is the schema $||||$. – But does arithmetic talk about the lines that I draw with pencil on paper? – Arithmetic doesn't talk about the lines, it *operates* with them.

A statement of number doesn't always contain a generalization or indeterminacy: "The line AB is divided into 2 (3, 4, etc.) equal parts."

If you want to know what $2 + 2 = 4$ means, you have to ask how we work it out. That means that we consider the process of calculation as the essential thing; and that's how we look at the matter in ordinary life, at least as far as concerns the numbers that we have to work out. We mustn't feel ashamed of regarding numbers and sums in the same way as the everyday arithmetic of every trader. In everyday life we don't work out $2 + 2 = 4$ or any of the rules of the multiplication table; we take them for granted like axioms and *use them* to calculate. But of course we could work out $2 + 2 = 4$ and children in fact do so by counting off. Given the sequence of numbers 1 2 3 4 5 the calculation is 1 2 1 2
1 2 3 4

Abbreviative Definitions:

$(\exists x).\,\varphi x : \sim(\exists x, y).\,\varphi x.\,\varphi y. \overset{\text{Def}}{=} .(\varepsilon x).\,\varphi x$

$(\exists x, y).\,\varphi x.\,\varphi y : \sim(\exists x, y, z).\,\varphi x.\,\varphi y.\,\varphi z. \overset{\text{Def}}{=} .(\varepsilon x, y).\,\varphi x.\,\varphi y,$ etc.

$(\varepsilon x).\,\varphi x. \overset{\text{Def}}{=} .(\varepsilon|x).\,\varphi x$

$(\varepsilon x, y).\,\varphi x.\,\varphi y. \overset{\text{Def}}{=} .(\varepsilon||x).\,\varphi x. \overset{\text{Def}}{=} .(\varepsilon 2 x).\,\varphi x,$ etc.

It can be shewn that
$$(\varepsilon||x).\,\varphi x.(\varepsilon|||x).\,\psi x.\underbrace{\sim(\exists x).\,\varphi x.\,\psi x.}_{\text{Ind.}} \supset .(\varepsilon|||||x).\,\varphi x \vee \psi x$$

is a tautology.

Does that prove the arithmetical proposition $2 + 3 = 5$? Of course not. It does not even show that

$(\epsilon||x) . \varphi x . (\epsilon|||x) . \psi x . \text{Ind.} . \supset . (\epsilon|| + |||x) . \varphi x \vee \psi x$ is tautologous, because nothing was said in our definitions about a sum $(|| + |||)$. (I will write the tautology in the abbreviated form "$\epsilon|| . \epsilon||| . \supset . \epsilon|||||$".) Suppose the question is, given a left hand side, to find what number of lines to the right of " $\supset$ " makes the whole a tautology. We can find the number, we can indeed discover that in the case above it is $|| + |||$; but we can equally well discover that it is $| + ||||$ or $| + ||| + |$, for it is all of these. We can also find an inductive proof that the algebraic expression

$$\epsilon n . \epsilon m . \supset . \epsilon \, n + m$$

is tautologous. Then I have a right to regard a proposition like

$$\epsilon 17 . \epsilon 28 . \supset . \epsilon (17 + 28)$$

as a tautology. But does that give us the equation $17 + 28 = 45$? Certainly not. I still have to work it out. In accordance with this general rule, it also makes sense to write $\epsilon 2 . \epsilon 3 . \supset . \epsilon 5$ as a tautology if, as it were, I don't yet know what $2 + 3$ yields; for $2 + 3$ only has sense in so far as it has still to be worked out.

Hence the equation $|| + ||| = |||||$ only has a point if the sign "$|||||$" can be recognised in the same way as the sign "5", that is, independently of the equation.

The difference between my point of view and that of contemporary writers on the foundations of arithmetic is that I am not obliged to despise particular calculi like the decimal system. For me one calculus is as good as another. To look down on a particular calculus is like wanting to play chess without real pieces, because playing with pieces is too particularized and not abstract enough. If the pieces really *don't* matter then one lot is just as good as another. And if the games are really distinct from each other, then one game is as good, i.e. as interesting, as the other. None of them is more sublime than any other.

Which proof of $\epsilon||.\epsilon|||. \supset .\epsilon|||||$ expresses our knowledge that this is a correct logical proposition?

Obviously, one that makes use of the fact that one can treat $(\exists x)\ldots$ as a logical sum. We may translate from a symbolism like

("if there is a star in each square, then there are two in the whole rectangle") into the Russellian one. And it isn't as if the tautologies in that notation expressed an idea that is confirmed by the proof after first of all appearing merely plausible; what appears plausible to us is that this expression is a tautology (a law of logic).

The series of propositions

$$(\exists x): aRx.xRb$$
$$(\exists x, y): aRx.xRy.yRb$$
$$(\exists x, y, z): aRx.xRy.yRz.zRb, \quad \text{etc.}$$

may perfectly well be expressed as follows:

"There is one term between a and b".

"There are two terms between a and b", etc.,

and may be written in some such way as:

$$(\exists 1x).aRxRb, \quad (\exists 2x).aRxRb, \quad \text{etc.}$$

But it is clear that in order to understand this expression we need the explanation above, because otherwise by analogy with $(\exists 2x).\varphi x. = .(\exists x, y).\varphi x.\varphi y$ you might believe that $(\exists 2x).aRxRb$ was equivalent to the expression $(\exists x, y).aRxRb.aRyRb$.

Of course I might also write "$(\exists 2x, y).F(x, y)$" instead of "$(\exists x, y).F(x, y)$". But then the question would be: what am I to take "$(\exists 3x, y).F(x, y)$" as meaning? But here a rule can be given; and indeed we need one that takes us further in the number series as far as we want to go. E.g.:

$$(\exists 3x, y).F(x, y). = .(\exists x, y, z): F(x, y).F(x, z).F(y, z)$$
$$(\exists 4x, y).F(x, y). = .(\exists x, y, z, u): F(x, y).F(x, z).\ldots$$

followed by the combinations of two elements, and so on. But we might also give the following definition:

$$(\exists 3x, y).F(x, y). = .(\exists x, y, z): F(x, y).F(y, x).F(x, z).$$
$$F(z, x).F(y, z).F(x, y), \quad \text{and so on.}$$

"$(\exists 3\ x, y).F(x, y)$" would perhaps correspond to the proposition in word-language "$F(x, y)$ is satisfied by 3 things"; and that proposition too would need an explanation if it was not to be ambiguous.

Am I now to say that in these different cases the sign "3" has different meanings? Isn't it rather that the sign "3" expresses what is common to the different interpretations? Why else would I have chosen it? Certainly, in each of these contexts, the same rules hold for the sign "3". It is replaceable by $2 + 1$ as usual and so on. But at all events a proposition on the pattern of $\varepsilon || \cdot \varepsilon ||| \cdot \supset \cdot \varepsilon |||||$ is no longer a tautology. Two men who live at peace with each other and three other men who live at peace with each other do not make five men who live at peace with each other. But that does not mean that $2 + 3$ are no longer 5; it is just that addition cannot be applied in that way. For one might say: 2 men who . . . and 3 men who . . ., each of whom lives at peace with each of the first group, $= 5$ men who . . .

In other words, the signs of the form $(\exists 1x, y).F(x, y)$, $(\exists 2x, y).F(x, y)$ etc. have the same multiplicity as the cardinal numbers, like the signs $(\exists 1x).\varphi x$, $(\exists 2x).\varphi x$, etc. and also like the signs $(\varepsilon 1x).\varphi x$, $(\varepsilon 2x).\varphi x$, etc.

"There are only 4 red things, but they don't consist of 2 and 2, as there is no function under which they fall in pairs". That would mean regarding the proposition $2 + 2 = 4$ thus: if you can see 4 circles on a surface, every two of them always have a particular property in common; say a sign inside the circle. (In that case of course every three of the circles too will have to have a sign in common etc.) If I am to make any assumption at all about reality, why not *that*? The

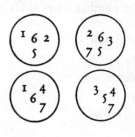

'axiom of reducibility' is essentially the same kind of thing. In this sense one might say that 2 and 2 do always make 4, but 4 doesn't always consist of 2 and 2. (It is only because of the utter vagueness and generality of the axiom of reducibility that we are seduced into believing that – if it is a significant sentence at all – it is more than an arbitrary assumption for which there is no ground. For this reason, in this and all similar cases, it is very illuminating to drop this generality, which doesn't make the matter any more mathematical, and in its place to make very specific assumptions.)

We feel like saying: 4 does not always have to consist of 2 and 2, but if it does consist of groups it can consist of 2 and 2, or of 3 and 1 etc.; but not of 2 and 1 or 3 and 2, etc. In that way we get everything prepared in case 4 is actually divisible into groups. But in that case arithmetic doesn't have anything to do with the actual division, but only with the possibility of division. The assertion might just as well be the assertion that any two of a group of 4 dots on paper are always joined by a line.

Or that around every 2 such groups of 2 dots in the real world there is always a circle drawn.

Add to this that a statement like "you can see two black circles in a white rectangle" doesn't have the form "($\exists$x, y), etc.". For, if I give the circles names, the names refer to the precise location of the circles and I can't say of them that they are either in this rectangle or in the other. I can indeed say "there are 4 circles in both rectangles taken together" but that doesn't mean that I can say of each individual circle that it is in one rectangle or the other. For in the case supposed the sentence "this circle is in this rectangle" is senseless.

But what does the proposition "there are 4 circles in the 2 rectangles taken *together*" mean? How do I establish that? By adding the numbers in each? In that case the number of the circles in the two rectangles *means* the result of the addition of the two numbers. – Or is it something like the result of taking a count through both rectangles? Or the number of lines I get if I correlate a line to a circle no matter whether it is in this rectangle *or* in the other? If "this circle" is individuated by its position, we can say "every line is correlated either to a circle in this rectangle or to a circle in the other rectangle" but not "this circle is either in this

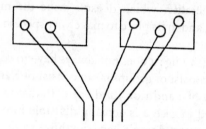

rectangle or in the other". *This* can only be *here* if "this" and "here" do not mean the same. By contrast *this* line can be correlated to a circle in this rectangle because it remains this line, even if it is correlated to a circle in the other rectangle.

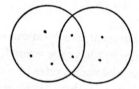

In these two circles together are there 9 dots or 7? As one normally understands the question, 7. But must I understand it so? Why shouldn't I count twice the points that are common to both circles?

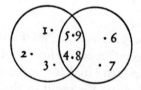

It is a different matter if we ask "how many dots are within the black lines?" For here I can say: in the sense in which there are 5 and 4 in the circles, there are 7.

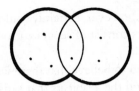

Now we might say: by the sum of 4 and 5 I mean the number of the objects which fall under the concept φx **v** ψx, if it is the case that $(E\ 4x)^1.φx.(E\ 5x).ψx.Ind$. That doesn't mean that the sum of 4 and 5 may only be used in the context of propositions like $(∃\ 4x).φx$; it means: if you want to construct the sum of n and m, insert the numbers on the left hand side of "⊃" in the form $(∃nx).φx.(∃mx).ψx$, etc., and the sum of m and n will be the number which has to go on the right hand side in order to make the whole proposition a tautology. So that is a method of addition – a very long-winded one.

Compare: "Hydrogen and oxygen yield water", "2 dots and 3 dots yield 5 dots".

So do e.g. 2 dots in my visual field, that I "see as 4" and not "as 2 and 2", consist of 2 and 2? Well, what does that mean? Is it asking whether in some way they are divided into groups of 2 dots each? Of course not (for in that case they would presumably have had to be divided in all other conceivable ways as well). Does it mean that they *can* be divided into groups of 2 and 2, i.e. that it *makes sense* to speak of such groups in the four? – At any rate it does correspond to the sentence $2 + 2 = 4$ that I can't say that the group of 4 dots I saw consisted of separate groups of 2 and 3. Everyone will say: that's impossible, *because* $3 + 2 = 5$. (And "impossible" here means "nonsensical".)

"Do 4 dots consist of 2 and 2?" may be a question about a physical or visual fact; for it isn't the question in arithmetic. The

---

1. For the explanation of this notation, see below, p. 343 f.

arithmetical question, however, certainly could be put in the form: "*Can* a group of 4 dots consist of separate groups of 2?"

"Suppose that I used to believe that there wasn't anything at all except one function and the 4 objects that satisfy it. Later I realise that it is satisfied by a fifth thing too: does this make the sign '4' become senseless?" – Well, if there is no 4 in the *calculus* then '4' is senseless.

If you say it would be possible when adding to make use of the tautology $(E\ 2x).\varphi x.(E\ 3x).\psi x.\ Ind. \supset .(\ E\ 5x).\varphi x \lor \psi x \ \ldots \ A)$ this is how it would have to be understood: first it is possible to establish according to certain rules that $(E\ x).\varphi x.(E\ x).\psi x.Ind..\supset.$ $(E\ x, y):\varphi x \lor \psi x.\varphi y \lor \psi y.$ is tautological. $(E\ x).\varphi x$ is an abbreviation for $(\exists x).\varphi x. \sim (\exists x, y).\varphi x.\varphi y.$ I will abbreviate further tautologies like A thus: $(E\ ).(E\ ).\supset.(E\ )$

Therefore

$(E\ x).(E\ x).\supset.(E\ x, y).(E\ x, y).(E\ x).\supset.(E\ x, y, z).$

and other tautologies follow from the rules. I write "and other tautologies" and not "and so on ad inf." since one doesn't yet have to use that concept.

[1]When the numbers were written out in the decimal system there were rules, namely the addition rules for every pair of numbers from 0 to 9, and, used appropriately, these sufficed for the addition of all numbers. Now which rule corresponds to these elementary

---

1. In the manuscript this paragraph is preceded by the remark: I can work out $17 + 28$ according to the rules, I don't need to give $17 + 28 = 45$ (α) as a rule. So if in a proof there occurs the step from $f(17 + 28)$ to $f(45)$ I don't need to say it took place according to (α); I can cite other rules of the addition table.

But what is this like in the $(((1) + 1) + 1)$ notation? Can I say I could work out e.g. $2 + 3$ in it? And according to which rules? It would go like this:
$$\{(1) + 1\} + \{((1) + 1) + 1\} = (((1) + 1\} + 1) =$$
$$\{((((1) + 1) + 1) + 1) + 1\} \ldots \sigma$$

rules? It is obvious that in a calculation like σ we don't have to keep as many rules in mind as in $17 + 28$. Indeed we need only *one* general rule. We don't need any rules like $3 + 2$; on the contrary, we now seem to be able to deduce, or work out, how many $3 + 2$ makes.

We are given the sum $2 + 3 = ?$ and we write

1, 2, 3, 4, 5, 6, 7
1, 2; 1, 2, 3

That is in fact how children calculate when they "count off". (And that calculus must be as good as any other.)

It is clear incidentally that the problem whether $5 + (4 + 3) = (5 + 4) + 3$ can be solved in *this* way:

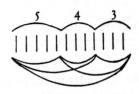

for this construction has precisely the same multiplicity as every other proof of that proposition.

A B C D E F G H I J K L M N O
A B C D E, A B C D
A   I, A B C
A   A B C D, A B C
A   A   G
A   E, A   G
A   L

If I name each number after its last letter, that is a proof that $(E + D) + C = E + (D + C) = L$

This is a good form of proof, because it shows clearly that the result is really worked out and because from it you can read off the general proof as well.

It may sound odd, but it is good advice at this point: don't do philosophy here, do mathematics.

Our calculus doesn't at all need to be acquainted with the construction of a series '(E x)', '(E x, y)', '(E x, y, z)' *etc.*; we can simply introduce two or three such signs without the "*etc.*". We can then introduce a calculus with a finite series of signs by laying down a sequence of certain signs, say the letters of the alphabet, and writing:

$$(E \ a).(E \ a). \supset .(E \ a, b)$$
$$(E \ a, b).(E \ a). \supset .(E \ a, b, c)$$
$$(E \ a, b).(E \ a, b). \supset .(E \ a, b, c, d)$$

etc. up to z.

The right hand side (the side to the right of "$\supset$") can then be found from the left hand side by a calculus like:

a	b	c	d	e	f	...z
a	b	–	–	–		
–	–	a	b	c		

$$\overline{}$$

a	b	c	d	e

B)

This calculus could be derived from the rules for the construction of tautologies as a simplification. – If I presuppose this law for constructing a fragment of the series out of two others, I can then introduce as a designation of that fragment the expression "sum of the two others", and thus give the definition:

$$a + a \overset{\text{Def}}{=} ab$$
$$a + ab \overset{\text{Def}}{=} abc$$

and so on up to z.

If the rules for the calculus B had been explained by examples, we could regard those definitions too as particular cases of a general rule and then set problems like "abc + ab = ?". It is now tempting to confuse the tautology

$$\alpha) \ (E \ a, b).(E \ a, b). \supset .(E \ a, b, c, d)$$

with the equation

$$\beta) \ ab + ab = abcd$$

But the latter is a replacement rule, the former isn't a rule but just a tautology. The sign "$\supset$" in α in no way corresponds to the "$=$" in β.

We forget that the sign "$\supset$" in α doesn't say that the two signs to the left and right of it yield a tautology.

On the other hand we might construct a calculus in which the equation $\xi + \eta = \eta$ was obtained as a transformation of the equation

γ) $(E\,\xi).(E\,\eta). \supset .(E\,\zeta) =$ Taut.

So that I as it were get $\zeta = \xi + \eta$ if I work out ζ from the equation γ.

In these discussions, how does the concept of sum make its entry? – There is no mention of summation in the original calculus that lays down that the form

δ) $(E\,\xi).(E\,\eta). \supset .(E\,\zeta)$

is tautologous where $\xi = xy$, $y = x$ and $\zeta = xyz$. – Later we introduce into the calculus a number system (say the system a, b, c, d, ... z), and finally we define the sum of two numbers as the number that solves the equation γ.

If we wrote "$(E\,x).(E\,x). \supset .(E\,x, y)$" instead of "$(E\,x).(E\,x). \supset .(E\,x+x)$" it would make no sense; unless the notation already went, not

ι) "$(E\,x)$, etc.", "$(E\,x, y)$ etc.", $(E\,x, y, z)$, etc."

but

ϰ) "$(E\,x)$, etc.", $(E\,x+x)$ etc.", "$(E\,x+x+x)$, etc."

For why should we suddenly write

"$(E\,x, y).(E\,x). \supset .(E\,xy+x)$"   instead of
"$(E\,x, y).(E\,x). \supset .(E\,x, y, z)$"?

That would just confuse the notation. – Then we say: it will greatly simplify the writing of the tautologies if we can write in the right bracket simply the expressions in the two left brackets. But so far that notation hasn't been explained: I don't know what $(E\,xy+x)$ means, or that $(E\,xy+x) = (E\,x, y, z)$.

But if the notation already went "$(E\,x)$", "$(E\,x+x)$", "$(E\,x+x+x)$" that would only give a sense to the expression "$(E\,x+x+x+x+x)$ and not to $(E\,(x+x)+(x+x))$.

The notation ϰ is in the same case as ι. A quick way of calculating whether you get a tautology of the form δ is to draw connecting lines, thus

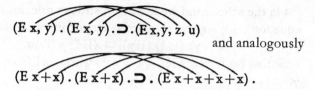

$$(E \; x, \overset{\frown}{y}) \cdot (E \; x, \overset{\frown}{y}) . \supset .(E \; x, y, z, u)$$

and analogously

$$(E \; x+x) \cdot (E \; x+x) . \supset . (E \; x+x+x+x) .$$

The connecting lines only correspond to the rule which we have to give in any case for checking the tautology. There is still no mention of addition; that doesn't come in until I decide – e.g. – to write "xy + yx" instead of "x, y, z, u" and adjoin a calculus with rules that allow the derivation of the replacement rule "xy + yx = xyzu". Again, addition doesn't come in when I write in the notation $\varkappa$ "(E x).(E x). $\supset$.(E x + x)"; it only comes in when I distinguish between "x + x" and "(x) + (x)" and write

$$(x) + (x) = (x + x)$$

I can define "the sum of ξ and η" "$(\xi + \eta)$" as the number (or "the expression" if we are afraid to use the word "number") – I can define "$\xi + \eta$" as the number ζ that makes the expression δ tautologous; but we can also define "$\xi + \eta$" (independently of the calculus of tautologies) by the calculus B and then *derive* the equation (E ξ).(E η). $\supset$.(E $\xi + \eta$) = Taut.

A question that suggests itself is this: must we introduce the cardinal numbers in connection with the notation $(\exists x, y, \ldots) . \varphi x . \varphi y \ldots$? Is the calculus of the cardinal numbers somehow bound up with the calculus of the signs "$(\exists x, y \ldots) . \varphi x . \varphi y \ldots$? Is that kind of calculus perhaps in the nature of things the only application of the cardinal numbers? So far as concerns the "application of the cardinal numbers in the grammar", we can refer to what we said about the concept of the application of a calculus. We might put our question in this way too: in the propositions of our language – if we imagine them translated into Russell's notation – do the cardinal numbers always occur after the sign "$\exists$"? This question is closely connected with another: Is a numeral always used in language as a characterization of a concept – a function? The answer to that is that our language does always use the numerals as attributes of concept-words – but that these concept-words belong to different grammatical systems that are so totally distinct from each other (as you see from the fact that some of them have meaning in contexts in which others are senseless), that a norm making them all concept-words is an uninteresting one. But the notation "$(\exists x, y \ldots)$ etc." is just such a norm. It is a straight translation of a norm of our word-language, the expression "there is . . .", which is a form of expression into which countless grammatical forms are squeezed.

Moreover there is another sense of numeral in which numerals are not connected with "$\exists$": that is, in so far as "$(\exists 3)_x \ldots$" is not contained in "$(\exists 2 + 3)_x \ldots$".

If we disregard functions containing "$=$" ($x = a . \mathbf{v} . x = b$, etc.), then on Russell's theory $5 = 1$ if there are no functions that are satisfied by only *one* argument, or by only 5 arguments. Of course at first this proposition seems nonsensical; for in that case how can one sensibly say that there are no such functions? Russell would have to say that the statement that there are five-functions and the statement that these are one-functions can only be separated if we have in our symbolism a five-class and a one-class. Perhaps he could say that his view is correct because without the paradigm of the class 5 in the symbolism, I can't say at all that a function is satisfied by five arguments. That is to say, from the existence of the sentence "$(\exists \varphi):(E_1 x) . \varphi x$" its truth already follows. – So you seem to be able to say: look at this sentence, and you will see that it is true. And in a sense irrelevant for our purposes that is indeed possible: think of the wall of a room on which is written in red "in this room there is something red". –

This problem is connected with the fact that in an ostensive definition I do not state anything about the paradigm (sample); I only use it to make a statement. It belongs to the symbolism and is not one of the objects to which I apply the symbolism.

For instance, suppose that "1 foot" were defined as the length of a particular rod in my room, so that instead of saying "this door is 6 ft high" I would say "this door is six times as high as *this* length" (pointing to the unit rod). In that case we couldn't say things like "the proposition 'there is an object whose length is 1 ft' proves itself, because I couldn't express the proposition at all if there were no object of that length". (That is, if I introduced the sign "*this* length" instead of "1 foot", then the statement that the unit rod is 1 foot long would mean "this rod has this length" (where I point both times to the same rod).) Similarly one cannot say of a group of strokes serving as a paradigm of 3, that it consists of 3 strokes.

"If the proposition isn't true, then the proposition doesn't exist" means: "if the proposition doesn't exist, then it doesn't exist". And one proposition can never describe the paradigm in another, unless it ceases to be a paradigm. If the length of the unit rod can be described by assigning it the length "1 foot", then it isn't the paradigm of the unit of length; if it were, every statement of length would have to be made by means of it.

If we can give any sense at all to a proposition of the form "~(∃φ):(E x).φx" it must be a proposition like: "there is no circle on this surface containing only *one* black speck" (I mean: it must have that sort of *determined* sense, and not remain vague as it did in Russellian logic and in my logic in the *Tractatus*).

If it follows from the propositions

ρ) ~(∃φ):(E x).φx

and σ) ~(∃φ):(E x, y).φx.φy

that 1 = 2, then here "1" and "2" don't mean what we commonly mean by them, because in word-language the propositions ρ and σ would be "there is no function that is satisfied by only one thing" and "there is no function that is satisfied by only two things." And according to the rules of our language these are propositions with different senses.

One is tempted to say: "In order to express '$(\exists x, y) . \varphi x . \varphi y$' we need 2 signs 'x' and 'y'." But that has no meaning. What we *need* for it, is, perhaps, pen and paper; and the proposition means no more than "to express 'p' we need 'p'."

If we ask: but what then does "$5 + 7 = 12$" mean – what kind of significance or point is left for this expression after the elimination of the tautologies, etc. from the arithmetical calculus? – the answer is: this equation is a replacement rule which is based on certain general replacement rules, the rules of addition. The content of $5 + 7 = 12$ (supposing someone didn't know it) is precisely what children find difficult when they are learning this proposition in arithmetic lessons.

No investigation of concepts, only insight into the number-calculus can tell us that $3 + 2 = 5$. That is what makes us rebel against the idea that

"$(E\ 3\ x) . \varphi x . (E\ 2\ x) . \psi x . Ind. : \supset . (E\ 5\ x) . \varphi x \vee \psi x$"[1]

could be the proposition $3 + 2 = 5$. For what enables us to tell that this expression is a tautology cannot itself be the result of an examination of concepts, but must be recognizable from the calculus. For the grammar is a calculus. That is, nothing of what the tautology calculus contains apart from the number calculus serves to justify it and if it is number we are interested in the rest is mere decoration.

Children learn in school that $2 \times 2 = 4$, but not that $2 = 2$.

---

1. Thus according to the typescript. The manuscript reads "$(\exists 3x) . \varphi x . (\exists 2x) . \psi x . Ind. : \supset . (\exists 5x) . \varphi x \vee \psi x$".

What distinguishes a statement of number about a concept from one about a variable? The first is a proposition about the concept, the second a grammatical rule concerning the variable.

But can't I specify a variable by saying that its values are to be all objects satisfying a certain function? In that way I do not indeed *specify* the variable unless I *know* which objects satisfy the function, that is, if these objects are given me in another way (say by a list); and then giving the function becomes superfluous. If we do not know whether an object satisfies the function, then we do not know whether it is to be a value of the variable, and the grammar of the variable is in that case simply not expressed in this respect.

Statements of number *in* mathematics (e.g. "The equation $x^2 = 1$ has 2 roots") are therefore quite a different kind of thing from statements of number outside mathematics ("There are 2 apples on the table").

If we say that A B admits of 2 permutations, it sounds as if we had made a *general* assertion, analogous to "There are 2 men in the room" in which nothing further is said or need be known about the men. But this isn't so in the A B case. I cannot give a more general description of A B, B A and so the proposition that no permutations are possible cannot say less than that the permutations A B, B A are possible. To say that 6 permutations of 3 elements are possible cannot say less, i.e. anything more general, than is shown by the schema:

$$
\begin{array}{ccc}
A & B & C \\
A & C & B \\
B & A & C \\
B & C & A \\
C & A & B \\
C & B & A \\
\end{array}
$$

For it's *impossible* to know the number of possible permutations without knowing which they are. And if this weren't so, the theory of combinations wouldn't be capable of arriving at its general formulae. The law which we see in the formulation of the permutations is represented by the equation p = n! In the same sense, I believe, as that in which a circle is given by its equation. – Of course I can correlate the number 2 with the permutations A B, B A just as I can 6 with the complete set of permutations of A, B, C, but that does not give me the theorem of combination theory. – What I see in A B, B A is an internal relation which therefore cannot be described. That is, *what* cannot be described is that which makes this class of permutations complete. – I can only count what is actually there, not possibilities. But I can e.g. work out how many rows a man must write if in each row he puts a permutation of 3 elements and goes on until he cannot go any further without repetition. And this means, he needs 6 rows to write down the permutations A B C, A C B, etc., since these just are "*the* permutations of A, B, C". But it makes no sense to say that these are all permutations of A B C.

We could imagine a combination computer exactly like the Russian abacus.

It is clear that there is a mathematical question: "How many permutations of – say – 4 elements are there?", a question of precisely the same kind as "What is 25 × 18?". For in both cases there is a general method of solution.

But still it is only with respect to this method that this question exists.

The proposition that there are 6 permutations of 3 elements is identical with the permutation schema and thus there isn't here a proposition "There are 7 permutations of 3 elements", for no such schema corresponds to it.

You could also conceive the number 6 in this case as another kind of number, the permutation-number of A, B, C. Permutation as another kind of counting.

If you want to know what a proposition means, you can always ask "How do I know that?" Do I know that there are 6 permutations of 3 elements in the same way in which I know that there are 6 people in this room? No. Therefore the first proposition is of a different *kind* from the second.

You may also say that the proposition "There are 6 permutations of 3 elements" is related to the proposition "There are 6 people in this room" in precisely the same way as is "$3 + 3 = 6$", which you could also cast in the form "There are 6 units in $3 + 3$". And just as in the one case I can count the rows in the permutation schema, so in the other I can count the strokes in

Just as I can prove that $4 \times 3 = 12$ by means of the schema

$$
\begin{array}{ccc}
\circ & \circ & \circ \\
\circ & \circ & \circ \\
\circ & \circ & \circ \\
\circ & \circ & \circ \\
\end{array}
$$

I can also prove $3! = 6$ by means of the permutation schema.

The proposition "the relation R links two objects", if it is to mean the same as "R is a two-place relation", is a proposition of grammar.

21

Sameness of number and sameness of length

How should we regard the propositions "these hats are of the same size", or "these rods have the same length" or "these patches have the same colour"? Should we write them in the form "(∃L).La.Lb"? But if that is intended in the usual way, and so is used with the usual rules, it would mean that it made sense to write "(∃L).La", i.e. "the patch has a colour", "the rod has a length". Of course I can write "(∃L).La.Lb" for "a and b have the same length" provided that I know and bear in mind that "(∃L).La" is senseless; but then the notation becomes misleading and confusing ("to have a length", "to have a father"). – What we have here is something that we often express in ordinary language as follows: "If a has the length L, so does b"; but here the sentence "a has the length L" has no sense, or at least not as a statement about a; the proposition should be reworded "if we call the length of a 'L', then the length of b is L" and 'L' here is essentially a variable. The proposition incidentally has the form of an example, of a proposition that could serve as an example for the general sentence; we might go on: "for example, if the length of a is 5 metres, then the length of b is 5 metres, etc." – Saying "the rods a and b have the same length" says nothing about the length of each rod; for it doesn't even say "that each of the two has a length". So it is quite unlike "A and B have the same father" and "the name of the father of A and B is 'N' ", where I simply substitute the proper name for the general description. It is not that there is a certain length of which we are at first only told that a and b both possess it, and of which '5m' is the name. If the lengths are lengths in the visual field we can say the two lengths are the same, without in general being able to "name" them with a number. – The written form of the proposition "if L is the length of a, the length of b too is L" is derived from the form of an example. And we might express the general proposition by actually enumerating examples and adding "etc.". And If I say, "a and b are the same length; if the length of a is L, then the length of b is L; if a is 5 m long then b is 5 m long, if a is 7 m long, then b is 7 m long, etc.", I am repeating the same proposition. The third formulation shows that the "and" in the proposition doesn't stand between two forms, as it does in "$(\exists x).\varphi x.\psi x$", where one can also write "$(\exists x).\varphi x$" and "$(\exists x).\psi x$".

Let us take as an example the proposition "there are the same number of apples in each of the two boxes". If we write this proposition in the form "there is a number that is the number of the apples in each of the boxes" here too we cannot construct the form "there is a number that is the number of apples in this box" or "the apples in this box have a number". If I write: $(\exists x).\varphi x. \sim (\exists x, y).\varphi x.\varphi y. = .(\exists_n 1x).\varphi x. = \varphi 1$, etc. then we might write the proposition "the number of apples in both boxes is the same" as "$(\exists n).\varphi n.\psi n$". But "$(\exists n).\varphi n$" would not be a proposition.

If you want to write the proposition "the same number of objects fall under φ and ψ" in a perspicuous notation, the first temptation is to write it in the form "$\varphi n.\psi n$". And that doesn't feel as if it were a logical product of φn and ψn, which would mean that it made sense to write $\varphi n.\psi 5$; it is essential that the same letter should follow ψ as follows φ, and $\varphi n.\psi n$ is an abstraction from the logical products $\varphi 4.\psi 4$, $\varphi 5.\psi 5$, etc., rather than itself a logical product. (So φn doesn't follow from $\varphi n.\psi n$. The relation of $\varphi n \cdot \psi n$ to a logical product is more like that of a differential quotient to a quotient.) It is no more a logical product than the photograph of a family group is a group of photographs. Therefore the form "$\varphi n.\psi n$" can be misleading and perhaps we should prefer a notation of the form "$\overline{\varphi n.\psi n}.$"; or even "$(\exists n).\varphi n.\psi n$", provided that the grammar of this sign is fixed. We can then stipulate $(\exists n).\varphi n = $ Taut., which is the same as $(\exists n).\varphi n.p. = .p$.

Therefore $(\exists n).\varphi n \vee \psi n. = .\text{Taut.}$, $(\exists n).\varphi n. \supset \psi n. = .\text{Taut.}$,
$(\exists n).\varphi n | \psi n. = \text{Cont.}$, etc.

$$\varphi 1.\psi 1.(\exists n).\varphi n.\psi n = .\varphi 1.(\exists n).\varphi n.\psi n$$
$$\varphi 2.\psi 2.(\exists n).\varphi n.\psi n. = .\varphi 2.(\exists n).\varphi n.\psi n$$
$$\text{etc. ad inf.}$$

And in general the calculation rules for $(\exists n)\varphi n.\psi n$ can be derived from the fact that we can write

$$(\exists n).\varphi n.\psi n. = .\varphi 0.\psi 0.\vee.\varphi 1.\psi 1.\vee.\varphi 2.\psi 2.\vee.\varphi 3.\psi 3$$

and so on ad inf.

It is clear that this is not a logical sum, because "and so on ad inf." is not a sentence. The notation $(\exists n).\varphi n.\psi n$ however is not proof against misunderstanding, because you might wonder why you shouldn't be able to put Φn instead of $\varphi n.\psi n$ though if you did $(\exists n).\Phi n$ should of course be meaningless. Of course we can clear that up by going back to the notation $\sim(\exists x).\varphi x$ for $\varphi 0, (\exists x)\varphi x.\sim (\exists x,y).\varphi x.\varphi x$ for $\varphi 1$, etc., i.e. to $(\exists_n ox).\varphi x$ for $\varphi 0, (\exists_n 1x).\varphi x$ for $\varphi 1$ respectively, and so on. For then we can distinguish between

$$(\exists_n 1x).\varphi x (\exists_n 1x).\psi x \quad \text{and} \quad (\exists_n 1x).\varphi x.\psi x$$

And if we go back to $(\exists n).\varphi n.\psi n$, that means $(\exists n):(\exists_n nx).\varphi x.(\exists_n nx).\psi x$ (which is not nonsensical) and not $(\exists n):(\exists_n nx).\varphi x.\psi x$, which is nonsensical.

The expressions "same number", "same length", "same colour", etc. have grammars which are similar but not the same. In each case it is tempting to regard the proposition as an endless logical sum whose terms have the form $\varphi n.\psi n$. Moreover, each of these words has several different meanings, i.e. can itself be replaced by several words with different grammars. For "same number" does not mean the same when applied to lines simultaneously present in the visual field as in connection with the apples in two boxes; and "same length" applied in visual space is different from "same length" in Euclidean space; and the meaning of "same colour" depends on the criterion we adopt for sameness of colour.

If we are talking about patches in the visual field seen simultaneously, the expression "same length" varies in meaning depending on whether the lines are immediately adjacent or at a distance from each other. In word-language we often get out of the difficulty by using the expression "it looks".

Sameness of number, when it is a matter of a number of lines "that one can take in at a glance", is a different sameness from that which can only be established by counting the lines.

Different criteria for sameness of number: in I and II the number that one immediately recognizes; in III the criterion of correlation; in IV we have to count both groups; in V we recognize the same pattern. (Of course these are not the only cases.)

We want to say that equality of length in Euclidean space consists in both lines measuring the same number of cm, both 5 cm, both 10 cm etc.; but where it is a case of two lines in visual space being equally long, there is no length L that both lines have.

One wants to say: two rods must always have either the same length or different lengths. But what does that mean? What it is, of course, is a rule about modes of expression. "There must either be the same number or a different number of apples in the two boxes." The method whereby I discover whether two lines are of the same length is supposed to be the laying of a ruler against each line: but do they have the same length when the rulers are *not* applied? In that case we would say we don't know whether during that time the two lines have the same or different lengths. But we might also say that during that time they have no length, or perhaps no numerical length.

Something similar, if not exactly the same, holds of sameness between numbers.

When we cannot immediately see the number of dots in a group, we can sometimes keep the group in view as a whole while we count, so that it makes sense to say it hasn't altered during the counting. It is different when we have a group of bodies or patches that we cannot keep in a single view while we count them, so that we don't have the same criterion for the group's not changing while it is counted.

Russell's definition of sameness of number is unsatisfactory for various reasons. The truth is that in mathematics we don't need any such definition of sameness of number. He puts the cart before the horse.

What seduces us into accepting the Russellian or Fregean explanation is the thought that two classes of objects (apples in two boxes) have the same number if they *can* be correlated 1 to 1. We imagine correlation as a check of sameness of number. And here we do distinguish in thought between being correlated and being connected by a relation; and correlation becomes something that is related to connection as the "geometrical straight line" is related to a real line, namely a kind of ideal connection that is as it were sketched in advance by Logic so that reality only has to trace it. It is possibility conceived as a shadowy actuality. This in turn is connected with the idea of ("∃x).φx" as an expression of the possibility of φx.

"φ and ψ have the same number" (I will write this "S(φ, ψ)" or simply "S") is supposed to follow from "φ5 . ψ5"; but it doesn't follow from φ5 . ψ5 that φ and ψ are connected by a 1–1 relation R (this I will write "Π(φ, ψ)" or "Π"). We get out of the difficulty by saying that in that case there is a relation like

$$\text{"}x = a . y = b . \mathbf{v} . x = c . y = d . \mathbf{v} ., \text{etc.''}$$

But if so, then in the first place why don't we define S without more ado as the holding of such a relation? And if you reply that this definition wouldn't include sameness of number in the case of infinite numbers, we shall have to say that this only boils down to a question of "elegance", because for finite numbers in the end I have to take refuge in "extensional" relations. But these too get us nowhere; because saying that between φ and ψ there holds a relation e.g. of the form $x = a . y = b . \mathbf{v} . x = c . y = d$ says only that

$$(\exists x,\ y) . φx . ψy . \sim (\exists x, y, z) . φx . φy . φz : (\exists x, y)\ ψx . ψy.$$
$$\sim (\exists x, y, z) . ψx . ψy . ψz.$$

(Which I write in the form

$$(\exists_n 2x) . φx . (\exists_n 2x) . ψx.)$$

And saying that between φ and ψ there holds *one* of the relations $x = a . y = b$; $x = a . y = b . \mathbf{v} . x = c . y = d$; etc. etc. means only that there obtains one of the facts φ1 . ψ1; φ2 . ψ2 etc. etc. Then we retreat into greater generality, saying that between φ and ψ there holds *some* 1–1 relation, forgetting that in order to specify this generality we have to make the rule that "some relation" includes also relations of the form $x = a . y = b$, etc. By saying more one does not avoid saying the less that is supposed to be contained in the more. Logic cannot be duped.

So in the sense of S in which S follows from $\varphi_5 . \psi_5$, it is not defined by Russell's definition. Instead, what we need is a series of definitions.

$$\left.\begin{array}{l} \varphi_0 . S = \varphi_0 . \psi_0 = \psi_0 . S \\ \varphi_1 . S = \varphi_1 . \psi_1 = \psi_1 . S \\ \qquad \text{etc. ad inf.} \end{array}\right\} \ldots \alpha$$

On the other hand Π is used as a criterion of sameness of number and of course *in another sense of S* it can also be equated with S. (And then we can only say: if in a given notation $S = \Pi$, then S means the same as Π.)

Though Π does not follow from $\varphi_5 . \psi_5$, $\varphi_5 . \psi_5$ does from $\Pi . \varphi_5$.

$$\Pi . \varphi_5 = \Pi . \varphi_5 . \psi_5 = \Pi . \psi_5$$
$$\text{etc.}$$

We can therefore write:

$$\Pi . \varphi_0 = \Pi . \varphi_0 . \psi_0 = \Pi . \varphi_0 . S$$
$$\Pi . \varphi_1 = \Pi . \varphi_1 . \psi_1 = \Pi . \varphi_1 . S \ldots \beta$$
$$\Pi . \varphi_2 = \Pi . \varphi_2 . \psi_2 = \Pi . \varphi_2 . S$$
$$\text{and so on ad inf.}$$

And we can express this by saying that the sameness of number follows from Π. And we can also give the rule $\Pi . S = \Pi$; it accords with the rules, or *the* rule, β and the rule α.

We could perfectly well drop the rule "S follows from Π", that is, $\Pi . S = \Pi$; the rule β does the same job.

If we write S in the form

$$\varphi_0 . \psi_0 . \mathbf{v} . \varphi_1 . \psi_1 . \mathbf{v} . \varphi_2 . \psi_2 . \mathbf{v} \ldots \text{ad inf.}$$

we can easily derive $\Pi . S = \Pi$ by grammatical rules that correspond to ordinary language. For

$(\varphi_0 . \psi_0 . \mathbf{v} . \varphi_1 . \psi_1 . \mathbf{v} \text{ etc. ad inf.}) . \Pi = \varphi_0 . \psi_0 . \Pi . \mathbf{v} . \varphi_1 . \psi_1$

$\Pi . \mathbf{v} . \text{ etc. ad inf.} = \varphi_0 . \Pi . \mathbf{v} . \varphi_1 . \Pi . \mathbf{v} . \varphi_2 . \Pi . \mathbf{v} . \text{etc. ad inf.}$

$= \Pi . (\varphi_0 \mathbf{v} \varphi_1 \mathbf{v} \varphi_2 \mathbf{v} \text{ etc. ad inf.}) = \Pi$

The proposition "$\varphi_0 \mathbf{v} \varphi_1 \mathbf{v} \varphi_2 \mathbf{v} . \text{etc. ad inf.}$" must be treated as a tautology.

: We can regard the concept of sameness of number in such
· a way that it makes no sense to attribute sameness of
· · number or its opposite to two groups of points except in
· · the case of two series of which one is correlated 1–1 to at
· · least a part of the other. Between such series all we can
· · talk about is unilateral or mutual inclusion.

This has really no more connection with particular numbers than equality or inequality of length in the visual field has with numerical measurement. We *can*, but need not, connect it with numbers. If we connect it with the number series, then the relation of mutual inclusion or equality of length between the rows becomes a relation of sameness of number. But then it isn't only that $\psi 5$ follows from $\Pi . \varphi 5$. We also have Π following from $\varphi 5 . \psi 5$. That means that here $S = \Pi$.

V MATHEMATICAL PROOF

22

In other cases, if I am looking for something, then even before it is found I can describe what finding it is; not so, if I am looking for the solution of a mathematical problem.
Mathematical Expeditions and Polar Expeditions

How can there be conjectures in Mathematics? Or better, what sort of thing is it that looks like a conjecture in mathematics? Such as making a conjecture about the distribution of the primes.

I might e.g. imagine that someone is writing primes in series in front of me without my knowing they are the primes – I might for instance believe he is writing numbers just as they occur to him – and I now try to detect a law in them. I might now actually form an hypothesis about this number sequence, just as I could about any sequence yielded by an experiment in physics.

Now in what sense have I, by so doing, made an hypothesis about the distribution of the primes?

You might say that an hypothesis in mathematics has the value that it trains your thoughts on a particular object – I mean a particular region – and we might say "we shall surely discover something interesting about these things".

The trouble is that our language uses each of the words "question", "problem", "investigation", "discovery", to refer to such basically different things. It's the same with "inference", "proposition", "proof".

The question again arises, what kind of verification do I count as valid for my hypothesis? Or can I *faute de mieux* allow an empirical one to hold for the time being until I have a "strict proof"? No. Until there is such a proof, there is no connection at all between my hypothesis and the "concept" of a prime number.

Only the so-called proof establishes any connection between the hypothesis and the primes *as such*. And that is shown by the fact that – as I've said – until then the hypothesis can be construed as one belonging purely to physics. – On the other hand when we have supplied a proof, it doesn't prove what was conjectured at all, since I can't conjecture to infinity. I can only conjecture what can be confirmed, but experience can only confirm a finite number of conjectures, and you can't conjecture the proof until you've got it, and not then either.

Suppose that someone, without having proved Pythagoras' theorem, has been led by measuring the sides and hypoteneuses of right angled triangles to "conjecture" it. And suppose he later discovered the proof, and said that he had then proved what he had earlier conjectured. At least one remarkable question arises: at what point of the proof does what he had earlier confirmed by individual trials emerge? For the proof is essentially different from the earlier method. – Where do these methods make contact, if the proof and the tests are only different aspects of the same thing (the same generalisation) if, as alleged, there is some sense in which they give the same result?

I have said: "from a single source only one stream flows", and one might say that it would be odd if the same thing were to come from such different sources. The thought that the same thing can come from different sources is familiar from physics, i.e. from hypotheses. In that area we are always concluding from symptoms to illnesses and we know that the most different symptoms can be symptoms of the same thing.

How could one guess from statistics the very thing the proof later showed?

How can the proof produce the same generalisation as the earlier trials made probable?

I am assuming that I conjectured the generalisation without conjecturing the proof. Does the proof now prove exactly the generalisation that I conjectured?!

Suppose someone was investigating even numbers to see if they confirmed Goldbach's conjecture. Suppose he expressed the conjecture – and it can be expressed – that if he continued with this investigation, he would never meet a counterexample as long as he lived. If a proof of the theorem is then discovered, will it also be a proof of the man's conjecture? How is that possible?

Nothing is more fatal to philosophical understanding than the notion of proof and experience as two different but comparable methods of verification.

What kind of discovery did Sheffer make when he found that $p \lor q$ and $\sim p$ can be expressed by $p|q$? People had no method of looking for $p|q$, and if someone were to find one today, it wouldn't make any difference.

What was it we didn't know before the discovery? (It wasn't anything that we didn't know, it was something with which we weren't acquainted.)

You can see this very clearly if you imagine someone objecting that $p|p$ isn't at all the same as is said by $\sim p$. The reply of course is that it's only a question of the system $p|q$, etc. having the necessary multiplicity. Thus Sheffer found a symbolic system with the necessary multiplicity.

Does it count as looking for something, if I am unaware of Sheffer's system and say I would like to construct a system with only *one* logical constant? No!

Systems are certainly not all in *one* space, so that I could say: there are systems with 3 and with 2 logical constants and now I am trying to reduce the number of constants *in the same way*. There is no "*same way*" here.

Suppose prizes are offered for the solution – say – of Fermat's problem. Someone might object to me: How can you say that this problem doesn't exist? If prizes are offered for the solution, then surely the problem must exist. I would have to say: Certainly, but the people who talk about it don't understand the grammar of the expression "mathematical problem" or of the word "solution". The prize is really offered for the solution of a scientific problem; for the *exterior* of the solution (hence also for instance we talk about a Riemannian *hypothesis*). The conditions of the problem are external conditions; and when the problem is solved, what happens corresponds to the setting of the problem in the way in which solutions correspond to problems in physics.

If we set as a problem to find a construction for a regular pentagon, the way the construction is specified in the setting of the problem is by the physical attribute that it is to yield a pentagon that is *shown by measurement* to be regular. For we don't get the concept of *constructive division into five* (or of a *constructive pentagon*) until we get it from the construction.

Similarly in Fermat's theorem we have an empirical structure that we interpret as a *hypothesis*, and not – of course – as the product of a construction. So in a certain sense what the problem asks for is not what the solution gives.

Of course a proof of the contradictory of Fermat's theorem (for instance) stands in the same relation to the problem as a proof of the proposition itself. (Proof of the impossibility of a construction.)

We can represent the impossibility of the trisection of an angle as a physical impossibility, by saying things like "don't try to divide the angle into 3 equal parts, it is hopeless!" But in so far as we can do that, it is not *this* that the "proof of impossibility" proves. That it is *hopeless* to attempt the trisection is something connected with physical facts.

Imagine someone set himself the following problem. He is to discover a game played on a chessboard, in which each player is to have 8 pieces; the two white ones which are in the outermost files at the beginning of the game (the "consuls") are to be given some special status by the rules so that they have a greater freedom of movement than the other pieces; one of the black pieces (the "general") is to have a special status; a white piece takes a black one by being put in its place (and vice versa); the whole game is to have a certain analogy with the Punic wars. Those are the conditions that the game is to satisfy. – There is no doubt that that is a problem, a problem not at all like the problem of finding out how under certain conditions white can win in chess. – But now imagine the problem: "How can white win in 20 moves in the war-game whose rules we don't yet know precisely?" – That problem would be quite analogous to the problems of mathematics (other than problems of calculation).

What is hidden must be capable of being found. (Hidden contradictions.)

Also, what is hidden must be completely describable before it is found, no less than if it had already been found.

It makes good sense to say that an object is so well hidden that it is impossible to find it; but of course the impossiblity here is not a logical one; i.e. it makes *sense* to speak of finding an object to describe the finding; we are merely denying that it will happen.

[We might put it like this: If I am looking for something, – I mean, the North Pole, or a house in London – I can *completely* describe what I am looking for before I have found it (or have found that it isn't there) and either way this description will be logically acceptable. But when I'm "looking for" something in mathematics, unless I am doing so *within* a system, what I am looking for cannot be described, or can only apparently be described; for if I could describe it in every particular, I would already actually *have* it; and before it is *completely* described I can't be sure whether *what* I am looking for is logically acceptable, and therefore describable at all. That is to say, the incomplete description leaves out just what is necessary for something to be capable of being looked for at all. So it is only an apparent description of what is being "looked for."][1]

Here we are easily misled by the legitimacy of an incomplete description when we are looking for a real object, and here again there is an unclarity about the concepts "description" and "object". If someone says, I am going to the North Pole and I expect to find a flag there, that would mean, on Russell's account, I expect to find something (an x) that is a flag – say of such and such a colour and size. In that case too it looks as if the expectation (the search) concerns only an indirect knowledge and not the object itself; as if that is something that I don't really know (knowledge by acquaintance) until I have it in front of me (having previously been only indirectly acquainted with it). But that is nonsense. There whatever I can perceive – to the extent that it is a fulfilment of my expectation – I can also describe in advance. And here "describe" means not saying something or other about it, but rather expressing it. That is, if I am looking for something I must be *able* to describe it *completely*.

The question is: can one say that at present mathematics is as it were jagged – or frayed – and for that reason we shall be able to round it off? I think you can't say that, any more than you can say that reality is untidy, because there are 4 primary colours, seven notes in an octave, three dimensions in visual space, etc.

You can't round off mathematics any more than you can say "let's round off the four primary colours to eight or ten" or "let's round off the eight tones in an octave to ten".

1. This paragraph is crossed out in the typescript.

The comparison between a mathematical expedition and a polar expedition. There is a point in drawing this comparison and it is a very useful one.

How strange it would be if a geographical expedition were uncertain whether it had a goal, and so whether it had any route whatsoever. We can't imagine such a thing, it's nonsense. But this is precisely what it is like in a mathematical expedition. And so perhaps it is a good idea to drop the comparison altogether.

Could one say that arithmetical or geometrical problems can always look, or can falsely be conceived, as if they referred to objects in space whereas they refer to space itself?

By "space" I mean what one can be *certain* of while searching.

23

Proof and the truth and falsehood of mathematical propositions

A mathematical proposition that has been proved has a bias towards truth in its grammar. In order to understand the sense of $25 \times 25 = 625$ I may ask: how is this proposition proved? But I can't ask how its contradictory is or would be proved, because it makes no sense to speak of a proof of the contradictory of $25 \times 25 = 625$. So if I want to raise a question which won't depend on the truth of the proposition, I have to speak of *checking* its truth, not of proving or disproving it. The method of checking corresponds to what one may call the sense of the mathematical proposition. The description of this method is a general one and brings in a system of propositions, for instance of propositions of the form $a \times b = c$.

We can't say "I will work out *that* it is so", we have to say "*whether* it is so", i.e., whether it is *so* or otherwise.

The method of checking the truth corresponds to the sense of a mathematical proposition. If it's impossible to speak of such a check, then the analogy between "mathematical proposition" and the other things we call propositions collapses. Thus there is a check for propositions of the form "$(\exists k)_m^n \ldots$" and "$\sim(\exists k)_n^m \ldots$" which bring in intervals.

Now consider the question "does the equation $x^2 + ax + b = 0$" have a solution in the real numbers?". Here again there is a check and the check decides between $(\exists \ldots)$, etc. and $\sim(\exists \ldots)$, etc. But can I in the same sense also ask and check "whether the equation has a solution"? Not unless I include this case too in a system with others.

(In reality the "proof of the fundamental theorem of algebra . . ." constructs a new kind of number.)

Equations are a kind of number. (That is, they can be treated similarly to the numbers.)

A "proposition of mathematics" that is proved by an induction is not a "proposition" in the same sense as the answer to a mathematical question unless one can look for the induction in a system of checks.

"Every equation G has a root." And suppose it has no root? Could we describe that case as we can describe its not having a rational solution? What is the criterion for an equation not having a solution? For this criterion must be given if the mathematical *question* is to have a sense and if the apparent existence proposition is to be a "proposition" in the sense of an answer to a question.

(What does the description of the contradictory consist of? What supports it? What are the examples that support it, and how are they related to particular cases of the proved contradictory? These questions are not side-issues, but absolutely essential.)

(The philosophy of mathematics consists in an exact scrutiny of mathematical proofs – not in surrounding mathematics with a vapour.)

In discussions of the provability of mathematical propositions it is sometimes said that there are substantial propositions of mathematics whose truth or falsehood must remain undecided. What the people who say that don't realize is that such propositions, *if* we can use them and want to call them "propositions", are not at all the same as what are called "propositions" in other cases; because a proof alters the grammar of a proposition. You can certainly use one and the same piece of wood first as a weathervane and then as a signpost; but you can't use it fixed as a weathervane and moving as a signpost. If some one wanted to say "There are also moving signposts" I would answer "You really mean 'There are also moving *pieces of wood*'. I don't say that a moving piece of wood can't possibly be used at all, but only that it can't be used as a signpost".

The word "proposition", if it is to have any meaning at all here, is equivalent to a calculus: to a calculus in which p ∨ ~p is a tautology (in which the "law of the excluded middle" holds). When it is supposed not to hold, we have altered the concept of proposition. But that does not mean we have made a discovery (found something that is a proposition and yet doesn't obey such and such a law); it means we have made a new stipulation, or set up a new game.

Mathematicians only go astray, when they want to talk about calculi in general; they do so because they forget the particular stipulations that are the foundations of each particular calculus.

The reason why all philosophers of mathematics miss their way is that in logic, unlike natural history, one cannot justify generalizations by examples. Each particular case has maximum significance, but once you have it the story is complete, and you can't draw from it any general conclusion (or any conclusion *at all*).

There is no such thing as a logical fiction and hence you can't work with logical fictions; you have to work out each example fully.

In mathematics there can only be mathematical troubles, there can't be philosophical ones.

The philosopher only marks what the mathematician casually throws off about his activities.

The philosopher easily gets into the position of a ham-fisted director, who, instead of doing his own work and merely supervising his employees to see they do their work well, takes over their jobs until one day he finds himself overburdened with other people's work while his employees watch and criticize him. He is particularly inclined to saddle himself with the work of the mathematician.

If you want to know what the expression "continuity of a function" means, look at the proof of continuity; that will show what it proves. Don't look at the result as it is expressed in prose, or in the Russellian notation, which is simply a translation of the prose expression; but fix your attention on the calculation actually going on in the proof. The verbal expression of the allegedly proved proposition is in most cases misleading, because it conceals the real purport of the proof, which can be seen with full clarity in the proof itself.

"Is the equation satisfied by any numbers?"; "It is satisfied by numbers"; "It is satisfied by all (no) numbers." Does your calculus have proofs? And what proofs? It is only from them that we will be able to gather the sense of these proportions and questions.

Tell me *how* you seek and I will tell you *what* you are seeking.

We must first ask ourselves: is the mathematical proposition proved? If so, how? For the proof is part of the grammar of the proposition! – The fact that this is so often not understood arises from our thinking once again along the lines of a misleading analogy. As usual in these cases, it is an analogy from our thinking in natural sciences. We say, for example, "this man died two hours ago" and if someone asks us "how can you tell that?" we can give a series of indications (symptoms). But we also leave open the possibility that medicine may discover hitherto unknown methods of ascertaining the time of death. That means that we can already describe such possible methods; it isn't their description that is discovered. What is ascertained experimentally is whether the description corresponds to the facts. For example, I may say: one method consists in discovering the quantity of haemoglobin in the blood, because this diminishes according to such and such a law in proportion to the time after death. Of course that isn't correct, but if it were correct, nothing in my imaginary description would change. If you call the medical discovery "the discovery of a proof that the man died two hours ago" you must go on to say that this discovery does not change anything in the grammar of the proposition "the man died two hours ago". The discovery is the discovery that a particular hypothesis is true (or: agrees with the facts). We are so accustomed to these ways of thinking, that we take the discovery of a proof in mathematics, sight unseen, as being the same or similar. We are wrong to do so because, to put it concisely, the mathematical proof couldn't be described before it is discovered.

The "medical proof" didn't incorporate the hypothesis it proved into any new calculus, so it didn't give it any new sense; a mathematical proof incorporates the mathematical proposition into a new calculus, and alters its position in mathematics. The proposition with its proof doesn't belong to the same category as the proposition without the proof. (Unproved mathematical propositions – signposts for mathematical investigation, stimuli to mathematical constructions.)

Are all the variables in the following equations variables of the same kind?

$$x^2 + y^2 + 2xy = (x + y)^2$$
$$x^2 + 3x + 2 = 0$$
$$x^2 + ax + b = 0$$
$$x^2 + xy + z = 0 \qquad ?$$

That depends on the use of the equations. – But the distinction between no. 1 and no. 2 (as they are ordinarily used) is not a matter of the extension of the values satisfying them. How do you prove the proposition "No. 1 holds for all values of x and y" and how do you prove the proposition "there are values of x that satisfy No. 2?" There is no more and no less similarity between the senses of the two propositions than there is between the proofs.

But can't I say of an equation "I know it doesn't hold for some substitutions – I've forgotten now *which*; but whether it doesn't hold in general, I don't know?" But what do you mean when you say you know that? How do you know? Behind the words "I know . . . " there isn't a certain state of mind to be the sense of those words. What can you do with that knowledge? That's what will show what the knowledge consists in. Do you know a method for ascertaining that the equation doesn't hold in general? Do you remember that the equation doesn't hold for some values of x between 0 and 1000? Or did someone just show you the equation and say he had found values of x that didn't satisfy the equation, so that perhaps you don't yourself know how to establish it for a given value? etc. etc.

"I have worked out that there is no number that . . . " – In what system of calculation does that calculation occur? – That will show us to which proposition-system the worked-out proposition belongs. (One also asks: "how does one work out *something like that*?")

"I have discovered that there is such a number."
"I have worked out that there is no such number."
In the first sentence I cannot substitute "no such" for "such a". What if in the second I put "such a" for "no such"? Let's suppose the result of a calculation isn't the proposition "~(∃n)" but "(∃n) etc." Does it then make sense to say something like "Cheer up! *Sooner or later* you must come to such a number, if only you try long enough"? That would only make sense if the result of the proof had not been "(∃n) etc." but something that sets limits to testing, and therefore a quite different result. That is, the contradictory of what we call an existence theorem, a theorem that tells us to look for a number, is not the proposition "(n) etc." but a proposition that says in such and such an interval there is no number which . . . What is the contradictory of what is proved? – For that you must look at the proof. We can say that the contradictory of a proved proposition is what would have been proved instead of it if a particular miscalculation had been made in the proof. If now, for instance, the proof that ~(∃n) etc is the case is an induction that shows that however far I go such a number cannot occur, the contradictory of this proof (using this expression for the sake of argument) is not an existence proof in our sense. This case isn't like a proof that one or none of the numbers a, b, c, d has the

property ε; and that is the case that one always has before one's mind as a paradigm. In that case I could make a mistake by believing that c had the property and after I had seen the error I would know that *none* of the numbers had the property. But at this point the analogy just collapses.

(This is connected with the fact that I can't eo ipso use the negations of equations in every calculus in which I use equations. For $2 \times 3 \neq 7$ doesn't mean that the equation $2 \times 3 = 7$ isn't to occur, like the equation $2 \times 3 = $ sine; the negation is an exclusion within a predetermined system. I can't negate a definition as I can negate an equation derived by rules.)

If you say that in an existence proof the interval isn't essential, because another interval might have done as well, of course that doesn't mean that not specifying an interval would have done as well. – The relation of a proof of non-existence to a proof of existence is not the same as that of a proof of p to a proof of its contradictory.

One should suppose that in a proof of the contradictory of "$(\exists n)$" it must be possible for a negation to creep in which would enable "$\sim (\exists n)$" to be proved erroneously. Let's for once start at the other end with the proofs, and suppose we were shown them first and then asked: what do these calculations prove? Look at the proofs and *then* decide what they prove.

I don't need to *assert* that it must be possible to construct the n roots of equations of the n-th degree; I merely say that the proposition "this equation has n roots" hasn't *the same* meaning if I've proved it by enumerating the constructed roots as if I've proved it in a different way. If I find a formula for the roots of an equation, I've constructed a new calculus; I haven't filled in a gap in an old one.

Hence it is nonsense to say that the proposition isn't proved until such a construction is produced. For when we do that we construct something new, and what we now mean by the fundamental theorem of algebra is what the present 'proof' shows us.

"Every existence proof must contain a construction of what it proves the existence of." You can only say "I won't call anything an 'existence proof' unless it contains such a construction". The mistake lies in pretending to possess a clear *concept* of existence.

We think we can prove a something, existence, in such a way that we are then convinced of it *independently of the proof*. (The idea of proofs independent of each other – and so presumably independent of what is proved.) Really, existence is what is proved by the procedures we call "existence proofs". When the intuitionists and others talk about this they say: "This state of affairs, existence, can be proved only thus and not thus." And they don't see that by saying that they have simply defined what *they* call existence. For it isn't at all like saying "that a man is in the room can only be proved by looking inside, not by listening at the door".

We have no concept of existence independent of our concept of an existence proof.

Why do I say that we don't discover a proposition like the fundamental theorem of algebra, and that we merely construct it? – Because in proving it we give it a new sense that it didn't have before. Before the so-called proof there was only a rough pattern of that sense in the word-language.

Suppose someone were to say: chess only had to be *discovered*, it was always there! Or: the *pure* game of chess was always there; we only made the material game alloyed with matter.

If a calculus in mathematics is altered by discoveries, can't we preserve the old calculus? (That is, do we have to throw it away?)

That is a very interesting way of looking at the matter. After the discovery of the North Pole we don't have two earths, one with and one without the North pole. But after the discovery of the law of the distribution of the primes, we do have two kinds of primes.

A mathematical question must be no less exact than a mathematical proposition. You can see the misleading way in which the mode of expression of word-language represents the sense of mathematical propositions if you call to mind the multiplicity of a mathematical proof and consider that the proof belongs to the *sense* of the proved proposition, i.e. determines that sense. It isn't something that brings it about that we believe a particular proposition, but something that shows us *what* we believe – if we can talk of believing here at all. In mathematics there are concept words: cardinal number, prime number, etc. That is why it seems to make sense straight off if we ask "how many prime numbers are there?" (Human beings believe, if only they hear words . . .) In reality this combination of words is so far nonsense; until it's given a special syntax. Look at the proof "that there are infinitely many primes," and then at the question that it appears to answer. The result of an intricate proof can have a simple verbal expression only if the system of expressions to which this expression belongs has a multiplicity corresponding to a system of such proofs. Confusions in these matters are entirely the result of treating mathematics as a kind of natural science. And this is connected with the fact that mathematics has detached itself from natural science; for, as long as it is done in immediate connection with physics, it is clear that *it* isn't a natural science. (Similarly, you can't mistake a broom for part of the furnishing of a room as long as you use it to clean the furniture).

The main danger is surely that the prose expression of the result of a mathematical operation may give the illusion of a calculus that doesn't exist, by bearing the outward appearance of belonging to a system that isn't there at all.

A proof is a proof of a particular proposition if it goes by a rule correlating the proposition to the proof. That is, the proposition must belong to a system of propositions, and the proof to a system of proofs. And every proposition in mathematics must belong to a calculus of mathematics. (It cannot sit in solitary glory and refuse to mix with other propositions.)

So even the proposition "every equation of nth degree has n roots" isn't a proposition of mathematics unless it corresponds to a system of propositions and its proof corresponds to an appropriate system of proofs. For what good reason have I to correlate that chain of equations etc. (that we call the proof) to *this* prose sentence? Must it not be clear— according to a rule – from the proof itself which proposition it is a proof of?

Now it is a part of the nature of *what we call propositions* that they must be capable of being negated. And the negation of what is proved also must be connected with the proof; we must, that is, be able to show in what different, contrasting, conditions it would have been the result.

25

Mathematical problems
Kinds of problem
Search
"Projects" in mathematics

Where you can ask you can look for an answer, and where you cannot look for an answer you cannot ask either. Nor can you find an answer.

Where there is no method of looking for an answer, there the question too cannot have any sense. – Only where there is a method of solution is there a question (of course that doesn't mean: "only where the solution has been found is there a question"). That is: where we can only expect the solution of the problem from some sort of revelation, there isn't even a question. To a revelation no question corresponds.

The supposition of undecidability presupposes that there is, so to speak, an underground connection between the two sides of an equation; that though the bridge cannot be built in symbols, it does exist, because otherwise the equation would lack sense. – But the connection only exists if *we* have made it by symbols; the transition isn't produced by some dark speculation different in kind from what it connects (like a dark passage between two sunlit places).

I cannot use the expression "the equation E yields the solution S" unambiguously until I have a method of solution; because "yields" refers to a structure that I cannot designate unless I am acquainted with it. For that would mean using the word "yields" without knowing its grammar. But I might also say: When I use the word "yields" in such a way as to bring in a method of solution, it doesn't have the same meaning as when this isn't the case. Here the word "yields" is like the word "win" (or "lose") when at one time the criterion for "winning" is a particular set of events in the game (in that case I must know the rules of the game in order to be able to say that someone has won) and at another by "winning" I mean something that I could express roughly by "must pay".

If we employ "yields" in the first meaning, then "the equation yield S" means: if I transform the equation in accordance with certain rules, I get S. Just as the equation $25 \times 25 = 620$ says that I get 620 if I apply the rules for multiplication to 25×25. But in this case these rules must already be given to me before the word "yields" has a meaning, and before the question whether the equation yields S has a sense.

It is not enough to say "p is provable"; we should say: provable according to a particular system.

And indeed the proposition doesn't assert that p is provable according to the system S, but according to its own system, the system that p belongs to. That p belongs to the system S cannot be asserted (that has to show itself). – We can't say, p belongs to the system S; we can't ask, to which system does p belong; we cannot search for p's system. "To understand p" means, to know its system. If p appears to cross over from one system to another, it has in fact changed its sense.

It is impossible to make discoveries of novel rules holding of a form already familiar to us (say the sine of an angle). If they are new rules, then it is not the old form.

If I know the rules of elementary trigonometry, I can check the proposition $\sin 2x = 2 \sin x . \cos x$, but not the proposition $\sin x = x - \frac{x^3}{3!} + \frac{x^5}{5!} - \ldots$ but that means that the sine function of elementary trigonometry and that of higher trigonometry are different concepts.

The two propositions stand as it were on two different planes. However far I travel on the first plane I will never come to the proposition on the higher plane.

A schoolboy, equipped with the armoury of elementary trigonometry and asked to test the equation $\sin x = x - \frac{x^3}{3!}$ simply wouldn't find what he needs to tackle the problem. He not merely couldn't answer the question, he couldn't even understand it.

(It would be like the task the prince set the smith in the fairy tale: fetch me a 'Fiddle-de-dee'. Busch, *Volksmärchen*).

We call it a problem, when we are asked "how many are 25 × 16", but also when we are asked: what is ∫ sin² x dx. We regard the first as much easier than the second, but we don't see that they are "problems" in different senses. *Of course* the distinction is not a psychological one; it isn't a question of whether the pupil can solve the problem, but whether the calculus can solve it, or which calculus can solve it.

The distinctions to which I can draw attention are ones that are familiar to every schoolboy. Later on we look down on those distinctions, as we do on the Russian abacus (and geometrical proofs using diagrams); we regard them as inessential, instead of seeing them as essential and fundamental.

Whether a pupil *knows a rule* for ensuring a solution to ∫sin²x.dx is of no interest; what does interest us is whether the *calculus* we have before us (and that he happens to be using) contains such a rule.
What interests us is not whether the pupil can do it, but whether the calculus can do it, and *how it* does it.

In the case of 25 × 16 = 370 the calculus we use prescribes every step for the checking of the equation.

"I *succeeded* in proving this" is a remarkable expression. (That is something no one would say in the case of 25 × 16 = 400).

One could lay down: "whatever one can tackle is a problem. – Only where there can be a problem, can something be asserted."

Wouldn't all this lead to the paradox that there are no difficult problems in mathematics, since if anything is difficult it isn't a problem? What follows is, that the "difficult mathematical problems", i.e. the problems for mathematical research, aren't in the same relationship to the problem "$25 \times 25 = ?$" as a feat of acrobatics is to a simple somersault. They aren't related, that is, just as very easy to very difficult; they are 'problems' in different meanings of the word.

"You say 'where there is a question, there is also a way to answer it', but in mathematics there are questions that we do not see any way to answer." Quite right, and all that follows from that is that in this case we are not using the word 'question' in the same sense as above. And perhaps I should have said "here there are two different forms and I want to use the word 'question' only for the first". But this latter point is a side-issue. What is important is that we are here concerned with two different forms. (And if you want to say they are just two different *kinds* of question you do not know your way about the grammar of the word "kind".)

"I know that there is a solution for this problem, although I don't yet know what kind of solution" – In what symbolism do you know it?

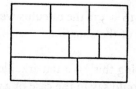

"I know that here there must be a law."[1] Is this knowledge an amorphous feeling accompanying the utterance of the sentence?

---

1. Perhaps the problem is to find the number of ways in which we can trace the joins in this wall without interruption, omission or repetition. Cf. *Remarks on the Foundations of Mathematics* p. 174.

That does not interest us. And if it is a symbolic process – well, then the problem is to represent it in a visible symbolism.

What does it mean to *believe* Goldbach's theorem? What does this belief consist in? In a feeling of certainty as we state or hear the theorem? That does not interest us. I don't even know how far this feeling may be caused by the proposition itself. How does the belief connect with this proposition? Let us look and see what are the consequences of this belief, where it takes us. "It makes me search for a proof of the proposition." – Very well; and now let us look and see what your searching really consists in. Then we shall know what belief in the proposition amounts to.

We may not overlook a difference between forms – as we may overlook a difference between suits, if it is very slight.

For us – that is, in grammar – there are in a certain sense no 'fine distinctions'. And altogether the word distinction doesn't mean at all the same as it does when it is a question of a distinction between two things.

A philosopher feels changes in the style of a derivation which a contemporary mathematician passes over calmly with a blank face. What will distinguish the mathematicians of the future from those of today will really be a greater sensitivity, and *that* will – as it were – prune mathematics; since people will then be more intent on absolute clarity than on the discovery of new games.

Philosophical clarity will have the same effect on the growth of mathematics as sunlight has on the growth of potato shoots. (In a dark cellar they grow yards long.)

A mathematician is bound to be horrified by my mathematical comments, since he has always been trained to avoid indulging in thoughts and doubts of the kind I develop. He has learned to regard them as something contemptible and, to use an analogy from psycho-analysis (this paragraph is reminiscent of Freud), he has acquired a revulsion from them as infantile. That is to say, I trot out all the problems that a child learning arithmetic, etc., finds difficult, the problems that education represses without solving. I say to those repressed doubts: you are quite correct, go on asking, demand clarification!

26

Euler's proof

From the inequality

$$1 + \tfrac{1}{2} + \tfrac{1}{3} + \tfrac{1}{4} + \ldots \neq$$
$$(1 + \tfrac{1}{2} + \tfrac{1}{2^2} + \tfrac{1}{2^3} + \ldots).(1 + \tfrac{1}{3} + \tfrac{1}{3^2} + \ldots)$$

can we derive a number which is still missing from the combinations on the right hand side? Euler's proof that there are infinitely many prime numbers is meant to be an existence proof, but how is such a proof possible without a construction?

$$\sim 1 + \tfrac{1}{2} + \tfrac{1}{3} + \ldots = (1 + \tfrac{1}{2} + \tfrac{1}{2^2} + \ldots).(1 + \tfrac{1}{3} + \tfrac{1}{3^2} + \ldots)$$

The argument goes like this: The product on the right is a series of fractions $1/n$ in whose denominators all multiples of the form $2^\nu 3^\mu$ occur; if there were no numbers besides these, then this series would necessarily be the same as the series $1 + \tfrac{1}{2} + \tfrac{1}{3} + \ldots$ and in that case the sums also would necessarily be the same. But the left hand side is ∞ and the right hand side only a finite number $2/1$. $3/2 = 3$, so there are infinitely many fractions missing in the right-hand series, that is, *there are* on the left hand side fractions that do not occur on the right.[1] And now the question is: is this argument correct? If it were a question of finite series, everything would be perspicuous. For then the method of summation would enable us to find out which terms occurring in the left hand series were missing from the right hand series. Now we might ask: how does it come about that the left hand series gives ∞? What must it contain in addition to the terms on the right to make it infinite? Indeed the question arises: does an equation, like $1 + \tfrac{1}{2} + \tfrac{1}{3} \ldots = 3$ above have any sense at all? I certainly can't find out from it *which* are the extra terms on the left. How do we know that all the terms on the right hand side also occur on the left? In the case of finite series I can't say that until I have ascertained it term by term; – and if I do so I see at the same time which are the extra ones. – Here there is no connection between the result of the sum and the terms, and only such a connection could furnish a proof. Everything becomes clearest if we imagine the business done with a finite equation:

1. Here and at one point further down, I have corrected a confusion in Wittgenstein's typescript between "left" and "right" (Tr.).

$$1 + \tfrac{1}{2} + \tfrac{1}{3} + \tfrac{1}{4} + \tfrac{1}{5} + \tfrac{1}{6} \neq (1 + \tfrac{1}{2}).(1 + \tfrac{1}{3}) = 1 + \tfrac{1}{2} + \tfrac{1}{3} + \tfrac{1}{6}$$

Here again we have that remarkable phenomenon that we might call proof by circumstantial evidence in mathematics – something that is absolutely never permitted. It might also be called a proof by *symptoms*. The result of the summation is (or is regarded as) a symptom that there are terms on the left that are missing on the right. The connection between the symptom and what we would like to have proved is a *loose* connection. That is, no bridge has been built, but we rest content with *seeing* the other bank.

All the terms on the right hand side occur on the left, but the sum on the left hand side is ∞ and the sum of the right hand side is only a finite number, *so there must* . . . but in mathematics nothing *must be* except what *is*.

The bridge has to be built.

In mathematics there are no symptoms: it is only in a psychological sense that there can be symptoms for mathematicians.

We might also put it like this: in mathematics nothing can be inferred unless it can be *seen*.

That reasoning with all its looseness no doubt rests on the confusion between a sum and the limiting value of a sum.

We do see clearly that *however far* we continue the right-hand series we can always continue the left hand one far enough to contain all the terms of the right hand one. (And that leaves it *open* whether it then contains other terms as well).

We might also put the question thus: if you had only this proof, what would you bet on it? If we discovered the primes up to N, could we later go on for ever looking for a further prime number – since the proof guarantees that we will find one? – Surely that is nonsense. For "if we only search long enough" has no meaning. (That goes for existence proofs in general).

Could I add further prime numbers to the left hand side in this proof? Certainly not, because I don't know how to discover any, and that means that I have no concept of prime number; the proof hasn't given me one. I could only add arbitrary numbers (or series).

(Mathematics is dressed up in false interpretations).

("Such a number *has to* turn up" has no meaning in mathematics. That is closely connected with the fact that "in logic nothing is more general or more particular than anything else").

If the numbers were all multiples of 2 and 3 then

$$\left(\lim_{n \to \infty} \sum_{\nu=0}^{\nu=n} \frac{1}{2^\nu} \right) \cdot \left(\lim_{n \to \infty} \sum_{\nu=n}^{\nu=n} \frac{1}{3^\nu} \right) \text{ would have to yield } \lim_{m \to \infty} \sum_{n=1}^{n=m} \frac{1}{n}$$

but it does not . . . What follows from that? (The law excluded middle). Nothing follows, except that the limiting values of the sums are different; that is, nothing. But now we might investigate how this comes about. And in so doing we may hit on numbers that are not representable as $2^\nu \cdot 3^\mu$. Thus we shall hit on larger prime numbers, but we will never see that *no* number of such original numbers will suffice for the formulation of all numbers.

$$1 + \tfrac{1}{2} + \tfrac{1}{3} + \ldots \neq 1 + \tfrac{1}{2} + \tfrac{1}{2^2} + \tfrac{1}{2^3}$$

However many terms of the form $1/2^\nu$ I take they never add up to more than 2, whereas the first four terms of the left-hand series already add up to more than 2. (So *this* must already contain the proof.) This also gives us at the same time the construction of a number that is not a power of 2, for the rule now says: find a segment of the series that adds up to more than 2: this must contain a number that is not a power of 2.

$$(1 + \tfrac{1}{2} + \tfrac{1}{2^2} + \ldots) \cdot (1 + \tfrac{1}{3} + \tfrac{1}{3^3} + \ldots) \ldots (1 + \tfrac{1}{n} + \tfrac{1}{n^2} \ldots) = n$$

If I extend the sum $1 + \tfrac{1}{2} + \tfrac{1}{3} + \ldots$ until it is greater than n, this part must contain a term that doesn't occur in the right hand series, for if the right hand series contained all those terms it would yield a larger and not a smaller sum.

The condition for a segment of the series $1 + \frac{1}{2} + \frac{1}{3} + \dots$
say $\frac{1}{n} + \frac{1}{n+1} + \frac{1}{n+2} + \dots \frac{1}{n+\nu}$ being equal to or greater than
1 is as follows.
To make:

$$\frac{1}{n} + \frac{1}{n+1} + \frac{1}{n+2} + \dots \frac{1}{n+\nu} \gtreqless 1.$$

transform the left hand side into:

$$\frac{1 + \dfrac{n}{n+1} + \dfrac{n}{n+2} + \dots \dfrac{n}{n+\nu}}{n} =$$

$$= \frac{1 + \left(1 - \dfrac{1}{n+1}\right) + \left(1 - \dfrac{2}{n+2}\right) + \dots \left(1 - \dfrac{n-1}{n+(n-1)}\right) + \dfrac{n}{2n} +}{n}$$

$$\frac{\dfrac{n}{2n+1} + \dfrac{n}{2n+2} + \dots \dfrac{n}{n+\nu}}{n} =$$

$$= \frac{n - \frac{1}{2}n(n-1)\dfrac{1}{n+1} + (\nu - n' + 1)\dfrac{n}{n+\nu}}{n} = 1 - \frac{n-1}{2n+2} +$$

$$\frac{\nu - n + 1}{n+\nu} \gtreqless 1$$

$$\therefore 2n\nu + 2\nu - 2n^2 - 2n + 2n + 2 - n^2 - n\nu + n + \nu \gtreqless 0$$

$$n\nu + 3\nu - 3n^2 + 2 + n \gtreqless 0$$

$$\nu \gtreqless \frac{3n^2 - (n+2)}{n+3} < 3n - 1$$

27

The trisection of an angle, etc.

We might say: in Euclidean plane geometry we can't look for the trisection of an angle, because there is no such thing, and we can't look for the bisection of an angle, because there is such a thing.

In the world of Euclid's Elements I can no more ask for the trisection of an angle than I can search for it. It just isn't mentioned.

(I can locate the problem of the trisection of an angle within a larger system but can't ask within the system of Euclidean geometry whether it's soluble. In what *language* should I ask this? In the Euclidean? – But neither can I ask in Euclidean language about the possibility of bisecting an angle within the Euclidean system. For in that language that would boil down to a question about absolute possibility, which is always nonsense.)

Incidentally, here we must make a distinction between different sorts of question, a distinction which will show once again that what we call a "question" in mathematics is not the same as what we call by that name in everyday life. We must distinguish between the question "how does one divide an angle into two equal parts?" and the question " is *this* construction the bisection of an angle?" A question makes sense only in a calculus which gives us a method for its solution; and a calculus may well give us a method for answering the one question without giving us a method for answering the other. For instance, Euclid doesn't shew us how to look for the solutions to his problems; he gives them to us and then proves that they are solutions. And this isn't a psychological or pedagogical matter, but a mathematical one. That is, the *calculus* (the one he gives us) doesn't enable us to look for the construction. A calculus which does enable us to do that is a *different* one.

(Compare methods of integration with methods of differentiation, etc.)

In mathematics there are very different things that all get called proofs, and the differences between them are *logical* differences. The things called 'proofs' have no more internal connection with each other than the things called '*numbers*'.

What kind of *proposition* is "It is impossible to trisect an angle with ruler and compass"? The same kind, no doubt, as "There is no F(3) in the series of angle-divisions F(n), just as there is no 4 in the series of combination-numbers $\dfrac{n.(n-1)}{2}$". But what kind of proposition is *that*? The same kind as "there is no $\frac{1}{2}$ in the series of cardinal numbers". That is obviously a (superfluous) rule of the game, something like: in draughts there is no piece that is called "the queen". The question whether trisection is possible is then the question whether there is such a thing in the game as trisection, whether there is a piece in draughts called "the queen" that has some kind of a role like that of the queen in chess. Of course this question could be answered simply by a stipulation; but it wouldn't set any problem or task of calculation, and so it wouldn't have the same sense as a question whose answer was: I will work out whether there is such a thing. (Something like: I will work out whether any of the numbers 5, 7, 18, 25 is divisible by 3). Now is the question about the possibility of trisecting an angle that sort of question? It is if you have a general system in the calculus for calculating the possibility of division into n equal parts.

Now why does one call *this* proof the proof of *this* proposition? A proposition isn't a name; as a proposition it belongs to a system of language. If I can say "there is no such thing as trisection" then it makes sense to say "there is no such thing as quadrisection", etc., etc. And if *this* is a proof of the first proposition (a part of its syntax), then there must be corresponding proofs (or disproofs) for the other propositions of the proposition-system, otherwise they don't belong to the same system.

I can't ask whether 4 occurs among the combination-numbers

if that is my number-system. And I can't ask whether $\frac{1}{2}$ occurs in the cardinal numbers, or show that it isn't one of them, unless by "cardinal numbers" I mean part of a system that contains $\frac{1}{2}$ as well. (Equally I can't either say or prove that 3 is one of the cardinal numbers.) The question really means something like this: "If you divide 1/2 do you get whole numbers?", and that can only be asked in a system in which divisibility and indivisibility is familiar. (The *working out* must make sense.)

If we don't mean by "cardinal numbers" a subset of the rational numbers, then we can't work out whether 81/3 is a cardinal number, but only whether the division 81/3 comes out or not.

Instead of the problem of trisecting an angle with straightedge and compass we might investigate a parallel, and much more perspicuous problem. There is nothing to prevent us restricting the possibilities of construction with straightedge and compass still further. We might for instance lay down the condition that the angle of the compass may not be changed. And we might lay down that the only construction we know – or better: that our calculus knows – is the one used to bisect a line AB, namely

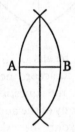

(That might actually be the primitive geometry of a tribe. I said above that the number series "1, 2, 3, 4, 5, many" has equal rights with the series of cardinal numbers[1] and that would go for this geometry too. In general it is a good dodge in our investigations to imagine the arithmetic or geometry of a primitive people.)

1. p. 321.

I will call this geometry the system α and ask: "in the system α is it possible to trisect a line?"

What kind of trisection is meant in this question? – that's obviously what the sense of the question depends on. For instance, is what is meant physical trisection – trisection, that is, by trial and error and measurement? In that case the answer is perhaps yes. Or optical trisection – trisection, that is, which yields three parts which look the same length? It is quite easily imaginable that the parts a, b, and c might look the same length if, for instance, we were looking through some distorting medium.

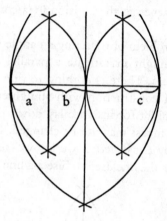

We might represent the results of division in the system α by the numbers 2, 2^2, 2^3, etc. in accordance with the number of the segments produced; and the question whether trisection is possible might mean: does any of the numbers in this series $= 3$? Of course that question can only be asked if 2, 2^2, 2^3, etc. are imbedded in another system (say the cardinal number system); it can't be asked if these numbers are themselves our number system for in that case we, or our system, are not acquainted with the number 3. But if our question is: is one of the numbers 2, 2^2, etc. equal to 3, then here nothing is really said about a *trisection* of the line. None the less, we might look in this manner at the question about the possibility of trisection. – We get a different view, if we adjoin to the system α a system in which lines are divided in the manner of this figure. It can then be asked: is a division into 180 sections a division of type α? And this question might again

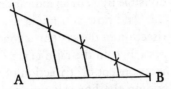

boil down to: is 108 a power of 2? But it might also indicate a different decision procedure (have a different sense) if we connected the systems α and β to a system of geometrical constructions in such a way that it could be proved in the system that the two constructions "must yield" the same division points B, C, D.

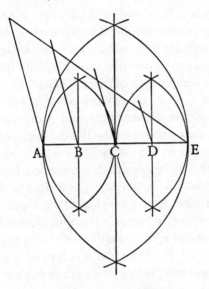

Suppose that someone, having divided a line AB into 8 sections in the system α, groups these into the lines a, b, c, and asks: is that a trisection into 3 equal sections? (We could make the case more easily imaginable if we took a larger number of original sections, which would make it possible to form groups of sections which

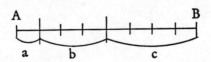

looked the same length). The answer to that question would be a proof that 2^3 is not divisible by 3; or an indication that the sections are in the ratio $1:3:4$. And now you might ask: but surely I do have a concept of trisection in the system, a concept of a division which yields the parts a, b, c, in the ratio $1:1:1$? Certainly, I have now introduced a new concept of 'trisection of a line'; we might well say that by dividing the line AB into eight parts we have divided the line CB into 3 equal parts, if that is just *to mean* we have produced a line that consists of 3 equal parts.

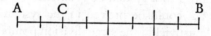

The perplexity in which we found ourselves in relation to the problem of trisection was roughly this: if the trisection of an angle is impossible – logically impossible – how can we ask questions about it at all? How can we describe what is logically impossible and significantly raise the question of its possibility? That is, how can one put together *logically* ill-assorted concepts (in violation of grammar, and therefore nonsensically) and significantly ask about the possibility of the combination? – But the same paradox would arise if we asked "is $25 \times 25 = 620$?"; for after all it's *logically* impossible that that equation should be correct; I certainly can't describe what it would be like if . . . – Well, a doubt whether $25 \times 25 = 620$ (or whether it $= 625$) has no more and no less sense than the method of checking gives it. It is quite correct that we don't here imagine, or describe, what it is like for 25×25 to be 620; what that means is that we are dealing with a type of question that is (logically) different from "is this street 620 or 625 metres long"?

(We talk about a *"division of a circle* into 7 segments" and also of a division of a cake into 7 segments).

If you say to someone who has never tried "try to move your ears", he will first move some part of his body near his ears that he has moved before, and either his ears will move at once or they won't. You might say of this process: he is trying to move his ears. But if it can be called trying, it isn't trying in at all the same sense as trying to move your ears (or your hands) in a case where you already "know how to do it" but someone is holding them so that you can move them only with difficulty or not at all. It is the first sense of trying that corresponds to trying "to solve a mathematical problem" when there is no method for its solution. One can always ponder on the apparent problem. If someone says to me "try by sheer will power to move that jug at the other end of the room" I will look at it and perhaps make some strange movements with my face muscles; so that even in that case there seems to be such a thing as trying.

Think of what it means to *search for* something in one's memory. Here there is certainly *something like* a search in the strict sense.

But trying to produce a phenomenon is not the same as *searching* for it.

Suppose I am feeling for a painful place with my hand. I am searching in touch-space not in pain-space. That means: what I find, if I find it, is really a place and not the pain. That means that even if experience shows that pressing produces a pain, pressing isn't searching for a pain, any more than turning the handle of a generator is searching for a spark.

Can one try to beat the wrong time to a melody? How does such an attempt compare with trying to lift a weight that is too heavy?

It is highly significant that one can see the group | | | | | in different ways (in different groupings); but what is still more noteworthy is that one can do it at will. That is, that there is a quite definite process of producing a particular "view" at will; and correspondingly a quite definite process of unsuccessfully attempting to do so. Similarly, you can to order see the figure below in such a way that first one and then the other vertical line is the nose, and first one and then the other line becomes the mouth; in certain circumstances you can try in vain to do the one or the other.

The essential thing here is that this attempt is the same kind of thing as trying to lift a weight with the hand; is isn't like the sort of trying where one does different things, tries out different means, in order (e.g.) to lift a weight. In the two cases the word "attempt" has quite different meanings. (An extremely significant grammatical fact.)

VI INDUCTIVE PROOFS AND PERIODICITY

29

How far is a proof by induction a proof of a proposition?

If a proof by induction is a proof of $a + (b + c) = (a + b) + c$, we must be able to say: *the calculation gives the result* that $a + (b + c)$ $= (a + b) + c$ (and no other result).

In that case the general method of calculating it must already be known, and we must be able to work out $a + (b + c)$ straight off in the way we can work out 25×16. So first there is a general rule taught for working out all such problems, and later the particular cases are worked out. – But what is the general method of working out here? It must be based on general rules for signs (– say, the associative law –).

If I negate $a + (b + c) = (a + b) + c$ it only makes sense if I mean to say something like: $a + (b + c)$ isn't $(a + b) + c$, but $(a + 2b) + c$. For the question is: In what space do I negate the proposition? If I mark it off and exclude it, what do I exclude it from?

To check $25 \times 25 = 625$ I work out 25×25 until I get the right hand side; – can I work out $a + (b + c) = (a + b) + c$, and get the result $(a + b) + c$? Whether it is provable or not depends on whether we treat it as calculable or not. For if the proposition is a rule, a paradigm, which every calculation has to follow, then it makes no more sense to talk of working out the equation, than to talk of working out a definition.

What makes the calculation possible is the system to which the proposition belongs; and that also determines what miscalculations can be made in the working out. E.g. $(a + b)^2$ is $a^2 + 2ab + b^2$ and not $a^2 + ab + b^2$; but $(a + b)^2 = -4$ is not a possible miscalculation in this system.

I might also say very roughly (see other remarks): "$25 \times 64 = 160$, $64 \times 25 = 160$; that proves that $a \times b = b \times a$" (this way of speaking need not be absurd or incorrect; you only have to interpret it correctly). The conclusion can be correctly drawn from that; so in *one* sense "$a.b = b.a$" can be proved.

And I want to say: It is *only* in the sense in which you can call working out such an example a proof of the algebraic proposition that the proof by induction is a proof of the proposition. Only to that extent is it a check of the algebraic proposition. (It is a check of its structure, not its generality).

(Philosophy does not examine the calculi of mathematics, but only what mathematicians say about these calculi.)

30

Recursive proof and the concept of proposition. Is the proof a proof that a proposition is true and its contradictory false?

Is the recursive proof of
$$a + (b + c) = (a + b) + c \dots A$$
an answer to a question? If so, what question? Is it a proof that an assertion is true and its contradictory false?

What Skolem[1] calls a recursive proof of A can be written thus;

$$\left. \begin{array}{l} a + (b + 1) = (a + b) + 1 \\ a + (b + (c + 1)) = a + ((b + c) + 1) = (a + (b + c)) + 1 \\ (a + b) + (c + 1) = ((a + b) + c) + 1 \end{array} \right\} \quad B$$

In this proof the proposition proved obviously doesn't occur at all. – What we have to do is to make a general stipulation permitting the step to it. This stipulation could be expressed thus

$$\left. \begin{array}{ll} \alpha & \varphi(1) = \psi(1) \\ \beta & \varphi(c + 1) = F(\varphi(c)) \\ \gamma & \psi(c + 1) = F(\psi(c)) \end{array} \right\} \quad \begin{array}{c} \Delta \\ \varphi(c) = \psi(c) \end{array}$$

If three equations of the from α, β, γ are proved, we say "the equation Δ is proved for all cardinal numbers". This is a definition of this latter form of expression in terms of the first. It shows that we aren't using the word "prove" in the second case in the same way as in the first. In any case it is misleading to say that we have proved the equation Δ or A. Perhaps it is better to say that we have proved its generality, though that too is misleading in other respects.

Now has the proof B answered a question, or proved an assertion true? And which is the proof B? Is it the group of three equations of the form α, β, γ or the class of proofs of these equations? These equations do *assert* something (they don't prove anything in the sense in which *they* are proved). But the proofs

1. *Begründung der Elementaren Arithmetik* von Th. Skolem, Skrifter utg. av. Vid.-Selsk i Kristiana 1923. I Mat.-nat. K. No. 6. p. ; Translated in van Heijenoort, *From Frege to Gödel*, Harvard University Press, 1967, pp. 302–333.

of α, β, γ answer the question whether these three equations are correct and prove true the assertion that they are correct. All I can do is to explain: the question whether A holds for all cardinal numbers is to mean: "for the functions

$$\varphi(\xi) = a + (b + \xi), \ \psi(\xi) = (a + b) + \xi$$

are the equations α, β, γ valid?" And then that question is answered by the recursive proof of A, if what that means is the proofs of α, β, γ (or the laying down of α and the use of it to prove β and γ).

So I can say that the recursive proof shows that the equation A satisfies a certain condition; but it isn't the kind of condition that the equation $(a + b)^2 = a^2 + 2b + b^2$ has to fulfil in order to be called "correct". If I call A "correct" because equations of the form α, β, γ can be proved for it, I am no longer using the word "correct" in the same way as in the case of the equations α, β, γ or $(a + b)^2 = a^2 + 2ab + b^2$.

What does "$1/3 = 0 \cdot 3$" mean? Does it mean the same as "$1/3 = 0 \cdot 3$"? – Or is that division the proof of the first proposition? That is, does it have the same relationship to it as a calculation has to what is proved?

"$1/3 = 0 \cdot 3$" is not the same kind of thing as
"$1/2 = 0 \cdot 5$";
what "$1/2 = 0 \cdot 5$" corresponds to is "$1/3 = 0 \cdot 3$" not
"$1/3 = 0 \cdot 3$"[1]

Instead of the notation "$1/4 = 0 \cdot 25$" I will adopt for this occasion the following "$1/4 = 0 \cdot 25$" So, for example, $3/8 = 0 \cdot 375$.

Then I can say, what corresponds to this proposition is not

---

1. The dash underneath emphasizes that the remainder is equal to the dividend. So the expression becomes the symbol for periodic division. (Ed.)

$1/3 = 0\cdot\dot{3}$, but e.g. "$\underset{=}{1/3} = 0\cdot333$" .$0\cdot\dot{3}$ is not a result of division

(quotient) in the same sense as $0\cdot375$. For we were acquainted with the numeral "$0\cdot375$" before the division $3/8$; but what does "$0\cdot\dot{3}$" mean when detached from the periodic division? – The assertion that the division a:b gives $0\cdot\dot{c}$ as quotient is the same as the assertion that the first place of the quotient is c and the first remainder is the same as the dividend.

The relation of B to the assertion that A holds for all cardinal numbers is the same as that of $\underset{1}{1/3} = 0\cdot3$ to $1/3 = 0\cdot\dot{3}$

The contradictory of the assertion "A holds for all cardinal numbers" is: one of the equations α, β, γ is false. And the corresponding question isn't asking for a decision between a (x).fx and a (∃x).~fx.

The construction of the induction is not *a* proof, but a certain arrangement of proofs (a pattern in the sense of an ornament). And one can't exactly say either: if I prove three equations, then I prove one. Just as the movements of a suite don't amount to a single movement.

We can also say: we have a rule for constructing, in a certain game, decimal fractions consisting only of 3's; but if you regard *this rule* as a kind of number, it can't be the result of a division; the only result would be what we may call periodic division which has the form a/d = c.

a

31

Induction. $(x).\varphi x$ and $(\exists x).\varphi x$. *Does the induction prove the general
proposition true and an existential proposition false?*

$$3 \times 2 = 5 + 1$$
$$3 \times (a + 1) = 3 + (3 \times a) = (5 + b) + 3 = 5 + (b + 3)$$

Why do you call this induction the proof that $(n):n > 2 . \supset .$
$3 \times n \neq 5$?! Well, don't you see that if the proposition holds for
$n = 2$, it also holds for $n = 3$, and then also for $n = 4$, and that it
goes on like that for ever? (What am I explaining when I explain
the way a proof by induction works?) So you call it a proof of
"$f(2).f(3).f(4)$, etc." but isn't it rather the form of the proofs of
"$f(2)$" and "$f(3)$" and "$f(4)$", etc.? Or does that come *to the same
thing*? Well, if I call the induction the proof of *one* proposition, I
can do so only if that is supposed to mean no more than that it
proves every proposition of a certain form. (And my expression
relies on the analogy with the relationship between the proposition "all acids turn litmus paper red" and the proposition
"sulphuric acid turns litmus paper red").

Suppose someone says "let us check whether $f(n)$ holds for all
n" and begins to write the series

$$3 \times 2 = 5 + 1$$
$$3 \times (2 + 1) = (3 \times 2) + 3 = (5 + 1) + 3 = 5 + (1 + 3)$$
$$3 \times (2 + 2) = (3 \times (2 + 1)) + 3 = (5 + (1 + 3)) + 3 = 5 + ((1 + 3) + 3)$$

and then he breaks off and says "I see it holds for all n" – So he has
seen an *induction*! But was he *looking for* an induction? He didn't
have any method for looking for one. And if he hadn't discovered
one, would he *ipso facto* have found a number which does not
satisfy the condition? – The rule for checking can't be: let's see
whether there is an induction or a case for which the law does not
hold. – If the law of excluded middle doesn't hold, that can only
mean that our expression isn't comparable to a proposition.

When we say that the induction proves the general proposition,
we think: it proves that this proposition and not its contradictory

is true. But what would be the contradictory of the proposition proved? Well, that $(\exists n) . \sim fn$ is the case. Here we combine two concepts: one derived from my current concept of the proof of $(n).fn$, and another taken from the analogy with $(\exists x).\varphi x$. (Of course we have to remember that "$(n).fn$" isn't a proposition until I have a criterion for its truth; and then it only has the sense that the criterion gives it. Although, before getting the criterion, I could look out for something like an analogy to $(x).fx^1$). What is the opposite of what the induction proves? The proof of $(a + b)^2 = a^2 + 2ab + b^2$ works out this equation in contrast to something like $(a + b)^2 = a^2 + 3ab + b^2$. What does the inductive proof work out? The equations: $3 \times 2 = 5 + 1$, $3 \times (a + 1) = (3 \times a) + 3$, $(5 + b) + 3 = 5 + (b + 3)$ as opposed to things like $3 \times 2 = 5 + 6$, $3 \times (a + 1) = (4 \times a) + 2$, etc. But this opposite does not correspond to the proposition $(\exists x).\varphi x$ – Further, what does conflict with the induction is every proposition of the form $\sim f(n)$, i.e. the propositions "$\sim f(2)$", "$\sim f(3)$", etc.; that is to say, the induction is *the common element* in the working out of $f(2)$, $f(3)$, etc.; but it isn't the working out of "all propositions of the form $f(n)$", since of course no class of propositions occurs in the proof that I call "all propositions of the form $f(n)$". Each one of these calculations is a checking of a proposition of the form $f(n)$. I was able to investigate the correctness of this proposition and employ a method to check it; all the induction did was to bring this into a simple form. But if I call the induction "the proof of a general proposition", I can't ask whether that proposition is correct (any more than whether the form of the cardinal numbers is correct). Because the things I call inductive proofs give me no method of *checking* whether the general proposition is correct or incorrect; instead, the method has to show me how to work out (check) whether or not an induction can be constructed for a particular case within a system of propositions. (If I may so put it, what is checked in this way is whether all n have this or that property; not whether all of them have it, or whether there are some that don't have it. For example, we work

---

1. ? $(x).\varphi x$. (Ed.)

out that the equation $x^2 + 3x + 1 = 0$ has no rational roots (that there is no rational number that . . .), and the equation $x^2 + 2x + 1/2 = 0$ has none, but the equation $x^2 + 2x + 1 = 0$ does, etc.)

Hence we find it odd if we are told that the induction is a proof of the general proposition; for we feel rightly that in the language of the induction we couldn't have posed the general question at all. It wasn't that we began with an alternative between which we had to decide. (We only seemed to, so long as we had in mind a calculus with finite classes).

Prior to the proof asking about the general proposition made no sense at all, and so wasn't even a question, because the question would only have made sense if a general method of decision had been known *before* the particular proof was discovered.

The proof by induction isn't something that settles a disputed question.

If you say: "the proposition '(n).fn' follows from the induction" only means that every proposition of the form f(n) follows from the induction and "the proposition (∃n). ∼ fn contradicts the induction" only means "every proposition of the form ∼ f(n) is disproved by the induction", then we may agree; but we shall ask: what is the correct way for us to use the expression "the proposition (n).f(n)"? What is its grammar? (For from the fact that I use it in certain contexts it doesn't follow that I use it everywhere in the same way as the expression "the proposition (x). φx.")

Suppose that people argued whether the quotient of the division 1/3 must contain only threes, but had no method of deciding it. Suppose one of them noticed the inductive property of $1 . 0/3$

$$= 0.3 \overset{1}{}$$ and said: now I know that there must be only threes in the quotient. The others had not thought of *that* kind of decision. I suppose that they had vaguely imagined some kind of decision by checking each step, though of course they could never have reached a decision in this way. If they hold on to their extensional

viewpoint, the induction does produce a decision because in the case of each extension of the quotient it shows that it consists of nothing but threes. But if they drop their extensional viewpoint the induction decides nothing, or nothing that is not decided by working out $1.0/3 = 0\cdot3$, namely that the remainder is the same
$$_1$$
as the dividend. But nothing else. Certainly, there is a valid question that may arise, namely, is the remainder left after this division the same as the dividend? This question now takes the place of the old extensional question, and of course I can keep the old wording, but it is now extremely misleading since it always makes it look as if having the induction were only a vehicle – a vehicle that can take us into infinity. (This is also connected with the fact that the sign "etc." refers to an internal property of the bit of the series that precedes it, and not to its extension.)

Of course the question "is there a rational number that is a root of $x^2 \times 3x + 1 = 0$?" is decided by an induction; but in this case I have actually constructed a method of forming inductions; and the question is only so phrased because it is a matter of constructing inductions. That is, a question is settled by an induction, if I can look for the induction in advance; if everything in its sign is settled in advance bar my acceptance or rejection of it in such a way that I can decide yes or no by calculating; as I can decide, for instance, whether in $5/7$ the remainder is equal to the dividend or not. (The employment in these cases of the expressions "all . . ." and "there is . . ." has a certain similarity with the employment of the word "infinite" in the sentence "today I bought a straightedge with an infinite radius of curvature").

The periodicity of $1/3 = 0\cdot3$ decides nothing that had been left
$$_1$$
open. Suppose someone had been looking in vain, before the discovery of the periodicity, for a 4 in the development of $1/3$, he

still couldn't significantly have put the question "is there a 4 in the development of 1/3 ?". That is, *independently of* the fact that he didn't actually discover any 4s, we can convince him that he doesn't have a method of deciding his question. Or we might say: quite apart from the result of his activity we could instruct him about the grammar of his question and the nature of his search (as we might instruct a contemporary mathematician about analogous problems). "But as a result of discovering the periodicity he does stop looking for a 4! So it does convince him that he will never find one." – No. The discovery of the periodicity will cure him of looking *if* he makes the appropriate adjustment. We might ask him: "Well, how about it, do you still want to look for a 4?" (Or has the periodicity so to say, changed your mind?)

The discovery of the periodicity is really the construction of a new symbol and a new calculus. For it is misleading to say that it consists in our having *realised* that the first remainder is the same as the dividend. For if we had asked someone unacquainted with periodic division whether the first remainder in this division was the same as the dividend, of course he would have answered "yes"; and so he did realise. But that doesn't mean he must have realised the periodicity; that is, it wouldn't mean he had discovered the calculus with the sign $\underset{a}{a/b} = c$.

Isn't what I am saying what Kant meant, by saying that $5 + 7 = 12$ is not analytic but synthetic *a priori*?

32

Is there a further step *from writing the recursive proof to the generalization? Doesn't the recursion schema already say all that is to be said?*

We commonly say that the recursive proofs show that the algebraic equations hold for all cardinal numbers; for the time being it doesn't matter whether this expression is well or ill chosen, the point is whether it has the same clearly defined meaning in all cases.

And isn't it clear that the recursive proofs in fact show *the same* for all "proved" equations?

And doesn't that mean that between the recursive proof and the proposition it proves there is always the same (internal) relation?

Anyway it is quite clear that there must be a recursive, or better, iterative "proof" of this kind (A proof conveying the insight that "that's the way it must be with all the numbers".)

I.e. it seems clear *to me*; and it seems that by a process of iteration I could make the correctness of these theorems for the cardinal numbers intelligible to someone else.

But how do I know that $28 + (45 + 17) = (28 + 45) + 17$ without having proved it? How can a general proof give me a particular proof? I might after all go through the particular proof, and how would the two proofs meet in it? What happens if they do not agree?

In other words: suppose I wanted to show someone that the associative law is really part of the nature of number, and isn't something that only accidentally holds in this particular case; wouldn't I use a process of iteration to try to show that the law holds and must go on holding? Well – that shows us what we mean here by saying that a law must hold for all numbers.

And what is to prevent us calling this process a proof of the law?

This concept of "making something comprehensible" is a boon in a case like this.

For we might say: the criterion of whether something is a proof of a proposition is whether it could be used for making it comprehensible. (Of course here again all that is involved is an extension of our grammatical investigation of the word "proof" and not any psychological interest in the process of making things comprehensible.)

"This proposition is proved for all numbers by the recursive procedure." That is the expression that is so very misleading. It sounds as if here a proposition saying that such and such holds for all cardinal numbers is proved true by a particular route, and as if this route was a route through a space of conceivable routes.

But really the recursion shows nothing but itself, just as periodicity too shows nothing but itself.

We are not saying that when $f(1)$ holds and when $f(c + 1)$ follows from $f(c)$, the proposition $f(x)$ is *therefore* true of all cardinal numbers; but: "the proposition $f(x)$ holds for all cardinal numbers" *means* "it holds for $x = 1$, and $f(c + 1)$ follows from $f(c)$".

Here the connection with generality in finite domains is quite clear, for in a finite domain that would certainly be a proof that $f(x)$ holds for all values of x, and *that* is the reason why we say in the arithmetical case that $f(x)$ holds for all numbers.

At least I have to say that any objection that holds against the proof B[1] holds also e.g. against the formula $(a + b)^n = $ etc.

Here too, I would have to say, I am merely assuming an algebraic rule that agrees with the inductions of arithmetic.

1. Above, p. 397.

$$f(n) \times (a + b) = f(n + 1)$$
$$f(1) = a + b$$
$$\text{therefore } f(1) \times (a + b) = (a + b)^2 = f(2)$$
$$\text{therefore } f(2) \times (a + b) = (a + b)^3 = f(3), \text{ etc.}$$

So far all is clear. But then: *"therefore $(a + b)^n = f(n)$"*!

Is a further inference drawn here? Is there still something to be established?

But if someone shows me the formula $(a + b)^n = f(n)$ I could ask: how have we got there? And the answer would be the group

$$f(n) \times (a + b) = f(n + 1)$$
$$f(1) = a + b$$

So isn't it a proof of the algebraic proposition? – Or is it rather an answer to the question "what does the algebraic proposition mean?"

I want to say: once you've got the induction, it's all over.

The proposition that A holds for all cardinal numbers is really the complex B plus its proof, the proof of β and γ. But that shows that this proposition is not a proposition in the same sense as an equation, and this proof is not in the same sense a proof of a proposition.

Don't forget that it isn't that we first of all have the concept of proposition, and then come to know that equations are mathematical propositions, and later realise that there are also other kinds of mathematical propositions.

33

How far does a recursive proof deserve the name of "proof"? How far is a step in accordance with the paradigm A justified by the proof of B?

(Editor's note: What follows between the square brackets we have taken from one of the manuscript books that Wittgenstein used for this chapter; although it is not in the typescript – "A" and "B" are given above, on p. 397.)

[(R) $\qquad a + (b + 1) = (a + b) + 1$

(I)

$$a + (b + (c+1)) \overset{R}{=} a + ((b+c)+1) =$$
$$\left.\begin{array}{l} \overset{R}{=} (a + (b + c)) + 1 \\ (a+b)+(c+1) \qquad \overset{R}{=} ((a+b)+c) + 1 \end{array}\right\} a + (b + c) = (a + b) + c$$

(II)

$$\left.\begin{array}{l} (a+1)+1 \overset{3}{=} (a+1)+1 \\ 1 + (a+1) \overset{R}{=} (1+a)+1 \end{array}\right\} a + 1 = 1 + a$$

(III)

$$a + (b+1) \overset{R}{=} (a+b)+1$$
$$\left.\begin{array}{l} (b+1)+a \overset{R}{=} (b+(1+a) \overset{II}{=} b+(a+1) \overset{R}{=} \\ \qquad\qquad\qquad\qquad = (b+a)+1 \end{array}\right\} a + b = b + a$$

$$a \cdot 1 = a \ldots (D)$$
$$a \cdot (b+1) = a \cdot b + a (M)$$

(IV)

$$a \cdot (b + (c+1)) \overset{R}{=} a \cdot ((b+c)+1) \overset{M}{=}$$
$$\left.\begin{array}{l} \qquad\qquad\qquad = a \cdot (b+c)+a \\ a \cdot b + (a \cdot (c+1)) \overset{M}{=} a \cdot b + (a \cdot c + a) \overset{I}{=} \\ \qquad\qquad\qquad = (a \cdot b + a \cdot c) + a \end{array}\right\} a \cdot (b+c) = a \cdot b + a \cdot c$$

(A step by step investigation of this proof would be very instructive.) The first step in I, $a + (b + (c+1)) = a + ((b+c)+1)$, if it is made in accordance with R, shows that the variables in R are not meant in the same way as those in the equations of I; since R would otherwise allow only the replacement of $a + (b + 1)$ by $(a + b) + 1$, and not the replacement of $b + (c+1)$ by $(b+c)+1$.[1]

---

1. See the appendix on p. 446. Cf. also *Philosophical Remarks*, p. 194 n.

The same appears in the other steps in the proof.

If I said that the proof of the two lines of the proof justifies me in inferring the rule $a + (b + c) = (a + b) + c$, that wouldn't mean anything, unless I had deduced that in accordance with a previously established rule. But this rule could only be

$$\left.\begin{array}{r} F_1(1) = F_2(1),\, F_1(x + 1) = f\{F_1(x)\} \\ F_2(x + 1) = f\{F_2(x)\} \end{array}\right\} \quad F_1(x) = F_2(x) \ldots (\rho).$$

But this rule is vague in respect of F_1, F_2 and f.]

We cannot appoint a calculation to be a proof of a proposition.

I would like to say: Do we *have to* call the recursive calculation the proof of proposition I? That is, won't another relationship do?

(What is infinitely difficult is to "see all round" the calculus.)

In the one case "The step is justified" means that it can be carried out in accordance with definite forms that have been given. In the other case the justification might be that the step is taken in accordance with paradigms that themselves satisfy a certain condition.

Suppose that for a certain board game rules are given containing only words with no "r" in them, and that I call a rule justified, if it contains no "r". Suppose someone then said, he had laid down only *one* rule for a certain game, namely, that its moves must obey rules containing no "r"'s. Is that a rule of the game (in the first sense)? Isn't the game played in accordance with the class of rules all of which have only to satisfy the first rule?

Someone shows me the construction of B and then says that A has been proved. I ask "How? All I see is that you have used $\alpha[\rho]$ to build a construction around A". Then he says "But when that is possible, I say that A is proved". To that I answer: "That only shows me the new sense you attach to the word 'prove'."

In one sense it means that you have used $\alpha[\rho]$ to construct the paradigm in such and such a way, in another, it means as before that an equation is in accordance with the paradigm.

If we ask "is that a proof or not?" we are keeping to the word-language.

Of course there can be no objection if someone says: if the terms of a step in a construction are of such and such a kind, I say that the legitimacy of the step is proved.

What is it in me that resists the idea of B as a proof of A? In the first place I observe that in my calculation I now here use the proposition about "all cardinal numbers". I used ρ to construct the complex B and then I took the step to the equation A; in all that there was no mention of "all cardinal numbers". (This proposition is a bit of word-language accompanying the calculation, and can only mislead me.) But it isn't only that this general proposition completely drops out, it is that no other takes it place.

So the proposition asserting the generalisation drops out; "nothing is *proved*", "nothing *follows*".
"But the equation A follows, it is that that takes the place of the general proposition." Well, to what extent does it follow? Obviously, I'm here using "follows" in a sense quite different from the normal one, because what A follows from isn't a proposition. And that is why we feel that the word "follows" isn't being correctly applied.

If you say "it follows from the complex B that $a + (b + c) = (a + b) + c$", we feel giddy. We feel that somehow or other you've said something nonsensical although outwardly it sounds correct.

That an equation follows, already has a meaning (has its own definite grammar).

If I am told "A follows from B", I want to ask: "*what* follows ?" That $a + (b + c)$ is equal to $(a + b) + c$, is something postulated, if it doesn't follow in the normal way from an equation.

We can't fit our concept of following from to A and B; it doesn't fit.

"I will prove to you that $a + (b + n) = (a + b) + n$." No one then expects to see the complex B. You expect to hear another rule for a, b, and n permitting the passage from one side to the other. If instead of that I am given B with the schema ρ^1 I can't call it a proof, because I mean something else by "proof".

I shall very likely say something like "oh, so that's what you call a 'proof', I had imagined . . ."

The proof of $17 + (18 + 5) = (17 + 18) + 5$ is certainly carried out in accordance with the schema B, and this numerical proposition is of the form A. Or again: B is a proof of the numerical proposition: but for that very reason, it isn't a proof of A.

"I will derive A_I, A_{II}, A_{III} from a single proposition."[2] – This

1. "The schema ρ" – or: the group of equations α, β and γ on p. 397. A little further on Wittgenstein refers to the same group as "R", p. 414 below. Later on p. 433, he speaks again of "the rule R" as here on p. 408, where it is: $a + (b + 1) = (a + b) + 1$. (Ed.)

2. This, probably, refers to those equations on p. 408 to the right of the brackets, that is: $a + (b + c) = (a + b) + c$, $a + 1 = 1 + a$, $a + b = b + a$. B_I, B_{II}, B_{III} . . . will then be the complexes of equations left of the brackets. On the meaning of the brackets, see below (Ed.)

of course makes one think of a derivation that *makes use of* these propositions – We think we shall be given smaller links of some kind to replace all these large ones in the chain.

Here we have a definite picture; and we are offered something quite different.

The inductive proof puts the equation together as it were crossways instead of lengthways.

If we work out the derivation, we finally come to the point at which the construction of B is completed. But at this point we say "therefore this equation holds"! But these words now don't mean the same as they do when we elsewhere deduce an equation from equations. The words "The equation follows from it" already have a meaning. And although an equation is constructed here, it is by a different principle.

If I say "the equation follows from the complex", then here an equation is 'following' from something that is not an equation.

We can't say: if the equation follows from B, then it does follow from a proposition, namely from $\alpha \cdot \beta \cdot \gamma$; for what matters is *how* I get A from that proposition; whether I do so in accordance with a rule of inference; and what the relationship is between the equation and the proposition $\alpha \cdot \beta \cdot \gamma$. (The rule leading to A in this case makes a kind of cross-section through $\alpha \cdot \beta \cdot \gamma$; it doesn't view the proposition in the same way as a rule of inference does.)

If we have been promised a derivation of A from α and now see the step from B to A, we feel like saying "oh, that isn't what was meant". It is as if someone had promised to give me something and then says: see, I'm giving you my trust.

The fact that the step from B to A is not an inference indicates also what I meant when I said that the logical product $\alpha \cdot \beta \cdot \gamma$ does not express the generalization.

I say that A_1, A_{11} etc. are used in proving $(a + b)^2 =$ etc. because the steps from $(a + b)^2$ to $a^2 + 2ab + b^2$ are all of the form A_1 or A_{11}, etc. In this sense the step in III from $(b + 1) + a$ to $(b + a) + 1$ is also made in accordance with A_1, but the step from $a + n$ to $n + a$ isn't!

The fact that we say "*the correctness* of the equation is proved" shows that not every construction of the equation is a proof.

Someone shows me the complexes B and I say "they are not proofs of the equations A". Then he says: "You still haven't seen the system on which the complexes are constructed", and points it out to me. How could that make the Bs into proofs?

This insight makes me ascend to another, a higher, level; whereas a *proof* would have to be carried out on the lower level.

Nothing except a definite transition to an equation from other equations is a proof of that equation. Here there is no such thing, and nothing else can do anything to make B into a proof of A.

But can't I say that if I have proved this *about* A, I have thereby proved A? Wherever did I get the illusion that by doing this I had proved it? There must surely be some deep reason for this.

Well, if it is an illusion, at all events it arose from our expression in word-language "this proposition holds for *all* numbers"; for on this view the algebraic proposition is only another way of writing the proposition of word-language. And that form of expression caused us to confuse the case of *all* the numbers with the case of 'all the people in this room'. (What we do to distinguish the cases is to ask: how does one verify the one and the other?)

If I suppose the functions φ, ψ, F exactly defined and then write the schema for the inductive proof:

$$
\begin{array}{c}
\mathrm{R} \\[4pt]
\mathrm{B} \quad
\left.
\begin{array}{l}
\alpha \quad \varphi(1) = \psi(1) \\
\beta \quad \varphi(c+1) = F\{\varphi(c)\} \\
\gamma \quad \psi(c+1) = F\{\psi(c)\}
\end{array}
\right\} \quad \ldots \quad
\begin{array}{c}
\mathrm{A} \\
\varphi n = \psi n
\end{array}
\end{array}
$$

Even then I can't say that the step from φr to ψr is taken on the basis of ρ (if the step in α, β, γ was made in accordance with ρ – in particular cases $\rho = \alpha$). It is still the equation A it is made in accordance with, and I can only say that it corresponds to the complex B if I regard that as another sign in place of the equation A.

For of course the schema for the step had to include α, β and γ.

In fact R isn't the schema for the inductive proof B_{III}; that is much more complicated, since it has to include the schema B_I.

The only time it is inadvisable to call something a 'proof' is when the ordinary grammar of the word 'proof' doesn't accord with the grammar of the object under consideration.

What causes the profound uneasiness is in the last analysis a tiny but obvious feature of the traditional expression.

What does it mean, that R justifies a step of the form A? No doubt it means that I have decided to allow in my calculus only steps in accordance with a schema B in which the propositions α, β, γ are derivable in accordance with ρ. (And of course that would only mean that I allowed only the steps A_1, A_{11} etc., and that those had schemata B corresponding to them).

It would be better to write "and those schemata had the form R corresponding to them". The sentence added in brackets was intended to say that the appearance of generality – I mean the generality of the concept of the inductive method – is unnecessary, for in the end it only amounts to the fact that the particular constructions B_I, B_{II}, etc. are constructed flanking the equations A_I, A_{II}, etc. Or that in that case it is superfluous to pick out the common feature of the constructions; all that is relevant are the constructions themselves, for there is nothing there except *these* proofs, and the concept under which the proofs fall is superfluous, because we never made any use of it. Just as if I only want to say – pointing to three objects – "put that and that and that in my room", the concept chair is superfluous even though the three objects are chairs. (And if they aren't suitable furniture for sitting on, that won't be changed by someone's drawing attention to a similarity between them.) But that only means, that the individual proof needs our acceptance of it as such (if 'proof' is to mean what it means); and if it doesn't have it no discovery of an analogy with other such constructions can give it to it. The reason why it looks like a proof is that α, β, γ and A are equations, and that a general rule can be given, according to which we can construct (and in that sense derive) A from B.

After the event we may become aware of this *general rule*. (But does that make us aware that the Bs are really proofs of A?) What we become aware of is a rule we might have started with and which in conjunction with α would have enabled us to construct A_I, A_{II}, etc. But no one would have called it a proof in this game.

Whence this conflict: "That isn't a proof!" "That surely is a proof."?

We might say that it is doubtless true, that in proving B by α I use α to trace the contours of the equation A, but not in the way I call "proving A by α".

The difficulty that needs to be overcome in these discussions is the difficulty of looking at the proof by induction as something new, *naively* as it were.

So when we said above we could begin with R, this beginning with R is in a way a piece of humbug. It isn't like beginning a calculation by working out 526×718. For in the latter case setting out the problem is the first step on the journey to the solution. But in the former case I immediately drop the R and have to begin again somewhere else. And when it turns out that I construct a complex of the form R, it is again immaterial whether I explicitly set it out earlier, since setting it out hasn't helped me at all mathematically, i.e. in the calculus. So what is left is just the fact that I now have a complex of the form R in front of me.

We might imagine we were acquainted only with the proof B_1 and could then say: all we have is this construction – no mention of an analogy between this and other constructions, or of a general principle in carrying out the constructions. – If I then see B and A like this I'm bound to ask: but why do you call that a proof of A precisely? – (I am not asking: why do you call it a *proof* of A)! What has this complex to do with A_1? Any reply will have to make me aware of the relation between A and B which is expressed in V.[1]

Someone shows us B_1 and explains to us the relationship with A_1, that is, that the right side of A was obtained in such and such a manner etc. etc. We understand him; and he asks us: is that a proof of A? We would answer: certainly *not*!

1. "V" denotes a definition which will be given below, p. 441. In the manuscript that passage comes somewhat earlier than the remark above. The passage runs: "And if we now settle by definition:
$[a + (b + 1) \overset{\alpha}{=} (a + b) + 1]$ & $[a + (b + (c + 1)) \overset{\beta}{=} (a + (b + c)) + 1)]$ &
& $[(a + b) + (c + 1) \overset{\gamma}{=}$
$= ((a + b) + c) + 1]$. $\overset{\text{Def}}{=} a + (b + c) . \mathfrak{J} . (a + b) + c \dots U)$
and in general: $[f_1(1) \overset{\rho}{=} f_2(1)]$ & $[f_1(c + 1) \overset{\beta}{=} f_1(c) + 1]$ &
& $[f_2(c + 1) \overset{\gamma}{=} f_2(c) + 1]$. $\overset{\text{Def}}{=} (f_1(c) . \mathfrak{J} . f_2(c) \dots V)$"
"$\mathfrak{J}$" is mentioned in the context below. V here is a definition of $\mathfrak{J}$). (Ed.)

Had we understood everything there was to understand about the proof? Had we seen the general form of the connection between A and B? Yes!

We might also infer from that that in this way we can construct a B from every A and *therefore conversely an A from every B as well.*

The proof is constructed on a definite plan (a plan used to construct other proofs as well). But this plan cannot make the proof a proof. For all we have here is one of the embodiments of the plan, and we can altogether disregard the plan as a general concept. The proof has to speak for itself and the plan is only embodied in it, it isn't itself a constituent part of the proof. (That is what I've been wanting to say all the time). Hence it's no use to me if someone draws my attention to the similarity between proofs in order to convince me that they are proofs.

Isn't our principle: not to use a *concept-word* where one isn't necessary? – That means, in cases where the concept word really stands for an enumeration, to say so.

When I said earlier "that isn't a proof" I meant 'proof' in an already established sense according to which it can be gathered from A and B by themselves. In this sense I can say: I understand perfectly well what B does and what relationship it has to A; all further information is superfluous and what is there isn't a proof. In this sense I am concerned only with A and B; I don't see anything beyond them, and nothing else concerns me.

If I do this, I can see clearly enough the relationship in accordance with the rule V, but it doesn't enter my head to use it as an expedient in construction. If someone told me while I was considering B and A that there is a rule according to which we could have constructed B from A (or conversely), I could only say to him "don't bother me with irrelevant trivialities." Because of course it's something that's obvious, and I see immediately that it doesn't make B a proof of A. For the general rule couldn't shew that B is a proof of A *and not of some other proposition,* unless it were a proof in the first place. That means, that the fact that the connection between B and A is in accordance with a rule can't show that B is a *proof* of A. Any and every such connection could be used as a construction of B from A (and conversely).

So when I said "R certainly isn't used for the construction, so we have no concern with it" I should have said: I am only concerned with A and B. It is enough if I confront A and B with each other and ask: "is B a proof of A?" So I don't need to construct A from B according to a previously established rule; it is sufficient for me to place the particular As – however many there are – in confrontation with particular Bs. I don't need a previously established construction rule (a rule needed to obtain the As).

What I mean is: in Skolem's calculus we don't *need* any such concept, the list *is sufficient*.

Nothing is lost if instead of saying "we have proved the fundamental laws A in this fashion" we merely show that we can co-ordinate with them constructions that resemble them in certain respects.

The concept of generality (and of recursion) used in these proofs has no greater generality than can be read immediately from the proofs.

The bracket } in R, which unites α, β, and γ^1 can't mean any more than that we regard the step in A (or a step of the form A) as justified

---

1. The schema R above, p. 414. In the manuscript shortly after this schema there follows the remark:
"I have put a bracket } between α, β, γ and A, as if it was self-evident what this bracket meant.
One might conjecture that the bracket meant the same as an equals sign. Such a bracket, incidentally, might be put between "1.0/0.3" and "1 : 3 = 0.3".
I

if the terms (sides) of the steps are related to each other in the ways characterized by the schema B. B then takes the place of A. And just as before we said: the step is permitted in my calculus if it corresponds to one of the As, so we now say: it is permitted if it corresponds to one of the Bs.

But that wouldn't mean we had gained any simplification or reduction.

We are given the calculus of equations. In that calculus "proof" has a fixed meaning. If I now call the inductive calculation a proof, it isn't a proof that saves me checking whether the steps in the chain of equations have been taken in accordance with *these* particular rules (or paradigms). If they have been, I say that the last equation of the chain is proved, or that the chain of equations is correct.

Suppose that we were using the first method to check the calculation $(a + b)^3 = \ldots$ and at the first step someone said: "yes, that step was certainly taken in accordance with a $(b + c) = a.b + a.c$, but is *that* right?" And then we showed him the inductive derivation of that equation. –

The question "Is the equation G right?[1]" means in one meaning: can it be derived in accordance with the paradigms? – In the other case it means: can the equations α, β, γ be derived in accordance with the paradigm (or the paradigms?) – And here we have put the two meanings of the question (or of the word "proof") on the same level (expressed them in a single system) and can now compare them (and see that they are not the same).

And indeed the new proof doesn't give you what you might expect: it doesn't base the calculus on a smaller foundation – as happens if we replace p∨q and ~p by p|q, or reduce the number of axioms, or something similar. For if we now say that all the basic equations A have been derived from ρ alone, the word "derived" here means something quite different. (After this promise we expect

1. Earlier version: . . . the question "is that too right?"

419

the big links in the chain to be replaced by smaller ones, not by two half links.[1]) And in one sense these derivations leave everything as it was. For in the new calculus the links of the old one essentially continue to exist as links. The old structure is *not* taken to pieces. So that we have to say the proof goes on in the same way as before. And in the *old* sense the irreducibility remains.

So we can't say that Skolem has put the algebraic system on to a smaller foundation, for he hasn't 'given it foundations' in the same sense as is used in algebra.

In the inductive proof doesn't α show a connection between the As? And doesn't this show that we are here concerned with proofs? – The connection shown is not the one that breaking up the A steps into ρ steps would establish. And *one* connection between the As is already visible before any proof.

I can write the rule R like *this*

$$\left|\begin{array}{ll} a+(1+1) = & (a+1)+1 \\ a+(\xi+1) & (a+\xi)+1 \\ a+((\xi+1)+1) & (a+(\xi+1))+1 \end{array}\right| \quad S$$

or like this:

$$a+(b+1)=(a+b)+1$$

if I take R or S as a definition or substitute for that form[2].

---

1. See below, p. 426.
2. Compare the form of the rule R on p. 433 below. In the manuscript Wittgenstein introduced this formulation thus: "Perhaps the matter will become clearer, if we give the following rule for addition instead of the recursive rule '$a+(b+1)=(a+b)+1$'

$$a+(1+1) = (a+1)+1$$
$$a+(1+1)+1 = ((a+1)+1)+1$$
$$a+(((1+1)+1)+1) = (((a+1)+1)+1)+1$$
$$\dots \text{etc.} \dots$$

If I then say that the steps in accordance with the rule R are justified thus:

$$\alpha \qquad a + (b + 1) = (a + b) + 1$$
$$\beta \quad a + (b + (c + 1)) = a + ((b + c) + 1) = (a + (b + c)) + 1 \quad \Big\} \quad B$$
$$\gamma \quad (a + b) + (c + 1) = ((a + b) + c) + 1$$

you can reply: "If that's what you call a justification, then you have justified the steps. But you haven't told us any more than if you had just drawn our attention to the rule R and its formal relationship to α (or to α, β, and γ)."

So I might also have said: I take the rule R in such and such a way as a paradigm for my steps.

Suppose now that Skolem, following his proof of the associative law, takes the step to:

$$a + 1 = 1 + a$$
$$a + (b + 1) = (a + b) + 1 \qquad \Big\} \quad C$$
$$(b + 1) + a = b + (1 + a) = b + (a + 1) = (b + a) + 1$$

If he says the first and third steps in the third line are justified according to the already proved associative law, that tells us no more than if he said the steps were taken in accordance with the paradigm $a + (b + c) = (a + b) + c$ (i.e. they correspond to the paradigm) and a schema α, β, γ was derived by steps according to the paradigm α. – "But does B justify these steps, or not?" – "What do you mean by the word 'justify'?" – "Well, the step is

We write this rule in the form, $|1, \xi, \xi + 1|$ thus

$$\begin{array}{c} a + (a + 1) = (a + 1) + 1 \\ \downarrow \qquad \downarrow \\ a + (\xi + 1) \quad (a + \xi) + 1 \\ a + ((\xi + 1) + 1) \; ((a + \xi) + 1) + 1 \end{array} \quad \Big| \quad R$$

In the application of the rule R . . . a ranges over the series $|1, \xi, \xi + 1|$."

He then says of *this* rule that it can be written also in the form S or in the form $a + (b + 1) = (a + b) + 1$.

justified if a theorem really has been proved that holds for all numbers" – But in what case would that have happened? What do you call a proof that a theorem holds for all cardinal numbers? How do you know whether a theorem is really valid for all cardinal numbers, since you can't test it? Your *only* criterion is the proof itself. So you *stipulate* a form and call it the form of the proof that a proposition holds for all cardinal numbers. In that case we really gain nothing by being first shown the general form of these proofs; for that doesn't show that the individual proof really gives us what we want from it; because, I mean, it doesn't justify the proof or demonstrate that it is a proof of a theorem for all cardinal numbers. Instead, the recursive proof has to be its own justification. If we really want to justify our proof procedure as a proof of a generalisation of this kind, we do something different: we give a series of examples and then we are satisfied by the examples and the law we recognize in them, and we say: yes our proof really gives us what we want. But we must remember that by giving this series of examples we have only translated the notations B and C into a different notation. (For the series of examples is not an incomplete application of the general form, but another expression of the law.) An explanation in word-language of the proof (of what it proves) only translates the proof into another form of expression: because of this we can drop the explanation altogether. And if we do so, the mathematical relationships become much clearer, no longer obscured by the equivocal expressions of word-language. For example, if I put B right beside A, without interposing any expression of word-language like "for all cardinal numbers, etc." then the misleading appearance of a proof of A by B cannot arise. We then see quite soberly how far the relationships between B and A and $a + b = b + a$ extend and where they stop. Only thus do we learn the real structure and important features of that relationship, and escape the confusion caused by the form of word-language, which makes everything uniform.

Here we see first and foremost that we are interested in the tree of the structures B, C, etc., and that in it is visible on all sides, like a particular kind of branching, the following form

$$\varphi(1) = \psi(1)$$
$$\varphi(n + 1) = F(\varphi n)$$
$$\psi(n + 1) = F(\psi n)$$

These forms turn up in different arrangements and combinations but they are not elements of the construction in the same sense as the paradigms in the proof of $(a + (b + (c + 1))) = (a + (b + c)) + 1$ or $(a + b)^2 = a^2 + 2ab + b^2$. The aim of the "recursive proofs" is of course to connect the algebraic calculus with the calculus of numbers. And the tree of the recursive proofs doesn't "justify" the algebraic calculus unless that is supposed to mean that it connects it with the arithmetical one. It doesn't justify it in the sense in which the list of paradigms justifies the algebraic calculus, i.e. the steps in it.

So tabulating the paradigms for the steps makes sense in the cases where we are interested in showing that such and such transformations are all made by means of those transition forms, arbitrarily chosen as they are. But it doesn't make sense where the calculation is to be justified in another sense, where mere looking at the calculation – independently of any comparison with a table of previously established norms – must shew us whether we are to allow it or not. Skolem did not have to promise us any proof of the associative and commutative laws; he could simply have said he would show us a connection between the paradigms of algebra and the calculation rules of arithmetic. But isn't this hair-splitting? Hasn't he reduced the number of paradigms? Hasn't he, for instance, replaced very pair of laws with a single one, namely, $a + (b + 1) = (a + b) + 1$? No. When we prove e.g. $(a + b)^4 =$ etc. (k) we can while doing so make use of the previously proved proposition $(a + b)^2 =$ etc. (l). But in that case the steps in k which are justified by l can also be justified by the rules used to prove l. And then the relation of l to those first rules is the same as that of a sign introduced by definition to the primary signs used to define it: we can always eliminate the definitions and go back to the primary signs. But when we take a step in C that is justified by B, we can't take the same step with $a + (b + 1) = (a + b) + 1$ alone. What is called proof here doesn't break a step in to smaller steps but does something quite different.

34

The recursive proof does not reduce the number of fundamental laws

So here we don't have a case where a group of fundamental laws is proved by a smaller set while everything else in the proofs remains the same. (Similarly in a system of fundamental concepts nothing is altered in the later development if we use definitions to reduce the number of fundamental concepts.)

(Incidentally, how very dubious is the analogy between "fundamental laws" and "fundamental concepts"!)

It is something like this: all that the proof of a *ci-devant* fundamental proposition does is to continue the system of proofs backwards. But the recursive proofs don't continue backwards the system of algebraic proofs (with the old fundamental laws); they are a new system, that seems only to run parallel with the first one.

It is a strange observation that in the inductive proofs the irreducibility (independence) of the fundamental rules must show itself after the proof no less than before. Suppose we said the same thing about the case of normal proofs (or definitions), where fundamental rules *are* further reduced, and a new relationship between them is discovered (or constructed).

If I am right that the independence remains intact after the recursive proof, that sums up everything I have to say against the concept of recursive "proof".

The inductive proof doesn't break up the step in A. Isn't it that that makes me baulk at calling it a proof? It's that that tempts me to say that whatever it does – even if it is constructed by R and α – it can't do more than show something *about* the step.

If we imagine a mechanism constructed from cogwheels made simply out of uniform wedges held together by a ring, it is still the cogwheels that remain in a certain sense the units of the mechanism.

It is like this: if the barrel is made of hoops and wattles, it is these, combined as they are (as a complex) that hold the liquid and form new units as containers.

Imagine a chain consisting of links which can each be replaced by two smaller ones. Anything which is anchored by the chain can also be anchored entirely by the small links instead of by the large ones. But we might also imagine every link in the chain being made of two parts, each perhaps shaped like half a ring, which together formed a link, but could not individually be used as links.

Then it wouldn't mean at all the same to say, on the one hand: the anchoring done by the large links can be done entirely by small links – and on the other hand: the anchoring can be done entirely by half large links. What is the difference?

One proof replaces a chain with large links by a chain with small links, the other shows how one can put together the old large links from several parts.

The similarity as well as the difference between the two cases is obvious.

Of course the comparison between the proof and the chain is a logical comparison and therefore a completely exact expression of what it illustrates.

35

Recurring decimals

$$1/3 = 0.\dot{3}$$

We regard the periodicity of a fraction, e.g. of 1/3 as consisting in the fact that something called the extension of the infinite decimal contains only threes; we regard the fact that in this division the remainder is the same as the dividend as a mere *symptom* of this property of the infinite extension. Or else we correct this view by saying that it isn't an infinite extension that has this property, but an infinite series of finite extensions; and it is *of this* that the property of the division is a symptom. We may then say: the extension taken to *one* term is 0.3, to two terms 0.33, to three terms 0.333 and so on. That is a *rule* and the "and so on" refers to the regularity; the rule might also be written" $|0.3, 0.\dot{3}, 0.\dot{3}3|$"
But what is proved by the division $\underset{1}{1/3} = 0.\dot{3}$ is *this* regularity in

contrast to another, not regularity in contrast to irregularity. The periodic division $\underset{1}{1/3} = 0.\dot{3}$ (in contrast to $\underset{1}{1/3} = 0.3$) proves *a*

periodicity in the quotient, that is it *determines* the rule (the repetend), it lays it down; it isn't a symptom that a regularity is "already there". *Where* is it already? In things like the particular expansions that I have written on this paper. But they aren't "*the* expansions". (Here we are misled by the idea of unwritten ideal extensions, which are a phantasm like those ideal, undrawn, geometric straight lines of which the actual lines we draw are mere tracings.) When I said "the 'and so on' refers to the regularity" I was distinguishing it from the 'and so on' in "he read all the letters of the alphabet: a, b, c and so on". When I say "the extensions of 1/3 are 0.3, 0.33, 0.333 and so on" I give three *three* extensions and – a rule. That is the only thing that is infinite, and only in the same way as the division $\underset{\underset{1}{|}}{1}/3 = 0\cdot3$

One can say of the sign $0\cdot\dot3$ that it is not an abbreviation.

And the sign "$|0\cdot3.0\cdot\xi, 0\cdot\xi3|$" isn't a substitute for an extension, but the undevalued sign itself; and "$0\cdot\dot3$" does just as well. It should give us food for thought, that a sign like "$0\cdot\dot3$" is *enough* to do what we need. It isn't a mere substitute in the calculus there are no substitutes.

If you think that the peculiar property of the division $\underset{\underset{1}{|}}{1}/3 = 0\cdot3$

is a symptom of the periodicity of the infinite decimal fraction, or *the* decimal fractions of the expansion, it is indeed a sign that something *is* regular, but *what?* The extensions that I have constructed? But there aren't any others. It would be a most absurd manner of speaking to say: the property of the division is an indication that the result has the form "$|0\cdot a, 0\cdot\xi, 0\cdot\xi a|$"; that is like wanting to say that a division was an indication that the result was a number. The sign "$0\cdot\dot3$" does not express its meaning from any greater distance than "$0\cdot333\ldots$", because this sign gives an extension of three terms and a rule; the extension $0\cdot333$ is inessential for our purposes and so there remains only the rule, which is given just as well by "$|0\cdot3, 0\cdot\xi, 0\cdot\xi3|$". The proposition "After the first place the division is periodic" just means "The first remainder is the same as the dividend". Or again: the proposition "After the first place the division will yield the same number to infinity", *means* "The first remainder is the same as the dividend", just as the proposition "This straightedge has an infinite radius" means it is straight.

We might now say: the places of a quotient of 1/3 are *necessarily all* 3*s*, and all that could mean would be again that the first remainder is like the dividend and the first place of the quotient is 3. The negation of the first proposition is therefore equivalent to the negation of the second. So the opposite of "necessarily all" isn't what one might call "accidentally all"; "necessarily all" is as it were one word. I only have to ask: what is the criterion of the necessary generalization, and what would be the criterion of the accidental generalization (the criterion for all numbers accidentally having the property ε)?

A "recursive proof" is the general term of a series of proofs. So it is a law for the construction of proofs. To the question how this general form can save me the proof of a particular proposition, e.g. $7 + (8 + 9) = (7 + 8) + 9$, the answer is that it merely gets everything ready for the proof of the proposition, it doesn't prove it (indeed the proposition doesn't occur in it). The proof consists rather of the general form plus the proposition.

Our normal mode of expression carries the seeds of confusion right into its foundations, because it uses the word "series" both in the sense of "extension", and in the sense of "law". The relationship of the two can be illustrated by a machine for making coiled springs, in which a wire is pushed through a *helically* shaped

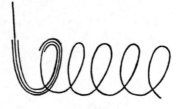

passage to make as many coils as are desired. What is called an infinite helix need not be anything like a finite piece of wire, or something that that approaches the longer it becomes; it is the law of the helix, as it is embodied in the short passage. Hence the expression "infinite helix" or "infinite series" is misleading.

So we can always write out the recursive proof as a limited series with "and so on" without its losing any of its rigour. At the same time this notation shows more clearly its relation to the equation A. For then the recursive proof no longer looks at all like a justification of A in the sense of an algebraic proof – like the proof of $(a + b)^2 = a^2 + 2ab + b^2$. That proof with algebraic calculation rules is quite like calculation with numbers.

$$5 + (4 + 3) = 5 + (4 + (2 + 1)) = 5 + ((4 + 2) + 1) =$$
$$= (5 + (4 + 2)) + 1 = (5 + (4 + (1 + 1))) + 1 =$$
$$= (5 + ((4 + 1) + 1)) + 1 = ((5 + (4 + 1)) + 1) + 1 =$$
$$= (((5 + 4) + 1) + 1) + 1 = ((5 + 4) + 2) + 1 = (5 + 4) + 3) \cdots (L)$$

That is a proof of $5 + (4 + 3) = (5 + 4) + 3$, but we can also let it count, i.e. use it, as a proof of $5(+ (4 + 4) = (5 + 4) + 4$, etc.

If I say that L is the proof of the proposition $a + (b + c) = (a + b) + c$, the oddness of the step from the proof to the proposition becomes much more obvious.

Definitions merely introduce practical abbreviations; we could get along without them. But is that true of recursive definitions?

Two different things might be called applications of the rule $a + (b + 1) = (a + b) + 1$: in one sense $4 + (2 + 1) = (4 + 2) + 1$ is an application, in another sense $4 + (2 + 1) = ((4 + 1) + 1) + 1 = (4 + 2) + 1$ is.

The recursive definition is a rule for constructing replacement rules, or else the general term of a series of definitions. It is a signpost that shows the *same* way to all expressions of a certain form.

As we said, we might write the inductive proof without using letters at all (with no loss of rigour). Then the recursive definition $a + (b + 1) = (a + b) + 1$ would have to be written as a series of definitions. As things are, this series is concealed in the explanation of its use. Of course we can keep the letters in the definition for the sake of convenience, but in that case in the explanation we have to bring in a sign like "$1, (1) + 1, ((1) + 1) + 1$ and so on", or, what boils down to the same thing, "$|1, \xi, \xi + 1|$". But here we mustn't believe that this sign should really be "$(\xi).|1, \xi, \xi + 1|$"!

The point of our formulation is of course that the concept "all numbers" is given only by a structure like "$|1, \xi, \xi + 1|$". The generality is *set out* in the symbolism by this structure and cannot be *described* by an $(x).fx$.

Of course the so-called "recursive definition" isn't a definition in the customary sense of the word, because it isn't an equation, since the equation "$a + (b + 1) = (a + b) + 1$" is only a part of it. Nor is it a logical product of equations. Instead, it is a law for the construction of equations; just as $|1, \xi, \xi + 1|$ isn't a number but a law etc. (The bewildering thing about the proof of $a + (b + c) = (a + b) + c$ is of course that it's supposed to come out of the definition alone. But α isn't a definition, but a general rule for addition).

On the other hand the generality of this rule is no different from that of the periodic division $\underset{1}{1/3} = 0\cdot3$. That means, there isn't anything that the rule leaves open or in need of completion or the like.

Let us not forget: the sign "$|1, \xi, \xi + 1|$" ... N interests us not as a striking expression for the general term of the series of cardinal numbers, but only in so far as it is contrasted with signs of similar construction. N *as opposed to* something like $|2, \xi, \xi + 3|$; in short, as a sign, or an instrument, in a calculus. And of course the same holds for $\underset{1}{1/3} = 0\cdot3$. (The only thing left open in the rule is its application.)

$$1 + (1 + 1) = (1 + 1) + 1, \; 2 + (1 + 1) = (2 + 1) + 1,$$
$$3 + (1 + 1) = (3 + 1) + 1 \ldots \text{and so on}$$
$$1 + (2 + 1) = (1 + 2) + 1, \; 2 + (2 + 1) = (2 + 2) + 1,$$
$$3 + (2 + 1) = (3 + 2) + 1 \ldots \text{and so on}$$
$$1 + (3 + 1) = (1 + 3) + 1, \; 2 + (3 + 1) = (2 + 3) + 1,$$
$$3 + (3 + 1) = (3 + 3) + 1 \ldots \text{and so on}$$

and so on.

We might write the rule "$a + (b + 1) = (a + b) + 1$", thus.[1]

$$\begin{array}{c} a + (1 + 1) = (a + 1) + 1 \\ \downarrow \qquad\qquad \downarrow \\ a + (\xi + 1) \quad (a + \xi) + 1 \\ a + ((\xi + 1) + 1) \quad ((a + \xi) + 1) + 1 \end{array} \quad R$$

In the application of the rule R (and the description of the application is of course an inherent part of the sign for the rule), a ranges over the series $|1, \xi, \xi + 1|$; and of course that might be expressly stated by an additional sign, say "$a \rightarrow N$". (We might call the second and third lines of the rule R taken together the operation, like the second and third term of the sign N.) Thus too the explanation of the use of the recursive definition "$a + (b + 1) = (a + b) + 1$" is a part of that rule itself; or if you like a repetition of the rule in another form; just as "$1, 1 + 1, 1 + 1 + 1$ and so on" means the *same* as (i.e. is translatable into) "$|1, \xi, \xi + 1|$". The translation into word-language *casts light on* the calculus with the new signs, because we have already mastered the calculus with the signs of word-language.

The sign of a rule, like any other sign, is a sign belonging to a calculus; its job isn't to hypnotize people into accepting an application, but to be used in the calculus in accordance with a system. Hence the exterior form is no more essential than that of an arrow $\rightarrow$; what is essential is the system in which the sign for the rule is employed. The system of contraries – so to speak – from which the sign is distinguished etc.

What I am here calling the description of the application is itself of course something that contains an "and so on", and so it can itself be no more than a supplement to or substitute for the rule-sign.

What is the contradictory of a general proposition like $a + (b + (1 + 1)) = a + ((b + 1) + 1)$? What is the system of propositions within which this proposition is negated? Or again, how, and in what form, can this proposition come into contradiction with others? What question does it answer? Certainly not the question

1. Cf. footnote, p. 420.

whether $(n).fn$ or $(\exists n). \sim fn$ is the case, because it is the rule R that contributes to the generality of the proposition. The generality of a rule is *eo ipso* incapable of being brought into question.

Now imagine the general rule written as a series

$$p_{11}, p_{12}, p_{13} \cdots$$
$$p_{21}, p_{22}, p_{23} \cdots$$
$$p_{31}, p_{32}, p_{33} \cdots$$
$$\cdots\cdots\cdots\cdots$$

and then negated. If we regard it as $(x).fx$, then we are treating it as a logical product and its opposite is the logical sum of the denials of p_{11}, p_{12} etc. This disjunction can be combined with any random product $p_{11} \cdot p_{21} \cdot p_{22} \cdots p_{mn}$. (Certainly if you compare the proposition with a logical product, it becomes infinitely significant and its opposite void of significance). (But remember that the "and so on" in the proposition comes after a comma, not after an "and" ("."). The "and so on" is not a sign of *incompleteness*.)

Is the rule R infinitely significant? Like an enormously long logical product?

That one can run the number series though the rule is a form that is given; nothing is affirmed about it and nothing can be denied about it.

Running the stream of numbers through is not something which I can say I can prove. I can only prove something about the form, or pattern, through which I run the numbers.

But can't we say that the general number rule $a + (b + c) = (a + b) + c \ldots$ A) has the same generality as $a + (1 + 1) = (a + 1) + 1$ (in that the latter holds for every cardinal number and the former for every triple of cardinal numbers) and that the inductive proof of A *justifies* the rule A? Can we say that we can give the rule A, since the proof shows that it is always right? Does $\underset{1}{1/3} = 0.3$

justify the rule

$\overset{1}{1/3} = 0.3$, $\overset{2}{1/3} = 0.333$, $\overset{3}{1/3} = 0.333$ and so on?" . . .P)

A is a completely intelligible rule; just like the replacement rule P. But I can't give such a rule, for the reason that I can already calculate the particular instances of A by another rule; just as I cannot give P as a rule if I have given a rule whereby I can *calculate* $1/3 = 0.3$ etc.

How would it be if someone wanted to lay down "$25 \times 25 = 625$" as a rule in addition to the multiplication rules. (I don't say "$25 \times 25 = 624$"!) – $25 \times 25 = 625$ only makes sense if the kind of calculation to which the equation belongs is already known, and it only makes sense in connection with that calculation. A only makes sense in connection with A's own kind of calculation. For the first question here would be: is that a stipulation, or a derived proposition? If $25 \times 25 = 625$ is a stipulation, then the multiplication sign does not mean the same as it does, e.g. in reality (that is, we are dealing with a different kind of calculation). And if A is a stipulation, it doesn't define addition in the same way as if it is a derived proposition. For in that case the stipulation is of course a definition of the addition sign, and the rules of calculation that allow A to be worked out are a different definition of the same sign. Here I mustn't forget that α, β, γ isn't the proof of A, but only the form of the proof, or of what is proved; so α, β, γ is a definition of A.

Hence I can only say "$25 \times 25 = 625$ is proved" if the method of proof is fixed independently of the specific proof. For it is this method that settles the meaning of "$\xi \times \eta$" and so settles *what* is proved. So to that extent the form $\underline{a} . b = c$ belongs to the method

$$\underline{a}$$

of proof that explains the sense of c. Whether I have calculated correctly is another question. And similarly α, β, γ belong to the method of proof that defines the sense of the proposition A.

Arithmetic is complete without a rule like A; without it it doesn't lack anything. The proposition A is introduced into arithmetic with the discovery of a periodicity, with the construction of a *new* calculus. Before this discovery or construction a question about the correctness of that proposition would have as little sense as a question about the correctness of "$1/3 = 0.3$, $1/3 = 0.33 \ldots$ ad inf."

The stipulation of P is not the same thing as the proposition "$1/3 = 0\cdot3$" and in that sense "$a + (b + \dot{c}) = (a + b) + \dot{c}$" is different from a rule (stipulation) such as A. The two belong to different calculi. The proof of α, β, γ is a proof or justification of a rule like A *only* in so far as it is the general form of the proof of arithmetical propositions of the form A.

Periodicity is not a sign (symptom) of a decimal's recurring; the expression "it goes on like that for ever" is only a translation of the sign for periodicity into another form of expression. (If there was something other than the periodic sign of which periodicity was only a symptom, that something would have to have a specific expression, which could be nothing less than the complete expression of that something.)

37

Seeing or viewing a sign in a particular manner. Discovering an aspect of a mathematical expression. "Seeing an expression in a particular way". Marks of emphasis.

Earlier I spoke of the use of connection lines, underlining etc. to bring out the corresponding, homologous, parts of the equations of a recursion proof. In the proof

$$a + (b + \overset{\gamma}{1}) = (a + b) + \overset{\alpha}{1}$$
$$a + (b + \overset{\delta}{(c + 1)}) = (a + (b + c)) + \overset{\beta}{1}$$
$$(a + b) + \overset{\xi}{(c + 1)} = ((a + b) + c) + \overset{\epsilon}{1}$$

the one marked α for example corresponds not to β but to c in the next equation; and β corresponds not to δ but to ϵ; and γ not to δ but to $c + \delta$, etc.

Or in

$$\overset{\alpha}{(\overset{\kappa}{a} + \overset{\lambda}{1})} + \overset{\beta}{1} = (\overset{\iota}{a} + \overset{\epsilon}{1}) + \overset{\zeta}{1}$$
$$\overset{\gamma}{1} + \overset{\delta}{(a + 1)} = (\overset{\mu}{1} + \overset{\eta}{a}) + \overset{\theta}{1}$$

ι doesn't correspond to κ and ϵ doesn't correspond to λ; it is β that ι corresponds to; and β does not correspond to ξ, but ξ corresponds to θ and α to δ and β to γ and γ to μ, not to θ, and so on.

What about a calculation like

$$(5 + 3)^2 = (5 + 3) \cdot (5 + 3) = 5 \cdot (5 + 3) + 3 \cdot (5 + 3) =$$
$$= 5 \cdot 5 + 5 \cdot 3 + 3 \cdot 5 + 3 \cdot 3 = 5^2 + 2 \cdot 5 \cdot 3 + 3^2 \dots \text{R})$$

from which we can also read a general rule for the squaring of a binomial?

We can as it were look at this calculation arithmetically or algebraically.

This difference between the two ways of looking at it would have been brought out e.g. if the example had been written

$$(5 + 2)^2 = 5^2 + \overset{\alpha}{2} . \overset{\beta}{2} . 5 + \overset{\beta}{2}{}^2$$

In the algebraic way of looking at it we would have to distinguish the 2 in the position marked α from the 2s in the positions marked β but in the arithmetical one they would not need to be distinguished. We are – I believe – using a different calculus in each case.

According to one but not the other way of looking at it the calculation above, for instance, would be a proof of $(7 + 8)^2 = 8^2 + 2.7.8 + 8^2$.

We might work out an example to make sure that $(a + b)^2$ is equal to $a^2 + b^2 + 2ab$, not to $a^2 + b^2 + 3ab$ – if we had forgotten it for instance; but we couldn't check in that sense whether the formula holds *generally*. But of course there is *that sort of* check too, and in the calculation

$$(5 + 3)^2 = \ldots = 5^2 + 2.5.3 + 3^2$$

I might check whether the 2 in the second summand is a general feature of the equation or something that depends on the particular numbers occurring in the example.

I turn $(5 + 2)^2 = 5^2 + 2.2.5$ into another sign, if I write

$$(\overset{\alpha}{5} + \overset{\beta}{2})^2 = \overset{\alpha-}{5^2} + \overset{\beta}{2}.2.\overset{\alpha}{5} + \overset{\beta-}{2}{}^2$$

and thus "indicate which features of the right hand side originate from the particular numbers on the left" etc.

(Now I realize the importance of this process of coordination. It expresses a new way of looking at the calculation and therefore a way of looking at a new calculation.)

'In order to prove A' – we could say – I first of all have to draw attention to quite definite features of B. (As in the division $1\cdot0/3 = 0\cdot\dot3$).

_I

(And α had no suspicion, so to speak, of what I see if I do.)

Here the relationship between generality and proof of generality is like the relationship between existence and proof of existence.

When α, β, γ are proved, the general calculus has still to be discovered.

Writing "$a+(b+c)=(a+b)+c$" in the induction series seems to us a matter of course, because we don't see that by doing so we are starting a totally new calculus. (A child just learning to do sums would see clearer than we do in this connection.)

Certain features are brought out by the schema R; they could be specially marked thus:[1]

$$\overbrace{a+(b+1)}^{f_1\ (1)}=\overbrace{(a+b)+1}^{f_2\ (1)}$$

$$\overbrace{a+(b+(c+1))}^{f_1\quad(c+1)}=\overbrace{\lceil a+(b+c)\rceil}^{f_1\quad(c)+1}+1$$

$$\overbrace{(a+b)+(c+1)}^{f_2\quad(c+1)}=\overbrace{\lvert(a+b)+c\rvert}^{f_2\quad(c)+1}+1$$

Of course it would also have been enough (i.e. it would have been a symbol of the same multiplicity) if we had written B and added

$$f_1\xi=a+(b+\xi),\ f_2\xi=(a+b)+\xi$$

(Here we must also remember that *every* symbol – however explicit – *can* be misunderstood.)

The first person to draw attention to the fact that B can be seen in that way introduces a new sign whether or not he goes on to attach special marks to B or to write the schema R beside it. In

---

1. The schema R as above on p. 414. Cf B on p. 397. (Ed.)

the latter case R itself is the new sign, or, if you prefer, B plus R. It is the way in which he draws attention to it that produces the new sign.

We might perhaps say that here the lower equation is used as $a + b = b + a$; or similarly that here B is used as A, by being as it were read sideways. Or: B was used as A, but the new proposition was built up from $\alpha . \beta . \gamma$, in such a way that though A is now read out of B, $\alpha . \beta . \gamma$ don't appear in the sort of abbreviation in which the premisses turn up in the conclusion.

What does it mean to say: "I am drawing your attention to the fact that the same sign occurs here in both function signs (perhaps you didn't notice it)"? Does that mean that he didn't understand the proposition? – After all, what he didn't notice was something which belonged essentially to the proposition; it wasn't as if it was some external property of the proposition he hadn't noticed (Here again we see what kind of thing is called "understanding a proposition".)

Of course the picture of reading a sign lengthways and sideways is once again a *logical* picture, and for that reason it is a perfectly exact expression of a grammatical relation. We mustn't say of it "it's a mere metaphor, who knows what the facts are really like?"

When I said that the new sign with the marks of emphasis must have been derived from the old one without the marks, that was meaningless, because of course I can consider the sign with the marks without regard to its origin. In that case it presents itself to me as three equations [Frege][1], that is as the shape of three equations with certain underlinings, etc.

---

1. Cf. perhaps: *Grundgesetze der Arithmetik*, II, p. 114, 115 §§ 107, 108. Waismann cited excerpts from these §§. (*Wittgenstein und der Wiener Kreis*, pp. 150–151). Cf here Wittgenstein's remarks on them (ibid. pp. 151–157). (Ed.)

It is certainly significant that this shape is quite similar to the three equations without the underlinings; it is also significant that the cardinal number 1 and the rational number 1 are governed by similar rules; but that does not prevent what we have here from being a new sign. What I am now doing with this sign is something quite new.

Isn't this like the supposition I once made that people might have operated the Frege-Russell calculus of truth-functions with the signs "~" and "." combined into "~p. ~ q" without anyone noticing, and that Sheffer, instead of giving a new definition, had merely drawn attention to a property of the signs already in use.

We might have gone on dividing without ever becoming aware of recurring decimals. When we have seen them, we have seen something new.

But couldn't we extend that and say "I might have multiplied numbers together without ever noticing the special case in which I multiply a number by itself; and that means x^2 is not simply $x.x$"? We might call the invention of the sign 'x^2' the expression of our having become aware of that special case. Or, we might have gone on multiplying a by b and dividing it by c without noticing that we could write $\dfrac{\text{"a.b"}}{c}$ as "a. (b|c)" or that the latter is similar to a.b. Or again, this is like a savage who doesn't yet see the analogy between ||||| and ||||||, or between || and |||||.

$$[a + (b + 1) \overset{\alpha}{=} (a + b) + 1] \ \& \ [a + (b + (c + 1)) \overset{\beta}{=} (a + (b + c)) + 1]$$
$$\& \ [(a + b) + (c + 1) \overset{\gamma}{=} ((a + b) + c) + 1].\overset{\text{Def}}{=}.a + (b + c).\mathfrak{J}.$$
$$(a + b) + c \ldots U)$$

and in general:

$$[f_1(1) \overset{\rho}{=} f_2(1)] \ \& \ [f_1(c + 1) \overset{\beta}{=} f_1(c) + 1] \ \& \ [f_2(c + 1) \overset{\gamma}{=}$$
$$= f_2(c) + 1].\overset{\text{Def}}{=}.f_1(c).\mathfrak{J}.f_2(c) \ldots V)$$

You might see the definition U, without knowing why I use that abbreviation.

You might see the definition without understanding its point. – But its point is something new, not something already contained in it as a specific replacement rule.

Of course, "$\mathfrak{Z}$" isn't an equals-sign in the same sense as the ones occurring in α, β, γ.

But we can easily show that "$\mathfrak{Z}$" has certain formal properties in common with =.

It would be incorrect – according to the postulated rules – to use the equals-sign like this:

$$\Delta \ldots \,|(a+b)^2 = a.(a+b) + b.(a+b) = \ldots =$$
$$= a^2 + 2ab + b^2|. = .|(a+b)^2 = a^2 + 2ab + b^2|$$

if that is supposed to mean that the left hand side is the proof of the right.

But mightn't we imagine this equation regarded as a definition? For instance, if it had always been the custom to write out the whole chain instead of the right hand side, and we introduced the abbreviation.

Of course Δ *can* be regarded as a definition! Because the sign on the left hand side is in fact used, and there's no reason why we shouldn't abbreviate it according to this convention. Only in that case either the sign on the right or the sign on the left is used in a way different from the one now usual.

It can never be sufficiently emphasized that *totally different* kinds of sign-rules get written in the form of an equation.

The 'definition' $x.x = x^2$ might be regarded as merely allowing us to replace the sign "$x.x$" by the sign "x^2," like the definition "$1 + 1 = 2$"; but it can also be regarded (and in fact is regarded) as allowing us to put a^2 instead of $a.a$, and $(a+b)^2$ instead of $(a+b).(a+b)$ and in such a way that any arbitrary number can be substituted for the x.

442

A person who discovers that a proposition p follows from one of the form q ⊃ p.q constructs a new sign, the sign for that rule. (I am assuming that a calculus with p, q, ⊃, has already been in use, and that this rule is now added to make it a new calculus.)

It is true that the notation "x^2" takes away the possibility of replacing one of the factors x by another number. Indeed, we could imagine two stages in the discovery (or construction) of x^2. At first, people might have written "$x^=$" instead of "x^2", before it occurred to them that there was a system x.x, x.x.x, etc.; later, they might have hit upon that too. Similar things have occurred in mathematics countless times. (In Liebig's sign for an oxide oxygen did not appear as an element in the same way as what was oxidized. Odd as it sounds, we might even today, with all the data available to us, give oxygen a similarly privileged position – only, of course, in the *form of representation* – by adopting an incredibly artificial interpretation, i.e. grammatical construction.)

The definitions $x.x = x^2$, $x.x.x = x^3$ don't bring anything into the world except the signs "x^2" and "x^3" (and thus so far it isn't necessary to write numbers as exponents).

|The process of generalization creates a new sign-system.|

Of course Sheffer's discovery is not the discovery of the definition ~ p.~ q = p|q. Russell might well have given that definition without being in possession of Sheffer's system, and on the other hand Sheffer might have built up his system without the definition. His system is contained in the use of the signs "~p.~p" for "~p" and "~(~p.~q).~(~p.~q)" for "p ∨ q" and all "p|q" does is to permit an *abbreviation*. Indeed, we can say that someone could well have been acquainted with the use of the sign "~(~p.~q). ~(~p.~q)" for "p ∨ q" without recognizing the system p|q.|.p|q in it.

It makes matters clearer if we adopt Frege's two primitive signs "~" and ".". The discovery isn't lost if the definitions are written ~p.~p = ~p and ~(~p.~p).~(~q.~q) = p.q. Here apparently nothing at all has been altered in the original signs.

But we might also imagine someone's having written the whole Fregean or Russellian logic in this system, and yet, like Frege, calling "~" and "." his primitive signs, because he did not see the other system in his proposition.

It is clear that the discovery of Sheffer's system in ~.p.~p = ~p and ~(~p.~p).~(~q.~q) = p.q corresponds to the discovery that $x^2 + ax + \dfrac{a^2}{4}$ is a specific instance of $a^2 + 2ab + b^2$.

We don't see that something can be looked at in a certain way until it is so looked at.
We don't see that an aspect is possible until it is there.

That sounds as if Sheffer's discovery wasn't capable of being represented in signs at all. (Periodic division.) But that is because we can't smuggle the *use* of the sign into its introduction (the rule is and remains a sign, separated from its application).

Of course I can only apply the general rule for the induction proof when I discover the substitution that makes it applicable. So it would be possible for someone to see the equations

$$(a + 1) + 1 = (a + 1) + 1$$
$$1 + (a + 1) = (1 + a) + 1$$

without hitting on the substitution

$$a = x, \; F_1(x) = x + 1, \; F_1(x + 1) = (x + 1) + 1,$$

$$F_2(x + 1) = 1 + (x + 1), \; F_2(x) = 1 + x$$

444

Moreover, if I say that I *understand* the equations as particular cases of the rule, my understanding has to be the understanding that shows itself in the explanations of the relations between the rule and the equations, i.e. what we express by the substitutions. If I don't regard that as an expression of what I understand, then nothing is an expression of it; but in that case it makes no sense either to speak of understanding or to say that I understand something definite. For it only makes sense to speak of understanding in cases where we understand *one* thing as opposed to another. And it is this contrast that signs express.

Indeed, seeing the internal relation must in its turn be seeing something that can be described, something of which one can say: "I see that such and such is the case"; it has to be really something of the same kind as the correlation-signs (like connecting lines, brackets, substitutions, etc.). Everything else has to be contained in the application of the sign of the general rule in a particular case.

It is as if we had a number of material objects and discovered they had surfaces which enabled them to be placed in a continuous row. Or rather, as if we discovered that such and such surfaces, which we had seen before, enabled them to be placed in a continuous row. That is the way many games and puzzles are solved.

The person who discovers periodicity invents a new calculus. The question is, how does the calculus with periodic division differ from the calculus in which periodicity is unknown?

(We might have operated a calculus with cubes without having had the idea of putting them together to make prisms.)

Appendix[1]

(On: The process of generalization creates a new sign-system)

It is a very important observation that the c in A is not the same variable as the c in β and γ. So the way I wrote out the proof was not quite correct in a respect which is very important for us. In A we could substitute n for c, whereas the cs in β and γ are identical.

But another question arises: can I derive from A that $i + (k + c) = (i + k) + c$? If so, why can't I derive it in the same way from B? Does that mean that a and b in A are not identical with a and b in α, β and γ?

We see clearly that the variable c in B isn't identical with the c in A if we put a number instead of it. Then B is something like

$$\left. \begin{array}{l} \alpha \quad 4 + (5 + 1) \qquad = (4 + 5) + 1 \\ \beta \quad 4 + (5 + (6 + 1)) = (4 + (5 + 6)) + 1 \\ \gamma \quad (4 + 5) + (6 + 1) = ((4 + 5) + 6) + 1 \end{array} \right\} \quad \ldots \text{W}$$

but that doesn't have corresponding to it an equation like A_w: $4 + (5 + 6) = (4 + 5) + 6$!

What makes the induction proof different from a proof of A is expressed in the fact that the c in B is not identical with the one in A, so that we could use different letters in the two places.

All that is meant by what I've written above is that the reason it looks like an algebraic proof of A is that we think we meet the same variables a, b, c in the equations A as in α, β, γ and so we

---

1. Remarks taken from the Manuscript volume. We must not forget that Wittgenstein omitted them. Even in the MS they are not set out together as they are here. (Ed.)

regard A as the result of a transformation of those equations. (Whereas of course in reality I regard the signs α, β, γ in quite a different way, which means that the c in β and γ isn't used as a variable in the same way as a and b. Hence one can express this new view of B, by saying that the c does not occur in A.)

What I said about the new way of regarding α, β, γ might be put like this: α is used to build up β and γ in exactly the same way as the fundamental algebraic equations are used to build up an equation like $(a + b)^2 = a^2 + 2ab + b^2$. But if that is the way they are derived, we are regarding the complex α β γ in a new way when we give the variable c a function which differs from that of a and b (c becomes the hole through which the stream of numbers has to flow).

38

Proof by induction, arithmetic and algebra

Why do we need the commutative law? Not so as to be able to write the equation $4 + 6 = 6 + 4$, because that equation is justified by its own particular proof. Certainly the proof of the commutative law can also be used to prove it, but in that case it becomes just a particular arithmetical proof. So the reason I need the law, is to apply it when using letters.

And it is this justification that the inductive proof cannot give me.

However, one thing is clear: if the recursive proof gives us the right to calculate algebraically, then so does the arithmetical proof L^1.

Again: the recursive proof is – of course – essentially concerned with numbers. But what use are numbers to me when I want to operate purely algebraically? Or again, the recursion proof is only of use to me when I want to use it to justify a step in a number-calculation.

But someone might ask: do we need *both* the inductive proof *and* the associative law, since the latter cannot provide a foundation for calculation with numbers, and the former cannot provide one for transformations in algebra?

Well, before Skolem's proof was the associative law, for example, just accepted without anyone's being able to work out the corresponding step in a numerical calculation? That is, were we previously unable to work out $5 + (4 + 3) = (5 + 4) + 3$, and did we treat it as an axiom?

If I say that the periodic calculation proves the proposition that justifies me in those steps, what would the proposition have been

1. Above, p. 431.

like if it had been assumed as an axiom instead of being proved?

What would a proposition be like that permitted one to put $5 + (7 + 9) = (5 + 7) + 9$ without being able to prove it? It is obvious that there never has been such a proposition.

But couldn't we also say that the associative law isn't used at all in arithmetic and that we work only with particular number calculations?

Even when algebra uses arithmetical notation, it is a totally different calculus, and cannot be derived from the arithmetical one.

To the question "is $5 \times 4 = 20$"? one might answer: "let's check whether it is in accord with the basic rules of arithmetic" and similarly I might say: let's check whether A is in accord with the basic rules. But with which rules? Presumably with α.

But before we can bring α and A together we need to stipulate what we want to call "agreement" here.

That means that α and A are separated by the gulf between arithmetic and algebra,[1] and if B is to count as a proof of A, this gulf has to be bridged over by a stipulation.

It is quite clear that we do use an idea of this kind of agreement when, for instance, we quickly work out a numerical example to check the correctness of an algebraic proposition.

And in this sense I might e.g. calculate

$$\frac{25 \times 16}{25} \qquad \frac{16 \times 25}{32}$$

$$\frac{150}{400} \qquad \frac{80}{400}$$

---

1. To repeat, α is: $a + (b + 1) = (a + b) + 1$
    A is: $a + (b + c) = (a + b) + c$. (Ed.)

and say: "yes, it's right, a.b is equal to b.a" – if I imagine that I have forgotten.

Considered as a rule for algebraic calculation, A cannot be proved recursively. We would see that especially clearly if we wrote down the "recursive proof" as a series of arithmetical expressions. Imagine them written down (i.e. a fragment of the series plus "and so on") without any intention of "proving" anything, and then suppose someone asks: "does that prove $a + (b + c) = (a + b) + c$?". We would ask in astonishment "How can it prove anything of the kind? The series contains only numbers, it doesn't contain any letters". – But no doubt we might say: if I introduce A as a rule for calculation with letters, that brings this calculus in a certain sense into unison with the calculus of the cardinal numbers, the calculus I established by the law for the rules of addition (the recursive definition $a + (b + 1) = (a + b) + 1$).

VII INFINITY IN MATHEMATICS
THE EXTENSIONAL VIEWPOINT

39
Generality in arithmetic

"What is the sense of such a proposition as '$(\exists n).3 + n = 7$'?" Here we are in an odd difficulty: on the one hand we feel it to be a problem that the proposition has the choice between infinitely many values of n, and on the other hand the sense of the proposition seems guaranteed in itself and only needing further research on our part, because after all we "know 'what $(\exists x)\varphi x$' means". If someone said he didn't know what was the sense of "$(\exists n).3+n=7$", he would be answered "but you do know what this proposition says: $3 + 0 = 7 . \mathbf{v} . 3 + 1 = 7 . \mathbf{v} . 3 + 2 = 7$ and so on!" But to that one can reply "Quite correct – so the proposition isn't a logical sum, because a logical sum doesn't end with 'and so on'. What I am not clear about is this propositional form '$\varphi(0) \mathbf{v} \varphi(1) \mathbf{v} \varphi(2) \mathbf{v}$ and so on' – and all you have done is to substitute a second unintelligible kind of proposition for the first one, while pretending to give me something familiar, namely a disjunction."

That is, if we believe that we do understand "$(\exists n)$ etc." in some absolute sense, we have in mind as a justification other uses of the notation "$(\exists \ldots) \ldots$", or of the ordinary-language expression "There is . . . " But to that one can only say: So you are *comparing* the proposition "$(\exists n) \ldots$ " with the proposition "There is a house in this city which . . ." or "There are two foreign words on this page". But the occurrence of the words "there is" in those sentences doesn't suffice to determine the grammar of this generalization, all it does is to indicate a certain analogy in the rules. And so we can still investigate the grammar of the generalisation "$(\exists n)$ etc." with an open mind, that is, without letting the meaning of "$(\exists \ldots) \ldots$" in other cases get in our way.

"Perhaps all numbers have the property ε". Again the question is:

what is the grammar of this general proposition? Our being acquainted with the use of the expression "all..." in other grammatical systems is not enough. If we say "you do know what it means: it means $\varepsilon(0) . \varepsilon(1) . \varepsilon(2)$ and so on", again nothing is explained except that the proposition is *not* a logical product. In order to understand the grammar of the proposition we ask: how is the proposition used? What is regarded as the criterion of its truth? What is its verification? – If there is no method provided for deciding whether the proposition is true or false, then it is pointless, and that means senseless. But then we delude ourselves that there is indeed a method of verification, a method which cannot be employed, but only because of human weakness. This verification consists in checking all the (infinitely many) terms of the product $\varepsilon(0) . \varepsilon(1) . \varepsilon(2) \ldots$ Here there is confusion between physical impossibility and what is called 'logical impossibility'. For we think we have given sense to the expression "checking of the infinite product" because we take the expression "infinitely many" for the designation of an enormously large number. And when we hear of "the impossibility of checking the infinite number of propositions" there comes before our mind the impossibility of checking a very large number of propositions, say when we don't have sufficient time.

Remember that in the sense in which it is impossible to check an infinite number of propositions it is also impossible to try to do so. – If we are using the words "But you do know what 'all' means" to appeal to the cases in which this mode of speech is used, we cannot regard it as a matter of indifference if we observe a distinction between these cases and the case for which the use of the words is to be explained. – Of course we know what is meant by "checking a number of propositions for correctness", and it is this understanding that we are appealing to when we claim that one should understand also the expression " . . . infinitely many propositions". But doesn't the sense of the first expression depend on the specific experiences that correspond to it? And these experiences are lacking in the employment (the calculus) of the second expression; if any experiences at all are correlated to it they are fundamentally different ones.

Ramsey once proposed to express the proposition that infinitely many objects satisfied a function $f(\xi)$ by the denial of all propositions like

$$\sim(\exists x).fx$$
$$(\exists x).fx.\sim(\exists x, y).fx.fy$$
$$(\exists x, y).fx.fy.\sim(\exists x, y, z).fx.fy.fz$$
and so on.

But this denial would yield the series

$$(\exists x).fx$$
$$(\exists x, y).fx.fy$$
$$(\exists x, y.z) \ldots, \text{etc., etc.}$$

But this series too is quite superfluous: for in the first place the last proposition at any point surely contains all the previous ones, and secondly even it is of no use to us, because it isn't about an infinite number of objects. So in reality the series boils down to the proposition:

$$\text{``}(\exists x, y, z \ldots \text{ad inf.}).fx.fy.fz \ldots \text{ad inf.''}$$

and we can't make anything of that sign unless we know its grammar. But one thing is clear: what we are dealing with isn't a sign of the form "$(\exists x, y, z).fx.fy.fz$" but a sign whose similarity to that looks purposely deceptive.

I can certainly define "$m > n$" as $(\exists x):m - n = x$, but by doing so I haven't in any way analysed it. You think, that by using the symbolism "$(\exists \ldots) \ldots$" you establish a connection between "$m > n$" and other propositions of the form "there is $\ldots$"; what you forget is that that can't do more than stress a certain analogy, because the sign "$(\exists \ldots) \ldots$" is used in countlessly many different 'games'. (Just as there is a 'king' in chess and draughts.) So we have to know the rules governing its use *here*; and as soon as we do that it immediately becomes clear that these rules are connected with the rules for subtraction. For if we ask the usual question "how do I know – i.e. where do I get it from – that there is a number x that satisfies the condition m – n = x ?" it is the rules for subtraction that provide the answer. And then we see that we haven't gained very much by our definition. Indeed we might just as well have given as an explanation of 'm > n' the rules for checking a proposition of that kind – e.g. '32 > 17'.

If I say: "given any n there is a δ for which the function is less than n", I am *ipso facto* referring to a general arithmetical criterion that indicates when $F(\delta) < n$.

If in the nature of the case I cannot write down a number independently of a number system, that must be reflected in the general treatment of number. A number system is not something inferior – like a Russian abacus – that is only of interest to elementary schools while a more lofty general discussion can afford to disregard it.

Again, I don't lose anything of the generality of my account if I give the rules that determine the correctness and incorrectness (and thus the sense) of 'm > n' for a particular system like the decimal system. After all I need *a* system, and the generality is preserved by giving the rules according to which one system can be translated into another.

A proof in mathematics is general if it is generally applicable. You can't demand some other kind of generality in the name of rigour. *Every* proof rests on *particular* signs, produced on a particular occasion. All that can happen is that one type of generality may appear more elegant than another. ((Cf. the employment of the decimal system in proofs concerning δ and η)).

"Rigorous" means: clear.[1]

---

1. (Remark in the margin in pencil.) A defence, against Hardy, of the decimal system in proofs, etc.

"We may imagine a mathematical proposition as a creature which itself knows whether it is true or false (in contrast with propositions of experience).

A mathematical proposition itself knows that it is true or that it is false. If it is about all numbers, it must also survey all the numbers. "Its truth or falsity must be contained in it as is its sense."

"It's as though the generality of a proposition like '(n) . ε(n)' were only a pointer to the genuine, actual, mathematical generality, and not the generality itself. As if the proposition formed a sign only in a purely external way and you still needed to give the sign a sense from within."

"We feel the generality possessed by the mathematical assertion to be different from the generality of the proposition proved."

"We could say: a mathematical proposition is an allusion to a proof."[1]

What would it be like if a proposition itself did not quite grasp its sense? As if it were, so to speak, too grand for itself? That is really what logicians suppose.

A proposition that deals with all numbers cannot be thought of as verified by an endless striding, for, if the striding is endless, it does not lead to any goal.

Imagine an infinitely long row of trees, and, so that we can inspect them, a path beside them. All right, the path must be endless. But if it is endless, then that means precisely that you can't walk to the end of it. That is, it does *not* put me in a position to survey the row. That is to say, the endless path does not have an end 'infinitely far away', it has no end.

Nor can you say: "A proposition cannot deal with all the numbers one by one, so it has to deal with them by means of the concept of number" as if this were a *pis aller*: "Because we can't do it like *this*, we have to do it another way." But it is indeed possible to deal with the numbers one by one, only that *doesn't*

1. *Philosophical Remarks,* 122, pp. 143–145.

lead to the totality. That *doesn't* lie on the path on which we go step by step, not even at the infinitely distant end of that path. (This all only means that "$\varepsilon(o) . \varepsilon(1) . \varepsilon(2)$ and so on" is not the sign for a logical product.)

"It cannot be a contingent matter that all numbers possess a property; if they do so it must be essential to them." – The proposition "men who have red noses are good-natured" does not have the same sense as the proposition "men who drink wine are good-natured" even if the men who have red noses are the same as the men who drink wine. On the other hand, if the numbers m, n, o are the extension of a mathematical concept, so that is the case that fm.fn.fo, then the proposition that the numbers that satisfy f have the property ε has the same sense as "$\varepsilon(m) . \varepsilon(n)\varepsilon . (o)$". This is because the propositions "f(m).f(n).f(o)" and "$\varepsilon(m) . \varepsilon(n) . \varepsilon(o)$" can be transformed into each other without leaving the realm of grammar.

Now consider the proposition: "all the n numbers that satisfy the condition $F(\xi)$ happen by chance to have the property ε". Here what matters is whether the condition $F(\xi)$ is a mathematical one. If it is, then I can indeed derive $\varepsilon(x)$ from $F(x)$, if only via the disjunction of the n values of $F(\xi)$. (For what we have in this case is in fact a disjunction). So I won't call this chance. – On the other hand if the condition is a non-mathematical one, we can speak of chance. For example, if I say: all the numbers I saw today on buses happened to prime numbers. (But, of course, we can't say: the numbers 17, 3, 5, 31 happen to be prime numbers" any more than "the number 3 happens to be a prime number"), "By chance" is indeed the opposite of "in accordance with a general rule", but however odd it sounds one can say that the proposition "17, 3, 5, 31 are prime numbers" is derivable by a general rule just like the proposition $2 + 3 = 5$.

If we now return to the first proposition, we may ask again: How is the proposition "all numbers have the property ε" supposed to be meant? How is one supposed to be able to know? For to settle its sense you must settle that too! The expression "by chance" indicates a verification by successive tests, and that is contradicted by the fact that we are not speaking of a finite series of numbers.

In mathematics description and object are equivalent. "The fifth number of the number series has these properties" says *the same* as "5 has these properties". The properties of a house do not *follow* from its position in a row of houses; but the properties of a number are the properties of a position.

You might say that the properties of a particular number cannot be foreseen. You can only see them when you've got there.

What is general is the repetition of an operation. Each stage of the repetition has its own individuality. But it isn't as if I use the operation to move from one individual to another so that the operation would be the means for getting from one to the other – like a vehicle stopping at every number which we can then study: no, applying the operation +1 three times yields and *is* the number 3.

(In the calculus process and result are equivalent to each other.)

But before deciding to speak of "all these individualities" or "the totality of these individualities" I had to consider carefully what stipulations I wanted to make here for the use of the expressions "all" and "totality".

It is difficult to extricate yourself completely from the extensional viewpoint: You keep thinking "Yes, but there must still be an internal relation between $x^3 + y^3$ and z^3 since at least extensions of these expressions if I only knew them would have to show the result of such a relation". Or perhaps: "It must surely be either *essential* to *all* numbers to have the property or not, even if I can't know it."

"If I run through the number series, I either eventually come to a number with the property ε or I never do." The expression "to run through the number series" is nonsense; unless a sense is *given* to it which removes the suggested analogy with "running through the numbers from 1 to 100".

When Brouwer attacks the application of the law of excluded middle in mathematics, he is right in so far as he is directing his attack against a process analogous to the proof of empirical propositions. In mathematics you can never prove something like *this*: I saw two apples lying on the table, and now there is only *one* there, so A has eaten an apple. That is, you can't by excluding certain possibilities prove a new one which isn't already contained in the exclusion because of the rules we have laid down. To that extent there are no genuine alternatives in mathematics. If mathematics was the investigation of empirically given aggregates, one could use the exclusion of a part to describe what was not excluded, and in that case the non-excluded part would not be equivalent to the exclusion of the others.

The whole approach that if a proposition is valid for one region of mathematics it need not necessarily be valid for a second region as well, is quite out of place in mathematics, completely contrary to its essence. Although many authors hold just this approach to be particularly subtle and to combat prejudice.

It is only if you investigate the relevant propositions and their proofs that you can recognize the nature of the generality of the propositions of mathematics that treat not of "all cardinal numbers" but e.g. of "all real numbers".

How a proposition is verified is what it says. Compare generality in arithmetic with the generality of non-arithmetical propositions.

It is differently verified and so is of a different kind. The verification is not a mere token of the truth, but determines the sense of the proposition. (Einstein: how a magnitude is measured is what it is.)

A misleading picture: "The rational points lie close together on the number-line."

Is a space thinkable that contains all rational points, but not the irrational ones? Would this structure be too coarse for our space, since it would mean that we could only reach the irrational points approximately? Would it mean that our net was not fine enough? No. What we would lack would be the laws, not the extensions.

Is a space thinkable that contains all rational points but not the irrational ones?

That only means: don't the rational numbers set a precedent for the irrational numbers?

No more than draughts sets a precedent for chess.

There isn't any gap left open by the rational numbers that is filled up by the irrationals.

We are surprised to find that "between the everywhere dense rational points", there is still room for the irrationals. (What balderdash!) What does a construction like that for $\sqrt{2}$ show? Does it show how there is yet room for this point in between all the rational points? It shows that the point *yielded* by the construction, yielded by *this* construction, is *not rational*. – And what corresponds to this construction in arithmetic? A sort of number which manages *after all* to squeeze in between the rational numbers? A law that is not a law of the nature of a rational number.

The explanation of the Dedekind cut pretends to be clear when it says: there are 3 cases: either the class R has a first member and L no last member, etc. In fact two of these 3 cases cannot be imagined, unless the words "class", "first member", "last member", altogether change the everyday meanings thay are supposed to have retained.

That is, if someone is dumbfounded by our talk of a class of points that lie to the right of a given point and have no beginning, and says: give us an example of such a class – we trot out the class of rational numbers; but that isn't a class of points in the original sense.

The point of intersection of two curves isn't the common member of two classes of points, it's the meeting of two laws. Unless, very misleadingly, we use the second form of expression to define the first.

After all I have already said, it may sound trivial if I now say that the mistake in the set-theoretical approach consists time and again in treating laws and enumerations (lists) as essentially the same kind of thing and arranging them in parallel series so that one fills in gaps left by another.

The symbol for a class is a list.

Here again, the difficulty arises from the formation of mathematical pseudo-concepts. For instance, when we say that we can arrange the cardinal numbers, but not the rational numbers, in a series according to their size, we are unconsciously presupposing that the concept of an ordering by size does have a sense *for rational numbers*, and that it turned out on investigation that the ordering was impossible (which presupposes that the *attempt* is thinkable). – Thus one thinks that it is possible to attempt to arrange *the real numbers* (as if that were a concept of the same kind as 'apple on this table') in a series, and now it turned out to be impracticable.

For its form of expression the calculus of sets relies as far as possible on the form of expression of the calculus of cardinal numbers. In some ways that is instructive, since it indicates certain formal similarities, but it is also misleading, like calling something a knife that has neither blade nor handle. (Lichtenberg.)

(The only point there can be to elegance in a mathematical proof is to reveal certain analogies in a particularly striking manner, when that is what is wanted; otherwise it is a product of stupidity and its only effect is to obscure what ought to be clear and manifest. The stupid pursuit of elegance is a principal cause of the mathematicians' failure to understand their own operations; or perhaps the lack of understanding and the pursuit of elegance have a common origin.)

Human beings are entangled all unknowing in the net of language.

"There is a point where the two curves intersect." How do you know that? If you tell me, I will know what sort of sense the proposition "there is . . . " has.

If you want to know what the expression "the maximum of a curve" means, ask yourself: how does one find it? – If something is found in a different way it is a different thing. We define the maximum as the point on the curve higher than all the others, and from that we get the idea that it is only our human weakness that prevents us from sifting through the points of the curve one by one and selecting the highest of them. And this leads to the idea that the highest point among a finite number of points is essentially the same as the highest point of a curve, and that we are simply finding out the same thing by two different methods, just as we find out in two different ways that there is no one in the next room; one way if the door is shut and we aren't strong enough to open it, and another way if we can get inside. But, as I said, it isn't human weakness that's in question where the alleged description of the action "that we cannot perform" is senseless. Of course it does no harm, indeed it's very interesting, to see the analogy between the maximum of a curve and the maximum (in another sense) of a class of points, provided that the analogy doesn't instil the prejudice that in each case we have fundamentally the same thing.

It's the same defect in our syntax which presents the geometrical proposition "a length may be divided by a point into two parts" as a proposition of the same form as "a length may be divided for ever"; so that it looks as if in both cases we can say "Let's suppose the possible division to have been carried out". "Divisible into two parts" and "infinitely divisible" have quite different grammars. We mistakenly treat the word "infinite" as if it were a number word, because in everyday speech both are given as answers to the question "how many?"

"But after all the maximum is higher than any other arbitrary points of the curve." But the curve is not composed of points, it is a law that points obey, or again, a law according to which points can be constructed. If you now ask: "which points?" I can only say, "well, for instance, the points P, Q, R, etc." On the one hand we can't give a number of points and say that they are all the points that lie on the curve, and on the other hand we can't speak of a totality of points as something describable which although we humans cannot count them might be called the totality of all the points of the curve – a totality too big for us human beings. On the one hand there is a law, and on the other points on the curve; – but not "*all* the points of the curve". The maximum is higher than any point of the curve that happens to be constructed, but it isn't higher than a totality of points, unless the criterion for that, and thus the sense of the assertion, is once again simply construction according to the law of the curve.

Of course the web of errors in this region is a very complicated one. There is also e.g. the confusion between two different meanings of the word "kind". We admit, that is, that the infinite numbers are a different *kind* of number from the finite ones, but then we misunderstand what the difference between different kinds amounts to in this case. We don't realise, that is, that it's not a matter of distinguishing between objects by their properties in the way we distinguish between red and yellow apples, but a matter of different logical forms. – Thus Dedekind tried to *describe* an infinite class by saying that it is a class which is similar to a proper subclass of itself. Here it looks as if he has given a property that a class must have in order to fall under the concept "infinite class" (Frege).[1] Now let us consider how this definition is applied. I am to investigate in a particular case whether a class is finite or not, whether a certain row of trees, say, is finite or infinite. So, in accordance with the definition, I take a subclass of the row of trees and investigate whether it is similar (i.e. can be co-ordinated one-to-one) to the whole class! (Here already the whole thing has become laughable.) It hasn't any meaning; for, if I take a "finite class" as a sub-class, the attempt to coordinate it one-to-one with the whole class must *eo ipso* fail: and if I make the attempt with an infinite class – but already that is a piece of nonsense, for if it is infinite, I cannot make an attempt to co-ordinate it. – What we call 'correlation of all the members of a class with others' in the case of a finite class is something quite different from what we, e.g., call a correlation of all cardinal numbers with all rational numbers. The two correlations, or what one means by these words in the two cases, belong to different logical types. An infinite class is not a class which contains more members than a finite one, in the ordinary sense of the word "more". If we say that an infinite number is greater than a finite one, that doesn't make the two comparable, because in that statement the word "greater" *hasn't the same meaning* as it has say in the proposition $5 > 4$!

That is to say, the definition pretends that whether a class is finite or infinite follows from the success or failure of the attempt to correlate a proper subclass with the whole class; whereas there just isn't any such decision procedure. – 'Infinite class' and 'finite class' are different logical categories; what can be significantly

---

1. Cf. *The Foundations of Arithmetic*, §84. (Ed.)

asserted of the one category cannot be significantly asserted of the other.

With regard to finite classes the proposition that a class is not similar to its sub-classes is not a truth but a tautology. It is the grammatical rules for the generality of the general implication in the proposition "k is a subclass of K" that contain what is said by the proposition that K is an infinite class.

A proposition like "there is no last cardinal number" is offensive to naive – and correct – common sense. If I ask "Who was the last person in the procession?" and am told "There wasn't a last person" I don't know what to think; what does "There wasn't a last person" mean? Of course, if the question had been "Who was the standard bearer?" I would have understood the answer "There wasn't a standard bearer"; and of course the bewildering answer is modelled on an answer of that kind. That is, we feel, correctly, that where we can speak at all of a last one, there can't be "No last one". But of course that means: The proposition "There isn't a last one" should rather be: it makes no sense to speak of a "last cardinal number", that expression is ill-formed.

"Does the procession have an end?" might also mean: is the procession a compact group? And now someone might say: "There, you see, you can easily imagine a case of something not having an end; so why can't there be other such cases?" – But the answer is: The "cases" in this sense of the word are grammatical cases, and it is they that determine the sense of the question. The question "Why can't there be other such cases?" is modelled on: "Why can't there be other minerals that shine in the dark"; but the latter is about cases where a statement is true, the former about cases that determine the sense.

The form of expression "m = 2n correlates a class with one of its proper subclasses" uses a misleading analogy to clothe a trivial sense in a paradoxial form. (And instead of being ashamed of

this paradoxical form as something ridiculous, people plume themselves on a victory over all prejudices of the understanding). It is
exactly as if one changed the rules of chess and said it had been
shown that chess could also be played quite differently. Thus we
first mistake the word "number" for a concept word like "apple",
then we talk of a "number of numbers" and we don't see that in
this expression we shouldn't use the same word "number" twice;
and finally we regard it as a discovery that the number of the even
numbers is equal to the number of the odd and even numbers.

It is less misleading to say "$m = 2n$ allows the possiblity of
correlating every time with another" than to say "$m = 2n$ correlates
all numbers with others". But here too the grammar of the meaning
of the expression "possibility of correlation" has to be learnt.

(It's almost unbelievable, the way in which a problem gets
completely barricaded in by the misleading expressions which
generation upon generation throw up for miles around it, so that it
becomes virtually impossible to get at it.)

If two arrows point in the same direction, isn't it in such a case
absurd to call these directions equally *long*, because whatever lies
in the direction of the one arrow, also lies in that of the other? –
The generality of $m = 2n$ is an arrow that points along the series
generated by the operation. And you can even say that the arrow
points to infinity; but does that mean that there is something –
infinity – at which it points, as at a thing? – It's as though the
arrow designates the possibility of a position in its direction. But
the word "possibility" is misleading, since someone will say: let
what is possible now become actual. And in thinking this we always
think of a temporal process, and infer from the fact that mathematics has nothing to do with time, that in its case possibility is
already actuality.

The "infinite series of cardinal numbers" or "the concept of
cardinal number" is only such a possibility – as emerges clearly

from the symbol "$|o, \xi, \xi + 1|$". This symbol is itself an arrow with the "o" as its tail and the "$\xi + 1$" as its tip. It is possible to speak of things which lie in the direction of the arrow, but misleading or absurd to speak of all possible positions for things lying in the direction of the arrow as an equivalent for the arrow itself. If a searchlight sends out light into infinite space it illuminates everything in its direction, but you can't say it illuminates infinity.

It is always right to be extremely suspicious when proofs in mathematics are taken with greater generality than is warranted by the known application of the proof. This is always a case of the mistake that sees general concepts and particular cases in mathematics. In set theory we meet this suspect generality at every step.

One always feels like saying "let's get down to brass tacks".

These general considerations only make sense when we have a particular region of application in mind.

In mathematics there isn't any such thing as a generalization whose application to particular cases is still unforseeable. That's why the general discussions of set theory (if they aren't viewed as calculi) always sound like empty chatter, and why we are always astounded when we are shown an application for them. We feel that what is going on isn't properly connected with real things.

The distinction between the general truth that one can know, and the particular that one doesn't know, or between the known description of the object, and the object itself that one hasn't seen, is another example of something that has been taken over into logic from the physical description of the world. And that too is where we get the idea that our reason can recognize questions but not their answers.

Set theory attempts to grasp the infinite at a more general level than the investigation of the laws of the real numbers. It says that you can't grasp the actual infinite by means of mathematical symbolism at all and therefore it can only be described and not represented. The description would encompass it in something like the way in which you carry a number of things that you can't hold in your hand by packing them in a box. They are then invisible but we still know we are carrying them (so to speak, indirectly). One might say of this theory that it buys a pig in a poke. Let the infinite accommodate itself in this box as best it can.

With this there goes too the idea that we can use language to *describe* logical forms. In a description of this sort the structures are presented in a package and so it does look as if one could speak of a structure without reproducing it in the proposition itself. Concepts which are packed up like this may, to be sure, be used, but our signs derive their meaning from definitions which package the concepts in this way; and if we follow up these definitions, the structures are uncovered again. (Cf. Russell's definition of "R*".)

When "all apples" are spoken of, it isn't, so to speak, any concern of logic how many apples there are. With numbers it is different; logic is responsible for each and every one of them.

Mathematics consists entirely of calculations.

In mathematics *everything* is algorithm and *nothing* is meaning; even when it doesn't look like that because we seem to be using *words* to talk *about* mathematical things. Even these words are used to construct an algorithm.

In set theory what is calculus must be separated off from what attempts to be (and of course cannot be) *theory*. The rules of the game have to be separated off from inessential statements about the chessmen.

In Cantor's alleged definition of "greater", "smaller", "+", "−"

Frege replaced the signs with new words to show the definition wasn't really a definition.[1] Similarly in the whole of mathematics one might replace the usual words, especially the word "infinite" and its cognates, with entirely new and hitherto meaningless expressions so as to see what the calculus with these signs really achieves and what it fails to achieve. If the idea was widespread that chess gave us information about kings and castles, I would propose to give the pieces new shapes and different names, so as to demonstrate that everything belonging to chess has to be contained in the rules.

What a geometrical proposition means, what kind of generality it has, is something that must show itself when we see how it is applied. For even if someone succeeded in meaning something intangible by it it wouldn't help him, because he can only apply it in a way which is quite open and intelligible to every one.

Similarly, if someone imagined the chess king as something mystical it wouldn't worry us since he can only move him on the 8×8 squares of the chess board.

We have a feeling "There can't be possibility and actuality in mathematics. It's all on *one* level. And is in a certain sense, *actual*. – And that is correct. For mathematics is a calculus; and the calculus does not say of any sign that it is merely *possible*, but is concerned only with the signs with which it *actually* operates. (Compare the foundations of set theory with the assumption of a possible calculus with infinite signs).

When set theory appeals to the human impossibility of a direct symbolisation of the infinite it brings in the crudest imaginable misinterpretation of its own calculus. It is of course this very misinterpretation that is responsible for the invention of the calculus. But of course that doesn't show the calculus in itself to

---

1. *Grundgesetze d. Arithmetik*, II, § 83, pp. 93, 94.

be something incorrect (it would be at worst uninteresting) and it is odd to believe that this part of mathematics is imperilled by any kind of philosophical (or mathematical) investigations. (As well say that chess might be imperrilled by the dicovery that wars between two armies do not follow the same course as battles on the chessboard.) What set theory has to lose is rather the atmosphere of clouds of thought surrounding the bare calculus, the suggestion of an underlying imaginary symbolism, a symbolism which isn't employed in its calculus, the apparent description of which is really nonsense. (In mathematics anything can be imagined, except for a part of our calculus.)

Like the enigma of time for Augustine, the enigma of the continuum arises because language misleads us into applying to it a picture that doesn't fit. Set theory preserves the inappropriate picture of something discontinuous, but makes statements about it that contradict the picture, under the impression that it is breaking with prejudices; whereas what should really have been done is to point out that the picture just doesn't fit, that it certainly can't be stretched without being torn, and that instead of it one can use a new picture in certain respects similar to the old one.

The confusion in the concept of the "actual infinite" arises from the unclear concept of irrational number, that is, from the fact that logically very different things are called "irrational numbers" without any clear limits being given to the concept. The illusion that we have a firm concept rests on our belief that in signs of the the form "o.abcd . . . ad infinitum" we have a pattern to which they (the irrational numbers) have to conform whatever happens.

"Suppose I cut a length at a place where there is no rational point (no rational number)." But can you do that? What sort of a length are you speaking of? "But if my measuring instruments were fine enough, at least I could approximate without limit to a certain point by continued bisection"! – No, for I could never tell whether my point was a point of this kind. All I could tell would always be that I hadn't reached it. "But if I carry out the construction of $\sqrt{2}$ with absolutely exact drawing instruments, and then by bisection approximate to the point I get, I *know* that this process will never reach the constructed point." But it would be odd if one construction could as it were prescribe something to the others in this way! And indeed that isn't the way it is. It is very possible that the point I get by means of the 'exact' construction of $\sqrt{2}$ is reached by the bisection after say 100 steps; – but in that case we could say: our space is not Euclidean.

The "cut at the irrational point" is a picture, and a misleading picture.

A cut is a *principle* of division into greater and smaller.

Does a cut through a length determine in advance the results of all bisections meant to approach the point of the cut? No.

In the previous example[1] in which I threw dice to guide me in the successive reduction of an interval by the bisection of a length I might just as well have thrown dice to guide me in the writing of a decimal. Thus the description "endless process of choosing between 1 and 0" does not determine a law in the writing of a decimal. Perhaps you feel like saying: the prescription for the endless choice between 0 and 1 in this case could be reproduced by a symbol like "0 $^{000}_{111}$ ... ad. inf.". But if I adumbrate a law thus '0·001001001 ... ad inf.', what I want to show is not the finite section of the series as a specimen of the infinite series, but rather the kind of regularity to be perceived in it. But in "0. $^{000}_{111}$ ... ad. inf." I don't perceive *any* law, – on the contrary, precisely that a law is absent.

(What criterion is there for the irrational numbers being complete? Let us look at an irrational number: it runs through a series of rational approximations. When does it leave this series behind? Never. But then, the series also never comes to an end.

Suppose we had the totality of all irrational numbers with one single exception. How would we feel the lack of this one? And – if

---

1. See below, p. 484

472

it were to be added – how would it fill the gap? Suppose that it's π. If an irrational number is given through the totality of its approximations, then up to *any* point taken at random there is a series coinciding with that of π. Admittedly for each such series there is a point where they diverge. But this point can lie arbitrarily far 'out', so that for any series agreeing with π I can find one agreeing with it still further. And so if I have the totality of all irrational numbers except π, and now insert π I cannot cite a point at which π is now really needed. At *every* point it has a companion agreeing with it from the beginning on.

To the question "how would we feel the lack of π" our answer must be "if π were an extension, we would never feel the lack of it". i.e. it would be impossible for us to observe a gap that it filled. But if someone asked us 'But have you then an infinite decimal expansion with the figure m in the r-th place and n in the s-th place, etc?' we could always oblige him.)

"The decimal fractions developed in accordance with a law still need supplementing by an infinite set of irregular infinite decimal fractions that would be 'brushed under the carpet' if we were to *restrict* ourselves to those *generated by a law*." Where is there such an infinite decimal that is generated by no law? And how would we notice that it was missing? Where is the gap it is needed to fill?

What is it like if someone so to speak checks the various laws for the construction of binary fractions by means of the set of finite combinations of the numerals o and 1? – The results of a law run through the finite combinations and hence the laws are complete as far as their extensions are concerned, once *all* the finite combinations have been gone through.

If one says: two laws are identical in the case where they yield the same result at every stage, this looks like a quite general rule. But in reality the proposition has different senses depending on what is the criterion for their yielding the same result at every stage. (For of course there's no such thing as the supposed generally applicable method of infinite checking!) Thus under a mode of speaking derived from an analogy we conceal the most various meanings, and then believe that we have united the most various cases into a single system.

(The laws corresponding to the irrational numbers all belong to the same type to the extent that they must all ultimately be recipes for the successive construction of decimal fractions. In a certain sense the common decimal notation gives rise to a common type.)

We could also put it thus: *every* point in a length can be approximated to by *rational* numbers by repeated bisection. There is no point that can only be approximated to by irrational steps of a specified type. Of course, that is only a way of clothing in different words the explanation that by irrational numbers we mean endless decimal fractions; and that explanation in turn is only a rough explanation of the decimal notation, plus perhaps an indication that we distinguish between laws that yield recurring decimals and laws that don't.

The incorrect idea of the word "infinite" and of the role of "infinite expansion" in the arithmetic of the real numbers gives us the false notion that there is a uniform notation for irrational numbers (the notation of the infinite extension, e.g. of infinite decimal fractions).

The proof that for every pair of cardinal numbers x and y $(\frac{x}{y})^2 \neq 2$ does not correlate $\sqrt{2}$ with a *single* type of number – called "the irrational numbers". It is not as if this type of number was constructed before I construct it; in other words, I don't know any more about this new type of number than *I* tell myself.

Kinds of irrational numbers
$(\pi'\ P, F)$

π' is a rule for the formation of decimal fractions: the expansion of π' is the same as the expansion of π except where the sequence 777 occurs in the expansion of π; in that case instead of the sequence 777 there occurs the sequence 000. There is no method known to our calculus of discovering where we encounter such a sequence in the expansion of π.

P is a rule for the construction of binary fractions. At the nth place of the expansion there occurs a 1 or a 0 according to whether n is prime or not.

F is a rule for the construction of binary fractions. At the nth place there is a 0 unless a triple x, y, z from the first 100 cardinal numbers satisfies the equation $x^n + y^n = z^n$.

I'm tempted to say, the individual digits of the expansion (of π for example) are always only the results, the bark of the fully grown tree. What counts, or what something new can still grow from, is the inside of the trunk, where the tree's vital energy is. Altering the surface doesn't change the tree at all. To change it, you have to penetrate the trunk which is still living.

I call "π_n" the expansion of π up to the nth place. Then I can say: I understand what π'_{100} means, but not what π' means, since π has no places, and I can't substitute others for none. It would be different if I e.g. defined the division $\overset{5\to3}{a/b}$ as a rule for the formation of decimals by division and the replacements of every 5 in the quotient by a 3. In this case I am acquainted, for instance, with the number $\overset{5\to3}{1/7}$. – And if our calculus contains a method, a law, to calculate the position of 777 in the expansion of π, then the law of π includes a mention of 777 and the law can be altered by the substitution of 000 for 777. But in that case π' isn't the same as what

I defined above; it has a different grammar from the one I supposed. In our calculus there is no question whether $\pi \gtreqless \pi'$ or not, no such equation or inequality. π' is not comparable with π. And one can't say "not *yet* comparable", because if at some time I construct something similar to π' that is comparable to π, then for that very reason it will no longer be π'. For π' like π is a way of denoting a game, and I cannot say that draughts is not *yet* played with as many pieces as chess, on the grounds that it might develop into a game with 16 pieces. In that case it will no longer be what we call "draughts" (unless by this word I mean not a game, but a characteristic of several games or something similar; and this rider can be applied to π and π' too). But since being comparable with other numbers is a fundamental characteristic of a number, the question arises whether one is to call π' a number, and a real number; but whatèver it is *called* the essential thing is that π' is not a number in the same sense as π. I can also call an interval a point and on occasion it may even be practical to do so; but does it become more like a point if I forget that I have used the word "point" with two different meanings?

Here it is clear that the possibility of the decimal expansion does not make π' a number in the same sense as π. Of course the rule for this expansion is unambiguous, as unambiguous as that for π or $\sqrt{2}$; but that is no proof that π' is a real number, if one takes comparability with rational numbers as an essential mark of real numbers. One can indeed abstract from the distinction between the rational and irrational numbers, but that does not make the distinction disappear. Of course, the fact that π' is an unambiguous rule for decimal fractions naturally signifies a similarity between π' and π or $\sqrt{2}$; but equally an interval has a similarity with a point etc. All the errors that have been made in this chapter of the philosophy of mathematics are based on the confusion between internal properties of a form (a rule as one among a list of rules) and what we call "properties" in everyday life (red as a property of this book). We might also say: the contradictions and unclarities are brought about by people using a single word, e.g. "number", to mean at one time a definite set of rules, and at another time a variable set, like meaning by "chess" on one occasion the definite game we play today, and on another occasion the substratum of a particular historical development.

"How far must I expand π in order to have some acquaintance with it?" – Of course that is nonsense. We are already acquainted with it without expanding it at all. And in the same sense I might say that I am not acquainted with π′ at all. Here it is quite clear that π′ belongs to a different system from π; that is something we recognize if we keep our eyes on the nature of the laws instead of comparing "the expansions" of both.

Two mathematical forms, of which one but not the other can be compared in my calculus with every rational number, are not numbers in the same sense of the word. The comparison of a number to a point on the number-line is valid only if we can say for every two numbers a and b whether a is to the right of b or b to the right of a.

It is not enough that someone should – supposedly – determine a point ever more closely by narrowing down its whereabouts. We must be able to construct *it*. To be sure, continued throwing of a die indefinitely restricts the possible whereabouts of a point, but it doesn't determine a point. After *every* throw (or every choice) the point is still infinitely indeterminate – or, more correctly, after every throw it is infinitely indeterminate. I think that we are here misled by the *absolute* size of the objects in our visual field; and on the other hand, by the ambiguity of the expression " to approach a point". We can say of a line in the visual field that by shrinking it is approximating more and more to a point – that is, it is becoming more and more similar to a point. On the other hand when a Euclidean line shrinks it does *not* become any more like a point; it always remains totally dissimilar, since its length, so to say, never gets anywhere near a point. If we say of a Euclidean line that it is approximating to a point by shrinking, that only makes sense if there is an already designated point which its ends are approaching; it cannot mean that by shrinking it *produces* a point. To approach a point has two meanings: in one case it means to come spatially nearer to it, and in that case the point must already be there, because in this sense I cannot approach a man who doesn't exist; in the other case, it means "to become more like a point", as we say for instance that the apes as they developed approached the stage of being human, their development produced human beings.

To say "two real numbers are identical if their expansions coincide in *all* places" only has sense in the case in which, by producing a method of establishing the coincidence, I have *given* a sense to the expression "to coincide in all places". And the same naturally holds for the proposition "they do not coincide if they disagree in *any one* place".

But conversely couldn't one treat π' as the original, and therefore as the first assumed point, and then be in doubt about the justification of π? As far as concerns their extension, they are naturally on the same level; but what causes us to call π a point on the number-line is its comparability with the rational numbers.

If I view π, or let's say $\sqrt{2}$, as a rule for the construction of decimals, I can naturally produce a modification of this rule by saying that every 7 in the development of $\sqrt{2}$ is to be replaced by a 5; but this modification is of quite a different *nature* from one which is produced by an alteration of the radicant or the exponent of the radical sign or the like. For instance, in the modified law I am including a reference to the number system of the expansion which wasn't in the original rule for $\sqrt{2}$. The alternation of the law is of a much more fundamental kind than might at first appear.

Of course, if we have the incorrect picture of the infinite extension before our minds, it can appear as if appending the substitution rule $7 \to 5$ to $\sqrt{2}$ alters it much less than altering $\sqrt{2}$ into $\sqrt{2 \cdot 1}$, because the expansions of $\overset{7 \to 5}{\sqrt{2}}$ are very similar to those of $\sqrt{2}$, whereas the expansion of $\sqrt{2 \cdot 1}$ deviates from that of $\sqrt{2}$ from the second place onwards.

Suppose I give a rule ρ for the formation of extensions in such a way that my calculus knows no way of predicting what is the maximum number of times an apparently recurring stretch of the extension can be repeated. That differs from a real number because in certain cases I can't compare $\rho - a$ with a rational number, so that the expression $\rho - a = b$ becomes nonsensical. If for instance the expansion of ρ so far known to me is 3·14 followed by an open series of ones (3·1411 11 . . .), it wouldn't be possible to say of the difference $\rho - 3 \cdot 14i$ whether it was greater or less than 0; so in this sense it can't be compared with 0 or with a point on the number axis and it and ρ can't be called number in the same sense as one of these points.

|The extension of a concept of number, or of the concept 'all', etc. seems quite harmless to us; but it stops being harmless as soon as we forget that we have in fact changed our concept.|

|So far as concerns the irrational numbers, my investigation says only that it is incorrect (or misleading) to speak of irrational numbers in such a way as to contrast them with cardinal numbers and rational numbers as a different kind of number; because what are called "irrational numbers" are species of number that are really different – as different from each other as the rational numbers are different from each of them.|

"Can God know all the places of the expansion of π?" would have been a good question for the schoolmen to ask.

In these discussions we are always meeting something that could be called an "arithmetical experiment". Admittedly the data determine the result, but I can't see *in what way* they determine it. That is how it is with the occurrences of the 7s in the expansion of π; the primes likewise are yielded as the result of an experiment. I can ascertain that 31 is a prime number, but I do not see the connection between it (its position in the series of cardinal numbers) and the condition it satisfies. – But this perplexity is only the consequence of an incorrect expression. The connection that I think I do not see does not exist. There is not an – as it were irregular – occurrence of 7s in the expansion of π, because there isn't any series that is called *the* expansion of π. There are expansions of π, namely those that have been worked out (perhaps 1000) and in those the 7s don't occur "irregularly" because their occurrence can be described. (The same goes for the "distribution of the primes". If you give as a law for this distribution, you give us a *new* number series, *new* numbers.) (A law of the calculus that I do not know is not a law). (Only what I *see* is a law; not what I *describe*. That is the only thing standing in the way of my expressing more in my signs that I can understand.)

Does it make no sense to say, even after Fermat's last theorem has been proved, that F = 0·11? (If, say I were to read about it in the papers.) I will indeed then say, "so now we can write 'F = 0·11'." That is, it is tempting to adopt the sign "F" from the earlier calculus, in which it didn't denote a rational number, into the new one and now to denote 0·11 with it.

F was supposed to be a number of which we did not know whether it was rational or irrational. Imagine a number, of which we do not know whether it is a cardinal number or a rational number. A description in the calculus is worth just as much as this particular set of words and it has nothing to do with an object given by description which may someday be found.

What I mean could also be expressed in the words: one cannot discover any connection between parts of mathematics or logic that was already there without one knowing.

In mathematics there is no "not yet" and no "until further notice" (except in the sense in which we can say that we haven't yet multiplied two 1000 digit numbers together.)

"Does the operation yield a rational number for instance?" – How can that be asked, if we have no method for deciding the question? For it is only in an established calculus that the operation *yields* results. I mean: "yields" is essentially timeless. It doesn't mean "yields, given time" – but: yields in accordance to the rules already known and established.

"The position of all primes must somehow be predetermined. We work them out only successively, but they are all already determined. God, as it were, knows them all. And yet for all that it seems possible that they are not determined by a law." – Always this picture of the meaning of a word as a full box which is given us with its contents packed in it all ready for us to investigate. – What *do* we know about the prime numbers? How is the concept of them given to us at all? Don't we ourselves make the decisions about them? And how odd that we assume that there must have been decisions taken about them that we haven't taken ourselves! But the mistake is understandable. For we use the expression "prime number" and it sounds similar to "cardinal number", "square number", "even number" etc. So we think it will be used in the same way, and we forget that for the expression "prime number" we have given quite different rules – rules *different in kind* – and we find ourselves at odds with ourselves in a strange way. – But how is that possible? After all the prime numbers are familiar cardinal numbers – how can one say that the concept of prime number is not a number concept in the same sense as the concept of cardinal number? But here again we are tricked by the image of an "infinite extension" as an analogue to the familiar "finite "extension. Of course the concept 'prime number' is defined by means of the concept 'cardinal number', but "the prime numbers" aren't defined by means of "the cardinal numbers", and the way *we* derived the concept 'prime number' from the concept 'cardinal number' is essentially different from that in which we derived, say, the concept 'square number'. (So we cannot be surprised if it behaves differently.) One might well imagine an arithmetic which – as it were – didn't stop at the concept 'cardinal number' but went straight on to that of square numbers. (Of course that arithmetic couldn't be applied in the same way as ours.) But then the concept "square number" wouldn't have the characteristic it has in our arithmetic of being essentially a part-concept, with the square numbers essentially a sub-class of the cardinal numbers; in that case the square numbers would be a complete series with a complete arithmetic. And now imagine the same done with the prime numbers! That will make it clear that they are not "numbers" in the same sense as e.g. the square numbers or the cardinal numbers.

Could the calculations of an engineer yield the result that the strength of a machine part in proportion to regularly increasing loads must increase in accordance with the series of primes?

Irregular infinite decimals

"Irregular infinite decimals". We always have the idea that we only have to bring together the words of our everyday language to give the combinations a sense, and all we then have to do is to inquire into it – supposing it's not quite clear right away. – It is as if words were ingredients of a chemical compound, and we shook them together to make them combine with each other, and then had to investigate the properties of the compound. If someone said he didn't understand the expression "irregular infinite decimals" he would be told "that's not true, you understand it very well: don't you know what the words "irregular", "infinite", and "decimal" mean? – well, then, you understand their combination as well." And what is meant by "understanding" here is that he knows how to apply these words in certain cases, and say *connects an image with them*. In fact, someone who puts these words together and asks "what does it mean" is behaving rather like small children who cover a paper with random scribblings, show it to grown-ups, and ask "what is that?"

"Infinitely complicated law", "infinitely complicated construction" ("Human beings believe, if only they hear words, there must be something that can be thought with them").

How does an infinitely complicated law differ from the lack of any law?

(Let us not forget: mathematicians' discussions of the infinite are clearly finite discussions. By which I mean, they come to an end.)

"One can imagine an irregular infinite decimal being constructed by endless dicing, with the number of pips in each case being a decimal place." But, if the dicing goes on for ever, no final result ever comes out.

"It is only the human intellect that is incapable of grasping it, a higher intellect could do so!" Fine, then describe to me the grammar of the expression "higher intellect"; what can such an intellect grasp and what can't it grasp and in what cases (in experience) do I say that an intellect grasps something? You will then see that describing grasping is itself grasping. (Compare: the solution of a mathematical problem.)

Suppose we throw a coin heads and tails and divide an interval AB in accordance with the following rule: "Heads" means: take the left half and divide it in the way the next throw prescribes. "Tails" says "take the right half, etc." By repeated throws I then

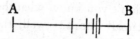

get dividing-points that move in an ever smaller interval. Does it amount to a description of the position of a point if I say that it is the one infinitely approached by the cuts as prescribed by the repeated tossing of the coin? Here one believes oneself to have determined a point corresponding to an irregular infinite decimal. But the description doesn't determine *any* point *explicitly*; unless one says that the words "point on this line" also "determine a point"! Here we are confusing the recipe for throwing with a mathematical rule like that for producing decimal places of $\sqrt{2}$. Those mathematical rules *are* the points. That is, you can find relations between those rules that resemble in their grammar the relations "larger" and "smaller" between two lengths, and that is why they are referred to by these words. The rule for working out places of $\sqrt{2}$ is itself the numeral for the irrational number; and the reason I here speak of a "number" is that I can calculate with these signs (certain rules for the construction of rational numbers) just as I can with rational numbers themselves. If I want to say similarly that the recipe for endless bisection according to heads and tails determines a point, that would have to mean that this recipe could be used as a numeral, i.e. in the same way as other numerals. But of course that is not the case. If the recipe were to correspond to a numeral at all, it would at best correspond to the indeterminate numeral "some", for all it does is to leave a number open. In a word, it corresponds to nothing except the original interval.

In June 1931 Wittgenstein wrote a parenthesis in his manuscript book: "(My book might be called: Philosophical Grammar. This title would no doubt have the smell of a textbook title but that doesn't matter, for behind it there is the book.)" In the next four manuscript volumes after this he wrote nearly everything that is in the present work. The second of these he called "Remarks towards Philosophical Grammar" and the last two "Philosophical Grammar".

The most important source for our text is a large typescript completed probably in 1933, perhaps some of it 1932. Our "Part II" makes up roughly the second half of this typescript. In most of the first half of it Wittgenstein made repeated changes and revisions – between the lines and on the reverse sides of the typed sheets – and probably in the summer of 1933 he began a "Revision" in a manuscript volume (X and going over into XI). This, with the "Second Revision" (which I will explain), is the text of our Part I up to the Appendix. – Wittgenstein simply wrote *"Umarbeitung"* (Revision) as a heading, without a date; but he clearly wrote it in 1933 and the early weeks of 1934. He did not write the "second revision" in the manuscript volume but on large folio sheets. He He crossed out the text that this was to replace, and showed in margins which parts went where. But it is a revision of only a *part*, towards the beginning, of the first and principal "Revision". The passages from the second revision are, in our text, §§1–13 and §§23–43. The second revision is not dated either, but obviously it is later than the passages it replaces; probably not later than 1934.

So we may take it that he wrote part of this work somewhat earlier, and part at the same time as his dictation of *The Blue Book*. Many things in the *Blue Book* are here (and they are better expressed). There are passages also which are in the *Philosophical Remarks* and others later included in the *Investigations*. It would be easy to give the reference and page number for each of these. We decided not to. This book should be compared with Wittgenstein's earlier and later writings. But this means: the method and the development of his discussion here should be compared with the *Philosophical Remarks* and again with the *Investigations*. The footnotes would be a hindrance and, as often as not, misleading. When Wittgenstein writes a paragraph here that is also in the *Remarks*, this does not mean that he is just repeating what he said there. The paragraph may have a different importance, it may belong to the discussion in a different way. (We know there is more to be said on this question.)

Wittgenstein refers to "my book" at various times in his manuscripts from the start of 1929 until the latest passages of the *Investigations*. It is what his writing was to produce. The first attempt to form the material into a book was the typescript volume he made in the summer of 1930 – the *Philosophical Remarks* (published in German in 1964). The large typescript of 1933 – the one we mentioned as a source of this volume – looks like a book. Everyone who sees it first thinks it is. But it is unfinished; in a great many ways. And Wittgenstein evidently looked on it as one stage in the ordering of his material. (Cf. the simile of arranging books on the shelves of a library, in *Blue Book* p. 44–45.)

Most of the passages which make up the text of the 1933 typescript (called "213" in the catalogue) he had written in manuscript volumes between July 1930 and July 1932; but not in the order they have in the typescript. From the manuscript volumes he dictated two typescripts, one fairly short and the other much longer – about 850 pages together. There was already a typescript made from manuscripts written *before* July 1930 – not the typescript which *was* the *Philosophical Remarks* but a typescript which he cut into parts and sifted and put together in a different way to *make* the *Philosophical Remarks*. He now used an intact copy of this typescript together with the two later ones in the same way, cutting them into strips: small strips sometimes with just one paragraph or one sentence, sometimes groups of paragraphs; and arranging them in the order he saw they ought to have. Groups of slips in their order were clipped together to form 'chapters', and he gave each chapter a title. He then brought the chapters together– in a definite order – to form 'sections'. He gave each section a title and arranged them also in a definite order. In this order the whole was finally typed. – Later he made a table of contents out of the titles of sections and chapter headings.

488

Certain chapters, especially, leave one feeling that he cannot have thought the typing of the consecutive copy had finished the work barring clerical details. He now wrote, over and over again, between the lines of typescript or in the margin: "Does not belong here", "Belongs on page ... above", "Belongs to 'Meaning', § 9", "Goes with 'What is an empirical proposition?' ", "Belongs with §14, p. 58 or § 89 p. 414", and so on. But more than this, about 350 pages – most of the first half of the typescript – are so written over with changes, additions, cancellations, questions and new versions, that no one could ever find the 'correct' text here and copy it – saving the author himself should write it over to include newer versions and make everything shorter.

He now makes no division into chapters and sections. He has left out paragraph numbers and any suggestion of a table of contents. We do not know why. (We do not find chapters or tables of contents anywhere else in Wittgenstein's writings. He may have found disadvantages in the experiment he tried here.) – The extra spaces between paragraphs and groups of paragraphs are his own; and he thought these important. He would have numbered paragraphs, probably, as he did in the *Investigations*. But the numbers in Part I here are the editor's, not Wittgenstein's. Neither is the division in chapters Wittgenstein's, nor the table of contents. – On the other hand, Part II has kept the chapters and the table of contents which Wittgenstein gave this part of the typescript. Perhaps this makes it look as though Part I and Part II were not one work. But we could not make them uniform in this (division and arrangement of chapters) without moving away from Wittgenstein's way of presenting what he wrote. Anyone who reads both parts will see connections.

And the appendix may make it plainer. Appendices 5, 6, 7, 8 and the first half of 4 are chapters of 'typescript 213'. Appendix 1, *Fact and Complex,* is also an appendix in *Philosophical Remarks*. But Wittgenstein had fastened it together with appendices 2 and 3 and given them a consecutive paging as one essay; with what intention we do not know. Each one of the eight appendices here discusses something connected with 'proposition' and with 'sense of a proposition'. The whole standpoint is somewhat earlier (the manuscripts often bear earlier dates) than that of

Part I here, but later than the *Philosophical Remarks*. – But the appendices also discuss questions directly connected with the themes of 'generality' and 'logical inference' in Part II.

Part I is concerned with the generality of certain expressions or concepts, such as 'language', 'proposition' and 'number'. For instance, § 70, page 113:

"Compare the concept of proposition with the concept 'number' and then on the other hand with the concept of cardinal number. We count as numbers cardinal numbers, rational numbers, irrational numbers, complex numbers; whether we call other constructions numbers because of their similarities with these, or draw a definitive boundary here or elsewhere, depends on us. In this respect the concept of number is like the concept of proposition. On the other hand the concept of cardinal number $|1, \xi, \xi + 1|$ can be called a rigorously circumscribed concept, that's to say it's a concept in a different sense of the word."

This discussion is closely related to the chapter on *'Kinds of Cardinal Numbers'* and on '$2 + 2 = 4$' in Part II; and with the section on *Inductive Proof*. These are the most important things in Part II.

London, 1969

Many passages in the *Philosophical Grammar* appear also in the *Philosophical Remarks,* the *Philosophical Investigations,* and the *Zettel.* In these cases I have used the translations of Mr Roger White and Professor G. E. M. Anscombe, so that variations between the styles of translators should not be mistaken for changes of mind on Wittgenstein's part. Rare departures from this practice are marked in footnotes. Passages from the *Philosophical Grammar* appear also in *The Principles of Linguistic Philosophy* of F. Waismann (Macmillan 1965): in these cases I have not felt obliged to follow the English text verbatim, but I am indebted to Waismann's translator.

Three words or groups of words constantly presented difficulties in translation.

The German word *"Satz"* may be translated "proposition" or "sentence" or (in mathematical and logical contexts) "theorem". I have tried to follow what appears to have been Wittgenstein's own practice when writing English, by using the word "proposition" when the syntactical or semantic properties of sentences were in question, and the word "sentence" when it was a matter of the physical properties of sounds or marks. But it would be idle to pretend that this rule provides a clear decision in every case, and sometimes I have been obliged to draw attention in footnotes to problems presented by the German word.

From the *Tractatus* onward Wittgenstein frequently compared a proposition to a *Maßstab.* The German word means a rule or measuring rod: when Wittgenstein used it is clear that he had in mind a rigid object with calibrations. Finding the word "rule" too ambiguous, and the word "measuring-rod" too cumbersome, I have followed the translators of the *Tractatus* in using the less accurate but more natural word "ruler".

Translators of Wittgenstein have been criticised for failing to adopt a uniform translation of the word *"übersehen"* and its derivatives, given the importance of the notion of *"übersichtliche Darstellung"* in Wittgenstein's later conception of philosophy. I have been unable to find a natural word to meet the requirement of uniformity, and have translated the word and its cognates as seemed natural in each context.

Like other translators of Wittgenstein I have been forced to retain a rather Germanic style of punctuation to avoid departing too far from the original. For instance, Wittgenstein often introduced *oratio recta* by a colon instead of by inverted commas. This is not natural in English, but to change to inverted commas would involve making a decision – often a disputable one – about where the quotation is intended to end.

I have translated the text of the Suhrkamp-Blackwell edition of 1969 as it stands, with the exception of the passages listed below in which I took the opportunity to correct in translation errors of transcription or printing which had crept into the German text. The pagination of the translation, so far as practicable, matches that of the original edition.

I am greatly indebted to Professor Ernst Tugendhat, who assisted me in the first draft of my translation; and to Mr John Thomas, Dr Peter Hacker, Mr Brian McGuinness, Professor G. E. M. Anscombe, Professor Norman Malcolm, Professor G. H. von Wright, Mr Roger White, Dr Anselm Müller, Mr and Mrs J. Tiles and Mr R. Heinaman who assisted me on particular points. My greatest debt is to Mr Rush Rhees, who went very carefully through large sections of a draft version and saved me from many errors while improving the translation in many ways. The responsibility for remaining errors is entirely mine.

I am grateful to the British Academy for a Visiting Fellowship which supported me while writing the first draft translation.

Oxford 1973

page 17 line 31 For "Gedanken" read "Gedanke".

24 15 For "selten" read "seltsam".

25 17 For "Vom Befehl" read "Von der Erwartung".

43 23 For "Carroll's" read "Carroll's Gedicht".

44 15 For "was besagt" read "was sagt".

52 13 For "uns da" read "uns da etwas".

52 27 For "geben" read "ergeben".

61 22 For "kann" read "kann nun".

72 4 There should be no space between the paragraphs.

75 28 For "übergrenzt" read "überkreuzt".

88 9 For "gezeichnet haben" read "bezeichnet haben, sie schon zur Taufe gehalten haben".

92 27 For "nun" read "nun nicht".

97 7 For "Jedem" read "jedem".

107 5 For "sie" read "sie von".

108 17 For "Körperlos" read "körperlos".

119 8 For "nun" read "um".

123 16 There should be no space between the paragraphs.

147 21 For "daß" read "das".

148 1 For "Zeichen" read "Zeichnen".

151 21 For "schreibt" read "beschreibt".

152 19 For "Auszahlungen" read "Auszahnungen".

152 30 For "hervorgerufen" read "hervorzurufen".

160 21 There should be a space between the paragraphs.

160 15 For "Ciffre" read "Chiffre".

163 30 There should be no space between the paragraphs.

171 12 For "systematischen" read "schematischen".

178 3 For "lügen:" read "lügen"".

205 9 For "in der" read "der".

215 3 For "Buches" read "Buches uns".

221 8 For "Erkenntis" read "Erkenntnis".

line 20   For "folgen" read "Folgen".

244   23   For "etwa" read "es dazu".

244   24   For "den" read "dem".

245   19   For "fy" read "fx".

251   12   For "dem" read "den".

251   13   For "mit" read "mir".

253   The "t1" in the figure is misplaced.

256   23   For "folge" read "folgte".

260   23   For "weh" read "nicht weh".

261   12   For "ist" read "ist da".

268   1ff   For 'f' read 'φ' *passim*.

278   31   For "Fall von f($\exists$) ist," read "Fall von f($\exists$) ist. Und nun kann mans uns entgegenhalten: Wenn er sieht, dass f(a) ein Fall von f($\exists$) ist,"

286   6   For "o·3" read "o·$\dot{3}$".

288   11   For "$1 + 1 + 1 + 1$" read "$1 + 1 + 1 + 1 + 1$".

288   30   For "ψx" read "φx".

292   5   For "wird" read "wird. Vom Kind nur die richtige Ausführung der Multiplikation verlangt wird".

294   13   For "uns" read "nun uns".

296   12   For "Ich habe gesagt" read "Ich sagte oben".

305   12   Insert new paragraph: "Wenn nachträglich ein Widerspruch gefunden wird, so waren vorher die Regeln noch nicht klar und eindeutig. Der Widerspruch macht also nichts denn er ist dann durch das Aussprechen einer Regel zu entfernen."

313   8   For "Hiweisen" read "Hinweisen".

316   21   For "unnötiges Zeichen für "Taut." geben" read "unnötiges – Zeichen für "Taut." gegeben".

317   6   For "den" read "dem".

317   15   For "Def." read "$\overset{\text{Def}}{=}$."

317   29   For "Sätze)." read "Sätze) und zwar eine richtige degenerierte Gleichung (den Grenzfall einer Gleichung)."

325   21   For "könne" read "könnte".